IT DID NOT START WITH JFK

THE DECADES OF EVENTS THAT LED TO THE ASSASSINATION OF JOHN F. KENNEDY

V O L U M E 1

WALTER HERBST

SUNBURY
P R E S S
Mechanicsburg, PA USA

Published by Sunbury Press, Inc.
Mechanicsburg, PA USA

SUNBURY
P R E S S

www.sunburypress.com

For information about special discounts for bulk purchases, please contact Sunbury Press Orders Dept. at (855) 338-8359 or orders@sunburypress.com.

To request one of our authors for speaking engagements or book signings, please contact Sunbury Press Publicity Dept. at publicity@sunburypress.com.

FIRST SUNBURY PRESS EDITION: October 2021

Set in Adobe Garamond Pro | Interior design by Crystal Devine | Cover by Lawrence Knorr | Edited by Lawrence Knorr.

Publisher's Cataloging-in-Publication Data
Names: Herbst, Walter, author.
Title: It did not start with JFK : the decades of events that led to the assassination of John F. Kenndy / Walter Herbst.
Description: First trade paperback edition. | Mechanicsburg, PA : Sunbury Press, 2021.
Summary : A right-wing movement is responsible for assassinating JFK. Understanding how this came to be is the key to unraveling the assassination riddle and can only be found by investigating the four decades before Kennedy's presidency. *It Did Not Start With JFK* is the first book to do so. And once "why" is understood, who was responsible becomes clear.
Identifiers: ISBN : 978-1-62006-874-8 (softcover).
Subjects: HISTORY / United States / 20th Century | POLITICAL SCIENCE / Corruption & Misconduct | POLITICAL SCIENCE / Political Ideologies / Nationalism & Patriotism | POLITICAL SCIENCE / Intelligence & Espionage.

Product of the United States of America
0 1 1 2 3 5 8 13 21 34 55

Continue the Enlightenment!

For Julia, Emily, Ryan, and Norah, the source of my inspiration.

Contents

Acknowledgments

Many years of research and writing passed before this book came to print, so naturally, I have many people to thank for making this possible.

First and foremost, I owe a tremendous debt of gratitude to my brother Robert, who has been there throughout the entire process. During my research, he was a sounding board off whom I could test theories and ideas and receive an unbiased reaction. While writing the manuscript, he read and edited every chapter and was a constant source of encouragement and support. His input in bringing this book to fruition was invaluable.

Thanks to David Aretha for providing professional editing services early on and helping me navigate through the book proposal submission process. David became a mentor when I needed one, and I will forever be grateful.

I also want to thank Lawrence Knorr, Marianne Babcock, Crystal Devine, Joe Walters, and the rest of the staff at Sunbury Press for all the assistance they have provided. Lawrence is a true history lover interested in the JFK assassination and was enthusiastic about publishing the book from the beginning. More importantly, he is a man of his word, and his passion and honesty made my decision to go with Sunbury Press an easy one.

My deepest thanks go to Mathew Selznick for all his hard work to ensure I professionally marketed the book. He has also become a mentor upon who I have come to rely increasingly more and more. His enthusiasm and belief in my work have far exceeded what I reasonably could have expected.

There were also countless people along the way who selflessly helped me research, write and present my manuscript for publication. They are too numerous to mention, but I am indebted to every one of them.

I would be remiss if I did not thank my family for all the support they have provided throughout the years. My parents Walter and Maria instilled a love of reading and an interest in history. My son Michael and his wife Debra, and my daughter Diana and her husband Philip, have listened to my rants about the JFK assassination conspiracy for years without complaint. They were always there for me, offering critical critique and assistance whenever I needed them, and I thank them for that.

Last but certainly not least, a most sincere thanks to my wife Margaret for the sacrifices she made, as she patiently watched me devote hours upon hours researching and writing, secreted in my study by myself. Many times, I know, she would have preferred to do something else, but she allowed me to pursue my dream of writing this book. Words cannot adequately express what that has meant to me.

Introduction

I was six years old when John F. Kennedy died, a first-grade student at Our Lady of Hope grammar school in the Middle Village section of Queens, New York. I vaguely remember a teacher coming into our classroom to make the grim announcement. School let out early, and once outside, I noticed a woman crying as she listened to a transistor radio held tightly against her ear. I was too young to process why she was so upset, unable to connect her visible emotions to the assassination.

As the years went by, I knew that not everyone accepted the Warren Commission's finding that Lee Harvey Oswald murdered President Kennedy, but I gave little attention to these reports. I blindly believed that such an impressive government body would uncover the truth with all the resources available to it and never lie to the American people. But around the age of twenty-five, I read my first book about a possible assassination conspiracy, and it was a revelation. I was captivated by what I read and angry that I was lied to, so I began my search to find the truth.

For thirty-eight years, I have devoted countless hours researching the events surrounding that fateful day in Dallas. And even though this American tragedy occurred many years ago, there is an emotional component to what happened that never goes away because America changed that day. We went from a people who had complete faith in our government to one that began to question authority. And all the civil disobedience this nation has struggled with in the years since can trace its roots back to November 22, 1963, including the social unrest we are experiencing today. If the events surrounding the assassination of a duly elected President can be covered up so that the truth is kept hidden, then "We the people" is nothing more than a fairy tale, and the American Dream is gone forever.

As my investigation into the assassination deepened, I began to realize that Lee Harvey Oswald was involved in the crime, but he did not act alone. The assassination of JFK was a domestic conspiracy consisting of an elite group that wanted to change the country at the expense of what most Americans wanted. For in the early 1960s, the United States was on the verge of accepting coexistence with Communist nations, promoting the inevitability of racial equality, and expanding social programs that elites believed destroyed self-determination, the belief that the Constitution guaranteed freedom of choice to the American people. The American landscape was changing, and the white, Christian, Anglo-Saxon American way of life was at stake. There were those willing to assassinate a President to prevent this from occurring.

The potential assassination suspects have garnered much attention over the years and are well known, even to those with just a passing interest in Kennedy's death. They include the CIA, the military, big business, anti-Communist paramilitary types, southern racists, Texas oilmen, crooked politicians, organized crime figures, and anti-Castro Cuban exiles. All could not be responsible for Kennedy's murder. Still, as my investigation deepened, I realized it was likely elements from various groups working together who had murdered the President. They had become familiar with each other long before most of the country even knew who JFK was, and a bond of trust developed between them. It would eventually lead them to the streets of Dallas on November 22, 1963.

I also began to consider assassination suspects through the lens of relative plausibility, which was the likelihood of any individual or group having assassinated Kennedy based on the strength of the evidence against them. It soon became abundantly clear that the discontent of the radical right during the early 1960s was born decades before and grew during the Cold War when numerous examples of treasonous behavior were evident, were one to take the time to look. So, I began to focus my research on the pre-Kennedy years, which would reveal, I believed, the most probable reasons for "why" Kennedy had to die. And once "why" was known, uncovering "who" was most likely responsible should naturally follow.

I also considered what else was happening around the world at the time of the assassination. I hoped that circumstances seemingly unrelated to JFK's death might provide additional clues to who was responsible and why murdering the President was the only option they were willing to entertain. It was an eye-opening experience, for I discovered that the assassination of President Kennedy did not occur in a vacuum. Numerous attempted assassinations and government overthrows were occurring throughout the world, all happening within twenty-six months of Kennedy's assassination, with an easily recognizable pattern. Consider the following:

- September 17, 1961—Turkey: Prime Minister Adnan Menderes was hanged following a coup the previous year because he had threatened to eliminate the profitable Turkish drug network. The CIA, along with their allies in the Turkish Mafia, the army high command, the rogue Turkish Secret Service, and violent far-right mercenaries, controlled the operation.

- August 22, 1962—France: A failed assassination attempt was perpetrated against Charles de Gaulle by supporters of anti-Algerian independence. The group allegedly had the support of the CIA.

- February 8, 1963—Iraq: The assassination of Prime minister General Abdul Karim Kassem occurred during a CIA-backed coup. An Iraqi Ba'ath leader stated, "We came to power on a CIA train." The CIA furnished the rebels with a list of alleged Communists, and extreme violence followed, resulting in the arrest of ten thousand Iraqis. It would result in the execution of five thousand.[1]

- March 8, 1963—Syria: A military coup successfully overthrew the government, inspired by the coup in Iraq the previous month.

- March 29, 1963—Guatemala: A military coup replaced President General Miguel Ydigoras Fuentes, whom the CIA feared might turn Communist. It resulted in the deaths of some 50,000 Guatemalans.

- April 1963—Italy: Communists amassed twenty-five percent of the vote in the national election. The Christian Democrat Party Prime Minister Aldo Morro fueled the fire by naming Socialists to cabinet posts. Italian General Giovanni de Lorenzo planned a silent coup d'état, in close cooperation with CIA's Vernon Walters, Rome CIA Station Chief William Harvey, and Colonel Renzo Rocca, the director of Italy's industrial counterespionage. Rocca recruited a paramilitary force that included members of the Mafia, Italian street gangs, and neo-Fascists, but a compromise between Socialists and right-wing Christian Democrats ended the coup.

The ensuing investigation accused Rocca of using secret funds provided by wealthy industrialists to recruit a terrorist squad. Before he could testify in 1968, Rocca was found dead from a gunshot wound to his head in his Rome office. It was ruled a suicide despite that his hands showed he had not fired a weapon. Undaunted, General Carlo Ciglieri, a former leader of the Carabinieri, the Italian national police, commissioned an investigation. However, on April 27, 1969, he would be found dead on a dirt road outside Padua in a mysterious car accident. General Giorgio Manis, who was to provide evidence to the commission, dropped dead on the streets of Rome on June 25, 1969. His assistant, Colonel Remo D'Ottario, allegedly shot himself in the heart a month later. Finally, in 1978, Prime Minister Morro was kidnapped and eventually assassinated by those who objected to his accommodation of Communists.[2]

- July 11, 1963—Ecuador: A successful CIA-backed military coup resulted in the widespread arrest of extreme leftists and ended communism throughout the country.

- September 25, 1963—Dominican Republic: A group of twenty-five senior military commanders, backed by the CIA, expelled President Orlando Bosch from the country because he had tried to introduce social reforms.

- October 3, 1963—Honduras: A military coup took control of the government ten days before the presidential election. According to the U.S. Ambassador, it "was justified due to the Communist infiltration into the [previous] government." On Kennedy's orders, the U.S. ended diplomatic relations with the new Honduras government, but Lyndon Johnson would recognize the new military government three weeks after JFK's assassination. U.S. companies took control of the fruit and mining industries, American companies acquired the two largest Honduran banks, unemployment rose, the national debt increased, and wealth inequality increased.

- November 2, 1963—South Vietnam: A CIA-backed military coup took over the government, resulting in the assassination of President Ngo Dinh Diem and his brother Ngo Dinh Nhu.

- February 17, 1964—Gabon: A military coup, believed to have involved the CIA, ousted the President and took over the government. Eventually, France intervened militarily and toppled the coup, restoring the President to power.

- March 1964—Cuba: A failed assassination attempt against Fidel Castro involved the Mafia and the CIA.

- April 1964—Brazil: A military coup toppled the Brazilian government. U.S. support of the coup included US Navy tankers from Aruba, 110 tons of ammunition, an aircraft carrier, four destroyers, and two destroyer escorts. The American ambassador acknowledged U.S. involvement in "covert support for pro-democracy street rallies . . . and encouragement [of] democratic and anti-communist sentiment in Congress . . ." CIA files regarding the coup remain classified.

- April 1964—Dominican Republic: Government forces and leftist rebels were engaged in a bloody civil war. Under the pretext of saving Americans stranded inside the country, 1,700 U.S. Marines were sent to the country and engaged in combat with the rebel forces.

- November 3, 1964—Bolivia: A military coup under the direction of Vice President Rene Barrientos and army commander-in-chief Alfredo Ovando Candia overthrew President Victor Paz Etenssoro. The CIA covertly financed the new right-wing government.[3]

Right-wing anti-Communists were involved in fifteen incidents against left-wing opponents, and in almost every case, the CIA and the U.S. military provided support. There seemed to be an organized effort throughout the world to remove pro-Communist governments from power, and when necessary, to assassinate leaders who stood in the way of this occurring. Meanwhile, authorities accused an alleged Communist and Castro supporter of assassinating a progressive U.S.

President. It did not make sense. So, with relative plausibility in mind, I realized that Kennedy's assassination was a right-wing conspiracy to take over the U.S. government, similar to what was happening around the world at the same time, and I found there was ample evidence pointing in that direction. The answer to "why" this had to happen could be found in the past.

* * *

As early as 1932, there was an attempt to overthrow the presidency of Franklin Roosevelt by Fascist elites. The story began in 1924 with the passage of the Bonus Bill by Congress, which provided World War I veterans with additional compensation to be paid in 1945. However, with the Great Depression taking its toll, by the summer of 1932, over 20,000 veterans and their families, dubbed the Bonus Army, marched on Washington demanding payment. One of those who addressed the crowd was retired Major General Smedley Butler. "They may be calling you tramps now," Butler said, "but in 1917, they didn't call you bums!" It was all for naught, for the Bonus Army was dispersed by force when General Douglas MacArthur led a military contingent into their camp, burned down their makeshift homes, and physically forced the protesters out.

Bill Doyle and Gerald C. MacGuire, two influential American Legion members, visited Butler at his home the following year. It was a group Butler distrusted. The Legion had a reputation of being union busters, arriving armed with baseball bats and other implements of destruction to scatter the "Communist" workers and squelch a strike. The two men wanted Butler to speak at an upcoming Legion convention in Chicago about FDR's abandonment of the gold standard, which delinked the dollar to gold. It gave Roosevelt a license to print money to fund his social programs, but opponents foresaw runaway inflation and widespread bankruptcy. FDR was called a Communist for pushing forward such a leftist agenda.

Butler did not commit to anything, but when FDR officially recognized the USSR on November 16, 1933, the potential for his violent overthrow became more serious. "We are facing a new and more dangerous foe today," said Richmond, Virginia American Legion Commander Frank N. Belgrano, Jr., in an October 1934 speech. "It has seeped quietly into our country and whispered into the ears of our workers and our people everywhere that our ideals of government are out of date. We of the Legion are mobilized to meet the enemy and, we are calling upon loyal Americans everywhere to join us in ridding our country of this menace." [4]

MacGuire had spent time in Europe studying how foreign veteran groups had enabled Fascists in Germany and Italy to come to power. In France, he witnessed the radical right-wing Criox de Feu's role in ending a strike that had paralyzed the country. Butler soon realized he was involved with a right-wing group of wealthy Fascist Americans whose intent was to overthrow the United States government.

Big-time money financed the group, including the Du Pont's and J.P. Morgan and Company, through the recently created anti-Roosevelt American Liberty League.

Butler considered it treason. Appearing before the House of Representatives on November 20, 1934, he confirmed there was ". . . an attempt to establish a fascist organization in this country . . ."[5] The *New York Times* confirmed, on November 21, 1934, that Butler "was to assemble his 500,000 men in Washington, possibly a year from now, with the expectation that such a show of force would enable it to take over the government peacefully in a few days."[6]

Paul Comly French reported in the *Philadelphia Record* and the *New York Post*, under the headline, "$3,000,000 Bid for Fascist Army Bared," that Butler ". . . has been asked by a group of wealthy New York brokers to lead a Fascist movement to set up a dictatorship in the United States . . ." MacGuire would tell French the conspirators wanted "a man on a white horse . . . a dictator who would come galloping in . . . [supported by] a group of organized veterans, to save the capitalistic system . . ." "We need a Fascist government in this country," MacGuire continued, "to save the Nation from the Communists who want to tear it down . . ."[7]

Despite the evidence presented, the story quietly disappeared without anyone arrested for attempting to overthrow the government. The men involved were much too powerful to be charged with something as frivolous as treason, but the hatred for Roosevelt remained. The American ambassador to Germany, William E. Dodd, who learned of a group of wealthy American industrialists who were pro-Nazi, wrote FDR that they were "hell-bent to bring a fascist state to supplant our democratic government."[8]

There were other attempts to remove FDR from power. The American Liberty League subsidized groups such as the fascist and anti-Semitic "Sentinels of the Republic" and the "Crusaders," who were instructed by their leader, George W. Christians, to consider lynching Roosevelt. One night, Christians threatened to cut off Chattanooga's electric power in anticipation of FDR's arrival. "Lots of things can happen in the dark!" he reportedly said. The Secret Service kept a watchful eye on him during the President's visit.[9]

Then there was the incident on February 15, 1933, when President-elect Roosevelt was at a political rally in Miami, which Chicago Mayor Anton Cermak also attended. The crowd included a thirty-three-year-old Italian immigrant named Giuseppe Zangara, who later admitted he was there to shoot and kill FDR. The large gathering made it impossible for him to get closer than twenty-five feet from his intended target, but he managed to get off five shots, hitting Cermak in the chest and wounding four others, but not FDR. Cermak would later die in the hospital of complications from his wound. Justice was quick for Zangara. He was tried, found guilty, and executed on March 20, a little over a month after the shooting. He maintained to the end that FDR was his intended target.[10]

In January 1940, the FBI arrested eighteen members of a "Christian Front" splinter group charged with overthrowing the U.S. government by seizing the

White House and installing Fascist Major General George Van Horn Moseley as a military dictator. Involved were the National Guard and high-ranking members of the U.S. Army. FDR's government was an "alien element in our midst." It was Moseley's code for Jews, as he believed World War II was about establishing Jewish hegemony throughout the world."[11]

Finally, consider Cornelius Vanderbilt Jr., a great-great-grandson of the famous industrialist, who reported after FDR's election in 1940 for a third presidential term that there was a Fascist plot to remove him from office. "I use the word 'conspiracy,'" Vanderbilt said, but "I really am talking of a plot—serious, long-discussed plan to—shall I say—[to] capture the president." The plot was "for the good of the country; to hold this dictator, this madman . . . while some persons set up emergency controls and saved America." Allegedly, Vanderbilt informed federal agencies of the plot, which put an end to the scheme.[12]

Wealthy elites in America wanted to stop anyone who supported a Socialist agenda. Louisiana Senator Huey Long was a prime example. There was a legitimate chance that Long could unseat FDR in the 1936 election. His "Share Our Wealth" program proposed such a radical redistribution of wealth that it made the New Deal appear conservative in comparison. According to H.W. Brands, the author of *Traitor to His Class*, "Share Our Wealth" would result in the "confiscation of fortunes above $8 million, would fund a guaranteed income for every family in America, as well as pensions for the elderly, aid to schools, and additional public works."[13]

According to Long, during the Great Depression, "Rockefeller, Morgan, and their crowd stepped up and took enough for 120 million people and left only enough for 5 million [people] for all the other 125 million to eat. And so many millions must go hungry and without these good things God gave us unless we call on them to put some of it back."[14]

Tensions ran high in Louisiana as the calendar turned to 1935. Like Roosevelt, Long was labeled a Communist and dictator by the far-right for forcing his Socialist agenda on Americans against their will. On September 8, he was in the State Capitol in Baton Rouge, surrounded by bodyguards, when Dr. Carl Weiss pulled out a handgun and shot Long, who died two days later. Weiss was killed on the spot, shot by Long's bodyguards, and there were immediate questions about what motivated the young doctor to kill the senator.

In January 1935, the Square Deal Association, a right-wing paramilitary group, was created because they believed the only way to stop Long's radical leftist policies was by armed revolt. The group's leadership was influential and included a former Louisiana governor and a mayor of New Orleans. Not surprisingly, Square Deal was affiliated with white supremacist groups and likened their movement to the 1874 uprising that pitted racist hate groups against Louisiana's Reconstruction government. Also telling was that on January 28, they joined forces with the Liberty League, the same group behind the Bonus Army government take-over that attempted to remove FDR from office.

That January, the Square Deal Association forcibly took over the courthouse in Baton Rouge. The National Guard defused the tense situation, but death threats against Long, arson attempts, and a drive-by shooting followed. He surrounded himself with bodyguards when he learned of an assassination plot that one of his associates had uncovered at a secret meeting held in New Orleans. It is unknown if Dr. Weiss was part of the Square Deal Association. However, it is very revealing that many Square Deal members paid their respects, making the funeral the largest service ever attended for an accused political assassin in the history of the U.S.[15]

* * *

Even before World War II, FDR called General Douglas MacArthur the most dangerous man in America. "You saw how he strutted down Pennsylvania Avenue," Roosevelt said. "You saw that picture of him in the *Times* after the troops chased all those [Bonus Army] vets out with tear gas and burned their shelters. Did you ever see anyone more self-satisfied? There's a potential Mussolini for you. Right here at home. The head man in the army. That's a perfect position if things get disorderly enough and good citizens work up enough anxiety. If all this talk comes to anything—about [the] government going to pieces and not being able to stop the spreading disorder—Doug MacArthur is the man . . ."[16]

The movement gained momentum after World War II, as the U.S. entered the Cold War era. In 1952, Herbert Hoover told the Republican Convention that Roosevelt and Truman had "distorted and violated" the Constitution. Around the same time, former ultra-right MacArthur protégé, General Pedro del Valle, wrote a letter to President Truman calling him a traitor for his handling of the Korean War.[17] MacArthur was even more emphatic. He said Democrats were setting "the national course unerringly toward the socialistic regimentation of a totalitarian state." The rhetoric was getting intense and personal.[18]

As time went by, MacArthur's disgust became abundantly clear. He warned about ". . . a new and heretofore unknown and dangerous concept that the members of our armed forces owe primary allegiance or loyalty to those who temporarily exercise the authority of the Executive Branch of the Government rather than to the country and to the Constitution which they are sworn to defend. No proposition could be more dangerous."[19]

To suggest the military was sworn to serve the Constitution and the people, and not the President, was excessive, but MacArthur was not alone. One military voice at the time, Colonel Robert Dwan, described how ". . . mature, professional officers appear convinced that the United States is losing the Cold War . . . and that inadequate steps are being taken to reverse the trend . . . Accompanying this pessimistic view is usually the clear implication that solutions are obvious if our people and their leaders only had the courage to act or were not somehow *under the insidious influences of the enemy and his accomplices*. If these attitudes are sincerely held by responsible officers . . . then *the consequences for the armed services and the Nation are potentially serious indeed.*"[20] (Author's Italics)

Similarly, an article written by George A. Kelley in *Army*, the official magazine of the U.S. Army, warned that the potential for a coup existed. "Once the nation's politics has been cast in doubt [by the military]," Kelley wrote, "there is no alternative source of allegiance to rally to, and one rallies instead to his own opinion and interpretation of events . . . [I]t is within this spectrum that numerous tragedies of military disobedience have occurred."[21]

The right-wing direction of the military also frightened those outside the armed services. Father John Cronin was a national figure and staunch anti-Communist. Regarding the dangerous trend he saw in the military, Cronin wrote: "When every discussion with the Communist powers is considered a sign of weakness or even treason, then we are left with only two stark alternatives: surrender or war. Common sense should tell us we should seek some middle course between these two extremes."[22]

The problem was there was no middle course, and it became clear to me that by 1963 the Fascist movement had evolved to where the assassination of JFK by the military and radical right was probable. And Oswald was part of it.

* * *

After his arrest, Oswald asked for a New York attorney named John Abt to represent him. "I don't know him personally," Oswald said, "but I know about a case that he handled some years ago, where he represented the people who had violated the Smith Act . . ."

Abt spent most of his career as chief counsel for the Communist Party USA (CPUSA), which has been the consensus for why Oswald wanted Abt to represent him, but that was not the case. The Smith Act interested the accused assassin because it was enacted in 1940 to make it *". . . a criminal offense to advocate the violent overthrow of the government or to organize or be a member of any group devoted to such advocacy."*[23] And in January 1955, John Abt had defended Claude Lightfoot, an African American Communist, who was tried in Chicago under the Smith Act for being part of a group that wanted to overthrow the U.S. government.

Oswald wanted someone with Abt's experience to represent him in Dallas because he was also involved in an attempt to overthrow the U.S. government. He was the only one in custody, and only Abt had the experience to try a case such as his.

Consider Oswald's words, spoken at the Jesuit House of Studies at Spring Hill College in Mobile, Alabama, in 1963, where his cousin Eugene Murret was a seminarian. "Americans are apt to scoff at the idea that a military coup in the U.S., as so often happens in Latin American countries, could ever replace our government," Oswald told those in attendance. "But that is an idea that has grounds for consideration." Four months before the assassination, Oswald publicly spoke about the possibility of a military take-over of the U.S. government.[24]

Then there was the information provided by Priscilla Johnson, a CIA-connected reporter who interviewed Oswald in Moscow after his "defection" to the Soviet Union. In her book *Marina & Lee*, Johnson described Oswald's political philosophy, which he put on paper in the spring of 1963, where he ". . . predicted that a 'total crisis' of some kind would soon destroy the capitalist system and the government of the United States." "We have no interest in violently opposing the U.S. government," Oswald said, or in ". . . assuming the head of government." To ". . . prevent foreign intervention [Soviet communism] and set up a 'separate, democratic, pure communist society,' he [Oswald] proposed the formation of a small party made up of disenchanted radicals, socialists, even remnants of the Republican Party, to *defend 'the right of private personal property*, religious tolerance and freedom of travel.'"[25] (Author's italics)

The reference to defending private property is critical because a Marxist should not have been concerned with this, as Oswald claimed to be. It was the radical right for whom this carried importance second to no other issue. They thought social programs, such as social security, welfare, unemployment insurance, and all the rest, violated their Constitutional rights. It was why the ultra-right believed Franklin Roosevelt, Harry Truman, Dwight Eisenhower, and John Kennedy were all Communists. I realized that Oswald's political philosophy coincided with this ultra-right tenet and that he was confused and came to believe that it was consistent with Marxist teachings.

There were "two world systems," according to Oswald. "One [was] twisted beyond recognition (communism) . . . the other decadent and dying (capitalism) . . . A truly democratic system would combine the better qualities of the two upon an American foundation . . ." He foresaw a final "conflict between the two world systems [that would leave] the country without defense or foundation of government . . ." The survivors would "seek an alternative to those systems which have brought them misery . . ." He wrote of a "readily foreseeable . . . economic, political or military crisis, internal or external, [which] will bring about the final destruction of the capitalist system . . ." He went on to note that ". . . only the intellectually fearless could even be remotely attracted too [sic] *our doctrine*, and yet this doctrine requires the utmost restraint, a state of being in itself majestic [sic] in power."[26] (Author's italics)

More than once, Oswald refers to "we" and "our." He wrote as if he were part of a group, not acting on his own. And this organization pointed in the direction of the radical right.

As we will see, Oswald had a connection to neo-Nazis in America. Their names were in his notebook, discovered after the assassination, and he primarily kept company with Fascists the last year of his life. A possible connection between Oswald and the right-wing is not a radical idea. The words of the Minutemen, a paramilitary Fascist group headed by Robert DePugh, were similar to Oswald's. "A life and death conflict is raging right now [at the time of the assassination]," DePugh said, "between the forces of freedom and advocates of slavery . . . that if the American people expect to be saved from slavery, they are going to have to do so themselves . . ."[27] Frank Ellsworth was an agent with the Treasury Department's Alcohol, Tobacco, and Firearms Division in Dallas in 1963. He testified before the Warren Commission that: "An organization known as the Minutemen is the right-wing group in Dallas most likely to have been associated with any effort to assassination the President . . ."[28]

Texas Congressman Henry B. Gonzalez made a special request to the Warren Commission to investigate a possible Minutemen/Oswald connection. Shortly after, the *New York Post* reported that the Warren Commission was investigating a potential Oswald—Minuteman link.[29]

In January 1964, California Attorney Stanley Mosk, addressing an audience in Anaheim, also noticed a similarity between Oswald and groups like the Minutemen. "We know he [Oswald] pursued political causes with fanaticism and without regard for democratic processes," Mosk said. "He was a political agitator who was alienated from our society and our political order. It is this alienation which is most disturbing in the attitudes of so-called Minutemen . . . [who] feel that our system has failed. They feel that our two major political parties are shams—simply a choice between two evils. They feel our processes have been totally perverted and are of no use. They admit looking forward to a time of armed conflict with an enemy they only vaguely identify . . ."[30]

* * *

The threat of the U.S. military, which began in 1932, continued to attract attention as the assassination neared. On June 18, 1961, the *New York Times* reported that ". . . officers of high and middle rank are indoctrinating their commands and the civilian population near their bases with political theories resembling those of the [radical right] John Birch Society. They are also holding up to criticism and ridicule some official policies of the United States Government." [31]

General Edwin Walker was a right-wing racist and anti-Kennedy zealot. He stated that the "public, to a certain extent, was in bewilderment at our peril and our national policy. You will find the military hunting a cause and a purpose, which natural[ly] originates from the people through Congress. So, there is . . . [an] instinct drawing [ ]the two together in search of an answer. There is a great vacuum, and the only solution brings these two areas together; the military, as the agency of implementing a national policy that basically should, and under the Constitution, originates with the people . . ."[32]

Then there were the retired generals who advocated a violent overthrow of the government, and they did so by aligning themselves with Fascist right-wing groups. In 1961, according to an informant within the radical-right National States' Right

Party, the party received a letter from retired General Pedro del Valle, who was associated with the organization. "When a free people find their elected servants following a destructive course of action regarding the Constitution," del Valle wrote, "the people must take effective action to restore same by taking the matter into their own hands and forcing the traitors out of power."[33]

Del Valle could not be more specific. Like Walker, he referenced a violation of the Constitution as justification for removing a so-called "traitor from power." That same year, he also wrote to Robert Welch of the John Birch Society, "The time has come for action. Treason sits enthroned in the seats of Power [*sic*], and treason will soon land us in the Red One-Worlder's Paradise unless we take steps to prevent it and do it now and with decisiveness."

Violent military dissent was seemingly everywhere. During a televised meeting of Project Alert, a right-wing anti-Communist group, the hanging of Chief Justice Earl Warren was called for by retired Marine Corps Colonel Mitchell Paige.[34]

Outright fear for where this all might lead set in as people began to take notice. On November 21, 1961, a Drew Pearson column warned of a "movement inside the armed forces and reservists not unlike in the French army which tried to topple President de Gaulle." Pearson noted that del Valle "has already come close to urging armed insurrection" and was threatening armed resistance.[35]

The potential for an armed military revolt prompted a concerned Congress to order an inquiry. Senator William Fullbright, a favorite target of the radical right himself, recognized the danger and the thin line that President Kennedy was treading. "The radicalism of the right," Fullbright cautioned,

> can be expected to have great mass appeal during such periods. It offers the simple solution, easily understood: [the] scourging of the devils within the body politic, or, in the extreme, lashing out at the enemy. If the military is infected with this virus of right-wing radicalism, the danger is worthy of attention. If it believes the public is, the danger is enhanced. If by the process of the military's educating the public, the fevers of both groups are raised, the danger is great indeed. Perhaps it is farfetched to call forth the revolt of the French generals as an example of the ultimate danger. Nevertheless, military officers, French or American, have some common characteristics arising from their profession, and there are numerous 'fingers on the trigger' throughout the world . . .[36]

According to the 1963 book *The Far Right*: "Concern has grown that a belligerent and free-wheeling military could conceivably become as dangerous to the stability of the United States as the mixture of rebelliousness and politics had in nations forced to succumb to juntas or fascism."[37]

The tension between Kennedy and the far-right generals prompted writers Fletcher Knebel and Charles Waldo Bailey II to pen a novel about an attempted military coup entitled *Seven Days in May*. Arthur Schlesinger, a Special Assistant to JFK, had the book in mind when he wrote the following in *Robert Kennedy and His Times*:

> . . . the military leaders were Cold War zealots. They had sedulously cultivated relations with powerful conservative legislators . . . They hunted and fished with right-wing politicians, supplied them [with] aircraft for trips home, and showed up at their receptions. The alliance between the military and the right disturbed the Kennedys. This was why the President backed [Robert] McNamara so vigorously in the effort to stop warmongering speeches by generals and admirals.
>
> Direct military excursions into politics was still more disturbing. Radicals of the right were conducting an impassioned crusade not only against negotiation with the Soviet Union but also against social measure at home . . . The John Birch Society was flourishing. The *Minutemen* were training their members in guerilla warfare. Major General Edwin A. Walker, the right-wing demagogue who . . . was in a sense the heir of Major General George Van Horn Moseley, who had gone, in the thirties, from high Army commands to the domestic fascist movement. When the popular thriller *Seven Days in May* depicted a Pentagon attempt to take over the government, the President [JFK] remarked, "It's possible. It could happen in this country, but the conditions would have to be just right. If, for example, the country had a young President, and he had a Bay of Pigs, there would be a certain uneasiness. If there were a second Bay of Pigs, the military would begin to feel it [was] their patriotic obligation to preserve the nation. Then, if there were a third Bay of Pigs, it could happen . . ."[38]

According to Schlesinger, the Fascist right included many right-wing generals, and they were also threatening violence. The ultra-right Congress of Freedom held its annual convention in New Orleans on April 4-6, 1963. Present was detective Lochart F. Gracey, Jr., who reported he was aware of talk regarding "the overthrow of the present government of the United States," and the plot included a plan ". . . to assassinate particular persons . . ." "High ranking members of the Armed Forces . . . secretly belonged to this organization."[39]

On October 10, 1963, the Constitution Party held a meeting in Indianapolis, Indiana. An informant told the FBI that they planned to form a violent underground army. There was talk of killing JFK, which was not the only information the FBI was given before the assassination that the right-wing was planning a coup.[40]

Richard Case Nagell was an American intelligence officer who claimed to be aware of the assassination plot that involved Lee Oswald. In 1963 he sent a letter to J. Edgar Hoover outlining the plan: "I advised Mr. Hoover of a conspiracy . . . involving Lee Harvey Oswald to murder the Chief Executive of the United States . . . I furnished a complete and accurate description of Mr. Oswald. I disclosed sufficient data about the conspiracy . . . to warrant an immediate investigation if not the arrest of Mr. Oswald . . . Nagell said the assassination was "a domestic-inspired, domestic formulated, and domestic sponsored conspiracy . . ."[41]

In an attempt to warn Robert Kennedy, Army private first class Eugene B. Dinkin wrote the Attorney General about "an attempt to assassinate President Kennedy on November 28, 1963, [and that] blame would be placed upon a Communist or Negro." Dinkin believed "that elements of the Military were engineering the conspiracy." An FBI report dated April 3, 1964, stated that "a conspiracy was in the making by the 'military' of the United States, perhaps combined with an 'ultra-right economic group."[42]

Joseph Milteer was a 61-year-old right-wing racist who was regional director of the Constitution Party and a member of the National States Rights Party. Thirteen days before the assassination, an informant tape-recorded him stating JFK was to be shot "from a tall building with a high-powered rifle." Milteer claimed that authorities "will pick up somebody within hours afterward[ ] . . . just to throw the public off." The FBI was given the tape recording before the assassination.[43]

On November 17, 1963, five days before the assassination, William Walter of the New Orleans FBI said his office received a teletype warning that ". . . a militant revolutionary group may attempt to assassinate President Kennedy on his proposed trip to Dallas . . . All receiving offices should immediately contact all . . . race and hate group informants and determine if any basis for threat. Bureau should be kept advised of all developments . . ."[44]

There were numerous warnings by the time of the assassination that the President's life was in danger. Those suspected of being involved included Oswald and various right-wing Fascist organizations, including the U.S. military and CIA.

Others sounded an alarm that went unheeded, such as Jack Ruby. When the Warren Commission interviewed him at the Dallas County Jail on June 7, 1964, he said, ". . . a whole new form of government is going to take over our country, and I know I won't live to see you another time . . ."[45] On a separate occasion, Ruby wrote, "So you must believe me, [there] is only one kind of people that would do such a thing, that would have to be the Nazis, and that is who is in power in this country right now . . . If those people were so determined to frame me . . . they had an ulterior motive. There is only one kind of people that would go to such extremes, and that would be the Master Race . . ."[46]

We also know that authorities in Dallas thought Oswald was part of an international conspiracy. Dallas District Attorney Henry Wade admitted this under oath to the Warren Commission. On the night of the assassination, Lyndon Johnson's advisers pressured him to drop the conspiracy allegations and charge Oswald as the lone assassin, which Wade did. When asked by reporters if Oswald was "simply a nut or a middleman" involved in a conspiracy, Wade answered, "I'll put it this way: I don't think he's a nut."[47]

Support for Wade's allegation came in November 1993, when the PBS show *Frontline* interviewed Dallas FBI Agent James Hosty, who admitted that Assistant District Attorney Bill Alexander's original indictment had charged Oswald "in furtherance of an international conspiracy."[48]

Wade and Alexander, prosecutors on the ground in Dallas who were privy to the actual evidence, were calling it an international conspiracy, a charge they would not have made lightly. But they were stopped from doing so by Lyndon Johnson's people, which is troubling because the new President may have known more than he was willing to tell, and he was trying to circumvent the investigation and hide the truth.

"This is the time when our whole public system could go awry," Lyndon Johnson said just three days after the assassination. "Not just the Republican party and Democratic party, but the American system of government."[49] It was peculiar for Johnson to say, considering the FBI had already concluded that a lone-nut, Communist sympathizer had assassinated the President by himself. Oswald, by himself, did not threaten the future of the American system of government. Only a domestic conspiracy, something along the lines of a military takeover involving people inside and outside government, could have jeopardized the American government.

Amazingly, J. Edgar Hoover reportedly said something similar. A year after the assassination, Hoover discussed the crime with the son of Texas oilman Billy Byars, who claimed Hoover said the following: "If I told you what I really know, it would be very dangerous to this country. Our whole political system could be disrupted."[50]

Considering all the information given to the FBI before the assassination, Hoover must have known a domestic conspiracy assassinated JFK, which could explain why he was so quick to say Oswald was the lone gunman. In November 1950, after an assassination attempt against President Truman by Puerto Rican nationalists, Hoover was asked by the attorney general to investigate if it was part of a conspiracy to overthrow the government. In reply, Hoover wrote he would ". . . conduct investigation as requested . . ."[51] There was no equivocation, and the FBI investigated a potential plot to destroy the United States government. Compare that to Hoover's response on November 24, 1963, just two days after the JFK assassination, when he wrote: "The thing I am most concerned about . . . is having something issued so we can convince the public that Oswald is the real assassin . . ."

The difference in Hoover's reaction is quite telling. When considered in conjunction with his statement that "our whole political system" was in jeopardy after

Kennedy's death, the only conclusion one can draw is that America was the victim of a coup d'état. And Hoover knew it.

Hoover gave a speech twelve days after the assassination, where he implied that Kennedy's murder was justified because he was unqualified to do the job he was elected to do. "Whenever politics and opportunism remain primary consider-ations in the appointment of . . . others charged with the administration of justice," Hoover said, "*the public should have more adequate guarantees for the immediate removal of those who prove by their unjustifiable actions that they cannot be entrusted with the important responsibilities of their office . . .*"[52] (Author's italics)

It is hard to believe that Hoover was not thinking of JFK when he wrote that speech.

* * *

President Kennedy's life was in danger as the clock ticked closer to Dealey Plaza, for there were rumblings of forcibly removing the President from office from various radical right-wing groups, the military, U.S. intelligence, and organized crime. In Dallas, there was talk of an international conspiracy, which could be con-sidered an overreaction. Unless one considers all the other right-wing government overthrows that happened around the world at the same time. How was it then that the immediate conclusion was that the assassin was an unstable Communist sympathizer who acted alone? There was no reason for this unless what Lyndon Johnson and J. Edgar Hoover said was correct. That disclosure of the truth would have destroyed the American system of government, so what happened in Dallas was suppressed for the country's good.

With the multitude of death threats against Kennedy, I became further con-vinced that the answer to "why" he had to die would be found in the years preced-ing his presidency, for the influential people responsible for his assassination did not come together overnight. By an analysis based on relative plausibility, those most likely involved in the assassination would become apparent. It was especially true of the Cold War years, when Presidents Truman and Eisenhower had to deal with treasonous behavior, such as the military and CIA creating foreign policy to circumvent what the presidents they supposedly served wanted to do. Consider that the Korean War was an act of treason, purposely started by the U.S. military to prevent Truman from allowing South Korea, Formosa (Taiwan), and Japan to fall to the Communists and prevent Communist China from becoming part of the United Nations. That an American-inspired coup to remove Fidel Castro in the summer of 1959 was thwarted when CIA Director Allen Dulles provided details of the coup to the Cubans, resulting in the deaths of the Americans involved. That CIA sabotaged a U-2 spy plane in the spring of 1960 to prevent President Eisenhower from signing a nuclear test ban treaty with the Soviets, which he and Khrushchev were about to do. Presidents who preceded JFK were undermined by those who opposed them, and this book will show that the answer to who killed Kennedy is found in the right-wing Fascist alliances formed long before Kennedy took office. Elements of the radical right, whose animosity festered decade after decade, reached a breaking point. As they watched one President after another take the country in a direction with which they disagreed, they were willing to forcibly remove a president from office before it was too late to reverse what he intended to do.

In summary, in examining past events, it is easily recognizable that there was a pattern of behavior by like-minded people from various groups, who were brought together in a common cause long before the assassination of JFK. And that is the essence of the subject of this book.

This book consists of two volumes, which cover the events before Kennedy's inauguration, focusing on the 1930s through 1960. It will show how various entities were brought together in the war against communism and the preservation of the American way of life, as they perceived it to be. That there was a Fascist movement which grew throughout the decades, culminating in the assassination to preserve the Constitution, which they believed was being rewritten by every President from FDR to Kennedy, and that anything was acceptable to keep America free from communism, the Godless enemy. The funding of domestic social programs at the expense of wealthy taxpayers, civil-rights initiatives that threatened a segregated South, and the appeasement of Communist countries were all signs that communism had infiltrated the U.S. government at the highest levels. These policies had to be stopped by any means possible. And after reading this book, it will become clear that groups wanted to create an international radical right-wing New World Order, which was why Kennedy had to die.

This book also explains how key individuals like Lee Harvey Oswald and Jack Ruby became known to the conspirators during the Cold War years and became part of the conspiracy and an inevitable date with destiny.

* * *

Two final points. First, the American history taught to us was a sanitized version of what those in power wanted us to believe the truth was, which applies to the Kennedy assassination and the events in the twentieth century that led to it. I ask the reader to keep this in mind as you read this book.

Second, as you read this book, I ask that you consider the evidence presented, which occurred before 1960, as if you are unaware that the JFK assassination ever took place. Then ask yourself the question—could the assassination of JFK have been considered a necessary evil by the radical right to preserve the American way of life and defend the country against the threat of communism, which they believed President Kennedy failed to recognize? If the answer to this questions is yes, then why Kennedy had to die, what happened in Dealey Plaza, and why the crime had to be covered up becomes much easier to comprehend. And in this author's opinion, yes is the only answer which an open-minded person can provide. And how this came to be can be found in the years before Kennedy became President.

Walter J. Herbst
Mahwah, NJ
October 2021

Acronyms

AID	Agency for International Development
AIFLD	American Institute for Free Labor Development
AINS	Agency Identification Numbers, CIA
AMGOT	Allied Military Government
ARC	Addiction Research Center
ARPA	Advanced Research Projects Agency
AVG	American Volunteer Group
BAAC	British—American—Canadian—Corporation, S.A.
BIS	Bank for International Settlements
BOB	Bureau of the Budget
BPF	Banca Privata Fiinanziaria
BRAC	Bureau of Repression of Communist Activities
BUF	British Union of Fascists
CACC	Christian Anti-Communist Crusade
CAP	Civil Air Patrol
CAT	Civil Air Transport
CENIS	Center for International Studies at MIT
CI	Counterintelligence, CIA
CIA	Central Intelligence Agency
CIC	Counterintelligence Corp, U.S. Army
CI/R&A	Counterintelligence Research and Analysis
CISC	Committee for International Student Cooperation
CFR	Council on Foreign Relations
CID	Criminal Investigations Division US Army
CIG	Central Intelligence Group
CIP	Corp of Intelligence Police
COI	Coordinator of Information
CORE	Congress of Racial Equality
CPUSA	Communist Party USA
CRAC	Crusade of Revolutionaries Against Communism
CRBM	Continental Range Ballistic Missile
CRC	Cuban Revolutionary Council

DDP	Deputy Director of Plans. CIA
DGI	Cuban Intelligence in the United States
DOD	Department of Defense
DRE	Cuban Student Directorate
EIN	Employee Identification Number, CIA
FBI	Federal Bureau of Investigation
FBN	Federal Bureau of Narcotics
FCC	Federal Communications Commission
FLN	Front de Liberation Nationale
FOI	Field Operations Intelligence
FPCC	Fair Play for Cuba Committee
FRD	Cuban Revolutionary Front
G-2	U.S. Army Intelligence
HAMPCO	Haitian-American Meat and Products Company
HSCA	House Select Committee on Assassinations
HUAC	House Un-American Activities Committee
IARF	International Association for Religious Freedom
ICBM	Intercontinental Ballistic Missile
ILO	International Labor Office
INCA	Information Council of the Americas
INR	Intelligence and Research Bureau, State Department
INRA	Instituto Nacional de Reforma Agraria
INS	Immigration and Naturalization Service
IO	International Organizations Division, CIA
IRCA	International Railways of Central America
JIC	Joint Intelligence Committee
JIOA	Joint Intelligence Objectives Agency
JCS	Joint Chiefs of Staff
KGB	Soviet Intelligence Group
KMT	Kuomintang, Chiang Kai Shek's troops
LTV	Ling-Temco-Vought
MGB	Ministry of State Security, Soviet Union
MI	Military Intelligence
MIT	Massachusetts Institute of Technology
MK/NAOMI	CIA Mind Control Program
MK/ULTRA	CIA Drug Experimentation Program
MRR	Movement of Revolutionary Recovery
MVD	Ministry of Internal Affairs, Soviet Union
NAACP	National Association for the Advancement of Colored People

NANA	North American Newspaper Alliance
NATO	North Atlantic Treaty Organization
NCFE	National Committee for a Free Europe
NDF	National Defense Fund
NIA	National Intelligence Authority
NIS	Naval Intelligence Service
NKVD	Soviet Domestic Law Enforcement Agency
NOPD	New Orleans Police Department
NORAD	North American Air Defense Command
NSA	National Security Agency
NSA	National Students Association
NSC	National Security Council
NYPD	New York Police Department
NYSPI	New York State Psychiatric Institute
OAS	Organisation Armee Secrete
OAS	Organization of American States
OCB	Operations Coordinating Board
OCI	Overseas Consultants, Inc
ONI	Office of Naval Intelligence
OPC	Office of Policy Coordination
OS	Office of Security, CIA
OSO	Office of Special Operations
OSS	Office of Strategic Services
PB-7	Program Branch 7, Assassination branch within OPC
PCF	French Communist Party
PCG	Planning Coordination Group
PCI	Italian Communist Party
PERMINDEX	Right-wing European CIA front company
POW	Prisoner of War
PPS	Policy Planning Staff
PRC	People's Republic of China
PSB	Psychological Strategy Board
PSI	Italian Socialist Party
QJ/WIN	CIA assassin.
QKENCHANT	CIA program to recruit civilians.
RPF	Rassemblement du Peuple Francais
SAC	Special Agent in Charge, FBI
SAC	Strategic Air Command, Air Force
SACEUR	Supreme Allied Commander Europe
SCEF	Southern Conference Education Fund

SCI	OSS's Secret Counterintelligence
SDECE	Service de Documentation Exterieure ey de Contre-Espionnage
SIC	Scientific Intelligence Committee
SIG	Special Investigations Group, CIA
SIGINT	Signals Intelligence, NSA
SIOP	Single Integrated Operational Plan
SISS	Senate Internal Security Subcommittee
SNFE	Second National Front of the Escambray
SOD	Special Operations Division
SOFINDUS	Sociedad Financiera Industrial
SRS	Security Research Staff, CIA
SS	Nazi Germany's Secret Police
SSU	Strategic Services Unit
SWP	Socialist Workers Party
TSS	Technical Services Staff, CIA
U-2	CIA High-Altitude Spy Plane
UGEMA	Union Generale des Etudiants Musulmans Algeriens
UN	United Nations
UNTCOK	United Nations Temporary Commission on Korea
UPI	United Press International
USC	Unitarian Service Committee
UWF	United World Federalists
WCC	World Commerce Corporation
WFDY	World Federation of Democratic Youth
X-2	OSS's Counterintelligence Branch
ZR/ALERT	CIA Hypnosis Program
ZR/AWARD	CIA Behavior-Modification Operations
ZR/RIFLE	CIA Assassination Program
ZSP	Polish Student Union

- 1 -

A New World Order

"Communism is merely a convenient bugaboo. It is the Fascist-minded men of America who are the real enemies of our institutions through their solidarity and their ability and willingness to turn the wealth of America against the welfare of America."

—Harold Ickes, FDR's Interior Secretary

At the time of JFK's assassination, there was an element of American society that still wanted to maintain the status quo. It was a country based on radical right-wing, anti-Communist, Christian, white supremacist principles. The movement began after World War I, one year after Communists took control in Russia. The world was changing then, as the Gilded Age gave way to the mass migration of "inferiors" and Communists from Slavic countries that threatened the Western way of life. This "Red Scare" was temporarily suppressed. Still, the fear remained because there was a long history of equating communism with Judaism and racial inferiority. Many Americans, Western Europeans, and the Vatican supported the rise of fascism in Europe. Fascists were anti-Communists. As a result, they were acceptable because radical right-wing elites passionately feared communism and its appeal to the oppressed masses, whom they considered a drain on society. And the only way to do this in the United States was by creating a new world order based on eugenics, class structure, Christian values, racial segregation, and the containment of communism. This radical Fascist new world order was propagandized as a war of good vs. evil during the Cold War, to the extent that it became a national ideology that would eventually lead to the assassination of JFK. And to understand this, it is necessary to know how this new world order came to be.

* * *

The rise of Marxism in Russia, which occurred as World War I veterans returned home to find that jobs were scarce, resulted in general strikes and political unrest throughout America and worldwide. European countries, devastated by war and economically depleted, were particularly vulnerable. In response, even though the Armistice had ended the war, both England and France involved themselves in the Russian Civil War, sending troops to fight the Bolsheviks. President Wilson was equally concerned and ordered thousands of American troops to remain in Russia as well. The containment of communism became a priority because the future of Western Europe was at risk. But it was not just Europe that worried Wilson. Back home, many of the disenfranchised who distrusted corporate America, who wanted improved working conditions and a livable wage, considered socialism and communism a means of ending the income inequality inherent in a Capitalist system. And if allowed to spread, the share-the-wealth mentality of communism had the potential to bring down any Western government, including the United States, for it offered an attractive alternative for the oppressed masses. It had to be contained, which was why American troops remained in Russia. Little did President Wilson know that controlling the Soviets would dominate American foreign policy for almost the remainder of the Twentieth Century.

In the United States, suppressing communism called for drastic measures, which was why in the two years following World War I, Congress passed the Espionage Act, the Sedition Act, and the Anarchist Act, all designed to keep the status quo in place. Something had to be done, for many were unemployed and disgruntled. Those that did have jobs had to endure unacceptable working conditions. As a result, by 1919, nearly twenty percent of American workers had already joined a picket line in an attempt to unionize, which those in power believed was the first step toward communism.[1] In February of that year, a general strike shutdown Seattle, a walkout occurred in Butte, Montana, and a textile strike hit Lawrence, Massachusetts. Over 1,800 strikes occurred between March and August, Boston's police walked off the job in September, a quarter-million steelworkers left their mills, and coal miners went on strike in November. The potential shift towards communism was a genuine concern, prompting U.S. Attorney General A. Mitchell Palmer to respond fast. On November 7, 1919, raids on the Union of Russian Workers offices occurred in twelve cities. In January 1920, agents raided Communist Party meeting halls in thirty-three cities, resulting in the arrest of approximately 4,000 suspected members. Over 500 people, many without probable cause, were deported.[2] Palmer considered the threat to the U.S. dangerous, and his violent response justified. He warned that a "blaze of revolution" threatened to destroy the American way of life, "licking the altars of churches, leaping into the belfry of the school bell, crawling into the sacred corners of American homes, seeking to replace marriage vows with libertine laws, burning up the foundations of society."[3]

The panic eventually died down, but by the mid-1930s, communism once again gained momentum as those suffering blamed capitalism for the Great Depression and the economic hardships the nation faced. Leftist writer Upton Sinclair unsuccessfully ran for governor of California on a Socialist platform. Congress proposed a lifetime yearly pension of $2,000 for every senior citizen. Huey Long pushed a "Share the Wealth" program, which would have crippled the U.S. economy. Radio personality Father Coughlin attacked bankers and the Federal Reserve System. Of course, FDR's New Deal elites were communists in disguise.[4]

The radical right was determined to stop this turn to the left. In Congress, Republicans joined forces with conservative Southern Democrats in opposition to FDR, who, in their eyes, was a Communist. Many outside politics agreed with this characterization. It was the Depression; times were terrible, and there were millions out of work and destitute. Yet, many right-wing elites believed these struggling people were a drain on the American economy and should be dealt with harshly, not provided handouts. For many, there was no sympathy, for they feared their property was in jeopardy of being taken away, as the New Deal threatened to force the well-to-do to subsidize, against their will, the so-called "freeloaders." Opponents of FDR pointed to the Declaration of Independence and that life, liberty, and the pursuit of happiness was every American's birthright. Taken from the English philosopher John Locke's *Second Treatise of Government*, which said it was a law of nature that everyone had the right to protect their "life, liberty, and property," it provided an almost religious justification for their callousness. The word "property" was the key here. Right-wing elites believed their God-given rights were in jeopardy when the government took money from American citizens without their consent. To them, the destruction of domestic communism was necessary, for the American way of life was at stake. And it was this, the preservation of the American way of life and self-determination, that the government did not have the right to take money from individuals without their consent, more than anything else, that formed the basis of Communist opposition in the United States. It would become the mantra of the radical right for the remainder of the Twentieth Century and was why any future President who proposed social programs would also be labeled a Communist.[5]

In the mid-1930s, Henry Luce's *Time* magazine reported that "today, with few exceptions, members of the so-called Upper Class frankly hate Franklin Roosevelt."[6] It was a strong word to use, but it did capture the intense hatred the radical right felt for FDR, and there was no mistake that Luce was an avid right-winger his entire life. His wife, Clare Boothe Luce, was an active anti-Communists throughout the Cold War. They had CIA connections, funded anti-Castro Cuban raids against Castro, and purchased the Zapruder film through *Life* magazine, which, of course, graphically depicted Kennedy's assassination. To spare the country from the film's gruesomeness, Henry Luce decided to lock the movie away. However, that the film does not support all shots coming from the Texas School Book Depository may have been the real reason. A case in point was *Life's* article describing the Zapruder film, obviously written to support the lone-gunman scenario:

Since by this time the limousine was 50 yards past Oswald and the President's back was turned almost directly to the sniper, it has been hard to understand how the bullet could enter the front of his throat [which the doctor's claimed]. Hence the recurring guess that there was a second sniper somewhere else. But the 8mm film shows the President turning his body far around to the right as he waves to someone in the crowd. *His throat is exposed–toward the sniper's nest–just before he clutches it.*[7] (Author's italics)

The last sentence is an outright lie, for JFK never turned even slightly, let alone toward the sniper's nest. The question is, who was the right-wing Luce protecting, and why would he be willing to suppress the truth? The only rational explanation was to bury a right-wing involvement in the assassination and perpetuate the myth that a single Communist had killed the President. Luce's decision to conceal the Zapruder film does not mean he knew who killed the President. The American way of life was at stake, and the radical right-wing elites protected their own.

* * *

Roosevelt's Interior Secretary, Harold Ickes, addressed a Town Hall forum in Detroit in 1935. and he took the opportunity to criticize FDR's wealthy opponents. Ickes blasted the President's elite detractors, who "were a "cruelly ruthless exploiting class looking to a return to power that will make it possible for them to grow even richer while the masses become poorer and poorer." "Communism is merely a convenient bugaboo," Ickes continued. "It is the Fascist-minded men of America who are the real enemies of our institutions through their solidarity and their ability and willingness to turn the wealth of America against the welfare of America."[8]

One did not use the term "Fascist-minded men" lightly in 1935, and it demonstrates how far to the right the opposition to FDR was positioned. These were people who approved of what Hitler was doing, and Ickes was not the only one who feared the consequences that could result from the rise of the Fascist-right in America. A left-leaning union official warned of a "conspiracy . . . to identify as Communist" anyone who dared "to assert independence in thought," and that the "great industrial and financial monopolists" intended to "control the economy of the United States in the interests of a few at the expense of many, to swell profits and beat down wages." But the fiery warnings made by Ickes and others failed to resonate with a large segment of the country, and in 1938 the fear of communism led to the creation of the House Committee on Un-American Activities (HUAC), which was authorized to investigate "subversive and un-American propaganda." Their mandate was to remove anything that even remotely hinted at a connection to communism, and they did not disappoint. They accused the Federal Theater Project of only putting on Communist plays and charged that guidebooks published by the Federal Writers Project contained Red propaganda. In 1939 John Steinbeck's *The Grapes of Wrath* was labeled pro-Communist. That same year, most Americans polled believed the CPUSA (Communist Party USA) took direct orders from the USSR, and by 1940 twenty-six percent wanted suspected Communists deported. Only eleven percent of those polled thought they should be left alone. Despite that Fascist states in Germany and Italy were ramping up their aggression, it was clear to the American people that communism was still the number one enemy of the United States. And a lean towards fascism continued to gain momentum within some factions in the country, for anything was acceptable if it suppressed the spread of communism.[9]

As early as 1930, the "American Fascisti" appeared in Atlanta with a "membership restricted to native-born white Americans." The *Baltimore Sun* reported they were "born out of the throes of unemployment and the canny exploitation of what its leaders term a Communistic threat to white supremacy." By 1934, 20,000 members of *The Friends of a New Germany* packed Madison Square Garden to support Hitler and the Nazis. They would eventually dissolve and reappear in 1936 as the *German American Bund*. That same year Herbert Hoover called for a "Holy Crusade for Freedom." According to Hoover, the country had to "fight again for a government founded upon ordered individual liberty and opportunity that was the American vision. If we lose, we will continue down this new deal road to some sort of personal government based upon collectivist [Socialist] theories . . ." The point is, there were many Americans who found fascism and its hateful message appealing.[10]

Fortune magazine criticized the New Deal in an editorial, writing that, "The spokesmen of the present Administration almost never mention liberty. They talk democracy, and they talk as if democracy were the core of the American Dream, rather than liberty." It was an important distinction, for liberty was synonymous with self-determination and democracy the founding fathers equated with mob rule.[11]

In 1936, newspaper columnist Dorothy Thompson wrote about "bands" of Fascist groups throughout America. A member of the group called *Christian Vigilantes* sent her a letter that included their motto: "Please learn by heart: Christian Nordic white America will keep the Jews and Negroes in their place of Jim Crow inferiority." Thompson wrote they were "white male Protestants" who justified their actions to "defend the United States and the Constitution." To do this, they intended to "exterminate Anarchists, Communists, Catholics, Negroes, and Jews; to restrict immigration and deport all undesirable aliens; to support and participate in lynch law; to arm its members for civil war . . . and eventually to establish a dictatorship in America."[12]

Many were indeed nothing more than Ku Klux Klan members who found fascism a means to promote their hatred. But it also included anti-New Dealers who were against FDR's social programs, which was why fascism was on the rise, and it would reach a fever pitch by the time of JFK's assassination. It was sometimes tricky, as one decade gave way to the next, to recognize who these people were and what they represented because, for the most part, they did not dress like Nazis or Mussolini henchmen. As author James Waterman Wise wrote in 1936, there were wealthy upper-class Fascists as well, who wanted to "enslave the masses." "Do not look to them to raise aloft the swastika," he warned. It would probably appear "wrapped up in the American flag and heralded as a plea for liberty and preservation of the constitution."[13]

In 1938, U.S. ambassador to Germany, William Dodd, wrote that "fascism is on the march today in America. A prominent executive of one of America's largest financial corporations told me point blank that if the progressive trend of the Roosevelt administration continued, he would be ready to take definite action to bring fascism to America."[14]

* * *

The 1920s were a turbulent time in Germany, as war reparations crippled the country's economy. In 1923 the German mark was a staggering 4.2 billion to the dollar, and as inflation soared, the Reichsbank printed money at a staggering rate, making it virtually worthless. Then, seemingly overnight, things began to change. Foreign investments, mainly from the United States, inundated Germany because interest rates charged there were far more significant than what could be obtained anyplace else in the form of short and long-term loans. And despite the atrocities that took place as the Nazis gained power, American business remained enthusiastic and did not perpetuate this profitable relationship.[15]

A prime example was the law firm Sullivan and Cromwell, who, through the auspices of the Dulles brothers, John Foster and Allen, represented various international banks and investment firms and was one of the leaders that rebuilt Germany after World War I. John Foster, an ardent right-wing cold warrior, would become Secretary of State under Eisenhower. Around the same time, Allen would head CIA during the Agency's Golden Years in the 1950s, only to be dismissed by JFK after the Bay of Pigs disaster. He would also serve on the Warren Commission, which investigated JFK's assassination, a very suspicious appointment.

John Foster Dulles' connection to Nazi Germany went far beyond an attempt to maximize profits for the company for whom he worked. As described by author David Talbot in his book, *The Devil's Chessboard*:

> Foster . . . funneled massive US investments into German industrial giants like IG Farben and Krupp. The profits generated . . . then flowed to France and Britain in the form of reparations and then back to the US to pay off war loans.

> [He] refused to shut down the Berlin office of Sullivan and Crom-
> well—whose attorneys were forced to sign their correspondence "Heil
> Hitler"—until his partners, fearful of a public relations disaster, insisted
> he do so.
>
> Even after the Nazi regime pushed through the anti-Semitic Nurem-
> berg Laws of 1935 and unleashed a wave of terror against the Jews,
> Foster clung to a sympathetic view of the Fuhrer. He could not help
> being impressed by a man 'who from humble beginnings . . . has attained
> the unquestioned leadership of a great nation,' Foster told a friend in
> 1937 . . .[16]

It was a strange dynamic as World War II approached. Communism was considered an evil that had to be eradicated from American society, while fascism was
supported by many of America's wealthiest citizens, regardless of how heinous German atrocities became. And the reason for this was quite simple, for if allowed to
gain momentum, communism could unite the working class against the wealthy.
Under fascism, the powerful flourished at the expense of the masses. The importance of preserving the American way of life varied depending on where one fell
on the economic ladder. Short of revolution, who had the upper hand was not in
question, And the intent was to ensure that revolution, whether like what happened
in the Soviet Union or figuratively, as in a transfer of power by the passage of laws to
make things more equitable, could not be allowed to happen. No matter how much
violence was needed to suppress it.

And nowhere was this more evident than in John Foster Dulles' support of
Nazi Germany. He took care of his German clients, hiding their U.S. assets and
protecting their U.S. subsidiaries from being confiscated by the federal government
as alien property. By the end of the war, there were accusations that Foster collaborated with the enemy, as many of his clients were under the watchful eye of the
Justice Department's antitrust division.[17]

Meanwhile, Allen Dulles, acting on behalf of President Roosevelt, met with
Adolph Hitler in March 1933 to learn what he could about the new German leader.
Still, his fundamental objective was to investigate how the Nazi rise to power would
affect his client's in Germany and the United States. He later told his brother that
he did not find Hitler particularly alarming, and he was "rather impressed" with
Goebbels' "sincerity and frankness." The younger Dulles eventually came to recognize the danger posed by the Nazis, but it did not stop him from continuing to do
business with Nazi financial and industrial giants. One example is that he joined
the board of J. Schroder Bank, the U.S. subsidiary of a London bank that *Time*
magazine in 1939 called "an economic booster of the Rome-Berlin axis."

Both Dulles brothers had a long history of working with Schroder. Representing
United Fruit Company in 1936, they involved the bank in a project in Guatemala,

where United Fruit took control of the International Railways of Central America (IRCA), which they needed to bring bananas to the U.S. Not coincidentally, the president of Schroder Bank remained a member of the IRCA board through 1954, when the CIA orchestrated a coup in Guatemala under Allen Dulles' leadership, once again on behalf of United Fruit, to oust a pro-Communist leader.[18]

Another close friend of Allen Dulles', Thomas McKittrick, was president of the Bank for International Settlements (BIS), which handled German reparation payments after World War I. By 1940, the Nazis controlled BIS, and after the war, the Allies charged five of its directors with war crimes, including Hermann Schmitz, the CEO of IG Farben. This chemical industrial giant used slave labor during the war and produced Zyklon B, the gas used in concentration camps.

Harry Dexter White, an aide to U.S. Treasury Secretary Henry Morgenthau, angrily said McKittrick was "doing business with the Germans while our American boys are fighting the Germans." Still, McKittrick hired John Foster as legal counsel, who successfully thwarted the effort. McKittrick made a business trip to the U.S. in the winter of 1942. Dozens of powerful financiers and industrialists, including the executives of several corporations such as General Motors and Standard Oil, companies that profited handsomely from doing business with the Nazis, gathered for a banquet in his honor at New York's University Club. Afterward, Morgenthau tried to prevent McKittrick from leaving the U.S., but he could depart only after Allen Dulles intervened.[19]

The reason the Dulles brothers, and others like them, were permitted to carry on business with Germany in the manner they did was quite simple. England and France were not paying their World War I debts to the U.S., and the Nazis were not considered a threat to American interests. As far as what was happening to the Jews, it was much easier to ignore the problem and look the other way. The truth is, anti-Semitism was prevalent in the U.S. and throughout Western Europe, and objections were few and far between regarding what the Germans were doing. Containing the spread of communism remained the number one concern of the radical right in the United States, not the curtailment of Nazi atrocities, and Joseph Kennedy, JFK's father, was a testament to this.

* * *

Joe Kennedy traveled in radical right-wing circles for most of his adult life. A supporter of Nazi Germany, he was accused of being a Fascist and an anti-Semite by his opponents, of whom there were many, and these accusations were not without merit. He advocated isolationism right up to the bombing of Pearl Harbor. He maintained a close relationship with the America First Committee, whose objective was for America not to fight in another European war. "I'm willing to spend all I've got to keep us out of the war," he said. ". . . Hitler has all the ports of Europe.

The German Stukas are already over Africa. Keep out of the war and keep the hemisphere out of it. If any of the Latin Americans act up, kick them in the teeth."[20]

Joe Kennedy did not see a problem in dealing with Hitler. He said, "it is unproductive for both democratic and dictator countries to widening the division now existing between them by emphasizing their differences . . . The democratic and dictator countries differ . . . but that should not preclude the possibility of good relations between them . . ."[21]

And a young JFK supported his father. He wrote, ". . . while it seemed to be unpopular with the Jews, etc. [Joe's speech] was considered to be very good by everyone who wasn't bitterly ant-Fascist . . ."[22]

Joe Kennedy was anti-Semitic. The German Ambassador to London, Herbert von Dirksen, later quoted him as saying: ". . . it was not so much that we [Germany] wanted to get rid of the Jews that was so harmful to us [in America], but rather the loud clamor with which we accomplished this purpose . . ."[23]

In the wake of Kristallnacht, Kennedy wrote to Charles Lindbergh, who shared his views. According to Joe, "even assuming that the reports from there are colored, isn't there some way to persuade them it is on a situation like this that the whole program of saving western civilization might hinge. It is more and more difficult for those seeking peaceful solutions to advocate any plan when the papers are filled with such horror."[24]

Kennedy's reference to the saving of western civilization was proof that he shared the views of Fascists in the United States and that the real villains of the world were the Soviet Union and Japan, not Nazi Germany. The latter was part of western civilization and warranted saving. In his mind, Germany did not have to curtail their attacks on Jews, just do it quietly, so the U.S. could turn a blind eye to what was occurring and maintain a business-as-usual relationship with the Third Reich. A large portion of America's right-wing felt the same way.

Perhaps another son of Joe Kennedy's, Joe Jr., explained the radical right regarding the Nazis better than anyone and reflected the circle in which they traveled. "They [the Jews] were at the heads of all big business . . . ," he wrote to his father during a visit to Germany in 1934. "It is all to their credit for them to get so far, but their methods had been quite unscrupulous . . . As far as the brutality is concerned, it must have been necessary . . . It was a horrible thing, but in every revolution, you have to expect some bloodshed." "Hitler is building a spirit in his men that could be envied in any country . . . he has passed the sterilization law, which I think is a good thing. I don't know how the [Catholic] Church feels about it, but it will do away with many of the disgusting specimens of men who inhabit this earth . . ."[25]

The Kennedy family was willing to ignore Nazi atrocities because Germany was against communism. They did not object to removing "disgusting specimens of men" from the planet forever, be they Jews or Slavic Communists. It was why they supported Germany and opposed the Soviet Union. The prevailing thought was that Jews were responsible for the rise of Bolshevism in Russia, and if communism were ever to spread throughout the western world, the Jews would be the conduit through which this would occur. Today we would consider this ridiculous, but that was not the case in the 1930s. So, the support of Nazi Germany, despite the atrocities they committed, was not surprising and was not restricted to the U.S. alone.

In England, Diana Mitford was one of the six Mitford sisters, a group of British socialites who gained prominence in the 1930s for their political views. Diana was very much pro-Nazi, and in October 1936, she married British Parliament member Oswald Mosley, who had founded the British Union of Fascists (BUF) in 1932. The couple had good connections in Germany, to the extent that Hitler attended their marriage at the home of Joseph Goebbels in Berlin. Two days before the wedding, over two thousand black-shirted BUF members, led by Mosley, had marched in London to support fascism. Mosley addressed his supporters when it was over: "The Government surrenders to Red violence and Jewish corruption. We never surrender . . . within us is the flame that shall light this country and shall later light this world."[26]

Another Mitford sister, Unity, was close to Adolph Hitler, who was smitten with her, and the two got together often. In a letter to her father after first meeting the Fuhrer, Unity wrote, "I'd suppose I am the luckiest girl in the world. For me, he is the greatest man of all time."

For the next five years, Unity was part of Hitler's inner circle. When Hitler announced the Anschluss in 1938, she appeared with him on the balcony in Vienna, and at a Hitler Youth festival, she gave a virulently anti-Semitic speech. She was so distraught in 1939 when Britain and Germany went to war that she shot herself in the head in an attempted suicide, but she survived, only to die a few years later.[27]

Lest one thinks the above is the isolated case of two misguided sisters, consider the writings of historian Andrew Roberts. "There was no shortage of people in 1930s Britain," Roberts wrote, "who would have viewed a British accommodation with Hitler positively, if not with enthusiasm. This feeling extended far beyond the lunatic fringe of anti-Semites. Perhaps most interestingly, a significant proportion of the British aristocracy had strong pro-German and sometimes even pro-Nazi leanings."[28]

There was a similar sentiment felt in Spain as Paul Preston wrote in *The Spanish Holocaust*: "In Spain, as in other European countries, anti-Semitism had reached even greater intensity after 1917. It was taken as axiomatic that socialism was a Jewish creation and that the Russian revolution had been financed by Jewish capital . . ."[29]

By the 1930s, a novel entitled *The Protocols of the Elders of Zion* became very popular in Spain. Its premise is that a secret Jewish government, the Elders of Zion, was plotting the destruction of Christianity with the goal of Jewish world domination. Meanwhile, Marques de Quintanar, the founder of an ultra-right pro-Monarchist journal *Accion Espanola,* claimed: "The great worldwide Jewish-Masonic conspiracy injected the autocratic Monarchies with the virus of democracy to defeat them . . ." To Monarchists and far-right radicals, democracy was equivalent to communism, and even fascism was preferable.[30]

The Spanish Civil War lasted from 1936-1939, resulting in the Fascists defeating Communists and Socialists for control of Spain. In his victory speech in Madrid on May 19, 1939, Generalissimo Franco warned that the fight was not yet over. "Let us not deceive ourselves," he said. "The Jewish spirit, which permitted the alliance of big capital with Marxism and which was behind so many pacts with the anti-Spanish revolution . . . still beats in the hearts of many . . ." And it was through unbridled violence that Franco intended to curtail the rise of communism in Spain.[31]

Most people are aware that in 1938, Britain's Prime Minister Neville Chamberlain traveled to Germany and signed the famous Munich Agreement with Adolph Hitler, which, in Chamberlain's words, was "symbolic of the desire of our two peoples never to go to war again." He returned to London triumphantly, waving the document as he exited his plane, but the continuation of Hitler's wave of terror ended the excitement. Many ridiculed Chamberlain, and generations have considered him naïve. However, highly respected author William Manchester had a different take in his three-volume masterpiece of Churchill entitled *The Last Lion.* He argued that Chamberlain signed the agreement because he fully expected Hitler to head east and attack the Soviet Union. From the Nazi perspective, the desire to exterminate the Jews had to include the destruction of Russia, for the Jews were responsible for that nation's very existence. Like his right-wing counterparts in the United States, Chamberlain considered the Soviet Union the world's greatest threat, and he was willing to get into bed with Hitler to stop them. And since the Jews were behind the rise of Bolshevism, their elimination by the Nazis prevented them from spreading communism throughout Western Europe.[32]

The view in Europe was well defined. That allowing Judaism to flourish increased the opportunity for communism to grow, which was why right-wing Fascists in the United States and European Monarchists supported fascism and Hitler's desire to eliminate the Jewish people. And although it was still many years away, the Darwinist objectives of racial purity shared by these right-wing European Monarchists and their White Nationalist American allies would be one of the leading causes behind the assassination of John F. Kennedy. As the years progressed, these trans-Atlantic allies would work closely together fighting communism and were motivated by a desire to maintain a class system based on racial segregation that also rejected wealth redistribution. And as the Presidency of JFK approached, their desire to rid the world of the Red Menace increased. Also certain was the sense of betrayal they would feel when their policies were opposed by one of their own who became President of the United States.

* * *

Socialism proliferated in Italy after the Russian Revolution in 1917, which the Catholic Church viewed with tremendous anxiety. More than one-half million Italians had died during World War I, and in the 1920s, socialism was on the rise, with the fear of communism gripping the Vatican.[33] So, it was not a surprise that the Vatican-sponsored Popular Party worked to lure people away from this looming menace that had the potential to take over Italian politics and potentially destroy the Vatican. And with Vatican support, by 1922, the Popular Party was among the country's largest. Meanwhile, Mussolini needed their help to overtake the Socialists in Parliament, who were growing in popularity. As a result, his Fascist Party adopted a platform that ended liberalism and imposed an authoritarian Catholic state which, he correctly believed, would be supported by the Vatican.

Only the Fascists, Mussolini proclaimed, could prevent Italy from following Russia's path. Pope Pius XI agreed, and when Mussolini became prime minister by appointment of the king, he did so with the Pope's blessing. There was still violence targeted against Catholics by Italian Fascist sectors, which the Vatican-sponsored publication *La Civilita Cattolica* continued to denounce. Still, they never again criticized Mussolini or fascism directly. And around the same time, Pius XI's first encyclical belittled the United Nations and its liberal, all-inclusive agenda, cementing his support for Mussolini. Mussolini responded by showering the Church with money and other gestures designed to ingratiate himself with Italian Catholics. However, by the spring of 1923, the Popular Party found itself abandoned. Mussolini no longer needed them because the support from the Vatican was enough for him to maintain power. As *La Civilta Cattolica* proclaimed: "The shouts of Mussolini's squads, 'down with Bolshevism!' are attracting supporters . . . all of Fascism consists simply of a protest and revolt against socialism." The Vatican's support of Mussolini was secure.[34]

Mussolini continued to work hard to appease the Vatican. The Italian government only used Church-approved books to teach religion in schools. Gambling halls were closed. Church holidays were included in the civil calendar. And the Bank of Rome, closely tied to the Vatican and on the verge of bankruptcy, was saved. In response, the Vatican issued a "Program of Collaboration of the Catholics with the Mussolini Government" in September 1923. It advised Catholics to ". . . think with terror of what might happen in Italy if the Honorable Mussolini's government were to fall, perhaps to an insurrection by subversive [Communist] forces, and so they [the Vatican] have every interest in supporting it."[35] The Vatican's motivation for aligning with Mussolini was clear—communism was their biggest threat, and they needed the Fascists to prevent a repeat of the Russian revolution in Italy.

In 1918, Pope Benedict XV ordered Vatican librarian Achille Ratti (the future Pope Pius XI) to go the Warsaw as his emissary. While there, Ratti heard clergy consistently calling Jews enemies of Catholic Poland, which was not surprising since the history of Jewish maltreatment by the Church was indisputable. As early as 1555, for murdering Jesus, Pope Paul IV had ordered all Jews under his control to live in ghettos and be confined to the most menial occupations. Conditions remained that way until Jews were liberated from the ghettos by the Italian conquest of Rome in 1870, but they continued to be mercilessly attacked by the Church. *La Civilta Cattolica* warned that "Jews, eternal insolent children, obstinate, dirty, thieves, liars, ignoramuses, pests and the scourge of those near and far . . . managed to lay their hands on . . . all public wealth . . . Oh, how wrong and deluded are those who think that Judaism is just a religion . . . and not in fact a race, a people, and a nation!" The publication charged there was a Jewish conspiracy to rule the world, and Ratti shared this view.[36]

In 1926, Tacchi Venturi, the pope's emissary to Mussolini, gave the Duce a recently published fifteen-page pamphlet entitled *Zionism and Catholicism.* "No one can doubt," its author warned, that the Jews, whom the Vatican equated with communism, sought revolution "to destroy current society and dominate the world by themselves, as their Talmud prescribes." In the United States, many were also concerned with a potential Communist revolution and supported the Vatican. America's Fascist radical right was in total agreement.

The Mussolini government shared the Vatican's concern. In 1933, a Genoese newspaper reported it was essential to "combat Jewish-Zionist-Masonic-Bolshevik—international sectarianism, which constitutes a huge and powerful reality, operating to the detriment of Christian civilization." The pope also thought that Jews and Communists were the same, and the Nazi reaction to both groups was appealing to Pius XI. "I have changed my opinion about Hitler," he told the French ambassador in early March 1933. "It is the first time that such a government voice has been raised to denounce Bolshevism in such categorical terms, joining with the voice of the Pope."

The Church even supported Mussolini after the world condemned Italy for invading Ethiopia, starting World War II. In a Sunday sermon, one archbishop said, ". . . the League of Nations is acting under the influence of occult force[s]," which were "Freemasonry, Bolshevism, Anglicanism." He added that the world could not tolerate a Fascist regime living "in perfect collaboration with the Catholic Church," Venturi seconded this belief directly to Mussolini: "Believe me, Excellency, we are dealing with a terrible trap plotted with the complicity of the League of Nations, which is under the domination of the Jews and the Masons." It was similar to what was being espoused by America's right-wing, who despised the League of Nations with an equal passion.[37]

As Jewish atrocities accelerated in Germany, the Vatican eventually attempted to separate itself from the Nazis. It tried to rationalize their position by saying the Church practiced "defensive anti-Semitism," which was necessary for the battle against "the Jewish invasion in politics, the economy, journalism, cinema, morals, and in all public life." It was a lame excuse. Jews and Communists were a threat; they believed because both intended to dominate the world, starting with Western Europe. This alliance could not be allowed to permeate Western society. As a result, Western Europe and the U.S. ignored what the Nazis were doing. They justified their position by equating the elimination of the Jewish population with preventing Communist expansion into their own countries.

This line of thinking was why Nazi Germany had many American supporters, some in high places. A strong Germany was the first line of defense against the Soviets, and to the right-wing Christian world in the U.S., supporting the Nazis over communism was the lesser of two evils.

* * *

One can understand the view of wealthy right-wing radicals in the United States that communism was their ultimate enemy, for it did have the potential to destroy the American way of life. What is difficult to comprehend is why some continued to support Germany even after Nazi atrocities became known unless one considers the prevailing attitude of right-wing Americans regarding race and ethnicity before World War II. History books have tried to hide this. However, in the name of science, ethnic cleansing began in the United States long before the Nazis came along.

It was a pseudoscience called eugenics. It intended to cleanse the U.S. population of all groups except Nordic, Germanic, and Anglo-Saxon peoples (The Nazis would eventually use the term Aryan, but the name difference does not hide the apparent similarity). Proponents believed middle and upper-class whites had "superior strains" of hereditary genes, which made them superior. Non-white races, other ethnicities, the disabled, even those who were poverty-stricken were all considered "unfit" and in need of population control and isolation from those deemed "fit." It all sounds ridiculous until one understands that groups like the Carnegie Institute and the Rockefeller Foundation provided extensive financing to respected scientists from prestigious universities such as Stanford, Yale, Harvard, and Princeton to support eugenics.

At Stanford, President David Starr Jordan's 1902 work *Blood of a Nation* stated that human blood determined an individual's ability to succeed. Two years later, the Carnegie Institute established a laboratory complex at Cold Spring Harbor, Long Island, that stockpiled millions of index cards on ordinary Americans, enabling researchers to carefully plot the removal of family bloodlines and whole peoples. By 1928, 376 separate university courses in some of the best American schools, with some school enrollments exceeding 20,000 students, included eugenics in their curriculum.

Sterilization laws were passed in Indiana and Virginia, compulsory for patients in mental institutions. California led the way, conducting 1,278 forced sterilizations in 1933 alone, 700 of which were done on women. Scientists could label anyone genetically inferior who did not fit neatly into a preconceived category. Forced sterilization became justified based on this—but it went further than that. Euthanasia was considered acceptable.

In 1918, World War I Army venereal disease specialist Paul Popenoe co-authored a widely used textbook, *Applied Eugenics*, which argued, "From a historical point of view, the first method which presents itself is execution . . . Its value in keeping up the standard of the race should not be underestimated." A chapter was devoted to "Lethal Selection," which proposed that nature cleansed itself "through the destruction of the individual by some adverse feature of the environment, such as excessive cold, or bacteria, or by bodily deficiency." A 1918 Carnegie Institute report suggested that an effective means of getting rid of "defective germ-plasms in the human population" was euthanasia. The most common method of carrying this out was establishing local gas chambers, a harbinger of things to come.[38]

After World War I, as many Europeans looked to flee the war-torn continent, the possibility that an influx of Eastern Europeans could pollute the American gene pool was a concern in the U.S. The 1920 House Committee on Immigration and Naturalization discussed the matter and brought in leading eugenicists as expert witnesses. Eugenics subsequently played a role in the Immigration Act of 1924, which essentially restricted immigration to Aryan and Nordic northern European countries.

Before the Nazi use of the term Aryan, or Anglo-Saxon after World War II, the name Nordic was the White Supremacist bloodline of choice in the U.S. As early as 1916, Madison Grant wrote in his influential eugenicist book, *The Passing of the Great Race: or The Racial Basis of European History*, "The Nordics are, all over the world, a race of soldiers, sailors, adventurers, and explorers, but above all, of rulers, organizers, and aristocrats . . . Chivalry and knighthood . . . are peculiarly Nordic traits, and feudalism, class distinctions, and race pride among Europeans are traceable for the most part to the north."

In 1921, Vice President Calvin Coolidge wanted to restrict immigration. He said, "The Nordics propagate themselves successfully. With other races, the outcome shows deterioration on both sides. Quality of mind and body suggests that observance of ethnic law is as great a necessity to a nation as immigration law."[39]

The *Saturday Evening Post* ran a series of articles in the 1920s promoting Nordicism. In 1922, they wrote about "certain biological laws which govern the crossing of different breeds, whether the breeds be horses or men. These laws should be of considerable interest . . . for so many millions of non-Nordic aliens have poured into this country since 1880 that in serval of America's largest cities these foreign-born and their children far outnumber the native Americans."[40]

The United States Supreme Court even considered eugenics in a 1927 decision. Justice Oliver Wendell Holmes wrote, "It is better for all the world if instead of waiting to execute degenerate offspring for crime, or to let them starve for their imbecility, society can prevent those who are manifestly unfit from continuing their kind . . . Three generations of imbeciles are enough." Years later, the Nazis at the Nuremberg trials quoted Holmes' words in their defense.

There was even a close personal relationship between Carnegie Institute eugenic scientists and Germany's Fascist eugenicists during the 1920s. "There is today one state," Hitler wrote, "in which at least weak beginnings toward a better conception [of immigration] are noticeable. Of course, it is not our model German Republic, but the United States." "I have studied with great interest," he told a fellow Nazi on another occasion, "the laws of several American states concerning prevention of reproduction by people whose progeny would, in all probability, be of no value or be injurious to the racial stock."[41]

When Hitler came to power, America eugenic scientists embraced the Nazi ethnic cleansing program, and California eugenicists republished Nazi propaganda for American consumption. In 1934, as Germany's sterilizations exceeded 5,000 per month, the California eugenics leader C. M. Goethe returned from Germany and told a colleague "that your work has played a powerful part in shaping the opinions of the group of intellectuals who are behind Hitler in this epoch-making program . . . I want you, my dear friend, to carry this thought with you for the rest of your life, that you have really jolted into action a great government of 60 million people."[42]

The fact that the U.S. laid the groundwork for Nazi ethnic cleansing is disturbing. What is outright frightening is that corporate America legitimized the practice through their relationship with the Nazis and their advancement of eugenics. The Rockefeller Foundation was a prime example.

By 1926, Rockefeller had donated some $410,000 (roughly $4 million today) to hundreds of German researchers and awarded $250,000 to the German Psychiatric Institute of the Kaiser Wilhelm Institute. A leading psychiatrist at the Institute, Ernst Rüdin, would become director of the murderous experimentation and research conducted on Jews, Gypsies, and others. Part of the Kaiser Wilhelm Institute's eugenic complex was the Institute for Brain Research. A 1929 grant resulted in the construction of a major center in German race biology. The Institute received additional contributions from the Rockefeller Foundation during the next several years. Another recipient was the Kaiser Wilhelm Institute for Anthropology, Human Heredity, and Eugenics in Berlin and Otmar Freiherr von Verschuer, the Institute for Anthropology, Human Heredity, and Eugenics. Verschuer wrote in *Der Erbarzt*, a eugenic doctor's journal he edited, that Germany's involvement in World War II would yield a "total solution to the Jewish problem." That Josef Mengele was his long-time assistant only adds to Rockefeller's guilt for providing financing to such people.[43]

Eugenics also found support in Franco's Spanish revolution. Major Antonio Vallejo Nagera was the head of psychiatric services for the rebel army and wrote a book in 1934 that called for the castration of psychopaths. His primary calling was the search for "the red gene," which was an attempt to link Marxism and mental deficiency. His book entitled *The Eugenics of Spanishness and the Regeneration of the Race* promoted race advancement based on "hierarchical, military and patriotic" factors. Anyone who disagreed with this, essentially Marxists, Communists, Jews, and Socialists, needed to be eradicated. Vallejo called it "the cleansing of our race" and called for a "modernized Inquisition" to purify the Spanish race of people. Fascists everywhere embraced eugenics.[44]

Charles Lindbergh was an early advocate for Nazi Germany and a leader in the America First movement, which wanted the U.S. to stay out of World War II. He was also a staunch proponent of eugenics. According to Lindbergh, Germany was not a threat to America, but the Soviet Union, that "Asian intruder," was who should concern the U.S. His position mirrored the Vatican's belief that the United States and Europe should join forces to "defend the white race against foreign invasion." He agreed that Northern and Western European whites were "the exemplar of the highest type of civilization yet evolved" and were inherently superior to "the black, brown, and yellow races."[45]

According to Lindbergh, America's bond to Europe, specifically Nazi Germany, was "a bond of race and not of political ideology . . . It is the European race we must preserve; political progress will follow. Racial strength is vital; politics, a luxury. If the white race is ever seriously threatened, it may then be time for us [the United States] to take our part in its protection to fight side by side with the English, French, and Germans, but not with one against the other for our mutual destruction."[46] His point was that the western European bloodline was superior. Those countries should be trying to limit the spread of other peoples, not exterminate their ethnicity by fighting amongst themselves.

The U.S. military at the time agreed with Lindbergh. Even in the late 1930s, books read at West Point and other Army institutions promoted white supremacy. The military taught officers that the white Nordic race always took "the leading part in the great drama of the world's progress," and the embodiment of true Americanism was the advancement of Anglo-Saxon society.[47] As we will see in the ensuing pages, in the year leading up to JFK's assassination, many retired and active military leaders trained under this racist creed aligned themselves with radical right-wing groups, southern race hate groups, and big business. All supported this line of thinking. The potential consequences of the union of such an unsavory alliance were dire indeed.

The U.S. military also had strong opinions regarding the nation's form of government. The Army training manual for 1928 listed the effects of democracy as "demagogism, license, agitation, discontent, anarchy." It was similar to the Vatican's opinion of the League of Nations and the European right-wing's desire to return to an age of monarchism. It coincided with the passion of eugenic scientists to suppress the birth rate of those deemed "unfit," and the right-wing's efforts to stop communism and socialism by any means possible. In short, they could not tolerate anything that jeopardized the American way of life and threatened the radical right-wing Fascist agenda. No wonder the American Liberty League thought they could rely on the Army in their plot to oust FDR from office in the early 1930s.[48]

* * *

The American Liberty League was formed in 1934 to "teach the necessity of respect for the rights of persons and property" and that "the duty of government [was] to encourage and protect individual and group initiative and enterprise." It was a cryptic message instructing the government to keep its hands off the money of the "haves" and to let the "have nots" fend for themselves. There was no compassion in the American Liberty League, and among its corporate sponsors were DuPont, General Motors, Sun Oil Associates, and, not surprisingly, Rockefeller Associates.

At a 1936 Liberty League gathering at Washington's Mayflower Hotel, ex-governor Al Smith, a life-long Democrat, told the crowd FDR was inciting "one class of our people against the other." He said, "if they [New Dealers] want to disguise themselves as Karl Marx or Lenin . . . but I won't stand for their allowing them to march under the banner of Jackson or Cleveland . . . There can only be one capital, Washington or Moscow . . ."[49]

J. Howard Pew, Jr., the president of Sun Oil, was a leading voice of conservatism in corporate America, and he was a driving force behind the American Liberty League. In 1944, Pew echoed the opinion of many when he wrote that "the New Deal is in a much stronger position than it has been for the last several years . . . [and] that within the next two years, America will determine whether our children are to live in a Republic or under National Socialism; and the present Administration is definitely committed to the latter course."[50] And Pew and his influential associates who thought the same as he did would never let that happen.

Pew also financed a group called the Sentinels of the Republic. They were fanatically anti-labor, openly Fascist, and closely connected to the American Liberty League. The Sentinels called the New Deal "Jewish Communism" and insisted "the old line of Americans of $1,200 a year [income] want a Hitler."[51]

Pew and Sun Oil remained closely affiliated with right-wing Fascist corporations and the Christian conservative religious groups they sponsored throughout the Cold War. He was an avid supporter of the radical right-wing John Birch Society, established in the 1950s. As we will see, Sun Oil and Pew would become involved with people in Dallas at the time of the JFK assassination, which, if not directly involved in the crime, associated with people who were. As JFK's assassination drew near, excessively violent, anti-Communist paramilitary groups, including ultra-right retired high-level military officers, racist hate groups, and radical right-wing business people, found each other. They perceived an American shift towards communism and the appeasement of foreign Communist governments by the President of the United States. It all created a sense of desperation among these parties to do something radical to stop such behavior before it was too late. And it was a White Supremacist Christian, racist, anti-Semitic and anti-Communist agenda, born in the fascism and eugenics of the 1930s, that united them.

Pew and the Rockefellers would also jointly fund translators to bring Christianity to third-world Latin American countries. Their fundamental objective was to create an alliance with right-wing dictators, whom they could exploit to generate significant wealth and ensure that the poverty-stricken masses, the "unfits," remained under control and unthreatening.[52]

The connection between Pew and the Rockefeller Foundation is of interest, considering Rockefeller's support of eugenics and each man's relationship to the Liberty League, which wanted to end FDR's New Deal programs designed to finance the less fortunate at the expense of the wealthy. Rockefeller also funded Nazi Germany's eugenics programs, while Pew was close to the Sentinels of the Republic, which claimed the American people wanted another Hitler to lead them. There was a central theme among America's leading radical right-wing citizens, which was suppressing groups perceived to drain society. And they would be accused of being controlled by Communists if these groups attempted to organize and revolt to improve their position, including labor unions, African Americans, Jews, or white liberals. As we have seen, the United States did not have a monopoly on this distorted line of thinking. European Monarchists and the Vatican were horrified by the prospect of a Jewish-inspired worldwide Communist revolt. They considered the elimination of unions the first step in preventing this from happening. One gets the impression that eugenics was a driving force behind all this because it provided a pseudo-scientific rationalization for a belief system based on simple greed, racism, and anti-Semitism, sometimes included extreme violence to promote its agenda.

In his 2002 book *Memoirs*, David Rockefeller wrote that "ideological extremists at either end of the political spectrum have seized upon well-publicized incidents . . . to attack the Rockefeller family for the inordinate influence they claim we have over American political and economic institutions. Some even believe we are part of a secret cabal working against the best interests of the United States, characterizing my family and me as 'internationalists' and with conspiring with others around the world to build a more integrated global political and economic structure—one world, if you will. If that's the charge, I stand guilty, and I am proud of it."[53]

Based on the causes we know the Rockefeller family contributed to, it is safe to say that the new world order included eugenics and the advancement of the white upper class, and nothing more. He was disingenuous by what he omitted from the proposed "secret cabal" that he and others in the United States and Europe wanted to create, for he had CIA connections and was close to Allen Dulles himself. And as David Brooks wrote in the *New York Times* that same year of 2002, Rockefeller "spent his life in the club of the ruling class and was loyal to members of the club, no matter what they did," and cut profitable deals with "oil-rich dictators," among others. "One world," as he wrote, or new world order, to put it another way, was to consist only of whites of Nordic and Anglo-Saxon heritage who contributed to the betterment of society. And other Rockefeller contemporaries shared this vision of new world order.

The FBI described Merwin Hart as "the alleged promoter of an American Fascist Movement." Charles Lindbergh was closely associated with Hart. As early as 1936, an FBI informant said a group connected to Hart approached Lindburgh to create a new "World Movement" based on fascism. And according to Max Wallace, author of *The American Axis, Henry Ford, Charles Lindbergh, and the Rise of the Third Reich*, there was a "clique—anti-Communist, anti-Semitic, and very conservative—made up primarily of military officers, intelligence agents, Republican politicians, and former diplomats. This group believed that Hitler could be useful. They were not necessarily pro-Nazi but believed that German aggression could be channeled eastward to rid Europe of the Soviet menace." [54]

Throughout the summer of 1940, after World War II had begun, but before America's entry, a group of men came together at the Century Club, just off Fifth Avenue in New York City. They all hailed from the east coast and were leaders in journalism, law, finance, and intellectual circles. They called themselves the Century Group. Their membership included Allen Dulles, Truman's future Secretary of State Dean Acheson, and publisher Henry Luce. Though not a member, John McCloy was involved with them and closely associated with people who were. Like Dulles, McCloy was a prominent New York attorney who worked for Cadwalader, Wickersham & Taft, one of the nation's most prestigious firms, and was without question the Twentieth Century's least recognizable national figure. Like Dulles, he did a great deal of work for corporations in Nazi Germany, such as I.G. Farben. And finally, he and Allen Dulles shared one other bond—both would serve as leaders on the Warren Commission. [55]

The men associated with the Century Group loathed FDR's domestic policies. However, as the Nazis became more aggressive and their brutal treatment of Jews gained publicity, even these members who did business in Germany realized that U.S. entry into the war was inevitable and the Nazis had to be defeated. On August 1, 1940, five members visited the White House to explain to President Roosevelt and several Cabinet members how they could get around the Neutrality Act to aid Britain. The next day their proposal was approved by the entire Cabinet. The Century Group had influence.

So, what was their motive for traveling to Washington to help FDR? According to James Conant, president of Harvard University, who began to attend Century Group meetings that fall, the group wanted America to be, in his words, "top dog." Another member, Lew Douglas, wrote to Conant in October. "Our endeavor and

England's endeavor," Douglas wrote, ". . . should be aimed at the reconstruction of a *world order* in which . . . the United States [would be] the dominant power . . ." Conant agreed and stated that, "I believe the only satisfactory solution for this country is for a majority of the *thinking* people to become convinced that we must be a world power, and the price of being a world power is willingness and capacity to fight when necessary . . ."[56] (Author's italics) Douglas' reference to a reconstructed world order goes along with Rockefeller's philosophy, as does Conant's reference to "thinking people" only. Undoubtedly, it was those of white, Christian, Anglo-Saxon, Nordic origin to whom Conant referred.

There were examples of others promoting this new world order as well. After World War II, fellow Centurion Henry Luce also argued that America was now positioned as the world's most significant power and called the postwar era "The American Century."[57] John McCloy was even more direct. In 1946, he wrote: "In the light of what has happened, I would take a chance on this country using its strength *tyrannously* . . . We need, if you will, a Pax Americana, and in the course of it, the world will become more receptive to the Bill of Rights viewpoint than if we do no more than devoutly wish for peace and freedom."[58] (Author's italics)

John McCloy became Assistant Secretary of War in April 1942 and would become President of the World Bank, U.S. High Commissioner to Germany in the post-war era, chairman of Chase Manhattan Bank from 1953-1960, chairman of the Ford Foundation from 1958-1965, a trustee of the Rockefeller Foundation from 1946-1949, and again from 1953 to 1958, chairman of the Council on Foreign Relations from 1954-1970 (to be succeeded by David Rockefeller), chairman or board director of the Atlantic Council, the American Council on Germany, the German-Marshall Fund, the Aspen Institute, and adviser to Presidents Eisenhower, Kennedy, Johnson, Nixon, Carter, and Reagan. The man was well connected. He did not wind up serving on the Warren Commission by accident. He knew how to keep a secret.[59]

John McCloy's new world order mirrored the others, but there was more. It was McCoy who, while working at the War Department when the attack on Pearl Harbor occurred, was the man most responsible for the internment of Japanese U.S. citizens. Americans of German origin were not subject to such treatment because McCloy and his right-wing associates still supported Germany. It was the Nazis they objected to. Was McCloy an advocate of eugenics? There is no evidence that he was, but he indeed traveled in an elite circle that did.

McCloy's willingness to use one's strength tyrannously is not subject to interpretation and can only mean the forced subjugation of foreign nations. It was the code for the rollback of communism, namely, the USSR. America was the only civilized nation still standing in a world of devastation, and the country had the opportunity to flex its muscles and create a world based on an American, Anglo-Saxon way of life, or so Luce, McCloy, and the others like them genuinely believed. It was this line of thinking that would lead to a prolonged Cold War with the USSR and China, who were America's two main Communist adversaries.

The Century Group was also closely aligned with the Council on Foreign Relations (CFR), founded in 1921 to analyze foreign policy issues. It soon became the first American think tank on international affairs and a regular meeting place for the Establishment's elite. As American financial interests became international, men of great wealth found it necessary to involve themselves more deeply in foreign policy matters. Today, it would be called the "Deep State."

John McCloy became involved with the CFR in 1939, which allowed him to interact with Allen Dulles once again, and numerous leaders in politics, finance, and big business. At the time, they wanted to develop a war-planning strategy and be directly involved with the U.S. foreign policy planning apparatus. Soon after Hitler invaded Poland in September 1939, Council members Hamilton Fish Armstrong and Walter H. Mallory traveled to Washington to propose a joint "War and Peace Project" with the State Department, the purpose being to provide global strategic planning. Three months later, the Rockefeller Foundation gave the CFR an initial $44,500 to begin the project. Allen Dulles was among those who started to draft policy papers, and before long, they were exerting influence on the White House. A CFR paper was given to FDR, recommending it was necessary "to achieve military and economic supremacy for the United States within the non-German world." It was clear that these men of power and inflated self-worth were not going to sit idly by and allow political operatives to determine the nation's fate.[60]

As the war neared its end, both the Century Group and the Council on Foreign Relations realized that Nazi Germany was doomed, as Communist Russia had once again become the dominant threat. Unions in Western Europe were considered Communist-inspired. Protecting elite European Monarchists from the rebelling masses who wanted a livable wage and economic security became a priority. And Germany would need to be brought back into the Capitalist fold of Western Europe in due time because their geographic location made them a natural buffer between the West and the USSR. And this suited the White Nationalists in the United States and Europe just fine. To them, a struggle between godless communism and the God-fearing free world was taking place, and it was up to America to ensure that the free world emerged victoriously.[61]

In later years, Senator Barry Goldwater was very critical of the CFR. "Their rational [sic] rests exclusively on materialism," he said. The goal was to contain communism and install right-wing dictators in third-world countries to keep the general masses suppressed, in true eugenics fashion, and keep these nations out of the Communist Bloc. A two-party system has always polarized this country, and the Council on Foreign Relations controlled both parties. "Since 1945, three different Republicans have occupied the White House for . . . sixteen years," Goldwater said. "With the exception of the first seven years of the Eisenhower administration, there has been no appreciable change in foreign or domestic policy direction . . . When a new president comes on board, there is a great turnover in personnel but no change in policy . . ."[62]

In other words, an invisible "Deep State" government has existed since the 1930s that strongly influenced, if not entirely controlled, foreign policy from one administration to the next. In the 1950s, Republican President Dwight Eisenhower called it the Military-Industrial Complex. As he said in his farewell address to the nation, "In the councils of government we must guard against the acquisition of unwarranted influence, whether sought or unsought . . . The potential for the disastrous rise of misplaced power exists and will persist." Around the same time, Democratic Senator Hubert Humphrey agreed. "We have transferred to some of these industrial giants, great power and influence," he said, "[and] the continued concentration of economic power and the loss of the government's decision-making power over aspects of defense policy should worry us."[63]

Misplaced power indeed, directed by those who wanted to control America's destiny. And to fulfill this destiny, everyone was expendable. Truman and Eisenhower would have to deal with this "Deep State" government. Still, it was not until JFK became President that the opposition began to get serious, for he was opposed to what the Deep State wanted to do on so many levels. He signed a nuclear test-ban treaty with the Soviets by bypassing Congress and going to the American people directly; he signed a deal to sell wheat to Russia, which enabled them to feed their people and delay the time when the Soviet economy would self-destruct; he publicly spoke of coexistence with the Soviets, an unspeakable misstep; he began a pullout of troops from Vietnam and intended to institute a complete withdrawal after he was reelected; he passed up the opportunity to invade Cuba during the Cuban Missile Crisis, even though this was what the hardliners around him advised he should do; he allowed the Soviets to remove missiles from Cuba after the Missile Crisis without verification, but agreed to remove U.S.; he decided to never invade Cuba; he initiated talks to normalize relations with Castro's Cuba, even though he knew that appeasement of Communists could not be tolerated; he refused to provide air support during the Bay of Pigs invasion, dooming many Cuban exiles to a certain death; he submitted a civil rights bill to Congress; he called on the National Guard to ensure that African American students were allowed to attend the University of Mississippi and the University of Alabama, and a host of other actions that the Deep State found unacceptable. It was why a Kennedy Presidency could no longer be allowed to continue. The proponents of a new world order wanted to achieve American superiority, preserve the American way of life, advance White Nationalism, contain communism, and maintain a segregated society at any cost. Anything was acceptable, and everyone was expendable in this endeavor, even an American President who disagreed with the Deep State's vision for the future of America.

- 2 -

Strange Bedfellows

"OSS responsibilities for Italian espionage were preempted by the Office of Naval Intelligence through a mysterious arrangement with the American Mafia."

—ex-CIA official R. Harris Smith

During World War II, Allen Dulles and William "Wild Bill" Donovan, Nazi generals, and the Vatican underground were involved together in attempts to assassinate Hitler. After the war, Dulles and Donovan created a private intelligence network designed to prevent communism from spreading through Western Europe. It was financed by Mafia drug operations, with the money laundered through the Vatican Bank, as anything became acceptable to control the spread of communism during the Cold War. When Dulles joined the CIA, and as the Agency grew, many anti-Communist covert operations bypassed Senate oversight and were financed in the same manner, establishing a dangerous precedent. Soon, the CIA was out of control. The Mafia and CIA developed a working relationship during World War II that lasted many years, well beyond the Presidency of John F. Kennedy. CIA wanted to keep this relationship hidden from the U.S. Senate.

* * *

A classmate of Franklin Roosevelt at Columbia Law School, William Donovan, joined a prestigious law firm upon graduation in 1907. Eventually, he established his law practice and became quite successful, but this was not enough to satisfy the desire for a more adventurous lifestyle burning inside him. In 1916, in the middle of World War I, he traveled to Berlin on behalf of the Rockefeller Foundation to persuade Britain and Germany to deliver food and clothing to eastern European countries in desperate need. Upon returning to the U.S., Donovan led a New York National Guard cavalry troop along the Mexico/Texas border, searching for Pancho Villa, the Mexican revolutionary leader whose band of outlaws were attacking

Americans. He did so alongside General Pershing, and before long, both men brought their fighting spirit to Europe as the U.S. entered World War I. Donovan served admirably and came home highly decorated, but his desire to be where the action was did not diminish.

After the war, Donovan returned to Europe, this time on behalf of J.P. Morgan. Like the Dulles brothers and John McCloy, Donovan was there to protect the interests of big business, which he did consistently between the two world wars, "establishing himself as a player in international affairs—and honing his skills as an intelligence gatherer overseas."[1] He met with Mussolini and developed connections with leading Nazis in Germany. On President Roosevelt's behalf, he traveled to Britain in the years immediately before America's entry into World War II and became close with Britain's intelligence service members. After World War I ended, the U.S. had abandoned a centralized intelligence agency, and Donovan pushed hard for FDR to reinstate it, which he did on July 11, 1941. He put Donovan in charge as Coordinator of Information (COI), answerable directly to the White House. Donovan quickly established COI headquarters in New York and asked Allen Dulles to head it. When the U.S. entered the war, Donovan got busy setting up front companies and espionage schools to catch up to his European counterparts, who were way ahead of the Americans in intelligence gathering. He developed a relationship with the Vatican, who maintained a network of priests used to spy against the Nazis throughout the war. After the war, Donovan and Allen Dulles symbolized what became known as the "Deep State," operating behind the scenes to circumvent what sitting Presidents were trying to accomplish, even though by doing so, they undermined the free election process that defined the United States.

Donovan remained in charge when COI became the Office of Strategic Services (OSS) in 1942. As the war progressed, he established connections to highly placed Germans who opposed Hitler, and Donovan secretly met with them to negotiate a peace treaty. The plan was to establish a democratic Germany under Allied occupation, with the rapidly approaching Soviets on the outside looking in. Still, for this to be successful required the assassination of Hitler. To pull this together, Donovan needed help, which he received from two primary sources. The first was Allen Dulles, the OSS lead agent in Bern, Switzerland. It was Dulles who had established initial contact with Germans interested in brokering an early peace. The second was the Vatican, whose network of spies within Germany were already plotting to assassinate Hitler. This inexplicable relationship between U.S. intelligence and the Catholic Church proved to be effective. It would continue long after World War II when the enemy changed from the Nazis to Communists. But first things first, for it is essential to understand how this unlikely marriage came into being.[2]

* * *

The Vatican's relationship with Nazi Germany started cordial enough. When the Nazis came to power in 1933, Pius XI praised Hitler's anticommunism and accepted his offer to formalize Catholic rights in Germany. The Church also received 500 million marks in annual tax revenues from the Nazis. The result was overwhelming support for Hitler by millions of German Catholics, which he had set out to accomplish. Vatican Secretary of State Eugenio Pacelli supported Germany. He hated Marxists and was enamored with the Nazi's Prussian orderliness and anticommunism. But within two years, things began to change. In 1937 Pacelli wrote a letter to Hitler complaining that the Nazis had "thwarted the Church's teaching, banned its organizations, censored its press, shuttered its seminaries, seized its properties, fired its teachers, and closed its schools." The Nazis did not take kindly to this and threatened that "after the defeat of Bolshevism and Judaism the Catholic Church will be the only remaining enemy." [3]

With the death of Pius XI in 1939, Pacelli became Pope Pius XII, and under his leadership, the secret war against Germany increased in intensity. Lay and clergy agents in Germany provided confidential intelligence reports to the Vatican. Albert Hartl, a defrocked priest who joined the SS, monitored the Catholic resistance. He reported that "a considerable quantity of weapons and ammunition were being kept hidden . . . There were rifles, machine guns, and two small artillery pieces." If need be, the Church intended to fight fire with fire.[4]

There were other groups in German-occupied countries throughout Europe that had similar underground and partisan resistance units. After the war, with fear rampant that the Soviets might march westward and take control of the continent, these groups remained in place and were employed by the U.S. military as a potential first line of defense. After its establishment in 1947, the CIA assumed the responsibility and expanded the role of these "stay-behind armies" to suppress local Communist uprisings whenever this arose. They became an integral part of the CIA's effort to contain the spread of communism, but more about them later.

The most prolific of the German couriers employed by the Vatican was a Munich lawyer named Josef Muller. He made over 150 trips between Germany and Italy during the war, flying a single-seated plane to Merano, Italy, where he transferred information to an agent who delivered the package to Father Robert Leiber at the Vatican.[5]

There were those in Germany who suspected Muller was secretly working with the Vatican, and in 1939 he was approached by Colonel Hans Oster, who told Muller there were German generals who wanted Hitler assassinated. They wanted Pope Pius to come to the Allies with a proposition to end the war in Europe. Muller delivered the message, and upon being advised of the plot, Pope Pius summoned D'Arcy Osborne, Britain's representative to the Vatican, and Osborne was told: "a part of the army would like a change of government and to get rid of Hitler." They intended to install a temporary military dictatorship, then replace it with a democratic state, and at that time, they would approach the Allies to broker peace. They were interested in ascertaining if such a scenario was of interest to the Allies.

What Muller said the Vatican found appealing, for he envisioned "a [united] European Economic Union, which would make war between separate states seemingly impossible." It would be a Union formed on Christian values. "We must think like Christians and must plan and prepare to rebuild again . . . We must fight and do everything to save what can be saved." German Jesuit and Dominican leadership concurred, pledging "to endure and preserve our Catholic honor, before our consciences, before the people, before history, the Church and the Lord God." They proposed a new world order, a united Europe that included western Christians but excluded Communists and Jews. It was similar to what was being considered by the radical right in the United States. As a result, it was inevitable that anti-Communists from both sides of the Atlantic would be drawn together after the war to pursue their common goal. And that still included the Vatican.[6]

* * *

The Catholic Church was willing to go to any length to end Nazi rule in Germany, but how could the Vatican approve of assassination, even someone as despicable as Hitler? As author Mark Riebling explains in *Church of Spies*, murder was an acceptable option for the Church under the right conditions, but the victim had to be a tyrant. He writes:

> Church teaching stated the conditions under which citizens could kill tyrants. Catholic doctrine permitted capital punishment; and though a priest himself could not shed blood, a Christian knight could wield the sword of justice at the bidding of a priest . . . They divided tyrants into two classes: usurpers, who seized power illegally, and oppressors, who used power unjustly.
>
> [In addition]. . . . the tyrant's executioners must have good grounds for believing his death would actually [*sic*] improve conditions and would not cause a bloody civil war . . . [and] his assassins must have sufficient reason to believe that those unjust policies would end with the tyrant's life . . .[7]

No wonder Hitler accused FDR of waging a "holy crusade" against the Third Reich.[8] However, we should take a moment to consider the JFK assassination in the context of this criteria, with the understanding that the Vatican did not have anything to do with JFK's death. We know the western world characterized the war against Communism as a war of good vs. evil and that the same groups who conspired to defeat the Nazis would later join forces to try and destroy the Russian bear, which included the U.S. military, CIA, and the Vatican. The question then becomes, were there individuals among these groups who met the Church's criteria that made assassination acceptable, who had the reason, the capability, and the motivation to assassinate an American President?

Consider the reference that an assassin had to be a "Christian knight" to kill a head of state and be deemed acceptable by the Vatican. Amazingly, the Church still had a legendary military society that dated back to the Crusades, called the Sovereign Military Order of Malta. One had to be knighted by the Church to become a member of this secret society. The Vatican bestowed this noble rank upon those who had performed duties on behalf of the Church, including assassinations. It sounds somewhat juvenile, but numerous American military and intelligence leaders in the years leading up to the JFK assassination considered the honor significant enough that the Vatican knighted them into this group. And the bond they all shared was an intense hatred for communism. The list included CIA Counterintelligence chief James Angleton, OSS head William Donovan, and future CIA directors John McCone, William Colby, and William Casey. An ex-Nazi spy chief was also on the list who became an organizer of stay-behind armies for the CIA in Europe, Reinhard Gehlen. The Allies should have executed Gehlen for the unspeakable wartime atrocities he had committed. Still, they were primarily against Jews and Communists, and as a result, what Gehlen did was ignored. The Vatican knighted Gehlen because the only criteria for this honor in the Church's eyes were rabid anti-communism, regardless of the crimes one may have committed in the past.[9]

A similar group was the Shickshinny Knights of the Order of St. John of Jerusalem, a radical right-wing Catholic organization founded in 1956, headquartered in Shickshinny, Pa., who claimed to be the real Knights of Malta. Their membership was not opposed to anything when it came to fighting communism, including assassination. Many members of the armed services belonged to this group. General Charles Willoughby, known as MacArthur's "Little Fascist" because of his far-right beliefs, was part of the group. So were Generals Pedro del Valle, Bonner Fellers, Lemuel Shepard, and Colonels Phillip Corso and Benjamin F. von Stahl. Sir Edward Domvile, an admiral in the British Royal Navy and a Nazi sympathizer, was also a member. These men could all be considered Fascists, and an intense hatred for communism characterized each of them.

Consider that during the 1950s, Willoughby, del Valle, and Fellers became associated with right-wing extremist hate groups plotting to take control of the U.S. government and were on record wanting to assassinate American political leaders as part of this. All three are suspects in the JFK assassination, as is Philip Corso, who spread a story that Oswald was an FBI informant immediately after the assassination.[10]

These men believed Communists inundated the U.S. government. We will discuss in the following pages the road they traveled in the years leading up to the assassination of JFK and how many of their paths crossed in pursuit of their right-wing, Christian, White Supremacist, anti-Communist agenda for the behavior they engaged in was treasonous. For now, it is essential to understand that it was likely not a coincidence they belonged to a Catholic organization, where knight-hood was a prerequisite to justify the assassination of a tyrant. To borrow the words of James Bond author Ian Fleming, what they obtained from the Church was a license to kill.

In conjunction with this, consider the writings of Father Aniceto de Castro Albarran, who, at the time of the Spanish Revolution, wrote there was a Catholic duty to resist tyranny, and a violent military overthrow was an acceptable means of accomplishing this. He defined a tyrant as "any oppressive or unjust government." In his 1938 book entitled *Guerra Santa* (Holy War), Castro Albarran argued that violence against an oppressor "was justified because it was a holy rebellion against tyranny, anarchy and Moscow-inspired Godlessness."[11] It was a consistent theme that transcended two continents—rebelling against the tyranny of a Godless enemy was doing God's work.

Just like General MacArthur, loyalty to the Constitution and the American way of life drove these American military leaders, not a President who temporarily passed through the White House with a distorted agenda. They had an allegiance to what the founding fathers believed in and would rather have died defending the basic tenets of self-government than succumbing to some convoluted interpretation of the Constitution. And in this context, the word tyrant takes on special meaning.

Thomas Jefferson called King George III a tyrant in the Declaration of Independence, but the connotation had a different meaning from what it does today. As described in Chapter One, in *Two Treatises of Government*, the English philosopher John Locke wrote that life, liberty, and the pursuit of property were natural rights guaranteed to everyone by God. But Locke also noted that any leader who denied these natural rights to the people he ruled was a tyrant. Jefferson changed the pursuit of property to the pursuit of happiness, but the intent remained the same. A tyrant was a despot who denied his subjects their God-given rights.

The Knights of Malta and the radical right were adherents to the founding fathers' basic principles that established the American republic. And following this, they would have equated tyranny with any President who denied fundamental Constitutional rights to the American people or subjected American citizens to laws and programs that were inconsistent with a way of life guaranteed under these God-given principles. They objected to was appeasement of communism, normalization of relations with the USSR, racial desegregation, and a disregard for self-determination by taking money from those who earned it without their consent. These policies denied Americans their unalienable rights, as the radical right interpreted it, and jeopardized their life, liberty, and pursuit of happiness without their approval, and as a result, satisfied the criteria for when the assassination of a political figure was acceptable. Under the Church's conditions and those of the

founding fathers, a political leader who denied these rights was a tyrant, which justified the attempted removal of FDR in the 1930s, the assassination of Huey Long,
and without question, the assassination of JFK. And regarding Kennedy, even the
Church's phrase, "assassins must have sufficient reason to believe that those unjust
policies would end with the tyrant's life," applied, considering who it was that was
waiting in the wings to replace him.

The Vatican considered it a moral duty to assassinate a tyrannical head of state,
which directly impacted the radical right-wing in the U.S. In 1954, FBI Director
J. Edgar Hoover warned Eisenhower about a conspiracy to have him replaced by
Senator Joseph McCarthy as President in the next election. The leaders of this conspiracy were Cardinal Spellman, Joe Kennedy, and numerous wealthy, influential
Catholics. The possibility that this story could be true is not as farfetched as one
might believe.[12]

We know that Cardinal Spellman and Joe Kennedy were close and that the
Vatican was aware of their relationship. Consider that after the 1948 elections in
Italy, when the Church spent a great deal of money to prevent Communists from
taking control of the government, the Pope sent a representative to the U.S. to
solicit the help of Spellman and Kennedy in getting Americans to pay for what the
Vatican had spent. The two men were successful. So if the Vatican ever wanted to
involve itself in an American Presidential election to ensure that an ardent anti-
Communist like McCarthy would be victorious, it would have been Joe Kennedy
and Cardinal Spellman to whom they would have turned.[13]

Not by coincidence, Spellman also controlled the Knights of Malta in America,
indicative of his closeness to the radical right and how vehemently he opposed communism. To call him a Fascist would not be an unreasonable accusation. He was
a supporter of Franco and admired the Spanish Revolution. And as John Cooney
wrote in *The American Pope*, "Spellman . . . came to know every wealthy Catholic
family . . . The most valuable of these was Joseph P. Kennedy . . . In his own way,
Kennedy was serious about his religion . . . In Spellman, he found a churchman
who met him on his own terms . . . They were politically attuned in their opposition to Communism and in almost everything else."[14]

Spellman would have welcomed the Presidency of Joe McCarthy. According
to Cooney, "As the American Church's political leader, he [Spellman] sought vengeance on the enemy of both Catholicism and the burgeoning American empire. In
doing so, he welded his Church and nation to the goal of obliterating Communism
wherever it appeared . . . [and] for two decades, Spellman's rabid anti-Communism
enhanced his power base at home."[15]

In summation, the radical right tried to remove FDR from power in the early
1930s without success. His vice president, Harry Truman, was supposed to lose the
1948 election to the Republican Thomas Dewey, but something went wrong, and
Truman won. Then, Eisenhower was going to be replaced by McCarthy, but this

also failed to materialize. If all this is true, is it any wonder that with JFK's election, if these misguided Fascists wanted to remove him from office, that they decided to assassinate him and leave nothing to chance?

There was also an event that occurred shortly after the Cuban Missile Crisis in 1962 that demonstrated the willingness of the Catholic Church to influence American affairs. Mario Garcia Kohly was a wealthy right-wing Cuban exile who wanted to get rid of Castro, and he worked with CIA's Howard Hunt in conjunction with this. In 1962 he wrote a letter to Hunt, which stated, ". . . I have again been in contact with the Vatican. As you know, they are very interested in my program, so much so that they will finance the greater part of my efforts for the liberation of Cuba . . ."[16]

The Vatican was very influential in the anti-Communist movement in the United States, to the extent that they were involved in Cuban affairs. It was a different time, and the threat of a Communist takeover of the world united those who opposed it. Right up to the death of President Kennedy, the Vatican was interested in halting the spread of communism anywhere in the world. It was something they would engage in repeatedly.

* * *

Returning once again to World War II and the German general's proposal to the Vatican to quickly end the war, in all, there were three unsuccessful attempts by German military plotters to assassinate Hitler. But when the war's outcome was no longer in doubt, the anti-Hitler German military contingent's objective changed from assassinating Hitler to signing a peace treaty with the Allies before it was too late. Negotiations had to be conducted before the Russians could control all of Germany, something both the anti-Hitler Germans and the Allies wished to avoid. It was here that Allen Dulles entered the picture, for he was well connected and aware of the assassination attempts against Hitler. "Groups working towards the elimination of Hitler have been greatly encouraged by the developments in Italy, where it has been shown that it is possible to remove a dictator [Mussolini]," Dulles wired Washington.

As previously mentioned, Dulles remained a strong supporter of his German business contacts even after the Nazis came to power. In the spring of 1939, he blamed FDR for "worsening the prospects of world peace" by supporting England and France in the conflict. That was probably why future Supreme Court Justice Arthur Goldberg called him "a traitor to his country." Once the war began, he still protected Germany, believing that only by staying out of the war could the U.S. "fulfill its destiny of showing the way to a permanent, constructive world peace." It was what he was still trying to do as he met with the Germans near the war's end.[17]

Dulles' Vatican contacts told him that SS chief Heinrich Himmler and Walter Schellenberg, head of the SS foreign intelligence service, were interested in discussing a separate peace with the U.S. The German High Command sent a Prussian aristocrat, Prince Max von Hohenlohe, to meet with him in Bern on their behalf. Hohenlohe was surprised to learn that Dulles believed a strong Germany was necessary as the first line of defense against the Soviets after the war. Dulles always considered the Soviet Union the true enemy of the United States.

Dulles reported directly to Donovan that the German army in northern Italy, which had been retreating as the Allied army continued to advance further north, wanted to discuss surrender. The leader in the discussions was General Karl Wolff, commander of all SS forces in Italy, but Field Marshall Albert Kesselring, the army's commander, had to approve whatever they agreed to. Time was of the essence because part of the plan was for Kesselring's army to redeploy to the eastern front to delay the Red Army's advance, allowing the Americans to reach Berlin first. The problem was negotiation terms of capitulation had to be handled by a U.S. military general. Enter Major General Lyman Lemnitzer.

Lyman Lemnitzer would become chairman of the Joint Chiefs of Staff roughly three months before JFK's inauguration. Their relationship would be a turbulent one, for Lemnitzer was a staunch anti-Communist who would recommend employing nuclear weapons against the Chinese and the Soviets on multiple occasions. And he did not respect the young President. "Here was a president with no military experience at all, sort of a patrol boat skipper in World War II," he said of Kennedy. Kennedy eventually tired of Lemnitzer's insubordination and appointed him to head NATO in November 1962. It was a demotion designed to remove Lemnitzer from Washington and decision-making responsibilities. Little did he and Dulles realize as they met in Switzerland near the end of World War II that both would rise to greatness in the ensuing years, only to be knocked off their pedestals by an upstart young President.

After World War II was over, like many other right-wing military zealots previously discussed, Lemnitzer envisioned a new world order driven by American might. "We cannot provide the necessary leadership to point the way if we are a weak nation . . . ," he said. "We must have force available, and we must have the courage and intelligence to use it if the situation demands."[18]

The attempt to forge a peace treaty with the German military was called Operation Sunrise. Lemnitzer secretly traveled to Bern with British Major General Terence S. Airey to take charge of the negotiations. "When I read the names and rank of the [Allied] men . . . I was astonished," Dulles recalled. "I wondered if I had made sufficiently clear just how bleak the situation was . . ." More senior Allied officers should have been sent to close the deal on the spot, in Dulles's opinion, for a delay could ruin any chance of an agreement.[19]

As mandated by FDR, Lemnitzer would accept only unconditional surrender, despite opposition from almost everyone who wasn't a New Dealer, including Winston Churchill, London director of OSS covert operations and future head of CIA,

William Casey, and General Omar Bradley. Dulles tried to convince Donovan to rescind unconditional surrender if they were to accomplish what they set out to do, but the U.S. would not waver. FDR wanted to punish Germany and the German people, and the ensuing delay proved to be fatal.[20]

On April 20, 1945, the Joint Chiefs of Staff cut off all contact with the Germans. The Soviet Union knew surrender discussions were underway, and they wanted a seat at the table, something the U.S. was not willing to permit. At the time, the Soviets were attempting to take over the port of Trieste before the Allies could get there. Meanwhile, Yugoslavia's Tito tried to link up with French Communists to create a Communist belt across northern Italy. If that were to occur, it would be disastrous for the future of Europe.

On April 26, SS General Wolff found himself a virtual prisoner in the Italian villa the SS used as their command post, surrounded by Italian partisans, the majority of whom were Communists. When Dulles learned of this, he violated FDR's direct order to break off contact with the Nazis, and he arranged for a subordinate, Gero von Schulze—Gaevernitz, to try and rescue Wolff. Gaevernitz was part of a prominent European family that helped finance Hitler's rise to power, but had become disillusioned with the Nazis and began working with Dulles against them. And like Dulles, he believed Europe would need "moderate" Nazis to reconstruct Germany after the war to prevent Communists from taking control of the country. Somehow Wolff, who the Allies would later charge in the murder of three hundred thousand men, women, and children for transporting Jews to concentration camps, satisfied their somewhat lenient criteria of what constituted a moderate Nazi. Gaevernitz arrived at the villa with a caravan of specially selected support troops, and at two in the morning, successfully orchestrated Wolff's removal.[21]

Meanwhile, things were getting desperate as the Soviets moved closer to Berlin. On April 27, the Joint Chiefs lifted their ban on direct peace discussions with the German army in Italy, and two days later, Wolff surrendered his army to the U.S. But it was too late, and by May 7, Germany officially surrendered. Dulles' effort to achieve an early peace settlement to slow the Russian advance toward Berlin had failed. The Soviets had reached the German capital before anyone else, a fact that would haunt the Western world for decades to come.[22]

*   *   *

With World War II over, the focus shifted from defeating Germany to preventing the Soviets from taking over the rest of Western Europe, a genuine concern considering the unbalanced relative strength of the Allied and Russian armies at that time. Allen Dulles had another contact who would be essential in preventing a Russian advance, which he was sure would soon be forthcoming. While trying to negotiate a peace treaty with Wolff, he also met secretly with the previously mentioned Knight of Malta, Nazi General Reinhard Gehlen. Sensing the war was nearly over,

Gehlen had approached Dulles to try and save himself. With his vast knowledge of anti-Soviet intelligence, and his responsibility for controlling various Eastern European groups that had fought on behalf of the Nazis against their pro-Soviet countrymen, Gehlen found Dulles interested in what he had to say. Gehlen proposed employing "stay-behind units" of German Fascists and pro-Nazi Eastern Europeans as a resistance force to oppose a potential Soviet invasion against West Germany and the previously Nazi-occupied countries that were now at risk. It was Dulles' worst nightmare. So, even though Gehlen's groups perpetrated some of the most vicious atrocities against Jews and Communists, for which they would have faced war crime trials if apprehended, he convinced Donovan that the OSS should provide military and strategic support for these stay-behind armies through Gehlen.[23]

"I have met Tracy Barnes . . . and am anxious to get him to Switzerland as soon as possible . . . We can find useful work for him," was how Dulles cabled David Bruce, the head of the OSS in London, on December 3, 1944.[24] Barnes arrived in Bern a few days later. He thus began a long relationship with Dulles, for Barnes would become a vital cog in the CIA's war against Castro, including assisting Richard Bissell in the plans leading up to the Bay of Pigs. In 1962 he would be placed in charge of the Domestic Operations Division, around the time that Lee Harvey Oswald returned to the U.S. from the Soviet Union. He would later be independently accused by ex-CIA agents Robert Morrow and Howard Hunt of involvement in JFK's assassination, so his introduction into Dulles's anti-Communist stay-behind army is relevant to our narrative.

Before the war, Barnes had been a lawyer at the New York law firm Carter Ledyard, where he worked alongside Frank Wisner, another OSS operative who would become a leading figure at CIA. After entering the war, Barnes became a member of an elite group known as the Jedberghs. His involvement with them was likely why Dulles summoned him from London, for his Jedburgh training made Barnes an asset in working with Gehlen.

The Jedburghs were a paramilitary unit that supported local resistance groups, mainly in France. Jedburgh teams would parachute in with a load of light arms, make contact with a preassigned resistance force, arrange for additional arm drops as required, and harass German operations near the front with surprise attacks from behind, all in conjunction with the movements of the regular Allied forces. Jedburgh training included instruction in blowing up bridges, code messaging, forging documents, silently strangling someone from behind, and other nefarious but practical skills when operating behind enemy lines. No wonder Dulles was attracted to Tracey Barnes. His experience during the war was what Gehlen was proposing to do.[25]

In February 1945, while Dulles was still hopeful of signing a peace agreement with Wolff and the Nazi army in Italy, the Yalta Conference details were announced. The conference was attended by an aging and visibly feeble FDR (he would die two months later), Winston Churchill, and Joseph Stalin, to discuss the postwar reorganization of Germany and Europe. They agreed to move the eastern border of Germany westward to the Oder and Neisse Rivers, cede parts of eastern Poland to the Soviets, and divide Germany into four occupation zones. Dulles was now confident that Gehlen's stay-behind forces would be needed to oppose the Red Army once the war was over, and the arrival of Tracy Barnes supported this idea. Dulles sent Gehlen and his top representatives to Fort Hunt, Virginia, where Donovan and other US officials entertained them. All agreed that Gehlen would return to Germany under U.S. protection to establish his clandestine force, which would receive total funding from US Army G-2 (intelligence) resources. Gehlen established stay-behind armies and recruited new guerilla soldiers from Third Reich veterans with staunch anti-Communist credentials. These men, primarily ex-Nazis, would be known as gladiators. The operation would be called Gladio, and, as will be seen, the United States' support for them would increase as the years passed. It was another example that communism was now the enemy, and anything was acceptable in containing its spread.[26]

* * *

James Angleton was another key OSS operative interested in maintaining stay-behind units in Germany after the war. Inducted into the US Army in 1943, Angleton was initially stationed in London, assigned to the Italian desk of X-2, OSS's counterintelligence branch. X-2 operated in complete secrecy, had overseas stations separate from regular OSS offices, and could veto OSS espionage and paramilitary operations without explanation.

Angleton had spent his childhood in Italy when his father Hugh moved the family there after purchasing the National Cash Register franchise in Milan. Hugh would also serve as president of the American Chamber of Commerce in Italy. He was an outspoken supporter of both Hitler and Mussolini and had extensive contacts with elite aristocrats and business people throughout Italy. These contacts would serve his son well, for James was transferred to Italy in November 1944, eventually becoming X-2 head for all of Italy. He was not averse to dealing with Fascists if it served the interests of the U.S. in the war against communism.[27]

James S. Plaut of the OSS visited the Vatican at the behest of James Angleton to meet with Albrecht von Kessel, still acting as First Secretary in the German embassy at the Vatican. Von Kessel wrote a manuscript detailing his role as German Colonel Claus von Stauffenberg's Vatican agent in the 1944 attempt to assassinate Hitler and take control of the Nazi government as Operation Valkyrie. He handed Plaut a copy of the manuscript, which was how Angleton became aware of the details involved in the attempt to remove Hitler from power.

The OSS sent Raymond Rocca to Italy in April 1944 as part of the X-2 counterintelligence team. On July 24, he visited the Church Secretariat of State Father

Vincent McCormick at the Vatican, who introduced Rocca to Monsignor Kaas. Kaas was of German ancestry and advised Pius XII on German affairs, which was the reason for Rocca's visit. He wanted to verify the claims made by some detained Nazis that they had abandoned the party and had been working to remove Hitler. Rocca was explicitly interested in von Kessel's allegation that the entire German embassy had been in on the assassination plot. Kaas not only confirmed that what von Kessel had said was true; he stunned the X-2 officer when he told Rocca there had been three attempts on Hitler's life. If Rocca wanted to know more, Kaas told him to speak to Father Leiber. Leiber eventually agreed to meet with Rocca on August 18 and not only confirmed that three attempts on Hitler's life were accurate but that he had also shared details of the plots with the pope.[28]

U.S. intelligence wanted to know more, which was why the OSS Research and Analysis Division in Washington began their investigation into the Catholic resistance movement. They were surprised by what they found, for as German émigré Willy Brandt, the future chancellor of West Germany, told them: "The Catholic Church is the most widespread and best-organized opposition in Germany."[29]

Meanwhile, James Angleton arrived in Italy and began helping the Carabinieri, the Italian military police, develop a counterintelligence unit, and recruit spies to penetrate the PCI (Italian Communist Party), the PSI (Italian Socialist Party), and the Vatican. And, of course, he would utilize his father's old aristocratic connections whenever he could.

Rabid anti-Communists, both Angleton and Allen Dulles thought it was essential to protect ex-Nazis needed to rebuild Germany. Dulles arrived in Rome in October 1945, hoping to establish a new Italian resistance, akin to what Gehlen had done during the war in Eastern Europe. And if Dulles had any doubts about Angleton, they were dismissed when Angleton assisted SS Colonel Eugen Dollmann, one of Wolff's principal intermediaries during Operation Sunrise, to escape Rome.[30]

Angleton, who by now had connections inside the Vatican, including priests known as "clerical fascists," arranged a secret meeting between Dulles and Pius XII. The Vatican had a resistance movement in place. Dulles, Angleton, and the Pope all believed they had to stop communism, the most significant threat the world faced, even if it meant collaborating with ex-Nazis. So, it was only natural that they began working together.[31]

An Italian aristocrat, Prince Junio Valerio Borghese, had been an associate of Angleton's father and a member of the Catholic Black Nobility, a prestigious aristocratic group with dual Italian and Vatican City citizenship. Their primary allegiance was to the Vatican, not Italy, hence the name Black Nobility.

After Italy surrendered, Borghese and his X MAS team had fought on the side of the Nazis, attacking pro-Communist Italian partisan bands throughout Italy. On April 13, 1945, with the war all but over, Borghese met with SS General Wolff and Angleton at a villa at Garda Lake, where they discussed using X MAS under the covert direction of the OSS. It occurred a couple of weeks before Gaevernitz orchestrated the rescue of Wolff from the Italian villa when pro-Communist partisans surrounded it. Then, sometime in May, Borghese was arrested and charged with war crimes. Still, Angleton secured his release into U.S. Army custody because Borghese and his 10,000 plus Fascists would be needed to help establish stay-behind units in the war against communism in Italy. OSS created a special training camp in Sardinia, off Italy's western coast. It was not long before anti-Communist resistance fighters from Germany, France, and Austria were training there. By 1946, hundreds of these Gladio units were in place throughout Western Europe, all under the control of U.S. intelligence.

Meanwhile, in early May, General Lemnitzer solicited Gaevernitz's help to investigate more than one hundred "Germans of a special brand" in Capri. They were being held as political prisoners at a local hotel by the U.S. Army. "Once within the hotel, I was surrounded instantly by an aggravated group of Germans," Graeveritz remembered: "Many of these prisoners had gone through hell, and their nerves were still shaking from their experiences, the most recent of which had been [an] escape from death at the hands of an SS murder squad." Among the detainees was Vatican super-spy Joseph Muller, who told Gaevernitz of the "barely known German Resistance . . ." Regarding Muller, Gaevernitz wrote in 1946: "Here, I felt, was a man who could be of immeasurable help in the task that faced our occupation army in Germany." Gaevernitz asked Mueller, 'Would you be willing to work with us and give to our forces the benefit of your experience and knowledge?" Mueller agreed.

"Some of these prisoners should be decorated instead of being interned," Gaevernitz wrote Lemnitzer on May 13. They had tried to kill Hitler and were indeed anti-Nazis. Gaevernitz thought they should be freed and returned to Germany, where they would have "a good influence" on other Germans in need of direction.

Muller came under the care of two American debriefers, Dale Clark and Joe Cox. He shared his vision of a new world order; a European economic union made up of right-wing Aryan and Anglo-Saxon Christians. As a U.S. intelligence agent, Muller eventually returned to Munich and cofounded the Bavarian wing of the Christian Democratic Party, which would come to dominate West German politics.[32]

Shortly after the war, U.S. intelligence officers like Dulles, Angleton, Barnes, and Donovan learned of the Vatican resistance movement inside Germany. They were captivated by their willingness to assassinate Hitler, their hatred for communism, and their support of a new world order based on pro-Christian and anti-Semitic values, and that there were Nazi officers who shared these views and worked with them. These were lessons they would not forget.

Funding these stay-behind units and secretly relocating ex-Nazis should have been a problem. Very few people in Washington knew this was taking place, which meant the money to support these operations would have to come from a different source, which is what occurred. The ever-accommodating Rockefeller Foundation and the Mellon provided the initial funding. Once Truman created the CIA, the process expanded. The means of acquiring money outside the watchful eye of Congress would bring together various sinister forces, including the CIA, the Vatican, organized crime, money launders, drug dealers, and international smugglers. But more about that later. For now, how the U.S. military and U.S. intelligence employed the services of organized crime during the war is a story unto itself.

* * *

If the American people knew the U.S. military and intelligence forces were employing the services of ex-Nazis shortly after World War II came to an end and that some of them were war criminals, it would have created an uproar. So, the facts surrounding this remained hidden, as were the details of an equally nefarious relationship that American forces fostered during the war.

In February 1942, shortly after America entered into the war, there were numerous incidents of sabotage in New York Harbor, which concerned the Office of Naval Intelligence (ONI). When a bomb exploded on the French ocean liner *Normandie* the day before it was supposed to set sail as an Allied troop transport ship, ONI decided to take drastic measures. They contacted New York District Attorney Frank S. Hogan. They asked for his help in finding low-level Mafia figures who would be willing to monitor activities along the piers on ONI's behalf. The hoods Hogan recommended were ready, but they needed approval from their boss, which led to a meeting between ONI officers and Moses Polakoff, the attorney for mobster Meyer Lansky. Lansky was an associate of Lucky Luciano, in prison at the Clinton Correctional Facility at Dannemora, New York.[33]

Luciano was born in Sicily in 1897 and emigrated to America in 1904. By 1916, the time of his first arrest for heroin possession, he was already involved in organized crime. He rose quickly through the ranks, and by 1929 he had established New York's five crime families and formed a national coalition of Mafia bosses, all of whom took their orders from Luciano. He brought in Lansky, known as the "Mob's Accountant," as a chief financial officer, and another longtime associate, Frank Costello, who hobnobbed with high-level members of society, which was why he was called "the Prime Minister."

The special prosecutor responsible for Luciano's conviction in 1936 of sixty-two counts of compulsory prostitution was future Republican presidential candidate Thomas E. Dewey, whose higher office aspirations were already evident. Although Luciano's thirty to fifty-year prison sentence was severe, he continued running his crime family behind bars, initially relaying orders through his acting boss, Vito Genovese. However, in 1937 Genovese fled to Naples, Italy, to avoid a pending murder indictment, so Luciano appointed Costello as Genovese's replacement. At the time, Costello managed gambling operations and casinos with Meyer Lansky and bookmaker Frank Erickson, including a casino in Louisiana with Carlos Marcello and Lansky's brother Jake.[34]

Meyer Lansky, who was Jewish, had a history of fighting Nazis by the time ONI approached him. During the 1930s, he and members of his Jewish gang would physically break up German American Bund pro-Nazi rallies. So, it was not surprising that he was willing to approach Luciano on behalf of ONI. Luciano agreed, suggesting that Polakoff and Lansky "act as a liaison between Luciano and the people . . . These mob surrogates knew that if Lansky said he was acting for Luciano, what he said could not be questioned."[35]

It was called the Luciano Project, or Operation Underworld, and it was surprising that the U.S. military went ahead with the project even after Luciano became part of the operation. In *Operation Gladio*, Paul L. Williams wrote that "Luciano imported heroin from the Chinese warlords in Shanghai and Tientsin that had been refined in laboratories controlled by the Corsican Mafia . . ." At the time, most Mafioso "shunned drug peddling as an 'immoral' and 'unmanly activity' [but] Lucky was the exception to this code of honor."

"Heroin represented a minute part of the Mafia's business," Williams continued. "Before World War II, America had less than twenty thousand heroin addicts . . . Use of the drug in America remained largely confined to Asian immigrants and black musicians . . . The combination of organized prostitution and drug addiction became a Luciano trademark. By 1936, he controlled two hundred New York City brothels, employing twelve hundred prostitutes, with an estimated annual income of $10 million."[36]

Even more surprising was that in 1943, one year after the *Normandie* affair, Lucky Luciano was approached by U.S. intelligence once again. On April 15, 1943, OSS was responsible for developing plans for the Allied invasion of Sicily. A Joint Chiefs of Staff report entitled *Special Military Plan for Psychological Warfare in Sicily* that called for the "Establishment of contact and communications with the [Sicilian] leaders . . . and clandestine radical groups, e.g., the Mafia, and giving them every possible aid," was given to Bill Donovan. He forwarded it to Earl Brennan, the OSS director in Italy. Not familiar with the mob in Sicily, Brennan contacted Monsignor Giovanni Montini, the Vatican Undersecretary of State and future Pope Paul VI, for help. Montini, apparently familiar with the Sicilian Mafia, told Brennan to approach Calogero "Don Calo" Vizzini, the boss of the Vizzini/Agostino crime family. According to ex-CIA official R. Harris Smith, Brennan advised Donovan what he had learned. Still, according to ex-CIA official R. Harris Smith, "OSS responsibilities for Italian espionage were preempted by the Office of Naval Intelligence through a mysterious arrangement with the American Mafia."[37]

Per Luciano's instructions, Lansky brought Sicilian Mafioso to ONI's Manhattan office, where they provided intelligence that proved to be helpful in the eventual amphibious landing into Sicily. Also, OSS obtained "the names of friendly Sicilian natives and even Sicilian underworld and Mafia personalities who could be trusted and used in the Sicilian campaign."[38]

Two days before the Sicilian invasion began, Luciano's written message was air-dropped near Don Calo's home. When American tanks landed on the beach in Palermo, Don Calo and his men spent the next six days guiding the Americans through western Sicily and organizing support among the local people. "One of the most important plans," recalled Commander Paul A. Alfieri, one of the ONI agents, "was to contact persons who had been deported for any crime from the United States . . . and one of my first successes after landing at Licata was in connection with this." Alfieri later told William B. Herlands, the New York State Commissioner of Investigation, that I "made it my business to make that [Mafia contact] my first stop" and found that these "criminal and underworld characters in Sicily who . . . were members of the Mafia . . . were 'extremely cooperative to me and also to various other intelligence officers.'"[39] Members of Brooklyn's Vincent Mangano's family led Alfieri to his Sicilian Mafiosi contacts, which is believable, considering that Naval Intelligence acquired the names of hundreds of informants from Mangano and fellow mobster Joe Adonis in Italy. Local Mafioso then guided Alfieri to a villa behind enemy lines that housed the Italian Naval Command. There he discovered documents detailing the location of Italian and German Naval forces in the Mediterranean Sea.[40]

Working with the Army's Civil Affairs Branch, the OSS installed Mafiosi in top positions in Sicily. Don Calo Vizzini was appointed mayor of Villalba and almost immediately murdered the local police chief, whom he found "too inquisitive." Giuseppe Genco Russo, Don Calo's second in command, became mayor of Mussomeli. Colonel Charles Poletti, the former lieutenant governor of New York and commander of the Allied Military Government (AMGOT), selected other Vizzini/Agostino crime family members to run many towns and villages across western Sicily. The Allies needed an iron hand in positions of power after removing the Nazi threat because they had to contain Italian Communists. But as the Federal Bureau of Narcotics would eventually learn, Vissini and Russo ran Sicilian Mafia narcotics operations, and putting them in power was the wrong thing to do.[41]

The military/Mafia alliance did not end in Sicily. In his 1954 report, Commissioner Herlands wrote that "Alfieri pursued the same technique of contacting former underworld characters in the subsequent invasions and operations on the [Italian] mainland with the same success." After the liberation of Naples in July 1944, the Army's Criminal Investigations Division (CID) learned that Poletti had appointed Vito Genovese as an interpreter for numerous Army officers. After the war, Luciano called Poletti "one of our good friends," which explains how Poletti could employ the services of such a notorious character as Genovese.

In addition to his Mafia activities, Genovese had previously befriended the secretary of Mussolini's Fascist Party in 1933 while setting up narcotics operations between Italy and the U.S. His contact with high-level members of Mussolini's government and a $25,000 donation to the Party proved beneficial, for he was allowed to remain in Italy, purchase a power plant near Naples, and manage a chain of banks controlled by the Fascist government. When he ordered the murder of anti-Fascist publisher Carlo Tresca in New York in 1943, he was awarded Italy's highest civilian title, presented personally by Mussolini.

Genovese's presence allowed the Italian Fascists to expand their narcotics operations. His connections reportedly enabled Mussolini's son-in-law to fly opium out of Turkey to refiners in Milan, who processed it into heroin. Genovese then transported the heroin to Nicolo Impostato, a Kansas City assassin who served as general manager of the Mafia's national drug syndicate in the U.S.

Genovese, who was untouchable because of his relationship with Poletti, used the Italian Mafia to establish black-market routes between Germany, Yugoslavia, and Sicily. It ended when CID Agent Orange Dickey arrested two Canadian deserters for having stolen U.S. Army trucks in June 1944, which led to the arrest of Genovese on August 27 of that year. When arrested, Genovese had letters of recommendation from three army officers, which concerned Dickey. He contacted the FBI, who told Dickey that Genovese was a suspect in the U.S. for Boccia's murder, but none of Dickey's superiors showed any sense of alarm. It prompted Dickey to write a report stating that several high-ranking Army officers were involved in a conspiracy to protect Genovese, which caused the U.S. consul to intervene. But the consul said Genovese was an Italian citizen and could not be held in an American jail, which left Dickey dissatisfied. He next went to see Poletti in Rome. He was surprised to find William O'Dwyer, the former Brooklyn District Attorney and a friend of Joe Adonis and Frank Costello, serving as the Judge Advocate General in Italy. O'Dwyer told Dickey that Genovese was no concern to the Army, which is hard to believe considering Genovese was running a black-market operation along with U.S. Army officers. Per O'Dwyer's instructions, Dickey contacted the current Brooklyn District Attorney, which resulted in the issuance of a passport for Genovese in November 1944 to return to New York for his murder trial. But in December, Genovese was still in Italy, transferred to a civilian prison in Bari. A general became involved in the case. There was no desire to send Genovese back to New York, where he could provide details of the relationship between U.S. forces and the Mafia in Italy, which the Army wanted to keep hidden.

Charles Siragusa of the Federal Narcotics Bureau interviewed Genovese at Bari, but it turned out to be a waste of time. Genovese knew too much, and the Army essentially protected him from prosecution. Dickey would eventually bring Genovese to New York but was unsuccessful because, amazingly, General O'Dwyer became the city's mayor.[42]

The OSS also had good reason to keep their relationship with the Mafia hidden. After the Allies took Sicily, the OSS controlled the Mafia, and according to

Richard Smith, "A very few OSS men had indeed been recruited directly from the ranks of Murder, Inc., and the Detroit 'Purple Gang.'"[43]

The OSS recruited underworld figures to perform assassinations on behalf of Division 19, a covert operation established on June 28, 1941, hidden within the National Defense Research Committee's Office of Scientific Research and Development. For example, OSS recruited professional killer Michael Milan through the recommendation of Manhattan's Republican boss, Sam Koenig. Mobster August "Little Augie" Del Grazio had trained Milan and was "running the skim" for Meyer Lansky and Benny Siegel. He claimed to have committed numerous assassinations under ONI Captain Roscoe McCall, who was part of the Luciano Operation.[44]

A group within OSS linked to assassinations were all ex-Federal Bureau of Narcotics officers, who left the FBN to join OSS when war broke out, including Charles Siragusa, Jean-Pierre Lafitte, and George Hunter White.

George White trained at Camp X, located on the Canadian shores of Lake Ontario. The camp taught students guerilla warfare, covert action, and assassination. Three days after arriving, White dubbed it "the school of murder and mayhem" in his diary. Charles Siragusa maintained ties to Mafia figures after World War II ended and would become a liaison between CIA and the mob, going so far as to set up assassination hit teams for the Agency. Lafitte was considered an expert in "close-quarter infiltration, disguise, and silent killing, and would work closely with White after the war in the U.S," when the two men involved themselves in the most unsavory of operations.[45]

George White would eventually qualify to train other agents in such clandestine tactics. According to author H.P. Albarelli in *A Terrible Mistake*, White's first OSS students were Richard Helms, Frank Wisner, James Angleton, Lyman Kirkpatrick, Thomas Karamessines, and William Colby. These men would lead the CIA in the years to come, and White would maintain a close relationship with the CIA long after World War II.

White worked with Angleton and had Mafia connections. As Douglas Valentine wrote in *The Strength of the Wolf*:

> In the summer and fall of 1943, as described in his diary, White attended several Mafia Plan meetings, including an August excursion into Chinatown [in New York City] with James J. Angleton . . . One month later, White escorted Angleton into Chinatown again, this time with his boss from the Mideast, Colonel Hoskins. Considering that the OSS was passing X-2 personnel through the FBN's New York office at the time, the purpose of these trips undoubtedly concerned the Mafia Plan—which translated into drug smuggling, espionage, and assassination.[46]

After World War II, OSS officers working with ex-Nazis, the Mafia, and stay-behind resistance units would eventually become leaders at the CIA. They considered assassination a legitimate option, and under the right conditions, was sanctioned by the Catholic Church. Anything was acceptable to neutralize the Russians. The Soviet Union's "evil empire" had to be contained, for to allow it to grow unchecked would potentially leave the U.S. a fortress unto itself, surrounded by a Communist world. True, the U.S. had sole possession of the atom bomb, but that would not last forever. Maintaining a conventional military large enough was not an option. The inherent cost would be too great, resulting in heavy taxation and decreased living standards for most Americans. Therefore, it would be up to the CIA to play a significant role through covert operations to maintain an acceptable balance of power.

CIA's mantra throughout the Cold War was that they could have saved millions of lives if someone had killed Hilter before World War II began. With such logic, one could rationalize anything. The question then becomes, if someone believed that they could save millions of American lives by assassinating a President, would it be justified to do so? Or, if assassination were the only means of protecting the American people from a President who intended to destroy the American way of life and take away their God-given rights, would this be deemed acceptable? As we will see, the answer to these questions is a resounding yes—the CIA would be willing to remove a President as a last resort. And the military and big business felt the same way. But the circumstances would have to be right—which would become a reality in 1963 as JFK took on the CIA, the military, and big business simultaneously. It appears that the first stop on the road to Dallas occurred during World War II, as U.S. intelligence, the military, and organized crime came together with the Vatican's blessing. And the Mafia's motivation was they believed it granted them immunity from prosecution, for the CIA and the military could never allow the Mafia to disclose what they knew. But with the emergence of the Kennedy brothers and Bobby's war on crime, the danger existed that the relationship with the Mafia could be revealed. To prevent this from happening was probably the last nail in the coffin that sealed JFK's fate.

- 3 -

The Evil Empire Emerges

"The Soviet Union was capable of 'varieties of skullduggery . . . including persuasion, intimidation, deceit, corruption, penetration, subversion, horse-trading, bluffing, psychological pressure, economic pressure, seduction, blackmail, theft, fraud, rape, battle, murder, and sudden death. Don't mistake that for a complete list.'"

—George Kennan—deputy head of the U.S. mission in Moscow

Soon after World War II ended, intolerable economic conditions resulted in a dramatic increase in communism in Western Europe, to the extent that a possible Communist takeover from within existed throughout the continent. And since military resistance was virtually nonexistent, the Allies feared that the Soviet Red Army might march across Europe to expand its sphere of influence. A policy of containment was introduced to combat this, which permitted communism to exist in the Soviet Union and its satellites but to go no further. Eventually, the CIA formed guerilla armies throughout Europe as the first line of defense, which included the employment of ex-Nazi forces, even though some were war criminals. They were valuable assets worthy of protection because the Soviet Union, an inferior subhuman race, had replaced the Nazis as the new enemy. And as John McCloy put it, the idea was to create a Pax Americana worldwide, starting in Western Europe. It was another name for a New World Order and had only one objective—for the radical right, appeasement of Communists was never acceptable. Roughly fifteen years later, John Kennedy would suffer the consequences for failing to realize this.

* * *

The war with Japan was nearing an end, the Land of the Rising Sun's navy and air force were essentially nonexistent, and the options left to defend themselves were severely limited. General MacArthur and the army wanted to blockade the island and starve the enemy into submission methodically. General LeMay thought incessant firebombing would force a surrender, which was what he wanted to do. But others thought a faster solution was in order, as time was running short. Stalin had become impossible to deal with in Europe. The United States desperately wanted to force a Japanese surrender before the Soviets could enter the fray and lay claim to territorial concessions they were not entitled to have. Already, just months after the fall of Berlin, the Soviet Union had replaced Germany as the enemy of the West.

The head of the Office of War Mobilization, James F. Byrnes, was a close friend of FDR who had accompanied the President to the Yalta Conference to meet with Churchill and Stalin at the beginning of February 1945. "We should get the Japanese affair over with before the Russians get in," Byrnes warned after the conference was over. "Once they are in, it will not be easy to get them out." He was not the only one who felt that way, but President Roosevelt, who was weak and on the verge of death, misjudged Stalin's intentions and conceded too much post-war European territory to the Russians at Yalta, much to the chagrin of many.[1]

Concern about the Soviets before the Yalta Conference began. As the Soviet army pushed back the Nazis and marched through Eastern Europe, they maintained an occupational force. They established puppet governments in the countries through which they advanced, such as Estonia, Latvia, Lithuania, Poland, Bulgaria, Hungary, Romania, Czechoslovakia, and Albania.[2] On January 6, the Red Army sealed off neighborhoods in many eastern European cities inhabited by people of German descent, and seventy thousand were loaded into boxcars and transported to Ural Mountain slave labor camps. The barbarity shocked OSS operatives stationed in these cities. By January 22, there was a report that Hungarian Communists, with Soviet support, planned to take over that government. The Soviets confiscated estates, Communist workers revolted in Budapest's largest metallurgical factory, and closed newspapers that supported prewar political parties.[3]

Despite these Soviet acts of aggression, the U.S. and Great Britain remained cautiously patient. Yalta agreed that democratic elections would be held in all Eastern European countries, the intent being to eliminate the "spheres of influence" that had already led Europe into two world wars. Western powers were confident that democratic elections would vote down communism, and the Soviet occupation of Eastern Europe would come to an end. But this was not to be, for the Soviets never intended to abide by the agreement they had signed at Yalta. On February 27, two weeks after Yalta, the Soviet deputy commissar for foreign affairs, Andrei Vyshinsky, arrived in Budapest, Hungary, with a choice for young King Michael. Dissolve the American-backed government and replace it with a Communist coalition or suffer the consequences.

Both Roosevelt and Churchill were shocked by this development, with Churchill cabling FDR, what Stalin was doing was "absolutely contrary to all democratic ideals." Even more alarming were the reports from Poland of forced "deportations" and "liquidations." Concerns grew when *Pravda,* the official Communist Party newspaper, declared that the U.S., Great Britain, and France interpreted the word "democracy" differently than the Soviets. According to *Pravda,* free people should be allowed to establish a so-called democratic government "according to their own choice," even if this involved coercion by force. It implied the Soviets had no intention of relying on elections to determine the fate of the countries they overtook. It became clear to Roosevelt and Churchill that their agreement with Stalin at Yalta was nothing more than a piece of paper.[4]

Meanwhile, Averell Harriman, the U.S. ambassador to the Soviet Union, sent a personal letter to the President and Secretary of State on March 21. Harriman wrote the Russians were "attempting to wear us down step by step" to expand their empire in postwar Europe. Before it was too late, the U.S. had to ". . . reorient our whole attitude and our methods of dealing with the Soviet Government . . . unless we wish to accept the 20th-century barbarian invasion of Europe." Repelling a potential Soviet advance across Western Europe was the real fear that gripped the Allies.[5]

The powers in Washington gave Harriman's warning the attention it warranted, but the ambassador may have had personal reasons for wanting to disrupt a potential Soviet advance. Like the Dulles brothers and John McCloy, he had extensive business dealings with Germany before the war and could lose everything if Germany became a Soviet satellite state. His banking business had been the primary Wall Street connection for numerous German companies, some of whom supported the Nazis. When Hitler declared war on the U.S., the government seized German interests in America, including Harriman's operations in New York City. So, it is indisputable that Harriman had a vested interest in keeping Germany out of the hands of the Soviets.

After Allen Dulles failed to broker a peace treaty with Nazi generals, he maintained contact with those Germans who opposed Hitler. He understood they were destined to play a significant role in rebuilding Germany and could act as the first line of defense against the Soviets. Near the end of 1945, Dulles returned to the U.S. On December 3, before leaving government service, he spoke about postwar Germany at the Council on Foreign Relations. The U.S. must not go too far in cleansing Germany of its Nazi past, Dulles told those in attendance. "Most men of the caliber required to [run the new Germany] suffer a political taint," he said, and ". . . we have already found out that you can't run railroads without taking in some [Nazi] Party members." And it was imperative to maintain a strong Germany because "the Russians are acting little better than thugs . . . The promises at Yalta to the contrary, probably eight to ten million people are being enslaved."[6] Most in the audience agreed with what Dulles had to say. Ex-Nazis were needed to protect Western Europe from the Soviets.

Returning to Harriman, his support of Germany may also have been motivated by something other than greed. The ambassador's father was E.H. Harriman, a wealthy railroad executive whose estate was valued at around $200 million when he died and left everything to his wife, who used some of the money to support causes dear to her heart, which included eugenics. She financed the creation of the Eugenics Record Office, purchasing eighty acres of land for its use about a half-mile from the Carnegie Institute's eugenic experimental station at Cold Springs Harbor, New York. Did Averell Harriman share the same views as his mother? His letter to the President and Secretary of State cited above may offer a clue, for he wrote that he favored "a forceful policy of supporting those people that have the same general outlook . . . and concept of life that we do." And many wealthy, high-ranking officials and business people felt the same way. They would rebuild Germany once the war was over, for it was essential to prevent the Soviets from contaminating the purity of the Nordic bloodline of Western Europe. To ignore the influence of eugenics regarding America's support of ex-Nazis would be to disregard the truth blatantly.

It may be difficult to comprehend today, but proponents of eugenics back then considered Russians and Eastern Europeans inferior to Nordic and Anglo-Saxon nationalities. Nazi war atrocities forced eugenics proponents and Fascist supporters to hide their true feelings after the war ended, but their attitudes had not changed. Consider the pre-war 1933 writings of the prestigious *Journal of the American Medical Association*, that "A foreign invasion, more particularly from the East, constitutes a menace to the German race. It is [imperative] that this menace be now suppressed and eliminated . . . Racial problems and questions dealing with hereditary biology must receive special consideration." The article promoted eugenics and called for the *"preservation of the German race and German culture."* (Author's Italics) It was at a time when the Nazis were already in power.[7]

And how did the U.S. government feel about this? A pre-war Congressional Committee on Selective Immigration reported that "Immigrants from northwestern Europe furnish us the best material for American citizenship and for the future upbuilding of the American race. They had higher living standards than the bulk of southeastern Europeans; are of [a] higher grade of intelligence; better educated; more skilled; better able to understand, appreciate and support our form of government." Not surprisingly, with this kind of thinking, preserving the racial purity of Germany became critically important to the United States, and the suppression of Russian expansion became a matter of national security.[8]

It is essential to recognize that this warped philosophy would play a role in the assassination of JFK, who was under tremendous pressure during his Presidency to present a civil rights bill to Congress, which he did in June 1963. It did not sit well with Southern racists. Equally displeased were those who wanted to maintain the American way of life through the Anglo-Saxon/Nordic European culture predominant in the United States.

JFK was also interested in coexistence with the Soviets to make the world a safer place. However, the radical right in 1963 did not trust the Russians, and they opposed extending an olive branch to America's sworn enemy. For coexistence not only meant the end of Communist containment, but it was also the first step towards the acceptance of a culture that eugenicists believed was inferior to Western Europe. Removing American troops from Vietnam would have had the same effect because the thought was that all Southeast Asia would become Communist once American was gone. As would an accommodation with Fidel Castro in Cuba, which Kennedy had initiated through backdoor discussions. The radical right believed it was better to leave Latin Americans in Latin America. They believed communism would lead to economic ruin and dilute the European bloodline they wanted to preserve. It was why containment of the Soviet Union became so important, for an Eastern European influx of Communists into American society would eventually become a drain on the country. The radical right believed people who were incapable of sustaining themselves should be purged from society, not supported, and socialism and communism were evil philosophies that threatened America, even if rejecting these systems was against what a "government by the people" was supposed to stand for. So, a significant reason why JFK had to die was to prevent this from happening. It is a relevant point to consider as we explore the period after World War II and the fear of God which the Soviets instilled in virtually every American.

The future assassination of JFK and concerns over eugenics notwithstanding, Winston Churchill was more worried about Britain's very survival at war's end. "An iron curtain is drawn upon their [the Soviets] front," he cabled President Truman on May 12, and the Russians could ". . . advance if they chose to the waters of the North Sea and the Atlantic." In anticipation of hostilities with the Soviets, Churchill ordered his military not to demobilize, or destroy any German weapons or planes, because Britain ". . . might have to fight the Russians with German help." That Churchill was already considering fighting alongside the Germans after two world wars against Germany just days after World War II ended in Europe underscores how serious the British Prime Minister perceived the Soviet threat. Incredibly, just days later, he authorized a preemptive, first strike against Russian forces that were to occur on July 1, 1945, but British generals said this was impossible. The Red Army had two and a half times the number of divisions as the combined Allied forces, with double the armored divisions. There was no choice but to scrap the operation.

Meanwhile, the Russians insisted they were more concerned with the protection of their own country. In a *Pravda* interview, Stalin stated, "The Germans made their invasion of the USSR through Finland, Poland, Rumania, Bulgaria, and Hungary . . . because, at the time, governments hostile to the Soviet Union existed in these countries." As a result, millions of Russians died, many more than from the United States and the United Kingdom combined. Stalin insisted this was the driving force behind Soviet aggression. "What can be surprising," Stalin fumed, "about the fact that the Soviet Union, anxious for its future safety, is trying to see to it that governments loyal in their attitude to the Soviet Union should exist in these countries?"[9]

Perhaps that is all that Stalin wanted, but the fact remained he violated post-war agreements made with his one-time Allies, and the addition of eastern satellite countries threatened Western Europe. And it is highly probable, despite attempts by historians to offer alternate explanations, that Soviet aggressiveness in Europe was the main reason the United States elected to drop atomic bombs on Japan. It was the only way to guarantee that the Soviets did not have time to join the fight in the Pacific, ensuring the U.S. would not have to deal with the same Russian hostility and desire for territorial expansion they now had to deal with in Europe. The shared occupation of Japan with the Soviets became unacceptable.

At the time, the Soviets were negotiating with the Chinese government to commence ground operations in Manchuria, which Stalin needed to launch an attack against Japan, which was considered imminent. However, on the night after the Hiroshima bombing, over one and a half million Soviet troops entered China without Chinese approval, which forced the occupying Japanese troops to evacuate. The Soviets also captured the Chinese puppet emperor, Pu Yi, and took him to Russia. Russian troops poured into Korea but stopped at the thirty-eight parallel, per a previous agreement with the United States. Considering the destructive power that the new American bombs had demonstrated, they were hesitant about proceeding further and possibly facing the wrath of their one-time ally.[10]

Unquestionably, dropping the bombs on Japan also served as a deterrent against a potential Soviet attack across Western Europe. Hiroshima "has shaken the world," Stalin said. "The balance of power has been destroyed." First Deputy Premier Vyacheslav Molotov was more direct. He said the bombs were "not aimed at Japan but rather at the Soviet Union." "Bear in mind you don't have an atomic bomb, and we do," Molotov portrayed the Americans as saying, "and this is what the consequences will be like if you make a wrong move!"[11]

The animosity between the United States and the Soviet Union was at a fever pitch. The Allies divided Berlin into four sectors, shared by the Soviet Union, Britain, France, and the U.S., with the city wholly located in the Soviet sector. The Russians became even more challenging to deal with as they tried to initiate confrontations with Allied forces. From June 1948 through May 1949, the Soviets denied the Allies land access to their sections of the city during the Berlin blockade, resulting in more than seven hundred incidents between Soviet and Allied aircraft. The death toll included thirty-nine British, thirty-one Americans, and five German airmen.[12]

It was clear that the period of cooperation between the Soviets and Allied nations had ended. Harriman called the Russians a "world bully," and said Stalin intended to establish a "sphere of influence" in Eastern Europe under his control. George Kennan, the deputy head of the U.S. mission in Moscow, knew what the Soviets were capable of and warned Washington repeatedly not to trust them.[13]

The fear was a potential spread of communism throughout the continent, and rightfully so. In *For the Soul Of Mankind, the United States, the Soviet Union, and the Cold War*, author Melvyn P. Leffler outlined the situation which confronted the Allies:

> In Belgium, the Communist Party grew from 9,000 in 1939 to 100,000 in November 1945; in Greece, from 17,000 in 1935 to 70,000 in 1945; in Italy from 5,000 in 1943 to 1.7 million at the end of 1945; in Czechoslovakia, from 28,000 in May 1945 to 750,000 in September 1945. In France, Italy, and Finland, communists were already getting 20 percent of the total vote; in Belgium, Denmark, Norway, Holland, and Sweden, it was close to 10 percent. In Eastern European countries, 20 to 50 percent . . . In Great Britain, the Labour Party emerged triumphant in 1945 and . . . unseated Churchill. Everywhere, people seemed to be clamoring for land reform, social welfare, and nationalization of industry . . .[14]

Europe was ripe for a Communist takeover as John McCloy visited there in April 1945. "There is a complete economic, social and political collapse going on in central Europe," he stated, "the extent of which is unparalleled in history." He told War Secretary Stimson that the situation in Germany was "worse than anything probably that ever happened in the world."[15]

Two years later, conditions would be no better, as millions of refugees still roamed Europe. As William Manchester and Paul Reid wrote in *The Last Lion, Volume III*, "Each morning in cities and towns of Germany and Austria the frozen bodies of the starved were picked up from streets and alleys by their starving fellow citizens and carted off to communal graves. Stalin would not give an inch [and] starvation was the only certainty for millions of Germans. And that was fine with Stalin . . ."[16]

From the U.S. perspective, the Soviets were the personification of evil, the European countries needed America for their very survival, and the fate of Western civilization hung in the balance. The U.S. was concerned, and rightfully so.

* * *

President Truman had no illusions regarding the threat the Soviets presented. Even though in the fall of 1945, there were leftover New Dealers who wanted to share the atomic bomb design with the Soviets in the name of peace, Truman held firm. In an October 27 speech, he called the bomb a "sacred trust" that the United States could not share with a "lawless world." In November, while he was reducing the size of his military force, Truman urged Congress to keep the United States safe through "the only kind of strength an aggressor understands—military power."[17]

In Moscow, George Kennan agreed with Truman and warned Harriman that "it would be a tragic folly for us to hand over the secrets of atomic energy production to the Russians." "There is nothing," Kennan wrote, ". . . which could justify us in assuming that the men who are now in power in Russia . . . would hesitate for a moment to apply this power against us if by doing so they thought that they might materially improve their own power position in the world."[18]

By 1946, the rhetoric between the two superpowers reached a dangerous level. In what was considered by many as the start of the Cold War, on February 9, Joseph Stalin addressed a national audience in his first major public speech since World War II. He said another world war was inevitable because of the "capitalist development of the world economy" and that the Soviets would have to concentrate on national defense in preparation for that war. Many in the U.S. took this as the official rejection of the wartime alliance. Supreme Court Justice William O. Douglas called it a "Declaration of World War III." Two weeks later, the U.S. learned that a Soviet spy ring was running espionage operations in the U.S. and Canada, whose purpose was to steal information related to the atomic bomb design.[19]

In response to these tensions, Truman asked George Kennan to put down on paper his thoughts regarding the Soviet system and the future of Soviet-American relations. He responded on February 22 with a 5,500-word telegram from Moscow to Secretary of State James Byrnes, and his comments laid the foundation for how the U.S. would deal with the Soviets throughout the Cold War.

Kennan began with the proclamation that the Soviets would never entertain "permanent peaceful coexistence" with the West, that they had a "neurotic view of world affairs," were "impervious to logic or reason," and perceived themselves to be in a "deadly struggle for [the] total destruction of rival power." There was no ambiguity—if, given the opportunity, the Russians intended to destroy America. He continued that those now in power had "instinctive fear of the outside world, for the dictatorship without which they did not know how to rule, for cruelties they did not dare not to inflict . . . It is a fig leaf of their moral and intellectual respectability. Without it, they would stand before history, at best, as only the last of that long succession of cruel and wasteful Russian rulers who have relentlessly forced the country on to even new heights of military power . . . to guarantee external security of their internally weak regimes." Kennan wrote that "We have here a political force [that thinks] it is desirable and necessary that the internal harmony of our society be disrupted, our traditional way of life be destroyed, the international authority of our state be broken, if Soviet power is to be secure."

He continued that the "health and vigor of our own society" had to be maintained because communism was "like [a] malignant parasite which feeds only on diseased tissue." To combat this, the U.S. should present "a much more positive and constructive picture of the sort of world we would like to see . . ." "We must have courage and self-confidence to cling to our own methods and conceptions of human society. After all, the greatest danger that can befall us . . . is that we shall allow ourselves to become like those with whom we are coping."[20]

It was called The Long Telegram, and Kennan's warnings resonated throughout Washington. Byrnes responded, ". . . If we are to be a great power, we must act as a great power, not only in order to ensure our own security but in order to preserve the peace of the world."[21] The Soviet ambassador to Washington sent Moscow a response stating that "the imperialist tendencies of American monopolistic capital" was one of "striving for world supremacy." Each side was accusing the other of looking to dominate the world, and there was every indication that things were only going to get worse.[22]

Kennan returned to the U.S. and continued his anti-Soviet onslaught when he spoke before the National War College on September 16, 1946. He talked about the Soviet reliance on "varieties of skullduggery . . . including persuasion, intimidation, deceit, corruption, penetration, subversion, horse-trading, bluffing, psychological pressure, economic pressure, seduction, blackmail, theft, fraud, rape, battle, murder, and sudden death." The United States needed a strong military with atomic weapons to contain the Soviets. "You have no idea how much it contributes to the general politeness and pleasantness of diplomacy when you have a little quiet armed force in the background . . . because the greater your strength, the less likelihood that you are ever going to use it." [23]

Then, in an October 1 speech before Yale's Institute of International Studies, Kennan accused the Soviets of committing "the most stupendous crimes in the history of mankind . . ." and all Communists, at all levels of importance, "have sold their souls to the theory that the outside world is threatening and hostile." He reiterated that the goal of the United States should be ". . . to contain the Russians indefinitely" and "to maneuver them back into the limits within which we would like them to stay."[24]

It was the introduction of the policy of containment, which believed the Soviets were economically unstable and would eventually succumb to internal unrest and self-destruct. "When exercised over a long period . . . [wisely]," containment would eventually provoke "discontent, trouble, and dissension within the totalitarian world." He was adamant that appeasement of the Soviets was unacceptable. It was why any President was called a Communist who wanted to normalize relations with the Soviet Union or China during the Cold War. As will be shown, even covert action and sabotage were resorted to when necessary if Truman, Eisenhower, or Kennedy began to waiver. The Cold War included many examples of treasonous conduct, which confirmed that this was true.

For instance, just before the Korean War, a treaty with Japan was being negotiated to determine if the U.S. would maintain a military presence in that country. At the same time, there was a debate over if Communist China should be officially recognized and allowed to join the United Nations. Should the U.S. defend Formosa in the event of a Communist Chinese attack, and should the U.S. continue to support South Korea so it would not fall to the Communists. The success of the containment policy was dependent on how the U.S. responded to these issues, and there was concern that President Truman might relent to international pressure and give the Communists what they wanted regarding any or all of these issues. The American right-wing position was clear that none could be allowed to occur, which was why the U.S. military purposely started the Korean War to ensure they did not.

In 1959, CIA Director Allen Dulles sabotaged an American-inspired coup to remove Fidel Castro because he was afraid of what the Soviets might do militarily in Europe in response. And when President Eisenhower was scheduled for a summit with Soviet Premier Khrushchev in May 1960 to negotiate a nuclear test ban treaty, the CIA sabotaged a U-2 flight over the Soviet Union to prevent any chance this treaty would be signed. There were other examples of treason to be covered in detail in the ensuing pages. A "Deep State" was acting within the United States that was determined to contain the spread of communism at any cost, even when it meant working in direct contradiction to what a President wanted to do.

And this applied to President Kennedy as well, for his memorable American University speech on June 10, 1963, five months before the assassination, totally contradicted George Kennan and was a rejection of containment, which had defined American foreign policy during the Cold War. "No government or social system is so evil that its people must be considered as lacking in virtue . . . So, let us not be blind to our differences—but let us also direct attention to our common interests and to the means by which those differences can be resolved. And if we cannot end now our differences, at least we can help make the world safe for diversity. For, in the final analysis, our most basic common link is that we all inhabit this small planet. We all breathe the same air. We all cherish our children's future. And we are all mortal."[25]

JFK's attempt at appeasement did not end there. The domestic opposition to his attempt at a nuclear test ban treaty was intense. Senate Republican leader Everett Dirksen called it a "give-away." The Joint Chiefs of Staff said they were opposed "under almost any terms." In July 1963, Kennedy sent Averell Harriman to Moscow as his chief negotiator, but Kennedy handled the negotiations himself from Washington. He spent hours editing the U.S. position as if he were at the negotiating table. No one outside a very tight circle knew what the President was doing, for Kennedy bypassed Congress. He took his case to the American people via an organized public relations campaign. Public pressure forced the Senate to approve the treaty, much to the chagrin of the military and the radical right. On August 5, an article in *U.S. News and World Report* stated that "many authorities in the military establishment . . ." believe that the "new strategy adds up to a type of *intentional* and *one-sided disarmament*." (Author's italics) Admiral Arthur Radford said, "I join with many of my former colleagues in expressing deep concern for our future security . . ." Kennedy was playing with fire.[26]

JFK approved the sale of surplus wheat to the Soviet Union the month before his assassination. It violated the policy of containment. He called it "one more hopeful sign that a peaceful world is both possible and beneficial to us all."[27]

JFK blatantly embraced appeasement in opposition to what his military and intelligence people believed. It was a slap in the face to those who supported containment, for a renewal of the Cold War was not possible—it had never ended. The right-wing accused Kennedy of reducing American military strength while building up the Soviet economy, which was the only way the Soviet Union could survive. Just like Truman and Eisenhower, the right-wing needed to stop JFK, but it would not be sabotage that reigned Kennedy in. His demise would be more deadly. For he had gone much further than either previous President had ever done, by unilaterally instituting changes that those who opposed him believed placed the United States in a dangerous position, from which there was potentially no recovery. And he had done so by bypassing the military and intelligence communities. Kennedy had put the nation at risk, threatened the American way of life, and undermined the Constitution, in violation of everything the country had stood for since its founding, something even a President was not allowed to do without consequences. And he paid the price. Containment had to be maintained at all cost, and to understand why this was so and how it would lead to JFK's assassination, we must return to the period immediately after World War II.

* * *

Kennan's anti-Soviet rhetoric had a profound effect on President Truman. His original plan had been to eliminate an intelligence agency after World War II ended, but he began to have second thoughts. The Soviets remained belligerent in Eastern Europe and posed a threat to invade the West. They had yet to remove troops from North Korea and kept a military government in place there. In August 1946, an American woman confessed she was a courier for Soviet spies, stealing classified information from various federal government departments. On September 5, Igor Gouzenko, a cipher clerk at the Soviet Embassy in Ottawa, Canada, defected and described Soviet espionage plots aimed at the United States. "I want someone to tell me what's going on around the world," an exasperated Truman exclaimed.[28]

Allen Dulles had pushed for an independent post-war intelligence organization from when the war ended, including covert action. Now out of government, he began assembling his private spy organization, using the Council on Foreign Relations to launch his intelligence offensive. Then, through his old business contacts, Dulles established a shadow intelligence service out of an office at 44 Wall Street. He arranged for the placement within the government of those loyal to him to work with front groups he controlled, and he used the media to inundate the public with evidence of the threat the Soviets posed to the United States.

"The Soviets were throwing everything they had at us. The NKVD [the Soviet domestic law enforcement agency] were eating us alive, and Washington could not make up its mind about what to do on intelligence," said Robert T. Crowley, a former aide to Dulles. Dulles, whose support for Germany never wavered, began a massive ex-Nazi recruitment campaign, using a State Department refugee office as a front. Wall Street investment bankers and lawyers were encouraged to reconnect with their old German contacts. In 1951, when he joined the CIA, Dulles brought these assets that he had recruited over to the Agency.[29]

Truman eliminated the OSS on January 24, 1946, and replaced it with the Central Intelligence Group (CIG). Its mandate was to "collect, coordinate, and analyze" foreign intelligence, but without "police, subpoena, law-enforcement powers, or internal security functions." There was no mention of covert operations. As a result, some thought the U.S. was not utilizing the new intelligence group properly, most notably Allen Dulles and William Donovan, the ex-head of the OSS. In October 1944, President Roosevelt had instructed Donovan to draft a proposal "for an intelligence service for the postwar period, which would be in overall supervision of all agencies of the Gov.t as to intelligence matters." Three weeks later, Donovan submitted his recommendation for a Central Intelligence Agency, which included the power to perform "other functions and duties relating to intelligence as the President from time to time may direct." It was an unstated but understood reference to covert operations. As head of OSS, Donovan knew this was necessry, but Truman was not ready to go that far. At least not yet, because the FBI and the Army's newly formed Strategic Services Unit (SSU) were applying pressure to maintain control of American intelligence.[30]

The military controlled CIG. Its first director, a temporary figurehead appointed because he was a Truman campaign contributor, was soon replaced by Lieutenant General Hoyt Vandenberg, the ex-intelligence chief of the War Department. Vandenberg brought in a staff of Pentagon colonels to help run CIG, and they established policy without input from any other group. Two-thirds of the ex-OSS officers who had joined CIG quit as a result and returned to the private sector. But by July 6, the U.S. government redirected funds formerly destined for OSS to CIG, and former OSS officers initially assigned to SSU were transferred back into CIG. The new group was called the Office of Special Operations (OSO), and their function remained intelligence gathering only.

By the summer of 1946, the President instructed a livid J. Edgar Hoover to shut down all FBI offices in Central and South America, with CIG assuming full responsibility for intelligence in these areas. He responded to Truman's decision by removing all personnel, equipment, and records from the Dominican Republic,

Costa Rica, Haiti, El Salvador, Honduras, and Brazil. "Hoover pursued a scorched earth policy," recalled future CIA Director Richard Helms. "He just cleaned the place out and went home in a sulk." Throughout the Cold War, Hoover would similarly conduct himself. He was more concerned with promoting the Bureau than upholding the interests of the United States.[31]

* * *

Meanwhile, Truman was busy digesting Kennan's Long Telegram. He had all his advisers review the document and sent a copy to every U.S. embassy worldwide. He asked White House counsel Clark Clifford to investigate Kennan's allegations. On September 24, 1946, Clifford submitted a report entitled "American Relations with the Soviet Union," supporting what Kennan had said. "Soviet leaders believe that a conflict is inevitable between the USSR and the capitalist states," the report stated, "and their duty is to prepare the Soviet Union for this conflict." Soviet policy was "designed to lead to eventual world domination," and the idea of "peaceful coexistence of communist and capitalist nations is impossible." There was no alternative but to use the "language of military power" as a deterrent.[32]

The Joint Intelligence Committee (JIC), established to produce intelligence reports for the Joint Chiefs, conducted a classified assessment of the Soviet threat. During the summer of 1946, they released JCS 1696, which offered a frightening appraisal of U.S.-Soviet relations. As described on the CIA's official website:

> The most ominous aspect of JCS 1696 was its alarming vision of a future war between the new superpowers . . . *"[I]n a war with the Soviet Union we must envisage complete and total hostilities unrestricted in any way on the Soviet part by adherence to any international convention or humanitarian principles.* Preparations envisaged on our part, and our plans must be on this basis." The United States had to be prepared for gas, bacteriological, and atomic warfare with the USSR. Intelligence was the key to US preparedness for a "total war" with the Soviets . . . "[o]ne of the most vital prerequisites to our future security is adequate intelligence from inside the USSR . . . [every] possibility of obtaining information concerning Soviet war-making potential and her vital areas should be exhausted."[33] (Author's italics)

The question was not if there would be a war with the Soviets, but when. And there would be no rules with an enemy described as the most despicable the U.S. would ever face. Coming one year after World War II, which included unspeakable atrocities, this was saying something. They understood the importance of obtaining intelligence from behind the Iron Curtain to learn the level of Russia's military strength. Throughout the Cold War, U.S. intelligence placed individuals inside Communist countries for that purpose. As will be shown in Volume Two, Lee Harvey Oswald participated in one of these programs.

* * *

In 1947, Great Britain withdrew its military from the eastern Mediterranean, putting Greece and Turkey in immediate jeopardy. As a result, warned Under Secretary of State for Economic Affairs, William Clayton, the leadership in the area would "be picked up either by the United States or by Russia." Hence, the U.S. had to act fast to ensure it would not be the Soviets.[34]

As Truman wrote in his memoirs: "If we were to turn our back on the world, areas such as Greece, weakened and divided as a result of the war, would fall into the Soviet orbit . . . and our avowed lack of interest would lead to the growth of domestic Communist parties in such European countries as France and Italy, where they already were significant threats."[35]

"If communism is allowed to absorb the free nations," Truman said, "then we would be isolated from our sources of supply and detached from our friends. Then we would have to take defense measures which might really bankrupt our economy and change our way of life so that we couldn't recognize it as American any longer."[36]

The importance of Greece was its location, and the Russians desperately wanted it to turn Communist. And what happened there became symbolic of American foreign policy throughout the Cold War, for it did not matter how brutally the Greek government treated their people. So long as they were not Communists, they would receive American support.

Those in power in Greece were Fascist Monarchists, who permitted most people to live in abject poverty while a small percentage of elites made fortunes at the expense of the poor. Opponents of the government were detained in camps, sometimes for years without trial. There were mass executions of captured Communists. It concerned Winston Churchill. who wrote that "it seems to me very unwise for the present Greek government to carry out mass executions of this character and it almost reduces us to the Communist level." He approached Greece's Queen Frederika, the thirty-year-old Greek monarch and granddaughter of the German Kaiser, about the executions, to which she responded: "Don't you believe in the law?" Churchill replied, "Yes, of course." The Queen then said that all those executed had been "properly tried and convicted," ending the discussion. She did not care how Greece treated suspected Communists. She just wanted American aid.[37]

On February 1, 1947, an article in *The New Statesman and Nation* reported that "Greece remains the one country in Europe, outside Spain, whose Army contains in positions of authority a greater number of ex pro-Nazis and collaborators than those identified with the Resistance." And they conducted themselves accordingly.[38]

The bottom line is that in Greece and other countries to follow, the only pre-requisite for receiving American aid was that those in power be anti-Communists. In the long term, such a policy would severely damage the U.S. Local populations developed a deep-seated hatred for the "leader of the free world" who provided blindly financial support without asking questions, as long as it kept right-wing Fascist governments in place. Communism was perceived to be cancer that could spread and infect the entire world, from which there was no cure. So, the U.S. supported Fascist regimes who treated their people just as cruelly, sometimes more so, than Communists would have, resulting in hatred for the U.S. in those countries. As we will, the United States was motivated by greed and a desire to keep communism off America's shores.

On March 12, 1947, Truman spoke before a joint session of Congress and requested financial aid for Greece and Turkey. He did not propose military action, but the threat was there, if not explicitly stated. "Nearly every nation must choose between alternative ways of life . . ." Truman said. "One way of life is based upon the will of the majority and is distinguished by free institutions, representative government, free elections, guarantees of individual liberty, freedom of speech and religion, and freedom from political oppression. [The other] is based upon the will of a minority forcibly imposed upon the majority. It relies upon terror and oppression, a controlled press and radio, fixed elections, and the suppression of personal freedoms. I believe that it must be the policy of the United States to support free peoples who are resisting attempted subjugation by armed minorities or by outside pressures . . ."[39]

It became known as the Truman Doctrine. His words indicated he had heeded the warnings of Kennan and others regarding the Soviet Union and the danger they posed to the American way of life. Then, in an April 18th speech before the American Society of Newspaper Editors, Assistant Secretary of State Dean Acheson described the US-Soviet conflict as the greatest since the era of "Athens and Sparta and Rome and Carthage." America's mandate was to hold onto the world's great "workshops," which included Germany and Japan. Even cooperation with their arch enemies during World War II was acceptable to prevent further Soviet expansion.[40]

With the need for obtaining information behind the Iron Curtain in mind, George Marshall, who became Secretary of State early in 1947, instituted the Policy Planning Staff (PPS) for "formulating and developing . . . long-term programs for the achievement of U.S. foreign policy objectives." In May, George Kennan became its first director.[41]

On May 23, Kennan sent Marshall PPS/1, the first paper to emerge from the Policy Planning Staff, which said the problem Europe faced was an "economic maladjustment" brought on by the ravages of war and made each European nation vulnerable to the rise of domestic communism. According to Kennan, the American objective was "to put us on the offensive instead of the defensive, to convince the European peoples that we mean business, to serve as a catalyst for their hope and confidence, and to dramatize for our people the nature of Europe's problems and the importance of American assistance." [42]

PPS/1 did not mention military support to counteract a potential Soviet invasion of Western Europe. For a good reason, for all the U.S. had at that time to hold back the Soviets was the threat of nuclear retaliation. When World War II ended, there were more than 12,000,000 U.S. troops available. By the end of 1947, it was less than 1,600,000. The approved military budget for 1946 was forty-two billion dollars. In 1947, it was fourteen billion. During the same period, the Navy was reduced to 343 combat vessels, down from 1,166 during the war, the Marine Corps from six combat-ready divisions to two, and the Army Air Force from sixty-three functional groups to eleven. The U.S. was in no position to provide military support to Europe.[43]

Secretary of Defense James Forrestal said the administration's objectives were "economic stability, political stability, and military stability . . . in about that order." He continued that "we are keeping our military expenditures below the levels which our military leaders [ensure are] the minimum which would in themselves ensure national security." The intent was to "follow a course which offers a prospect of eventually achieving national security and also long-term world stability."[44]

Calculated risks were not something the military embraced. They were not pleased with cuts in military spending, and in April 1947, the Joint Chiefs made this clear. "Faith in the ability of the United Nations as presently constituted to protect," the JCS stated, "the security of the United States would mean only that the faithful have lost sight of the vital security interest of the United States and could quite possibly lead to results fatal to that strategy."[45] It was the first sign of blatant military discontent with Truman.

On June 5, 1947, George Marshall spoke at Harvard University about the need for the U.S. to economically support Europe. He cited a united Europe as one of the plan's objectives. Not surprisingly, Winston Churchill was also promoting a similar program, which he called the United States of Europe, which involved rebuilding Germany and aligning that nation with France and Britain. It was all part of the policy of containment, designed to keep the Soviets bottled up within their borders and reduce the likelihood that communism would rise in western European countries.[46]

Eighteen European countries eventually received aid under the Marshall Plan, with the United Kingdom, France, and West Germany receiving the most money. The United States also included Soviet satellites in the list of countries eligible for assistance, but Stalin rejected the offer. The first step in keeping Western Europe free from communism was underway.[47]

* * *

Hoyt Vandenberg became CIG Director on June 10, 1946. Three days later, he was advised by CIG's legal counsel, Lawrence Houston, that in a few months, CIG would essentially be illegal because an agency set up by the Executive Branch could only remain operational for one year without congressional approval which the CIG did not have. Houston drafted legislation to replace the group based on Bill Donovan's original plan for a Central Intelligence Agency. Truman presented to generals working on a different central intelligence plan, and they incorporated Houston's program into their own. To the military, the ability to control central intelligence was essential.[48]

For Truman, considering the warnings of Kennan and others regarding the Soviets and the public's increased Red Scare paranoia, the time was right not only to establish a more permanent central intelligence agency but also to restructure overall U.S. intelligence and military branches. He did just that with the National Security Act of 1947. The Department of the Army merged with the Department of the Navy into the National Military Establishment. The Department of the Air Force became a new branch of government. All military departments were now under a new Cabinet officer, the Secretary of Defense. There were two items of importance here. First, Truman eliminated the War Department because the national defense was now a full-time requirement. Hence the name change. Second, the Joint Chiefs no longer had direct access to the President. They would now have to go through the Secretary of Defense, who would be a civilian. Isolating the military from the President was done by design. They wanted civilians to create foreign policy.

And last but not least, Truman established two intelligence agencies—the National Security Council (NSC), which replaced the NIA, and the Central Intelligence Agency (CIA), which replaced CIG. Rear Admiral Roscoe Hillenkoetter became CIA's first director to appease the military, and the new agency remained an intelligence-gathering organization only, but Truman knew this had to change.

The State Department and George Marshall dominated the NSC, with George Kennan named Marshall's representative on the NSC staff. Subsequently, the Policy Planning Staff became the primary source of ideas for NSC; thus, George Kennan essentially became the man who would direct the nation's foreign policy.[49]

NSC's first order of business was NSC 1/1, which called for removing U.S. troops from Italy and recommended that the President issue a public warning that the United States would not allow Italy's democratic government to fall. And that if there were a Communist attempt to do this, the U.S. "would be obliged to consider what measure would be appropriate for the maintenance of peace and security." Truman listened to Kennan and issued the public warning.[50]

The next item of importance occurred in December 1947. In retaliation for the Marshall Plan, the Soviets created the Cominform, which consolidated eastern European satellite governments into one organization. This new Communist alliance caused a sense of urgency in the U.S. It led to the approval of NSC-4, which warned that the Soviets were "employing coordinated psychological, political, and economic measures . . . to weaken and divide world opinion." Also, it called for "the immediate strengthening" of programs designed to influence foreign opinion towards democracy. The State Department was responsible for coordinating the various programs that were already underway throughout different government departments. Telling was the fact that the CIA was not mandated to spearhead this.

Interestingly, an annex to NSC-4 approved covert psychological operations, which indicates the Truman administration was ready to take American intelligence to the next level. But there would be opposition on Capitol Hill to fund such procedures, so going through the CIA was not an option. "We are handicapped," Kennan told Clark Clifford, "by the lack of ability to use the techniques of under-cover political operation[s as are] used against us." He said Secretary of Defense Forrestal that he knew the American people would disapprove of such methods. "I do feel, however," Kennan said, "that there are cases where it might be essential to our security that we fight fire with fire." Another means of funding had to be found, one that was free of congressional scrutiny.[51]

* * *

In addition to establishing a private intelligence agency, Allen Dulles was busy advising various government groups interested in creating a central intelligence agency themselves. He prepared a nine-page memo for the Senate Armed Services Committee regarding intelligence and laid out a plan for a central intelligence agency. When the CIA became a reality, Dulles hoped to be named director, but it did not happen since he was a Republican in a Democratic administration. In the long run, this may have been a blessing in disguise, for instead, President Truman turned to Allen Dulles and his private covert intelligence network to carry out secret espionage activities, independent of congressional scrutiny.[52]

Returning to the period when the war in Europe was ending, both the British Security Coordinator, Sir William Stephenson, and the head of the OSS, William Donovan, realized it meant the termination of their respective intelligence branch-es. Both men knew this was a major mistake because the threatening presence of the Soviet Union had to be dealt with, and not necessarily on the battlefield. As a result, in May 1945, Stephenson and a small group of associates formed a private corpo-ration under a Panamanian registry, the British-American-Canadian-Corporation, S.A. (BACC). Based in New York, most of its officers and rank and file were former members of intelligence services. One of Stephenson's past senior intelligence of-ficers, Sir Charles Hambro, who was now a partner in BACC, had early in the war coordinated with Bill Donovan on the start-up of an American organization for covert action. Donovan's law firm was now acting as the corporate legal adviser for BAAC, so there was every indication that Donovan, who was also a staunch

Republican who wanted to remain part of U.S. intelligence, was directly involved in the formation of this new organization. It was an export company on paper, but it was an intelligence group offering its services in post-war Europe in actuality.[53]

In September 1945, two days after the government shut down OSS, Stephenson and Donovan started another Panamanian registered company called the World Commerce Corporation (WCC). They soon placed former OSS and British MI6 officers in forty-seven different countries. It was a mercenary intelligence network, with an office was in New York City that maintained contact with intelligence personnel worldwide. Precisely what they were up to can be deduced from an August 1947 warning Donovan gave to Defense Secretary Forrestal. It said, "Our French Friends" needed help if they were to continue "making a fight" against the Communists, and Donovan raised "the possibility of dealing with this matter independent of government action." Nine months later, a CIA officer reported that "various remnants of OSS personnel who had previously operated in and around Paris, France were operating in that same locality on a private commercial basis under the leadership of their former director, William Donovan . . . [who] had made a trip to Paris for the purpose of surveying and inspecting the activities of the group."

Donovan did travel to Paris in 1948, where he met with numerous ex-OSS officers, including Howard Hunt, Donovan's former Far Eastern operative, who was supposedly in town as part of a Marshall Plan contingent. A staunch anti-Communist, the future Watergate burglar, would become involved in a series of attempted CIA coups in foreign countries over the next decade. It suggests that Hunt's meeting with his old OSS boss in Paris was not coincidental, and he was part of Donovan's new international mercenary network. The fact that Hunt has long been a JFK assassination suspect increases the importance of this intelligence group, which operated outside the laws of the U.S. government. Donovan also met in Paris with William Casey, a future CIA director, an ex-OSS officer who now worked for Donovan's law firm. Years later, Casey would be Director of the CIA and provide Oliver North with instructions on setting up a Panama-registered company. It was a private anti-Communist network dealing in drugs for weapons transactions that, as we will see, was what Donovan's group was involved in here. The idea was to promote pro-U.S. political parties in foreign countries, regardless of the cost.[54]

The primary function of the WCC was to assist foreign underground groups, which included Chiang Kai Shek's army in Taiwan, the Mafia in Italy, Monarchists in Greece, among others. Funding came from various sources who had a history of supporting anti-Communist ventures, including Nelson Rockefeller, Joseph C. Grew, Alfred DuPont, and BRAC founder Charles Hambro. There is little doubt that the private intelligence network that Allen Dulles put together was the same organization with which Donovan was involved.[55]

Providing weapons to underground groups throughout Europe is worth noting, considering that Donovan met with William Colby while in Paris. Like Tracy Barnes, during the war, Colby was a member of the Jedburghs. This elite group supplied weapons to underground resistance fighters working against the Nazis, who would then parachute into Europe to train these local groups in paramilitary techniques. It suggests that WCC provided weapons and technical assistance to the groups they helped, as the Jedburghs had done during the war. Consider also that the Jedburghs supported groups primarily in France, making Donovan's reference to Forrestal regarding their "French Friends" even more suspicious.

Another connection to this group was James Angleton, who had remained in Italy after the war, using ex-Nazis to fight against the Communists. Angleton had headed X-2, the counter-espionage branch of the OSS, and had brought Tracy Barnes to Italy to help train stay-behind armies.

Ricardo Sicre operated in Spain during the war and set up a training school for spies who would travel from Spain to Vichy, France. He was also part of X-2 and was one of Donovan's top agents, which is why Donovan brought him in to become a vice president at the WCC.[56]

Sicre's wife, Betty Lussier, a.k.a. Aline, Countess of Romanones, was also an X-2 alumnus who went to work at WCC. She later reported that what they did "seems to have been a precursor to the Iran-Contra situation." Her observation supports the possibility that William Casey learned what he needed to know years later regarding the Iran-Contra affair from the WCC.

Finally, there is the story of Frank Wisner, another Wall Street lawyer who became head of OSS operations in southeastern Europe during World War II. In March 1945, Wisner was in Wiesbaden, Germany, where he served as the OSS liaison to the Reinhard Gehlen Group (which we will cover in detail in the next chapter). He remained in Germany for a short while after the war ended, working under Allen Dulles and setting up the first post-war cover networks, but eventually, he returned to the U.S. to practice law.[57]

Back in New York, William Colby was working on the case of a Romanian exile financier accused of being a spy for Donovan's law firm. Representing the opposing counsel was none other than Frank Wisner. Interestingly, Wisner's law office was at 2 Wall Street, the same building as Donovan's, three floors up. It could hardly be coincidental. Wisner, Donovan, and Dulles were already working together in the new spy group[58]

By 1948 Wisner would return to government service, working for George Kennan at the State Department. Wisner wanted to assist "native anti-communist elements" in "psychological warfare, clandestine warfare, subversion, sabotage, and miscellaneous operations such as assassination . . . ," However, the ground rules had not changed. Additional funding was needed and had to be obtained "in such a manner as to conceal the fact that their source is the United States Government." As Wisner would later say, there was a need for some "private American organization" to "dovetail with this plan . . ." This, of course, is where Donovan's group and the WCC came in, working in conjunction with Allen Dulles's group in a private intelligence organization that was answerable to no one. FBI files describe a 1949 "controversy between Admiral Hillenkoetter, Director of CIA, and Frank Wisner [at State] . . . over the possibility of Wisner's outfit transmitting information to General 'Wild Bill' Donovan." So, even after the government established the CIA, it was clear that the Donovan group, with WCC funding, handled sensitive and illegal projects the Agency could not perform. And Frank Wisner was in the middle of it all.[59]

* * *

To understand Donovan's connection with the CIA, one need not look any further than the case of George Polk. Polk was an American CBS foreign correspondent, murdered in Greece in May 1948. Locals found his lifeless body floating in Salonika Bay, shot in the back of the head with his hands and feet bound with rope. The immediate response of the Greek government was that Communists had committed the murder, but all evidence pointed to authorities within the Monarchist government being responsible. Polk, who had written articles accusing government officials of corruption and embezzling American funds, threatened to disrupt the Truman Doctrine funding that Greece received from the United States. When he tried to obtain an interview with the Communists' leader, and at the same time, expose Greek Prime Minster Constantine Tsaldaris with proof that he was depositing large sums of money in his private bank account, they had to silence Polk.

The Greek Monarchist government and the CIA were united in their desire to blame Polk's murder on Greek Communists. Any other outcome put Truman Doctrine funding in jeopardy and opened the door for a Communist takeover of Greece. The murder of an American reporter trying to get at the truth was a small price to pay to prevent communism from expanding into the Mediterranean region. "We had made a policy decision on Greece," said Presidential counsel Clark Clifford, and "it was the responsibility of competent people to make sure that policy was carried out . . . Without our intervention, they [Greece] would have fallen to the Soviets." Enter Bill Donovan.[60]

Despite not being associated with the Truman government, Donovan remained close to those at the CIA. Many Agency agents had served under him at OSS and shared his anti-Communist passion. "The CIA continued to rely on him," recalled his law partner James Withrow. "And Donovan would do anything the CIA asked. That was his first loyalty." Donovan would call CIA's legal counsel Lawrence Houston at 3:00 AM with regularity, with ideas on how to best battle communism around the globe. In 1948, Secretary of Defense James Forrestal asked Donovan to serve on a secret committee to investigate the ability of the U.S. to defend itself against an unconventional attack. Truman probably did not know Donovan was on the new committee, but it did not matter. CIA understood it was advantageous to utilize the spymaster's services for sensitive assignments, and as a result, he had never really left the Agency but worked covertly under the radar. And the Polk murder was a delicate assignment. U.S. intelligence knew that Greek Monarchists had murdered Polk, and they blamed the crime on a Communist. And Donovan was the right man to ensure this happened.

However, the media knew the truth and formed the Newsmen's Commission to Investigate the Murder of George Polk, which included many who were close to the slain reporter. One such man was NBC reporter John Donovan (no relation to Bill Donovan). His network fired him for trying to learn the truth. The *New York Daily News* demoted William Price to covering the police beat, and his career was also essentially over. Even Edward R. Murrow, CBS's superstar broadcaster for whom Polk had worked, was told to hand over his Polk file to CBS executives. Someone had gotten to the media giants and told them to suppress the story. It was probably Bill Donovan.

In his Washington Merry-Go-Round column in the nation's capital, only Drew Pearson kept the story alive. On May 23, 1948, he wrote that "Evidence points to the probability that rightist forces within the [Greek] government were responsible for Polk's murder . . . Only they knew how critical he [Polk] had been of Greek rightist attempts to sabotage the American reconstruction program. The Greek [Communist] guerillas had everything to gain from the interview with Polk. The Greek government did not want him in Greece and did everything to get him out."[61]

The American investigation was a whitewash from the start. William Colby and his wife conveniently befriended Polk's Greek widow Rea when she traveled to the U.S. Rea told Colby all she knew about her husband's murder and the likelihood that the right-wing was responsible. Still, Colby worked for Bill Donovan, and what she had to say died with him. Later, when Rea needed an attorney to represent her, she accepted Bill Donovan's offer. What the widow of the slain reporter had to say was kept quiet.

The Greek police were corrupt, but one man, John Panopoulos, investigated and concluded that the Monarchists had killed Polk. He provided William Donovan with evidence supporting his belief, but Donovan passed this information on to Greek or American officials. Donovan's job was to suppress the truth, not expose it.

Lieutenant Colonel James Kellis, another ex-OSS man, was Donovan's choice to go to Greece and investigate Polk's murder. When Kellis concluded that the Greek government was responsible, he reported this to Donovan, others at the CIA, the FBI, and the chief of the British Police Mission in Greece. But what he said fell on deaf ears, and he realized there was an Anglo-American attempt to cover up the murder. Shortly after that, he was recalled to Washington, essentially taken off the case. He was probing too hard.

Eventually, authorities framed an innocent local Greek reporter from Salonika named Gregory Staktopoulos for taking part in the murder of George Polk. The evidence against him was fabricated and flimsy. Still, he was imprisoned under harsh conditions and tortured until he confessed to being a Communist and being present when Polk was shot by others, even though one of the others accused had been dead for over a month before the death of Polk.

Staktopoulos was convicted and given a life sentence. He would be pardoned and released in 1961 because it was clear he had done nothing wrong. Unfortunately for him, like George Polk, he was just another expendable casualty in the war against communism. In the big picture, his life was worth sacrificing to ensure the Soviet Union remained contained. John Kennedy would die for essentially the same reason. Evidence was doctored to create a false narrative. And a so-called Communist scapegoat would similarly get arrested and be blamed for the President's assassination. It was a simple blueprint to follow, for most of the western world was convinced that a Communist could be guilty of committing any atrocity

Bill Donovan was present during Polk's trial and pleased with the outcome, even though he knew that right-wing Monarchists within the Greek government had killed him. Also present was Bill Polk, who hounded Donovan with questions to try and obtain justice for his brother, but to no avail. "Young man," Donovan said to him, "there is a war on. Stop asking these troublesome questions. You'll end up spoiling your chances for a good future." But Bill Polk did not stop, which was why Donovan told the State Department that the young Polk was a Communist, an accusation leveled against anyone who did not accept the official American position. They had accused his dead brother of being a Communist himself because he refused to accept the lies about conditions on the ground in Greece. The U.S. Embassy in Ankara would cable the Secretary of State asking if William Polk was "a [Communist] fellow traveler [like his brother]." It was all lies but perceived to be a necessary evil in the war against communism.[62]

The murder and coverup of George Polk dispelled any question regarding Bill Donovan's continued connection to U.S. intelligence and to what extent he was willing to go in the war against communism.

* * *

An arrangement existed between Donovan, Dulles, the WCC, and the CIA. It would continue and expand in size. It was not a coincidence that many of those associated with the Donovan/Dulles group would eventually wind up with the CIA, engaged in the most infamous operations, in violation of U.S. law. These operations would continue to be funded by proponents of a new world order, which meant an American-led world that isolated communism but not a world intent on improving the status of those less fortunate. In the words of John McCloy, it would be a Pax Americana, where the U.S. would be the leader in the anti-Communist crusade. There were no limitations as to what was acceptable to ensure that this new world order would be allowed to flourish. Even the assassination of an American President, if necessary, would eventually be justified in their distorted pursuit of a better future.

The Enemy of My Enemy is My Friend

"We knew what we were doing. It was a visceral business of using any bastard as long as he was anti-communist . . ."

—CIA Soviet expert Harry Rositzke

In 1948, Italy held elections, and there was a chance the Communists could take control of the government. Nothing was off the table to prevent this from happening. With help from the Mafia, the CIA used drug money to bribe voters, assassinated Communist leaders, and intimidation tactics were employed wherever possible to defeat the Communists. And shortly after that, the same thing happened in France with the help of the Corsican Mafia. It was a precursor of things to come and opened a new era for the CIA. Program Branch 7 began, "responsible for assassinations and kidnapping as well as other 'special operations.'" Nazi scientists, who were well advanced in all areas of unconventional fighting, such as chemical and biological warfare, were secretly sent to the U.S., and leading imprisoned Nazis were pardoned and released as the U.S. continued to employ the services of ex-Nazis. The Russian Research Center and the Center for International Studies were two groups in the U.S. that worked closely with the CIA and the military. They were heavily involved with what was going on in Europe, including placing immigrants behind the Iron Curtain to learn what life was like in a Communist country. It is of interest to our narrative because the evidence suggests that these two groups would be involved in Lee Harvey Oswald's "defection" to the Soviet Union in 1959. It was all part of the war against communism.

* * *

Following the JFK assassination, if you wanted someone to serve on the Warren Commission who, along with Allen Dulles, would protect the interests of U.S. intelligence and the military and ensure that past secrets which were better kept hidden remained that way, John McCloy was your man. He knew when to stay quiet and what was best for the United States, which was why he maintained a position of prominence for seemingly the entire Twentieth Century. As much as anyone, McCloy knew where the dead bodies were and who had put them there.

Bill Donovan was told by Commander Ian Fleming, the British intelligence officer and future James Bond spy thriller novelist, to hire John McCloy as his chief of staff. Still, Donovan knew that Secretary of War Henry Stimson would never release McCloy from the War Department. As Stimson wrote in his diary, "McCloy knows more about subversive-German agents in this country, I believe, than any other man." Something about the multitalented John McCloy made people believe he was best suited to work for an intelligence branch.[1]

After the war, in September 1949, McCloy became U.S. high commissioner of Allied Germany. According to author Kai Bird in *The Chairman, John J. McCloy The Making of the American Establishment*, at the time, "occupied Germany was the primary domicile for a host of covert intelligence operations aimed at containing, if not rolling back, the Soviet empire in Eastern Europe."[2]

Frankfurt, Germany was the headquarters of the high commissioner's office in the complex of the industrial giant IG Farben, a past client of John McCloy. In the same building, a few floors down, CIA maintained an office as well, and one suspects that the proximity of the two offices, so close to each other, was not an accident.[3]

Two years before McCloy's arrival, the U.S. Army realized Germany would be vital in containing the Soviet Union. As a result, they created numerous programs designed to take advantage of ex-Nazi SS and German military intelligence expertise to revitalize past U.S.-German relationships that were more important than exacting punishment for wartime atrocities. The largest and most effective program of all was Operation Paperclip.[4]

It started with Joint Chiefs of Staff directive JCS 1076, which ensured that Germany could never rebuild its war machine, put a halt to all German military research, and relocated German scientists to detention centers for evaluation. At its peak, they housed over fifteen hundred people. There was a benefit to this, for it allowed the U.S. to take advantage of German scientific knowledge in areas where America was lagging. It prevented these scientists in U.S. custody from falling into the hands of the Soviet Union. There were already intelligence reports that "eight out of ten leading German scientists in the field of guided missiles" were missing. The military assumed they were captured by the Soviets and taken back to Russia. It could not be allowed to happen.[5]

The expertise of the German scientists was extensive, including atomic energy, biological warfare, chemical warfare, guided missiles, aircraft design, and other areas in which the United States needed to gain expertise. After a prolonged debate, on July 6, 1945, the Joint Chiefs approved a program to utilize Nazi scientist expertise to expand America's knowledge in important defense-related areas. The Joint Chiefs did not tell President Truman about this, which underscores the sensitivity of this operation. G-2 military intelligence was given oversight responsibility, with the mandate that "no known or alleged war criminals should be brought to the United States." The project was called Operation Overcast. Shortly after that, the newly created Joint Intelligence Objectives Agency (JIOA) became responsible for Overcast. The JIOA was a subcommittee of the Joint Intelligence Committee (JIC). It was a clever way to camouflage what was happening.[6]

A subsequent JCS memo warned that ". . . the Soviet Union within a relatively short time may equal United States developments in the field of atomic research and guided missiles and may [already] be ahead of US developments in other fields of great military importance," which created concern in the halls of Washington. By March 1946, in the name of "national interest," the U.S. initiated a program where they brought one thousand German scientists to the United States, among whom were many hard-core ex-Nazis, but known or alleged war criminals were excluded. Questionable characters would have a paperclip attached to their file, hence the name Operation Paperclip. Eventually, even war criminals would come to the United States, the thought being that anything was acceptable to keep them out of Russian hands. After 1947, the CIA also became involved when the Scientific Intelligence Committee (SIC) came into existence.[7]

John McCloy was aware that ex-Nazi scientists were being sent to the United States with their families and given visas and allowed to live there permanently. He also knew many were war criminals responsible for the deaths of tens of thousands. They had used chemical weapons, employed slave labor camps, engaged in germ warfare testing, experimented on live human beings in the name of science, committed outright murder, and partook in a host of other unspeakable atrocities. McCloy, the high commissioner of Allied Germany, never raised an objection, which is not surprising, considering what else he was up to at that time.

The Nuremberg trials of suspected Nazi war criminals resulted in many convictions, including death sentences and long-term incarcerations. It did not deter McCloy, who inexplicably pardoned many convicted ex-Nazis. Perhaps his most sensational decision was to reduce the prison sentence given to Alfred Krupp. His company had supervised the production of artillery, submarines, and other military equipment, while Germany was engaged in an illegal rearmament program before the war. By all accounts, he was an avid admirer of Hitler and produced fuses from a plant in Auschwitz, where concentration camp inmates were nothing more than slave laborers. Thousands died of malnutrition, beatings, and disease under his watch. But McCloy let him go.

McCloy released one-third of the Nazi war criminals held at Landsberg Prison, the main detention center. It included Krupp and eight members of his board of directors convicted along with him. But that was not all. McCloy also commuted

Baron Ernst von Weizsacker, who had deported some six thousand Jews from France to Poland in 1942. Then there was the Einsatzgruppen, a mobile killing squad that carried out large-scale murders of Jews on the eastern front. Some of these men "have committed crimes that are historic in their magnitude and horror," McCloy told his staff, yet this did not deter him. McCloy freed two prisoners out of twenty immediately, and an additional thirteen had their sentences reduced. In another case, he reduced the sentences of doctors who had experimented on concentration camp inmates. One was paroled immediately for time served. Four of the seven high-ranking Nazi judges who had administered Gestapo justice were freed by McCloy outright. He even attempted to have Albert Speer, the Nazi Minister of Armaments and War Production who was part of Hitler's inner circle, freed from prison.[8]

West Germany supported what McCloy was doing, and undoubtedly that played a part in his decisions, but there was more at work here. Consider that for the most part, those pardoned were leaders of business, high-ranking officers, and in some cases, members of the German aristocracy. In other words, these were from the upper crust of Germany, albeit diehard Nazis. Simultaneously, the victims of these war criminals were primarily Slavs and Jews, those deemed to be expendable by proponents of eugenics. Once again, there is no evidence that McCloy supported eugenics, but sometimes actions speak for themselves. Quite frankly, this was all part of the New World Order American elites embraced, a white supremacist, globalist approach to geopolitics, which included the reintroduction of Germany into the non-Communist western world. And John McCoy was, without question, a proponent of that. It explains why a man closely linked to U.S. intelligence with a checkered past would someday serve on the Warren Commission. It was because he had already demonstrated he would be willing to ignore the truth for the good of the country if that were necessary. And it once again confirmed that to the Fascist right in America, the life of those opposed to their way of thinking had no value and could be extinguished if doing so kept the world safe from Communist expansion and the preservation of the American way of life.

* * *

George Kennan also believed that utilizing the services of ex-Nazis was necessary for the rebuilding and protection of Western Europe. "Whether we like it or not," he wrote, "nine-tenths of what is strong, able and respected in Germany . . ." includes "more than nominal members of the Nazi Party." It was preferable to "teach [ex-Nazis] the lessons we wish [them] to learn" rather than just locking them away.[9]

Early in 1948, numerous incidents confirmed Kennan's thinking was correct. In February, the coalition government of Czechoslovakia collapsed partly because the U.S. failed to support President Edvard Benes, who was not an ardent enough anti-Communist. The Czech Communist Party, with support from the Red Army, took control, but only after they gunned down protesting students in the street. The prime minister allegedly fell to his death from a balcony, but very few in the West believed it was a suicide. In March, the Hungarian government nationalized significant industries, putting 90 percent of heavy industry in state hands. Stalin initiated a new "Great Terror," akin to the Russian purge of 1937-38, filling Gulags and containment camps back home with anti-Communist Hungarians. That same month, Britain, France, Belgium, the Netherlands, and Luxembourg formed the Western Union, a precursor to NATO. Each nation pledged to defend one another from external (i.e., Soviet) attacks. In June, the Berlin Blockade by the Soviets cut off all land and rail access to the American zone in Berlin, forcing the U.S. to airlift supplies into the beleaguered city.[10]

Meanwhile, the Truman administration continued to cut military spending. The number of U.S. troops in Europe approached dangerously low levels, as the U.S. defense policy to contain the Soviet Union became reliant upon nuclear weapons. It was a flawed strategy, and in 1949 the Joint Chiefs formed a committee, chaired by U.S. Air Force Lieutenant General Hubert R. Harmon, to determine the effectiveness of an atomic attack on the Soviet Union. The Harmon Report concluded that if seventy different Soviet cities, with a combined population of 34.7 million people, were struck with atomic bombs, 2.7 million would die, and another 4 million would be injured. Still, the attacks would fail to disrupt a potential Soviet ground and retaliatory air offensive against Western Europe. The Soviets would quickly recover from any industrial damage that the United States would inflict.[11]

Inexplicable to the military, the response to the Harmon Report was not to increase the number of ground troops in Europe but to build more bombs. The idea was not for the United States to win a war against the Soviets but to deter the Russians from starting an altercation in the first place. The Truman administration believed that massive nuclear deterrence was the answer. The military begged to differ.

In later years, through a Freedom of Information Act inquiry by Christopher Simpson, the author of *Blowback, The First Full Account of America's Recruitment of Nazis, and Its Disastrous Effect On Domestic Foreign Policy*, a top-secret 1949 military planning estimate was declassified. It was an attempt to convince the Truman administration that building additional nuclear weapons was not enough. It was imperative to dramatically increase U.S. ground troops and conventional weaponry to maintain a balance of power with the Soviets. Clearly, in doing this, the military overstepped its authority and, in effect, told the President he was making defense-related decisions that were harming the security of the United States. Within the JCS's collective mind, only the military was qualified to make these decisions. For the President to ignore their recommendations meant he was not a competent leader. That this was borderline treason is indisputable. It was true that during World War II, the military was essentially free to do whatever they wanted, but this was peacetime. Washington now made foreign policy and military-related decisions. In a sense, the war had not ended; the only difference was the enemy had changed from Germany and Japan to the Soviet Union. The Truman administration tried to prevent another war, and the JCS wanted to start one from a position of strength. It was a position they would maintain throughout the Cold War. Their willingness to circumvent presidential foreign policy and military directives they disagreed with was destined to get worse and was always treasonous.

Air Force General Curtis LeMay summed up the Joint Chiefs of Staff's condescending position regarding politicians who involved themselves in military affairs. "In my opinion," LeMay said, "a general nuclear war will grow through a series of political miscalculations and accidents rather than through any deliberate attack by either side. Let me stress the point that I said political accidents, not military accidents. The dominant school of thought believes that . . . a commander might exceed his authority and independently start a nuclear war. [In America], military instigated war has never occurred . . . and I am hard-pressed to think of an instance when it has happened elsewhere unless the military leader was acting within his authority as concurrent chief-of-state. Military leaders are not prone to start wars. Politicians are." [12]

The 1949 military planning estimate prepared by the military stated that in the event of war, the Soviet Union would simultaneously initiate "a campaign against Western Europe (including Italy and Sicily, but not the Iberian Peninsula initially) to gain the Atlantic seaboard in the shortest possible time and to control the central Mediterranean;" "an aerial bombardment against the British Isles; a campaign to seize control of the Middle East, including Greece and Turkey, and the Suez Canal area; a campaign against China, and South Korea, and air and sea operations against Japan and the United States bases in Alaska and the Pacific, insofar as the Soviet Union can support such operations without prejudice to those in other areas; small scale one-way air attacks against the United States and Canada, and possibly small-scale two-way air attacks against the Puget Sound area; a sea and air offensive against Anglo-American sea communications; subversive activities and sabotage against Anglo-American interests in all parts of the world; a campaign against Scandinavia and air attacks on Pakistan may also be undertaken concurrently with the foregoing, or as necessary; on successful conclusion of the campaign in Western Europe (and possibly Scandinavia) a full-scale air and sea offensive would be directed against the British Isles; the Soviet Union will have sufficient armed forces to undertake campaigns simultaneously in the theaters indicated and still have sufficient armed forces to form an adequate reserve."[13]

The Joint Chiefs claimed the Soviets could do the impossible, but they wanted to make a point. The nuclear bombing wasn't sufficient to stop the Soviets. Truman had to increase military spending, not reduce it, because the military's estimates reported that the Soviets were strong enough to take over Western Europe and whatever other territories they wanted to go after. There was nothing the U.S. could do to stop the Soviet Union with the current plans in place by all appearances.

The Truman administration recognized the danger they faced and publicly began a global propaganda program to demonstrate the evils of communism to the world. Privately, however, Truman authorized U.S. intelligence to carry out secret programs as long there was no potential for repercussions against the United States. Kennan supported this covert approach. Early in 1948, he called for "organized political warfare" against communism and established groups that would create "resistance to tyranny in foreign countries . . ." Kennan wanted to accomplish this by having U.S. intelligence train Soviet bloc refugees to instigate resistance against Communist regimes.[14] It sounded similar to the stay-behind armies privately stationed throughout Europe. Kennan was probably aware of what Dulles and Donovan were doing when he requested the government to consider covert operations.

Kennan's call to resist Communist tyranny culminated with NSC 10/2, the first official directive to authorize covert operations, including "propaganda, economic warfare, direct preventive action, including sabotage, anti-sabotage, demolition and evacuation measures, subversion against hostile states, including assistance to underground resistance movements, guerillas and refugee liberation groups; and support of indigenous anti-communist elements in threatened countries of the free world." The NSC's only condition was that plausible deniability had to be maintained. [15]

President Truman approved NSC 10/2 in June 1948 and created a new organization named the Office of Special Projects to engage in the activities outlined in the document. Including Special Projects in the name was not vague enough for some, so the NSC quickly changed it to the Office of Policy Coordination (OPC). There was some debate over where to place this new group, the concern being that things could spiral out of control if it became part of the newly formed CIA. The military was also not an option, for as the *Washington Post* reported in March 1947: "Dominance by the military could . . . leave the country once again with the same warped one-sided interpretation of intelligence that led to Pearl Harbor."[16] The result was a compromise. OPC did become part of the CIA, but its head would be chosen by the Secretary of State, with the CIA Director's approval. The CIA would remain an intelligence-gathering organization only.[17]

The State Department ran OPC. Not surprisingly, George Kennan became overseer of all covert operations. Per his suggestion, which undoubtedly was at the behest of William Donovan or Allen Dulles, Kennan chose OSS veteran Frank Wisner to head OPC. Kennan demonstrated the concern those at State felt when he told Wisner from the beginning that he wanted "specific knowledge of the objectives of every operation and also of the procedures and methods employed in all cases where those procedures and methods involve political decisions."[18]

Kennan worried about State's ability to control the new intelligence group and instructed his people that "while this Department should take no responsibility for [Wisner's] operations, we should nevertheless maintain a firm guiding hand." Not that Kennan was averse to pursuing an aggressive covert action policy, for he had already supported the immigration to the U.S. of ex-Nazis. He was willing to use Germans and Eastern Europeans as a resistance force against the Soviets and provide intelligence. But he did not realize how far Wisner intended to go. Wisner immediately brought in many of his old OSS agents who had fought the Nazis with an anything-goes mentality. He had remained close to the Dulles/Donovan WCC group operating a private intelligence organization with outside funding. There is no doubt as to where Wisner's allegiances lied and that he had no intention of keeping the State Department apprised of everything he intended to do, for OPC was more connected to the secret intelligence group that operated outside of government supervision. It became even more apparent in November 1948 with the approval of NSC 20/4. It redefined U.S. policy from one of containment to the "gradual retraction of undue Russian power and influence from the present perimeter areas around the traditional Russian boundaries and the emergence of the satellite countries as entities independent of the USSR." Rollback, the removal of Soviet control of its satellite countries, was now an acceptable option to pursue, which suited Wisner just fine.[19]

* * *

The main reason the NSC created OPC was the Italian national election in April 1948, which was in danger of being lost to the Communists. America intended to thrust itself into the internal affairs of a foreign nation, which created a high degree of nervousness among those who wanted the United States consistently to maintain plausible deniability in such matters. It all started in March, a month before the election. The Communists were on the verge of taking power in Italy, so James Angleton flew from Rome to Washington to meet with Allen Dulles. It is pretty telling that Angleton elected to meet with Dulles, who was out of government at the time, not the CIA, for whom Angleton worked. It demonstrated that the Donovan/Dulles private intelligence organization was responsible for sensitive covert operations. So, while the CIA officially was involved with propaganda efforts like Radio Free Europe, the old OSS group within CIA and OPC seemingly worked for Donovan and Dulles, specializing in risky covert operations as they had done during the war. Did this ensure plausible deniability, or did it create a rogue agency where disaster lurked on the horizon? The evidence will show it was the latter.[20]

The Vatican was willing to do whatever it could to sway the election, for the future of the Catholic Church in Italy was in jeopardy if the Communists took control of the government. Pope Pius XII instructed Jesuit General de Boynes to find proof that the Soviet Union was financing the Italian Communists. Concerned, he told more than 300,000 people in St. Peter's Square that "the opposing fronts in the religious and moral fields are becoming even more clearly defined . . ." The next day, the Pope told a Catholic women's group that it was a sin not to vote. His Christmas Eve broadcast made his position abundantly clear: "He is a deserter and a traitor who would give his material support, his services, his talents, aid or vote to parties and to forces which deny God . . . [21]

Meanwhile, the Truman administration had already funneled $350 million to the Vatican Bank to create Catholic Action, an organization designed to thwart the atheistic Communists, by the time Angleton met with Dulles. However, more was needed because fifty percent of Italians supported the Communists. This was why it was the Mafia that Wisner, Dulles, Donovan, and Angleton turned to once again—Luciano in the United States and Don Calo in Italy. There were no rules here, for as George Kennan said, "Italy is . . . the key point. If communists were to win [the] election there, our whole position in the Mediterranean and possibly Western Europe as well would probably be undermined."[22]

In the months leading up to the election, $65 million of black money (untraceable, untaxed revenue) was deposited into the Vatican Bank, much hand-delivered by Luciano's syndicate, which included Catholic clerics affiliated with the Sicilian Mafia. Meanwhile, hundreds of Mafia "made men" arrived in Italy to assist Luciano and Don Calo. The Vatican Bank paid out black money in exchange for mob muscle from religious organizations, including Catholic Action, which nurtured the relationship between the Vatican and the Sicilian Mafia.

The Mafia wasted little time. Don Calo and his minions, including Vito Genovese's cousin Giovanni Genovese, burned down eleven Communist branch offices and tried four times to assassinate Communist leader Girolamo Li Causi. Detroit's Frank Coppola, brought in by Angleton to work with Sicilian henchman Salvatore Giuliano, fired on a crowd celebrating May Day in Portella della Ginestra, killing eleven and wounding fifty-seven (The WCC reportedly provided the funds for the massacre). A leading labor organizer, Placido Rizzotto, was found dead at the bottom of a cliff—legs and arms chained and a bullet through his brain. Throughout 1948 in Sicily alone, killings occurred at an average of five people per week.[23]

With the Pope's blessing, Monsignor Don Giuseppe Bicchierai assembled a group that physically beat Communist candidates, smashed left-wing political gatherings, and intimidated voters. On Election Day, Don Calo's men stuffed ballot boxes and bribed voters with freshly laundered drug money. At the same time, Pope Pius remained in his chambers "hunched-up, almost physically overcome" while he awaited the election results.[24] The onslaught was too much for the Communists to deal with, and the Christian Democrats remained in power.

Lest the Pope's determination to rid Europe of communism be underestimated, considering that in 1949, Pius XII issued a solemn decree which excommunicated not only members of the Church who supported communism but also all Catholics who read or sold publications that upheld Communist ideology. An internal CIA memo opined that "Communist governments . . . will have to accept the issue as now posed . . . [and although they would] have preferred to carry on their anti-church campaign at their own pace, the power of decision has now [removed]. The conflict can be pressed on them with a speed and comprehensiveness that may well affect the satisfactory development of other Communist policies . . ."[25]

The Vatican's anti-Communist credentials were well defined and clearly displayed, as was their connection to the Mafia and U.S. intelligence. The combined efforts of these three groups had begun during World War II and continued without missing a beat. The only difference being the enemy shifted from the Nazis to the Soviet Union.

* * *

France was faced with the same problem trying to prevent a Communist takeover of their government at the same time as Italy. The French Communist Party (PCF) was part of General Charles de Gaulle's forces in exile during World War II. After the war, De Gaulle was elected president but resigned in January 1946, unhappy with the limitations placed on his presidency. It opened the door for the PCF, which had infiltrated the post-war government at high levels, including the military and French intelligence services. In response, Bill Donovan instituted a plan under cover of WCC to form private paramilitary resistance groups made up of former American, British, Canadian, and French operatives, which partnered with the Service d'Ordre du RPF. This privately-run French intelligence service was part of a larger organization called the Rassemblement du Peuple Francais (RPF). Wealthy industrialists secretly funded the RFP. They had a non-Communist vision to maintain French colonial rule throughout the third world. It operated independently, with the French government unaware of its existence. So, two intelligence organizations worked together as the war against communism was waged in France—the WCC and the Service d'Ordre, operating independently of their respective governments and funded by wealthy right-wing financiers. Recall from the previous chapter that in 1947 Donovan warned Secretary of Defense Forrestal that "our French friends" needed help. It was undoubtedly the Service d'Ordre to whom he was referring.[26]

The problems in France reached a boiling point in November 1947 when wildcat strikes and demonstrations involving millions of workers took place across the country, paralyzing the French economy. The government feared that French Communists might take advantage of the situation and attempt a coup. Things were particularly precarious in Marseilles, where 80,000 striking workers shut down the docks. In response, money and arms were sent from American intelligence sources to the Corsican Mafia, who then assaulted Communist picket lines, harassed union leaders, and murdered striking workers. In conjunction with this, a significant propaganda effort inundated the striking workers with radio broadcasts, posters, and pamphlets, creating division among their ranks. The strike eventually ended in

Marseilles on December 9 when the U.S. threatened to ship 65,000 sacks of food back to America unless dockworkers unloaded the food immediately. The striking dockworkers had no choice but to comply, and in short order, the remaining labor force throughout France went back to work as well. The final touch occurred on Christmas Eve when eighty-seven box cars arrived at a Marseilles train station carrying foodstuffs as "gifts from the American people" to the underfed people of France. [27]

So, as the end of the 1940s drew to a close, in France and Italy, there were two secret intelligence services, the WCC and the Service d'Ordre, operating outside government control, working with organized crime in both countries, laundering money through the Vatican Bank, all in the name of keeping Western Europe free of communism. If ever there was an example of the ends justifying the means, this was it. And it was only the beginning, for, in short order, things would get dramatically worse.

* * *

Emboldened by successes in Italy and France, America's secret spy network continued the fight communism. In June 1949, Allen Dulles and Bill Donovan established the National Committee for a Free Europe. The board included such anti-Communist notables as General Dwight Eisenhower, Henry Luce, and C.D. Jackson from *Life* magazine, the Mellon Bank, and Texas oilman George C. Mc-Ghee. It was a CIA front, and along with the American Committee for Liberation from Bolshevism, they funded anti-Communist European émigrés and financed significant propaganda efforts against the Soviets, much of which came from outside channels, including Nazi gold which Dulles had confiscated after the war.[28]

Supporting Eastern European émigrés was something dear to Frank Wisner's heart. While stationed in Bucharest, Romania with OSS near the end of the war, he witnessed first-hand the brutality of communism as he watched the Red Army detain and ship away all capable men and women "of German ethnic origin, regardless of citizenship." Transylvanian families who had been in Romania for generations were dragged from their homes, placed in boxcars, and sent to Russian work camps. Wisner had become close to many of these people, and he drove around the city in a jeep trying to stop the mass exodus (the U.S. and the Soviet Union were still allies at this time) without success. There was no doubt in Wisner's mind who America's real enemy was. If the West ignored the Communist threat, all of Europe could face a similar fate as Romania.[29]

When he took control of OPC after the war, Wisner accelerated Eastern European and German operations to counteract local Communists. CIA operatives would remain in-country and become resistance fighters as a first line of defense when the Soviet Union marched against Western Europe while still providing intelligence on local conditions. Anti-Communist émigré governments in exile would return to their native country after internal revolutions toppled the existing Communist governments.

Operation Bloodstone was part of NSC 10/2, which meant George Kennan and the State Department had to sign off on the program. Its official mandate was to increase defections and utilize "social, labor union, intellectual, moderate right-wing groups, and others" to distribute anti-Communist "handbills, publications, magazines . . . radio," but there was more to what they wanted to accomplish.[30] According to Wisner, "Unvouchered funds of $5,000,000 should be made available by Congress for the fiscal year 1949," and ". . . Disbursements should be handled in such a manner as to conceal the fact that their source is the US government." [31]

Congress approved the money, which, among other things, Bloodstone used to assist refugees from the Soviet Union and Iron Curtain countries to establish themselves in the United States, providing OPC with an avenue for gathering valuable intelligence. The Tolstoy Foundation, established in 1939, was one organization that profited from Bloodstone's support. Alexandra Tolstoy, the youngest daughter of Russian writer Leo Tolstoy, started the organization. When Lee Harvey Oswald and his wife Marina returned to the U.S. in 1962, they became close with an anti-Communist White Russian (Russian Monarchists who supported the tsar) émigré community in Dallas. Paul Raigorodsky was a member of that group. He told the Warren Commission the Tolstoy Foundation took care of "Russian refugees throughout the world . . . [and] know all about them before they come here . . . anybody who comes to the Tolstoy Foundation you know right off the bat [has] been checked, rechecked, and double-checked. There is no question about them. I mean, that's the No.1 stamp."[32]

George Kennan understood the importance of obtaining intelligence from behind the Iron Curtain, so in 1951 he arranged for the Tolstoy Foundation to receive funding through the Ford Foundation via the East European Fund. There were other groups with similar agendas that the OPC supported as well. The American Committee for the Liberation of Russia, Committee for a Free Latvia, Committee for a Free Albania, United Lithuanian Relief Fund of America, American Friends of Anti-Bolshevik Nations, Bulgarian National Front, and a host of others.

The Russian Research Center at Harvard was an organization established with a grant from the Carnegie Corporation, whose primary objective was to study Russian institutions and behavior to determine the policies of the Soviet Union. Per the requirements of Operation Bloodstone, one of the ways they obtained this was to conduct in-depth interviews, either covertly or overtly, of members in organizations like the Tolstoy Foundation.[33]

The FBI was responsible for uncovering Communist activity within the United States. They were always on the lookout for an agency that overstepped its bounds, which was why they investigated the Research Center. An FBI report stated that "the close contact made between Harvard professors and government officials during the war were emphasized as a link binding the research group to the State Department." In other words, during World War II, Harvard professors worked with the State Department to defeat Nazi Germany, and the Russian Research Center was just a continuation of that relationship in the war against communism. It is an important point, for OPC was under State Department jurisdiction, suggesting the Research Center was working with OPC.[34]

In 1950, the Air Force joined forces with the Russian Research Center to "develop a method for (a) understanding how a relatively inaccessible foreign social system 'looks from within' and (b) predicting how it would react to various strains and stresses placed on the pattern of interrelationships among the social institutions . . ." It was in line with what the Research Center was supposed to investigate.[35] However, a later FBI report dated May 1, 1951, stated the Russian Research Center wanted to know what life was like behind the Iron Curtain. So, it expanded its operation by ". . . conducting a mass interview project of Russian escapees and defectors coming from Eastern Germany into Western Germany to do a mass sampling proposition for the benefit of the government . . ."[36]

George Fischer was a crucial figure in Russian Research Center operations in Germany and was a devout believer in the Center's work. The purpose was to determine what the Soviet Union looked like "from within." The findings were made available to the intelligence community. A unique "restricted" Guide for Interviewing Soviet Escapees, written by Alice H. Bauer, was prepared "for the use of the military intelligence operator." The MIT Center for International Studies and other research groups serving "the Military establishment" received the results.[37]

According to a Senate Select Committee on Intelligence report in 1976, the CIA allocated $300,000 in 1951 to establish the Center for International Studies (CENIS) "to research worldwide political, economic and social change . . . in the interest of the entire intelligence community." CENIS, located at MIT because of Harvard's ban on classified research, drew on scholars throughout Cambridge. It was not your typical research facility, as armed guards stood on continuous duty at the entrance door. Its first director was MIT economics professor Walt Rostow, who would become director of the Policy Planning Staff during the Kennedy administration, taking George Kennan's old job. Under Lyndon Johnson, Rostow became National Security Adviser and one of the nation's leading war hawks regarding Vietnam. He was succeeded as CENIS director by Max Millikan, another MIT economics professor. In 1946, Millikan was chief economist for the State Department in the Intelligence Bureau Division, Research for Europe. In 1951 and 1952, he took a leave of absence from MIT to serve as Assistant Director of the CIA. These two men were not your average college economics professors.

In the mid-1950s, Millikan explained, "there has been some continuing ambiguity as to whether we were the creatures of the CIA or [was CIA] acting as an administrative office for other agencies." The latter point seemed to be an admission by Millikan that the CIA acted as an intermediary for another entity that wanted to utilize the services of CENIS. The Dulles/Donovan WCC secret intelligence group comes to mind as a possible candidate.

Harvard's Russian Research Center and MIT's Center for International Studies were linked and worked closely together. Of this, there is no doubt. Raymond A. Bauer worked closely with both groups. In 1959 he wrote in *Nine Soviet Portraits*: "The raw material for these vignettes [in the book] came from hundreds of interviews with Soviet refugees [Bauer traveled to Germany with travel permits supplied by the military], conducted by the Harvard Refugee Interview project in 1950-1951." And "the employees of the Russian Research Center fell into this category."[38]

Military and intelligence assets working together was not uncommon. Fletcher Prouty was a senior aide to the Air Force Chief of Staff in the 1940s, who would later become the top liaison between the Pentagon and CIA. There was a common goal that intelligence and the military aspired to attain, which was the defeat of the Soviet Union. Protecting Europe from the Soviets in a nuclear war necessitated that the military and U.S. intelligence work together. They "knew that if there was a nuclear exchange in those days," Prouty recalled, "you would destroy the communications and lifeblood of a country, but the country would still exist." It concurred with the Joint Chiefs report previously cited that a nuclear attack against the Soviet Union would not eliminate Russia's ability to wage a ground attack against Western Europe. As conventional military spending continued to decline, the Army, Air Force, and CIA began preparing for this inevitability. They developed special forces responsible for setting up anti-Communist political leaders backed by guerilla armies inside the USSR and Eastern Europe. The U.S.could call upon these special forces in a nuclear attack against the Soviet Union. They would be the first line of defense—capture political power in satellite countries, eliminate any remaining Communist resistance, and prevent the Red Army from generating a counterattack.

"The Eastern Europeans and Russian émigré groups we had picked up from the Germans were the centers of this," Prouty claimed. "The CIA was to prepare these forces in peacetime; stockpile weapons, radios, and Jeeps for them to use; and keep them ready in the event of war. A lot of this equipment came from military surplus. The CIA [had] contacts inside worked out ahead of time for use when we got there, and that was also the job of the émigré groups . . . In the meantime, they were useful for espionage and covert action."[39]

A public description of intelligence work was limited to propaganda, such as radio broadcasts into Communist countries, designed to hide what was happening. Because behind the scenes, unknown to Congress and the public, the military and U.S. intelligence worked together to turn émigré groups in Communist satellite countries into a resistance guerilla army. How this came about requires further investigation.

* * *

Camp King was an interrogation center utilized by the German Air Force during World War II. After the war, the U.S. Army used it to gather intelligence from detained prisoners of war. The previously mentioned Reinhart Gehlen came to the attention of General Edwin Sebert, the highest-ranking U.S. Army intelligence officer in Europe, and Walter Bedell Smith, the Chief of Staff of the Supreme Allied Command and future CIA Director. Meanwhile, Bill Donovan and Allen Dulles knew about Gehlen and were interested in him as well.

Gehlen and three assistants were sent to Washington D.C. for debriefing in August 1945. Dulles still maintained direct access to Gehlen, while Frank Wisner remained connected to WCC and ran OPC. Wisner also headed the coordination team. Gehlen furnished them with reports on Russian military strategy and capabilities obtained from four million Soviet prisoners of war during World War II. The ex-Nazi promised the Americans he would not employ former SS, SD, and Gestapo men if he were to work for the U.S., but he lied. At least a half dozen of his first staff of fifty officers were former SS or SD men, including Hans Sommer, who had set seven Paris synagogues on fire in October 1941. Once again, past atrocities did not concern U.S. intelligence or the military in the war against communism.

Red Army General Andrey Vlasov defected to the Nazis during the war. He created an anti-Communist army composed of German-held POWS, refugees, and reassigned Nazis and their Eastern European collaborators, some of the most notorious elements of the Third Reich's killing machine. These were men who were responsible for the mass extermination of Jews throughout Eastern Europe. It was these same ex-Nazis and Nazi collaborators, now held as prisoners of war themselves by the U.S., who would become part of Gehlen's postwar stay-behind armies throughout Germany and eastern Europe, modeled after what Vlasov had done. Initially, they were the first line of defense against a potential Soviet advance on the west. Still, as time went on, Vlasov's army suppressed the rise of communism in countries throughout Europe, and eventually, they became an integral part of America's nuclear military strategy. In the event of a U.S. nuclear attack against the Soviets, they would provide resistance and encouraged the local populace to overthrow the Communist governments the Soviets had installed.[40]

In the U.S., part of Frank Wisner's responsibility was to vet émigrés imported by the CIA, some of whom had questionable backgrounds like those Gehlen was employing. Wisner arranged to have these émigrés exempted from immigration laws, which had previously barred war criminals. "We knew what we were doing, "said Harry Rositzke, a Soviet expert at CIA. "It was a visceral business of using any bastard as long as he was anti-communist . . . ," a recurring theme. "Some of the people Frank [Wisner] brought in were terrible guys, but he didn't focus on it," said James Critchfield, a CIA officer who served as liaison to the Gehlen group. And clearly, what these Nazis had done did not matter, for they were putting together a resistance army made up of unsavory characters and void of government oversight.[41]

According to Vladimir Petrov, a leading Russian scholar in the U.S. and a one-time Vlasov Army adviser, these émigrés trained in the U.S. "were ready to go back [to eastern Europe] at any time." There emerged among these groups "one vocal and not uninfluential element that not only wanted war with Russia . . ." for selfish reasons. George Kennan noted that "Their idea . . . was simply that the United States should, for their benefit, fight a war against the Russian people to achieve the final breakup of the traditional Russian state and the establishment of themselves as the regimes of the various 'liberated' territories."

"It became an article of faith that the USSR was going to fall apart at any time," noted Vladimir Petrov. "Communists killed people to maintain their power, so the first chance [the people] had there would be a rebellion."[42] Eventually, the United States formed anti-Communist governments in exile for each satellite country. They waited for the post-nuclear day of reckoning after resistance armies took control of Soviet puppet regimes. It was when these governments would return to Europe. But the Soviet Union had nuclear weapons, with the quantity and quality unverifiable, so the United States starting a war with them was doubtful. Yet the émigrés groups remained optimistic, unaware that their American handlers were misleading them for the most part.

Returning POWs held in Europe, the problem faced by the WCC was how to organize a resistance army that could secretly penetrate Soviet satellite countries without U.S. authorities learning what they were doing. The answer was simple. POWs were incorporated into the U.S. Army's Labor Service and used to guard POW camps, clear debris from bombed-out cities, locate graves of casualties, etc. The rationale was this was an inexpensive source of labor when budget cutting and troop demobilization in Europe was what Congress wanted. However, Congress was unaware of what WCC intended to do. Though prohibited from hiring ex-Nazis, the Labor Service began recruiting Waffen SS veterans and one-time Nazi collabora-tors, such as Latvians, Lithuanians, and Estonians, who found themselves serving under the same SS officers in the Labor Service they supported during the war.[43]

The next hurdle was to finance this army, hide stashes of weapons in each country, and train these people, both in Europe and the United States, without gov-ernment assistance. Fortunately, the solution to the problem was already in place.

* * *

Paul Helliwell joined the Army during World War II and eventually trans-ferred to OSS. In 1943, he became OSS head of the Secret Intelligence Branch, eventually rising to chief of the Far East Division of the War Department's Stra-tegic Service Unit. Two years later, with Chiang Kai-shek in need of funding to keep his Chinese government in exile alive, Wisner sent Helliwell to Formosa to assist Chiang in preparation for a future invasion of Communist China. Under Helliwell's direction, with the help of fellow spooks Howard Hunt and Lucien Conein, they created Civil Air Transport (CAT), an airline based in Formosa, and Sea Supply Corporation shipping company in Bangkok, to raise money for Chiang. Helliwell used Sea Supply to import arms for Chiang's army, the Kuomintang (KMT), so they could stave off the Burmese military, which was giving them problems. CAT planes delivered the arms into Burma, and the aircraft were used on the return trip to fly drugs from Burma to Formosa, Bangkok, and Saigon. The drugs were processed, and the proceeds derived from the sale of these narcotics were used to finance the KMT and Chiang Kai-shek's corrupt government in Formosa, keeping the whole operation secret from the U.S. Congress. It was an unsavory business, but nothing was off-limits in the war against communism, as we have seen many times.

Helliwell approached William Donovan, who contacted James Angleton, Allen Dulles, and British spymaster William Stephenson, to discuss the sale of drugs scenario used in Southeast Asia to generate the financing they needed in Europe. They approved and arranged for Helliwell, who controlled the pipeline of covert funds for secret operations throughout Asia, to use laundered Nazi gold money through the World Commerce Corporation to buy heroin. Most troubling was that the drugs were to be sold only in inner-city African American neighborhoods in the U.S. because these people were considered expendable. No one would notice if there were a spike in drug addiction in these locations. Eugenics was still alive and well in America.

Donovan, Angleton, and Dulles signed off on the plan, knowing it would provide U.S. intelligence with the steady supply of revenue they needed. To process the opium into heroin and distribute it, they turned again to Lucky Luciano, who had a history of working the drug trade in Southeast Asia. Luciano had imported heroin into the U.S. from Chinese warlords in Shanghai and Tientsin at the end of prohibition. He refined it in laboratories controlled by the Corsican Mafia, another group well acquainted with the WCC. So, the mobster knew what to do.

To move things forward, New York Governor Thomas Dewey, who was close to Dulles and Donovan, was pressured by them to commute Luciano's prison sentence in the name of national security. Dewey deported him to Italy to oversee the drug operation, even though Luciano was a U.S. citizen and not subject to deportation. The distribution problem was addressed by returning Vito Genovese to the U.S. from Italy, despite that he was a fugitive wanted for the murder of fellow mobster Ferdinand Boccia. On June 2, 1945, Genovese was arraigned in New York City and pled not guilty. One week later, a key witness for the prosecution, Peter LaTempa, was found poisoned in his solitary cell. A second witness was murdered shortly after that, alongside a Norwood, New Jersey road. Authorities dropped all charges against Genovese.

Luciano arrived in Sicily in the summer of 1946. The CIA did not exist yet, so this was strictly an OPC/WCC operation. In October, he traveled to Cuba, where he met fellow mobsters Frank Costello, Genovese, Albert Anastasia, Meyer Lansky, and Santos Trafficante Sr. to discuss the Helliwell plan. The operation was large, and Luciano would need additional mobsters to make it work. The OPC/WCC connection decided that Lansky and Helliwell would handle financial details through General Development Corporation, a shell company in Miami. Angleton would be responsible for any legal disputes between the two groups through an associate, New York lawyer Mario Brod. The Mafia would ship drugs to Trafficante in Cuba, where he took control of the illicit cargo. From Cuba, the mob forwarded the drugs to the U.S. for distribution.

NYPD Colonel Albert Carone protected the group in the United States. Among other things, he bribed law enforcement officials so they would ignore the illegal drug operation. Carone collected the drug money and sent it to Italy, where the Vatican Bank laundered it. He would eventually become a Grand Knight of the Sovereign Military of Malta which, as has been shown, was quite an exclusive club, whose only prerequisite for membership the Vatican required was the willingness to fight communism.

* * *

An Illegal drug operation was not the only questionable endeavor the OPC/WCC/Mafia triumvirate engaged in. Colonel Boris Pash, the son of Russian immigrants, was born in San Francisco in 1900. Two years later, the family returned to Russia and sided with the White Russians against the Bolsheviks during the Russian Revolution. The experience left its mark on young Boris, who maintained an intense hatred for Communists for the rest of his life. In the 1920s, he returned to the United States and became a reserve officer with military intelligence and served with them when called to active duty during World War II. After the war, Pash served under General MacArthur in Japan during 1946 and 1947 and remained loyal to MacArthur throughout his career. In 1948, he was the Army's representative on Bloodstone and assigned to OPC, where he became involved in all kinds of questionable activity, much of which was illegal.

OPC wanted to keep hidden what type of work Pash. However, thirty-year after the fact, it came to light. According to what Watergate burglar Howard Hunt told the *New York Times,* "in 1954 or 1955," Pash ran a unit the "CIA set up to arrange for the assassination of suspected double agents and similar low-ranking foreign officials." Hunt had nothing to gain from incriminating Pash, so this was probably a warning that authorities should tread softly investigating his prosecution because he could disclose much more.

Before a Senate Select Committee in 1976 investigating CIA, in response to Hunt's allegations, Pash denied ever assassinating anyone. Still, a witness disclosed

Pash had served as Chief of Program Branch 7 (PB/7) when OPC came into existence. The former Director of Operations Planning for OPC told the committee that PB/7 "was responsible for assassinations and kidnapping as well as other 'special operations.'" Consider also that Bloodstone's "special operations," as defined by the Pentagon, could "include clandestine warfare, subversion, sabotage and . . . assassination," according to the 1948 records of the Joint Chiefs of Staff.[44]

Pash's denial notwithstanding, it is known that PB/7 included at least five former OSS assassins, and, likely, OPC would have hired these men to perform a similar service. Hunt claimed that while he was with the Southeast European Division, he strongly suspected that one of Wisner's émigré warriors, a former bodyguard for Albania's deposed King Zog, was acting as a double agent. Hunt asked his superior, Tracy Barnes, the ex-Jedburgh who was now Special Assistant for Paramilitary Psychological Operations, how he should "dispose" of this double agent. Barnes sent him to Pash.[45]

There is support for Hunt's allegation. In *Blowback, The First Full Account of America's Recruitment of Nazis, and its Disastrous Effect on Our Domestic and Foreign Policy*, Christopher Simpson writes that U.S. intelligence encouraged insurgents to "eliminate the command and other dangerous personnel of the MVD and the MGB [Soviet secret police]."

Other assigned tasks included "organizing for the destruction of industry, communications and other factors in Soviet war-making capacity; engaging in sabotage wherever and whenever it disrupts enemy action, and creating panic and terror."[46]

"In the international clandestine business, it was part of the code that the only remedy for the unfrocked double agent was to kill him," the CIA's Director of Operations Planning during the Truman administration testified before Congress in 1976, "and all double agents knew that. That was part of the occupational hazard of the job."[47]

Consider that in 1950, the Army's Counterintelligence Corps (CIC) in Germany began training a hundred members of a neo-Fascist group called the League of Young Germans. Led by former Luftwaffe officer Gerhard Peters, these mainly were Waffen-SS and Wehrmacht veterans. The CIC provided them with arms and guerilla training and placed them inside the Soviet Union. In 1952, German police arrested one of Peter's men carrying a hit list of two hundred leftist Social Democratic politicians from West Germany. They were to be assassinated before they could take control of the West German government in the event of a Soviet invasion. U.S. officials had to admit to the *New York Times* that the allegation was true and that the U.S. had been funding the paramilitary training of these "young Germans, many of them former soldiers . . . ".[48]

Frank Wisner estimated that from the end of the war until 1951, OPC-funded guerilla groups in Ukraine alone had eliminated 35,000 Soviet police troops and

Communist party members. And this did not include assassinations that took place in other countries.[49]

We know that the OSS was involved in assassination training, supporting the assertion that PB/7 had their won assassination group. Division 19 was a highly secret, World War II operation within the National Defense Research Committee's Office of Scientific Research and Development. They began recruiting underworld figures who were adept at "close-in killing methods" through the OSS. In conjunction with this, the OSS also operated an "assassination and elimination" training program at Camp X near Oshawa, Ontario, which was conducted by George Hunter White, as previously described.

Evidence exists that the OPC and the Donovan/Dulles WCC secret intelligence organization employed assassination assets. It included Mafia killers, U.S. intelligence assassination training camps, ex-Nazi murderers, and their one-time eastern European collaborators who were just as vicious. Corsicans in Marseilles, drug money for arms to finance a resistance army as the first line of defense against the Soviets, money laundering by the Vatican, and drug distribution through American inner-city black neighborhoods, to state that anything was acceptable in the war against communism is an understatement. It makes the murder of an American president almost pale in comparison.

* * *

There is evidence that intelligence operatives connected to the Donovan and Dulles group played a role in Lee Harvey Oswald's 1959 "defection" to the Soviet Union. Volume Two will cover this in detail. It is worth touching upon it briefly here to underscore the potential relevance to Oswald and the assassination.

The Russian Research Center's Raymond Bauer was investigated by the FBI, CIA, military intelligence, and the House Committee on Un-American activities. They suspected him of being an undercover Communist. The FBI, in particular, kept a close eye on him, noting that he attempted to obtain a passport for travel to France, Switzerland, and Austria "[to carry] on studies in connection with the Russian Research Center, Harvard University."[50]

Similarly, when Oswald applied for his passport before he defected to the Soviet Union, he stated he was a student. He planned "to attend the College of A[lbert] Schweitzer, Switzerland, and the University of Turku, Turku, Finland," and travel to England, France, Switzerland, Germany, Finland, Russia, Cuba, and the Dominican Republic. It was all untrue, and even though Oswald did apply to Albert Schweitzer, he never attended.

As was the case with Bauer, the FBI was very suspicious of Oswald. For one thing, Albert Schweitzer College was an extremely liberal, borderline Communist school. It garnered the support of numerous far-left groups, which prompted both the FBI and CIA to monitor the school's correspondence (The CIA, FBI, and State

Department kept track of Schweitzer). The concern over why Oswald never appeared at Albert Schweitzer College was worrisome and went as high as J. Edgar
Hoover, who notified all FBI personnel that an impostor might be posing as Oswald in the Soviet Union. They should be on the lookout for his possible return.
Secretary of State Dean Rusk became involved as well.

This comparison with Bauer is not incriminating on its own, but consider
Oswald's mysterious cousin, Dorothy Murret. She left for Japan by steamer while
Oswald was planning his defection to the Soviet Union, with a travel itinerary
like Bauer's and Oswald's. She intended to work her way around the world as a
schoolteacher. Murret returned to the United States three-and-one-half years later,
in January 1963, having worked in Japan for one year. She also visited Hawaii,
Hong Kong, Australia, New Zealand, Singapore, Thailand, India, Iran, the Holy
Land, and England. In East Berlin, the police detained her for twelve hours.

When she first arrived in Japan, Murret immediately visited Lee Oswald's half-
brother, John Pic, stationed with the Air Force in Tashikawa. Pic later told the Warren Commission that he asked Murret about Lee, to which she responded, "Oh,
He's in Russia, don't you know?" It was before Oswald's defection became public
knowledge, so how did she know?

A most revealing thing occurred in 1970, when a misfiled document dated
May 22, 1964, entitled "MARILYN DOROTHEA MURRET," was inadvertently
discovered by a researcher in the National Archives. Inexplicably, the report did not
contain a word about Murret. Instead, although supposedly related to the assassination of JFK (for what other reason would there have been for an intelligence file
kept on Murret), the file dealt exclusively with a person named Harold Isaacs. At
the time of the assassination, Isaacs was a relatively unknown research associate at
the previously mentioned MIT Center for International Studies. He specialized in
worldwide youth movements (Potentially relevant because Isaacs taught the course
Changing Outlook and Identities in the World every year throughout the 1960s except for 1963). The file also stated that Isaacs "specialized in Far Eastern Affairs, was
a *Newsweek* correspondent in the Far East . . . [and] much of Isaacs' work takes him
away from MIT and consists of international travel and concentration on [study-
ing] India." During the 1930s, Isaacs lived in Shanghai and was the editor of a
weekly periodical that supported the Communist uprising of Mao. He became a
close friend of Agnes Smedley, who worked for Soviet spy Richard Sorge. Sorge
was a German diplomat who worked undercover for the Soviets and developed a
network of spies in Japan that kept the Soviets informed of Japanese military and
industrial capabilities. Although reported to be a Trotsky supporter and a proponent of worldwide revolution (like Oswald), Isaacs told the FBI that he no longer
felt this way when working at the Center for International Studies.[51]

An FBI document stated that "Murret was linked in some manner with the . . .
apparatus of Professor Harold Isaacs," which would have been through the MIT

Center for International Studies. And it would naturally follow that the MIT Center was responsible for Murret's extensive travel through third-world countries, which involved studying student movements worldwide of interest to U.S. intelligence. Murret's connection to Isaacs, her suspicious travel itinerary, and the MIT Center only came to light during an investigation into the JFK assassination. Therefore, Oswald's mysterious travel itinerary was possibly connected to the Center for International Studies as well. For why else would Dorothy Murret's link to Isaacs be of concern to the FBI unless Oswald had a connection to him? The apparent explanation is that the MIT Center for International Studies sent Oswald to the Soviet Union as part of an intelligence operation, which would have involved the Russian Research Center at Harvard.

There was another report that connected Isaacs to Oswald. It involved an FBI interview of Richard Giesbrecht and a conversation between two men he had overheard at a Winnipeg airport in February 1964, just three months after the assassination. According to Giesbrecht, they were concerned about Oswald, what he may have told his wife about the assassination plot, and wondered why Isaacs was involved with a "psycho" like Oswald.

Giesbrecht later identified David Ferrie as one of the two men. Ferrie suffered from alopecia, which rendered the body utterly void of hair. He compensated for his condition by wearing an ill-fitting wig and painted-on eyebrows that looked ridiculously artificial, making him a person one would not soon forget. It added a degree of credibility to Giesbrecht's story, as did the fact that Oswald and David Ferrie knew each other in New Orleans. By all accounts, the two men were close. And considering the public was not aware of an Oswald/Ferrie relationship in February 1964 and that a possible connection between Oswald and Issacs was also unknown, Giesbrecht's story has merit.[52]

The reference to what Oswald may have told his wife is also revealing. Russian-born Isaac Don Levine was a post-World War II editor of an anti-Communist monthly periodical called *Plain Talk*. In 1948, Levine told Assistant Secretary of State Adolf A. Berle, Jr. that Whittaker Chambers said Alger Hiss was a Communist. Levine likely had intelligence connections. In 1951 he was hired by Frank Wisner to develop a secret program to export Russian and Ukrainian émigrés into Germany from other countries. It meant there was a connection between Wisner, the WCC anti-Communist resistance armies Wisner was involved with, and Levine.

In 1963, Levine was *Life* magazine's representative in Dallas, which Henry Luce owned. After the assassination, he obtained exclusive access to Marina Oswald, Lee's wife, and C.D. Jackson, who also worked for Luce, directed the taping of Marina's story and had local Russian émigré Ilya Mamantov transcribe it. Before Marina testified before the Warren Commission on February 3, 1964, Levine spent an entire week with her, which one informed source characterized as witness coaching. Levine had also testified before the Commission in January, asked to do so by Allen Dulles himself., and told the Commission that Marina claimed to have been contacted by Russian intelligence, an assertion that one finds hard to believe. Marina was afraid of being deported, so admitting she had a connection to Soviet intelligence, even an innocent one, was unlikely. At any rate, Levine's allegation to the Warren Commission ensured that *Life* would never publish Marina's story, which suggests that the need to suppress what she had to say was the reason Levine approached her in the first place.

Levine may have also worked with Wisner and Dulles regarding the émigré resistance armies, which suggests keeping Marina quiet may have been related to distancing Oswald from this group. In 1953, the Russian-born Levine was "a veteran China Lobbyist who had previously collaborated on anti-Soviet projects with CIA and the CIA-subsidized Tolstoy Foundation." What a staunch anti-Communist would be doing lobbying China raises questions, but considering that Harold Isaacs also had an interest in Red China, perhaps there was a connection between the two men. In any event, around the same time, Levine set up the American Committee for the Liberation of the Peoples of Russia, which OPC ran. Finally, Levine was a board member of the American Friends of Paix et Liberte, where Paix et Liberte was the private intelligence group operating in France connected to Donovan and Dulles's WCC.

Levine was a player in the world of intelligence who became involved with Marina Oswald to suppress her story, while *Life* magazine was writing about JFK turning around to face the sniper's nest (see Chapter One). Meanwhile, Henry Luce purchased the Zapruder film to lock it away so the public could not see it. It would be irresponsible to accept that this was innocent or a mere coincidence.[53]

As mentioned above, Ilya Mamantov was the person chosen to translate Marina's taped interview into English. He was a geologist with Sun Oil Company, whose owners, the Pew family, had donated over $1,000,000 to right-wing organizations. Recall from Chapter One that Sun Oil President J. Howard Pew was the driving force behind the American Liberty League in 1944, financed the openly Fascist Sentinels of the Republic, and was a member of the John Birch Society. It would be hard to imagine that Mamantov could work for such a man and not share his views, which turned out to be the case.

Testifying before the Warren Commission, Oswald's curious acquaintance, George De Mohrenschildt, said Mamantov was the one "excessive rightist" among the Russian émigré community in Dallas. Consider also that Jack Crichton was the person who approached Mamantov to be Marina's translator. A former OSS officer who had served in Europe, Crichton, who by 1956 had organized the 488th Military Intelligence Detachment, a U.S. Army Intelligence unit that operated out of Dallas. How was it that an Army Intelligence officer had immediate access to Marina Oswald and arranged for her interpreter while the police and FBI stood idly by? There had to have been a relationship between Crichton and Levine, for it was through Crichton that Levine became Marina's interpreter. These men did not arrive on the scene by accident.[54]

Mamantov was also a close friend of Peter Gregory, a White Russian who had befriended Lee and Marina Oswald in Dallas. Mamantov and Gregory helped establish an anti-Communist Orthodox parish in the Dallas-Fort Worth area, which the Tolstoy Foundation funded. Recall that the previously mentioned Paul Raigorodsky was another White Russian associate of the Oswalds, who was on the Board of Directors of the Tolstoy Foundation, one of Wisner's émigré groups funded by WCC, to which Levine was connected.[55]

There was also Spas Raikin, who worked for Traveler's Aid Society. He met the Oswalds at the dock in Hoboken, N.J., when they first returned from Russia in 1962. This innocent description of Raikin was a convenient shield to hide the truth about him. He was also secretary-general of the American Friends of the Anti-Bolshevik Bloc of Nations, a fanatically anti-Communist, pro-Fascist, pro-Nazi organization. The CIA worked with Raikin through this group.[56]

George de Mohrenschildt was a petroleum geologist with friends in high places and intelligence connections, and it was de Mohrenschildt who introduced the Oswalds to the Dallas White Russian community. In April 1963, de Mohrenschildt left Dallas to pursue a project in Haiti, but before leaving the country, he stopped in Washington, D.C. While there, he met with Nicholas A. Anikeeff, who discussed their encounter in a post-assassination interview. "Yes, I knew George," Anikeeff said. "From young manhood before World War II, back in the 30s, we were close friends."[57]

De Mohrenschildt arrived in the United States in 1938 and stayed with his older brother Dimitri, a staunch anti-Communist who would become an OSS operative and one of the founders of Radio Free Europe and Radio Liberty, both OPC operations. British intelligence reportedly told the U.S. government that they suspected George was working for German intelligence. There was also documentation indicating he was under FBI surveillance for much of the 1940s. At the time, de Mohrenschildt worked for the Shumaker Company in New York City, as did Pierre Fraiss. Fraiss had connections to French intelligence, and according to de Mohrenschildt, he and Fraiss would obtain information about people involved in "pro-German" activities for the French.

After the war, Nicholas Anikeeff worked for the CIA and was likely also involved in U.S. intelligence in the 1930s when he first met de Mohrenschildt. Consider that World War II began in 1939, only one year after de Mohrenschildt arrived in the U.S. Is it plausible that Anikeeff would have said that he and George were "close friends" in the 1930s if they first met in the U.S. in 1939? Most likely not, for they would not have known each other long enough. Also, Anikeef said he knew de Mohrenschildt "from young manhood." George was born in 1911, which meant that if he had met Anikeeff for the first time in 1939 in the U.S., he would have been around twenty-eight years old. Young manhood is not a description one would apply to someone that age. The early twenties would be more appropriate, which meant that Anikeeff and de Mohrenschildt first met in Europe in the early 1930s, while de Mohrenschildt was in his early twenties and had not yet arrived in America. This is importance because Anikeeff and de Mohrenschildt were probably working for an intelligence organization in Europe before the war. And there is no reason to believe that after the war ended, with both living in the United States, they did not begin working for U.S. intelligence once again.

During the early 1950s, we know that Anikeeff worked on a CIA operation that dispatched two groups of Lithuanian infiltrators into Poland, which would have been part of the WCC émigré resistance operation in Europe. In *The Red Web*, author Tom Bower wrote that "In preparing both operations, the CIA case officer [Nicholas] Mike Anikeef has liaised in detail with the Reinhard Gehlen group . . ." In another book, *The Invisible Government,* author David Wise lists the CIA chain of command related to the Soviet Union as Wisner (DDP) to Helms (A/DDP) to John Maury (chief of the Soviet Russian Division) and to N.M. Anikeef, who appeared to have been a branch chief in the Soviet Russian Division. A connection to the Gehlen group by a branch chief of the Soviet Russian Division of CIA, who dispatched Lithuanian infiltrators into Poland, puts Anikeef at the heart of Wisner's émigré resistance movement in Europe, as well as a connection to Donovan and Dulles' WCC.[58]

Based on this, it is plausible that de Mohrenschildt was involved in the OPC/WCC émigré resistance movement in the early 1950s, run by Frank Wisner. It is also conceivable that Oswald worked with Harold Issacs and MIT Center for International Studies. Don Levine, C.D. Jackson, and Ilya Mamantov attempted to suppress Marina's story after the assassination. With the Dallas White Russian connection to the Tolstoy Foundation and the fortuitous appearance of Spas Rankin as the first person to meet the returned defector Oswald when he first stepped onto U.S. soil, it is easy to see that a common thread united them all. They all may have been part of Wisner's émigré resistance operation. Since Oswald's connection to all these people couldn't have been by coincidence, the only logical explanation is that Oswald's subsequent "defection" was a WCC operation connected to the MIT Center for International Studies and the Harvard Research Group. Why else would various people try to prevent Marina from telling her story if not to hide a relationship between these groups and Lee Oswald that had to remain hidden?

People associated with the Dulles/Donovan WCC operation before Oswald defected had to be protected. In the following chapters, the evidence provided will show that Oswald's "defection" was an undercover assignment. He was not an ordinary Marine, but his relationship with these people does not imply they were involved in the JFK assassination. However, it suggests that they were involved with Oswald in an independent operation unrelated to the assassination that they had to conceal. In the war against communism, many illegal and immoral operations were rationalized and justified. Maybe that is why those who had something to hide had Oswald killed quickly after the assassination, and a written record of what he said during his interrogation does not exist because his past had to remain hidden. One thing is sure. The CIA, the Russian Research Center, and the Center for International Studies at MIT tied this together. But more about that later at the appropriate time.

- 5 -

A Difference of Opinion
Defending the Pacific

"You can depend on it that I will defend South Korea as I would defend the shores of my own native land."
—General Douglas MacArthur, 1949 (before the Korean War began)

The year 1949 was a defining moment because a series of events occurred which, had they been prevented, the assassination of JFK would likely never have happened. The Truman administration was willing to abandon both Formosa and South Korea to the Communists. Meanwhile, the U.S. was negotiating a treaty with Japan. The possibility existed that the United States would have to leave Japan and abandon its military bases there, dooming Japan to eventual Soviet or Chinese subjugation. The Pentagon considered all three countries essential and had no intention of leaving, so General MacArthur and the Joint Chiefs resorted to treason to ensure that the U.S. remained. Their success encouraged the military and CIA and led to future examples of insubordination, as they had foreign policy objectives that often were contrary to what a sitting President wanted, including the overthrow of foreign governments run by Communists. The overthrow of the U.S. government and the elimination of John F. Kennedy would become part of this.

American innocence died with the Korean War, for after it ended, anything was acceptable in support of a plan that was perceived to be in the best interest of the American people. Even the murder of an American President. It was not what the Founding Fathers meant when they included "provide for the common defense" in the Preamble to the Constitution, for that was supposed to lead to "domestic Tranquility." Instead, the exact opposite happened, and we are still paying the price for it today. Domestic tranquility has become a pipe dream, and it all started with lies and deceit in Korea.

* * *

In a speech before the Press Club on January 12, 1950, Secretary of State Dean Acheson said that U.S. foreign policy in Southeast Asia needed to be changed. The military would only defend "essential parts" of the region behind a "defensive perimeter" that ran from the Aleutian Islands to Japan, to the Ryukyus' and the Philippines. Acheson emphasized this did not include Formosa and South Korea. The U.S. defense policy would only rely on air and naval power from critical locations like Japan, Okinawa, and the Philippines. Those two countries could fall to the Communists, for the U.S. did not intend to provide them with any protection.

NSC-48/2 was adopted around the same time, which loosely committed the administration to the continued recognition of Chiang's forces on Formosa until its situation was "clarified," which was a cryptic way of saying until Red China took it over. The paper stated that only a significant U.S. military intervention could save Formosa, which the administration had no interest in doing. And regardless of what happened to Chiang, the People's Republic of China (PRC) would not be formally recognized by the U.S. until it was in their best interest to do so.[1]

Under Secretary of State, Robert Lovett was more emphatic. He said spending had to be limited, "or the United States would find itself in the position of underwriting the security of the whole world . . . [W]e must be careful not to over-extend ourselves. We lack sufficient financial and economic resources simultaneously to finance the economic recovery of Europe, to furnish arms and equipment to all individual countries or groups of countries which request them, and to build up our [ ] military strength."[2]

Meanwhile, there were rumblings out of Korea. On October 12, 1949, the American Commander-in-Chief, Far East, G-2, reported that the North Koreans were preparing to attack the South on October 15, but nothing happened. Another report on December 30 stated an invasion was to occur in March or April 1950, as did separate reports dated January 1 and February 19, 1950. In all cases, the U.S. government ignored these reports, which did not matter, for there was no interest in assisting South Korea if an invasion from the North were to occur.[3]

Despite the administration's position, there were signs of discontent brewing, as evidenced by NSC-68, which the Policy Planning Staff put out in the spring of 1950 in opposition to the new limited containment policy. NSC-68 considered all points along the perimeter having equal importance and worth defending. "The assault on free institutions is worldwide now," stated NSC-68, "and in the context of the present polarization of power, a defeat of free institutions anywhere is a defeat everywhere." As a result, the U.S. should retaliate with boots on the ground against any sign of Communist aggression, including Formosa and South Korea. Still, this military build-up would merely be "a shield behind which we must deploy all our nonmilitary resources in the campaign to roll back the power of the USSR and to frustrate the Kremlin's design."[4] What the authors advocated was "a rapid build-up" of both nuclear and conventional forces to increase American "political, economic, and military strength" to attain "clearly superior overall power" over the Soviets. NSC-68 recognized that money was an issue, but it was imperative to remember "that our independence as a nation may be at stake." What the U.S. needed was the ability to deter Soviet aggression by maintaining nuclear superiority over them, with a conventional army that was strong enough to stand up to the Red Army.[5]

"The fundamental design of those who control the Soviet Union and the international communist movement," NSC-68 continued, "is to retain and solidify their absolute power, first in the Soviet Union and second in the areas now under their control." But this was not enough. NSC-68 Soviet leaders believed "achievement of this design requires the dynamic extension of their authority and the ultimate elimination of any effective opposition to their authority." [6]

"Without superior aggregate military strength . . . a policy of 'containment' . . . is no more than a policy of bluff," NSC-68 strongly warned. Conventional military force capabilities had "to increase as rapidly as possible . . . ," but it was still imperative that the U.S. stay ahead of the Soviets in the number and quality of nuclear weapons, including the much more powerful hydrogen bomb. Total military superiority was the objective.[7]

President Truman was shocked when he was given NSC-68 on April 7, 1950, for it estimated military spending cost be around $50 billion. Truman would never agree to this. His military budget projection for 1951 was only $13 billion, and he had no intention of increasing it. So, the administration ignored NSC-68 for the time being.

General Omar Bradley, chairman of the Joint Chiefs, told the House Armed Services Committee in October 1949 that he understood Truman would disapprove of NSC-68 due to financial constraints. But he also said something quite revealing, that "obviously, if war is thrust upon us, the American people will spend the amount necessary to provide for national defense, and to carry out their international obligations." The investigation that would become NSC-68 began in January 1950. Bradley had spoken to the Armed Services Committee *three months before* when the false alarms of a potential North Korean invasion into South Korea were known. In June, the Korean War began, and it was this that resulted in the approval of NSC-68, which forever dramatically increased the amount the United States would spend on the military. The timing was not an accident. And Truman took the bait.

There were three main areas of concern in the spring of 1950. South Korea and a potential Communist invasion from North Korea; Chiang Kai-Shek and a possible attack against Formosa by Red China; a peace treaty with Japan would keep U.S. military bases and missiles there permanently. A deception to initiate a war between the U.S. and North Korea involved the U.S. military, Chiang Kai-Shek, and South Korean President Syngman Rhee. It was treason. Before discussing the Korean War, it is crucial to examine these three critical areas and explain the importance each played as the war with Korea loomed on the horizon and what the military did to ensure that the outcome they wanted would come to fruition.

* * *

Korea

Syngman Rhee was acting provisional president of Korea during the 1920s in Shanghai, while the Japanese occupied Korea, but alleged misuse of power resulted in the removal of Rhee. Despite this, he continued lobbying for Korean independence, including participation in a League of Nations investigation into the matter in 1933. Rhee was a hardline anti-Communist and ardent supporter of the United States and remained in the good graces of the U.S. military. In 1939, he moved to Washington D.C. When World War II started, the ex-Korean President helped OSS establish anti-Japanese strategies while convincing FDR to formally recognize his provisional Korean government. When the Japanese surrendered on September 2, 1945, he remained a staunch anti-Communist. Rhee rejected the Soviet Union and United States' proposal that a trusteeship based upon the cooperation of the Communist left-wing and right-wing Nationalist parties would govern Korea. Most of all, he refused to negotiate with the Communists from the North.[8]

Rhee was flown to Tokyo by U.S. military plane and issued a passport by the American military government in Japan, something the State Department, which was in favor of the Korean trusteeship, had refused to do. After a secret meeting with General MacArthur, Rhee flew to Seoul aboard MacArthur's personal airplane in mid-October. The divide between the U.S. military and the politicians in Washington was evident.

For years, factionalism characterized the Korean Nationalist movement. Rhee, who had lived for decades in the United States, had converted to Christianity and was an anti-Communist, was considered the logical candidate to run the country by the conservatives in the U.S. military. And he spoke English, which none of his rivals did, so he was the obvious choice.

In June 1946, Rhee still maintained that Korea must be established free of American and Soviet domination, so he moved briefly to Washington, D.C., to promote his agenda. While he was there, the Truman Doctrine was announced, which protected South Korea, solidified Rhee's support in America, and reinforced his anti-Communist beliefs.

By 1947 South Korea was in economic distress, with widespread famine and unemployment. A new and stronger right-wing group had formed, made up of anti-Communists who supported a government-run by wealthy elites, and youth gangs terrorized Communist leftists. Meanwhile, the United Nations recognized Korea's independence and established the United Nations Temporary Commission on Korea (UNTCOK) to ease their transition into becoming a united government.

However, the Soviets and North Koreans did not recognize UNTCOK's authority and refused to participate in a nationwide election to establish a new government. Rhee seized the moment and said elections should go ahead anyway, which they did. On May 10, 1948, the election of the Republic of Korea's first Korean National Assembly election took place. The new assembly filled two hundred seats, with one hundred seats reserved for Koreans from the North when they decided to join the new government.

On August 15, 1948, Rhee was elected president and immediately cracked down on those who had opposed him, using the national police to do his bidding. The government enacted laws to curtail political descent. Freedom of the press was restricted, leftist opponents were arrested and tortured, assassinations were a regular occurrence, and the Rhee government oversaw outright massacres. That fifty-three percent of South Korean police officers had served in the National Police during the Japanese occupation only added to the terror. It all served to alienate Rhee's countrymen from the North further, prompting them to hold independent elections, which resulted in a new North Korean government on September 9, 1948, with Kim Il Sung, a popular guerilla leader, elected as premier. Sung claimed to be the legitimate leader of all Korea, citing underground elections in the South that supported him as proof. Later that year, the Soviets removed all their troops from the North, and the U.S. did the same in the South, leaving behind only a five-hundred-man Korean Military Advisory Group to train the South Korean army.[9]

The situation worsened in October 1948, when a group of South Korean soldiers, sent to engage leftist rebels in an armed conflict, decided instead to turn against their government. They took control of the port city of Yosu and executed some Rhee supporters, but the South Korean army regained control within a week, causing many locals who supported the rebels to flee. Some remained, and government troops killed more than five hundred. Others were beaten and tortured. Syngman Rhee's army, backed by American advisors, killed an estimated six thousand guerrillas between November 1949 and March 1950, jailed thirty thousand suspected Communists, and enrolled 300,000 suspected sympathizers in what was called a "re-education" movement.

Through all this, General MacArthur supported Rhee. At the Seoul ceremonies which established the Rhee regime, he proclaimed: "In this hour, as the fortunes of righteousness advance, the triumph is dulled by one of the great tragedies of contemporary history—an artificial barrier has divided your land. This barrier must and will be torn down." When Rhee went to Tokyo in 1949, MacArthur saw him off with a pat on the back and a declaration: "You can depend on it that I will defend South Korea as I would defend the shores of my own native land." But it remained unclear if the U.S. government supported this declaration by MacArthur.[10]

In 1949 Rhee was determined to go to war with the North to create a unified Korea, something Kim Il Sung also wanted to do. Rhee attacked the North that year, but Sung was well prepared, for in 1947, he had sent 30,000 troops to China to assist Mao Zedong in the Chinese civil war, and those troops, who had returned from China, were battle-tested. Kim had also been buying military equipment from the Soviets, which gave him a distinct advantage. A bloody border battle took place in May, and hostilities would continue until the actual Korean War began.

By 1950 the U.S. policy of limited containment was in place, and Rhee knew full well that the U.S. would not get involved when the North invaded South Korea. Early in May, Rhee made an appeal to the U.S. for combat planes, saying, "May and June may be the crucial period in the life of our nation." On May 10, Captain Sihn Sung Mo, Defense Minister of South Korea, held a press conference in Seoul stating "that North Korean troops were moving in force toward the 38th Parallel and that there was imminent danger of [an] invasion from the North." Robert T. Oliver, an American adviser to Rhee, also appealed for planes in the June 9 issue of *Periscope on Asia*, warning without the aircraft, "the next Soviet advance in Asia could be down the Korean peninsula." The pleas for help were ignored by the United States, an ominous sign for Rhee.

Under this uncertainty, the North saw an opportunity and initiated a campaign for unification, urging the South to throw Rhee and his supporters out. But Rhee's problems were exacerbated when the U.S. Congress threatened to suspend American aid to South Korea "in the event of the formation . . . of a coalition government which includes one or more members of the Communist Party or the party now in control of the government of North Korea."[11]

While warning South Korea that they would cut off aid were Communists to make inroads into their government, the U.S. continued to call for elections to reunite Korea, which Rhee repeatedly postponed, fearing the worst. It was not until Dean Acheson threatened to suspend aid unless elections were held on May 30 that Rhee relented, which proved to be a disaster for him. Ninety percent of eligible Koreans voted, resulting in 128 of 210 seats won by independents, while Rhee's popularity dwindled. It was as if the State Department was looking for an excuse to cut off aid to Rhee.

Rhee was receiving mixed signals from the United States. After visiting MacArthur in Japan, John Foster Dulles, at MacArthur's urging, traveled to Korea and addressed the Korean National Assembly on June 19, which created optimism just six days before the Korean War began. Dulles said that "in the front line of freedom, under conditions that are both dangerous and exciting [we] encounter a new menace, that of Soviet Communism . . . [which] has seized in its cruel embrace the Korean people to the north of the 38th Parallel and . . . seeks by terrorism, fraudulent propaganda, infiltration, and incitement to civil unrest, to enfeeble and discredit your new Republic." He assured them, "You are not alone . . . so long as you continue to play . . . your part in the great design of human freedom."[12]

Elections in South Korea showed that Rhee's popularity was waning as Communists gained seats in the government. Guerilla activity in South Korea opposed to Rhee was on the increase, and the population wanted unification. The North's underground elections showed the people of the South supported a Communist government over Rhee's. It was only a matter of time before the Rhee government would be gone, and a united Korean Communist government would replace it. Why then would the North Koreans invade South Korea, as the official record says they did, and take the chance that the United States could have a change of heart, especially after the speech given by Dulles less than a week before. It did not make sense.

On the other hand, Rhee was at a point of desperation. His government was floundering; he could not match the military strength of the North, the opposition he faced internally continued to grow. Rhee faced the possibility of being removed from office. The U.S. was ambivalent and insisted on elections they knew would be unfavorable for him, demonstrating that the Americans considered his small nation expendable. But he had one trump card left to play. MacArthur, who had nothing short of disdain for politicians, was on record saying he would help Rhee militarily against North Koran aggression. Then, six days before hostilities began, John Foster Dulles arrived in Korea, fresh from a meeting in Japan with MacArthur. He told the South Koreans they were not alone, as long as they continued to play their part. Considering that people like Dulles and MacArthur equated communist subjugation with slavery, the grand design of human freedom can only be resistance to communism. The question is, what exactly was the part Dulles expected the South Koreans to play to ensure they would get MacArthur's support? Simultaneously, there were repeated rumors that North Korea was preparing to invade the South, almost as if to prepare Washington that if hostilities occurred, the North were the instigators. Dulles undoubtedly arrived in Seoul with a message for Rhee from MacArthur that Rhee should initiate an attack against the North; it would surely result in a retaliatory invasion by the North in return. Aid from the U.S. for South Korea would follow. It is what occurred.

FORMOSA

On October 1, 1949, having driven Chiang Kai-shek and his Chinese Nationalist forces off the mainland onto Formosa, Communist Chinese leader Mao Zedong established the People's Republic of China (PRC), ending the bloodiest civil war in modern history. It lasted twenty-two years and resulted in more than three million military casualties and at least twelve million civilian casualties. Seeing no possible hope for a Nationalist resurgence, the U.S. cut off aid to Chiang, which did not sit well with American supporters who viewed Chiang as a heroic anti-communist fighter. The President and the State Department were labeled Communist sympathizers and accused of abandoning China to the Communists.[13]

There was an immediate push to reinstate aid to Chiang. On January 2, 1950, Herbert Hoover and Senator Robert Taft demanded that the U.S. Navy defend Formosa from a "Communist invasion." However, the following day the *United Press International* released a State Department directive dated December 23 they had secretly obtained, sent to American diplomats abroad, saying that Formosa's fall to the Red Chinese was inevitable and that the U.S. would not interfere. Left with no choice, on January 5, Truman issued a written statement to the press confirming that "military aid or advice" would not be given to Chiang and the U.S. would not "pursue a course which would lead to involvement in the civil conflict in China." It remained official U.S. policy until the outbreak of the Korean War.[14]

The Truman administration expected the American China Lobby to support Chiang. Taft blamed the State Department, saying they were "guided by a left-wing group who . . . wanted to get rid of Chiang and were willing at least to turn China over to the Communists for that purpose." MacArthur echoed Taft, writing that "the decision to withdraw previously pledged American support was one of the greatest mistakes ever made in our history."[15]

To understand why Chiang garnered such deeply rooted support in the United States, we must return briefly to the beginning of World War II while he was still in power in mainland China. Claire Chennault was a retired U.S. Army Air Corps officer who served as a military aviation advisor to Chiang during the Sino-Japanese War. In 1940, the looming threat of Japanese aerial attacks against mainland China was on the horizon. Chennault received approval from President Roosevelt (sympathetic to the Chinese plight since his family had made their fortune in the Chinese opium trade) to organize a private air squadron to assist the Chinese. The American Volunteer Group (AVG), nicknamed the Flying Tigers, was made up of non-military pilots, a necessity since the U.S. was not at war and could not violate its neutral status. The group saw combat from December 1941 through July 1942 and was highly successful, downing 296 Japanese aircraft in support of China.

William Pawley was also instrumental in the formation of AVG. Pawley was a wealthy American who will be revisited many times through our story due to his close relationship with the Eisenhower administration, his CIA connections, and his involvement with Cuban exiles in the war against Fidel Castro. Pawley established an assembly plant in Burma to service AVG planes. It was later relocated to Loiwing, China, after the Japanese invaded Burma, and then onto India when the Japanese capture Loiwing. Problems arose when Chennault accused Pawley of involvement in black market activities and stealing from AVG, and based on Pawley's character, it was an accusation that most likely had merit. Public pressure forced Pawley to dissociate himself from AVG, but the battle with Chennault continued as Pawley inflated his importance. A 1942 *Time* magazine article referred to him as the "China Swashbuckler" and described his contribution "to help sell the US Government on the idea of the now-legendary A.V.G.," which started when "he began touting the scheme in

1939." In closing, the article quoted Pawley as unabashedly saying, "Unquestionably, I have been one of the prime contributors to China's defense."[16]

After the war and Chiang's departure to Formosa, Pawley maintained an interest in China, pleading with President Truman on several occasions to back the Nationalist government with arms and financial aid. A cadre of State Department foreign officers who wanted to abandon Chiang opposed him because they believed a Red Chinese takeover of Formosa was inevitable. In Pawley's unpublished memoir, he wrote that matters came to a head in December 1949, six months before the Korean War began. He met with Truman at that time and warned the President that, "Unless we go all out, right now, to back up the Nationalist movement in China, in which Chinese will do their own fighting for their freedom, you've lost China." "On top of that," he continued, "you'll have a war on your hands in Burma, Indochina, or Korea within a year . . . most likely Korea, where the Reds are strongest. That will leave you a choice of committing America to a ground war, or you will lose all of Asia."[17]

One can understand Truman's reluctance to support Chiang. He hoped to launch an invasion of China with his 70,000 KMT soldiers stationed on two small islands called Quemoy and Matsu, one hundred miles west of Formosa and just a few miles off the Chinese coast. It was a suicide mission unless he received U.S. support, and he publicly stated that they were abandoning him. In short, Chiang was in desperate trouble, but he still had friends.[18]

In June 1947, while Chiang was still in China, the Joint Chiefs had called for a significant effort to support his Nationalist forces. Mao Zedong and his Communist horde were "tools of Soviet policy," they said. The administration had to apply pressure to Soviet aggression anywhere it occurred if the Truman Doctrine remained relevant. General Albert C. Wedemeyer, who had served as Chiang's Chief of Staff during World War II, was sent to China to evaluate the situation. When he returned, Wedemeyer concurred with the Joint Chiefs that Chiang should be supported, which prompted George Kennan to have the Policy Planning Staff conduct an independent study. They concluded that only massive American aid, more than what the U.S. sent to Western Europe, could save Chiang, which was impossible. However, for political reasons, roughly $570 million of non-military aid was sent to the Nationalists. It was a token gesture, a mere pittance compared to the $17 billion allocated for the Marshall Plan in Europe.[19]

Wedemeyer, testifying before Congress after Chiang fled the mainland, said what was needed were experienced American military advisers who could offer immediate tactical assistance, but Congress did nothing. The U.S. was abandoning Chiang, and a chasm had grown between the State Department and the military, as the latter considered Chiang too important to turn their back on him.

Despite being left for dead by the State Department, Chiang continued to receive support from familiar names. In mid-1947, fighting erupted in Thailand over the opium trade, where Chiang's Nationalist Chinese made desperately needed money serving as the middleman in the production and transportation of narcotics. Communists were involved, so to limit the damage, William Donovan traveled to Bangkok to gather the various fighting factions into a single, united force fighting against the Communists. Chiang benefited greatly from Donovan's intervention, and it demonstrated how well U.S. intelligence worked with Chiang's forces, albeit through Donovan's private intelligence group. U.S. intelligence and the U.S. military supported the Nationalist Chinese leader.[20]

Others felt the same way. "China asked for a sword," declared Senator Styles Bridges, "and we gave her a dull paring knife." Then there was Henry Luce, who became Chiang's most devoted foreign friend. The son of a Presbyterian missionary in Shandong, he was born in China. Luce persistently badgered the State Department and used all his resources to sway public opinion, putting Chiang on the cover of *Time* magazine a half dozen times. He was part of the China Lobby that was pressuring Truman to support the Chinese Nationalists.

But the issuance of the famous White Paper by the State Department on July 29, 1949, removed any doubt about how the administration expected to deal with Chiang. "The ominous result of the civil war in China," the paper warned, "was beyond the control of the government of the United States . . . We will not help the Chinese or ourselves by basing our policy on wishful thinking."[21]

Pawley publicly opposed the White Paper, for he could not understand that if Roosevelt supported the AVG before World War II, Truman refused to help Chiang. MacArthur agreed and fed information to pro-Chiang Republicans in Congress while encouraging Japanese pilots to go to Formosa and support Chennault, who was looking for volunteers to attack mainland China.

Pawley's concern gained some traction. He received permission from the Secretary of State to lead a group of retired military officers, led by Admiral Charles Cooke, to Formosa to advise the Nationalist forces on security affairs. Before he arrived, Bill Donovan again got involved, meeting with Chiang's defense minister and police chief on Pawley's behalf. In December, ex-U.S. diplomat William Bullitt began raising funds for the so-called Pawley-Cooke Advisory Mission, the lion's share of which a group of Texas oilmen, including right-wing fanatic H.L. Hunt, provided. It was clear that the China Lobby, which now included conservative Texas oilmen, intended to support Chiang, even if the U.S. government was willing to abandon him. More importantly, Pawley's connection to Donovan must have meant he was working with WCC as well, which had to include Allen Dulles and James Angleton, via WCC's connection to CIA.

By the spring of 1950, the Truman administration continued to apply pressure. John Foster Dulles stated that with the continued pursuit of the Pacific Rim strategy, third-world countries feared they could be abandoned by the U.S. as well. Only Western Europe could feel secure. On May 11, 1949, Chiang's ambassador in Washington suggested to Acheson that they establish a Pacific Pact, similar to NATO, which had bound the United States and all NATO nations to come to each other's defense as needed. Two days later, South Korea's Syngman Rhee approached the State Department with the same request. On May 18, Acheson stated publicly that the time was not suitable for such an alliance in Asia. Both Chiang and Rhee knew that this spelled disaster for them, and if they were to survive, they would have to do something to force Truman's hand. Fortunately for them, they had supporters who were willing to do just that.[22]

JAPAN

Dealing with the Soviets was a point of contention between General MacArthur, who had become the effective ruler of post-war Japan, and the Truman administration. In October 1945, John McCloy traveled to Japan to speak with him because Washington wanted the general to agree to an Allied Advisory Council, which would include the Soviets, and advise MacArthur on occupation policy in Japan. A similar advisory council was in place in Germany, whose existence could be in jeopardy if MacArthur refused to play ball with the Russians. McCloy would say they argued for days, often engaged in shouting matches, with MacArthur pacing the floor, threatening to resign. Eventually, the general conceded, and an Allied Advisory Council with Russian representation became a reality. But it was a council in name only, exercising virtually no authority over Japanese affairs.[23]

The occupation of Japan was the most significant foreign policy operation ever undertaken by the United States. The War Department, not State, ran it, for this was a military operation. All orders from Washington first passed through the Joint Chiefs to minimize State Department interference, and many a State Department directive never made it to MacArthur. The military had just soundly defeated Germany and Japan. They were not going to be undermined by politicians with diplomatic surprises and compromises that did not serve America's best interests. To the military, they dictated policy in Asia. They were staying faithful to the Constitution and protecting the American people from an ineffective President; at least, that is how they justified their behavior.

More than any other country, the Russians worried the U.S. military because they had moved into Manchuria and North Korea and showed no signs of moving out. In February 1946, Averill Harriman visited Japan and warned MacArthur that the Russians were demanding that their troops be allowed to occupy the northernmost island of Japan, Hokkaido and that the country be divided into separate zones of occupation, as had been done in Germany. MacArthur threatened military retaliation if they did, and the Soviets backed down. Tensions were high.

MacArthur planned to rebuild Japan with a democratic constitution, not as a military garrison governing a conquered people. The Russians had different ideas.

They wanted to treat the emperor as a war criminal, jail anyone suspected of war profiteering, redistribute the wealth, and deny the vote to anyone who was not a Communist. They encouraged mob violence and supported demonstrations instigated by Japanese Communists. In response, MacArthur limited Russian travel outside Tokyo to twenty-five miles, thus keeping the Soviets away from the general population as much as possible.

From 1946 to 1948, inflation in Japan was 1200 percent. Joseph Dodge, MacArthur's financial adviser, developed a plan to impose fiscal austerity, balance the Japanese budget, establish a single exchange rate for the yen, and abolish the black market. The Communists called it the "road to fascism" that created a "semicolonial regime." Unrelenting, MacArthur instituted the so-called Red Purge. It resulted in the removal of twenty thousand alleged Communists from the workforce. MacArthur had developed an intense hatred for the Soviets, and democratic constitution or not, he would suppress them by any means possible. The Communists would not become a force to be reckoned with in Japan.[24]

During a January 6, 1948 speech, Army Secretary Kenneth Royall stated that "the men who were most active in building up and running Japan's war machine" were the ones most qualified to "contribute to the economic recovery of Japan." A fully functional Japan could "serve as a deterrent against any other totalitarian war threat [Soviet Union] which might hereafter arise in the Far East." But Royall was a civilian, not a military man, and the military was unwilling to arm an enemy responsible for the loss of so many American lives. Japan was also not Germany, and they were considered an inferior race. MacArthur made sure the Japanese would not play a role in defending Japan from the Soviets.

In March, George Kennan traveled to Tokyo to meet with MacArthur and discuss the limited containment policy. He would describe the encounter in his memoirs as like being "an envoy charged with opening up communications and establishing diplomatic relations with a hostile and suspicious foreign government." He was not talking about Japan—he was referring to MacArthur. The two men viewed Japan from different perspectives, but they did agree on one thing. The U.S. could not sign a peace treaty with Japan and leave the country defenseless.[25]

In April 1949, a *Fortune* magazine article was very critical of MacArthur's job in Japan. He responded two months later with a six-thousand-word reply, admitting that Japan's economy had become "in effect a large concentration camp" under his supervision. Without a peace treaty, he said, "Japan would remain . . . in the strait jacket of an economic blockade." The problem was the President and Secretary of State wanted to rearm Japan and remove American troops, which MacArthur had little tolerance for, believing that "Japanese rearmament is contrary to many of the fundamental principles which have guided [the American position] ever since the Japanese surrender." "Abandonment of these principles now," he said, "would dangerously weaken our prestige in Japan and place us in a ridiculous light before the Japanese people." What he wanted was for America to maintain its military presence in Japan.

By late 1949, despite opposition from the Joint Chiefs and MacArthur, the continued occupation costs increased the unpopularity of the American presence among the Japanese people. It also created pressure from allies that the U.S. should pull out. A fear that the Russians might propose a separate treaty to the United Nations resulted in Secretary of State Acheson believing that an American treaty with Japan was needed. John Foster Dulles, brought into the administration in May 1950, was given the responsibility to make this happen, with one condition—under no circumstances would a treaty be signed that would eventually allow Russia to gain control of Japan. "Were Japan added to the Communist bloc," said Acheson, "the Soviets would acquire skilled manpower and industrial potential capable of significantly altering the balance of world power."[26]

But even the State Department was conflicted. They believed the risks of negotiating with the Russians regarding Japan outweighed the benefits. "[W]e were in favor of working out a Treaty soon," Acheson told French and British foreign ministers in September 1949. But "our interests were so great in Japan that we would not get ourselves in a position in which we had to approve a treaty we did not like." Several months later, Acheson called "neutrality [ ] an illusion . . . while Western Powers honored their obligation to observe Japanese neutrality, the Soviets would continue to pursue infiltration tactics, permitting them ultimately to turn Japan into an aggressive military threat." And since the new constitution forbade Japanese rearmament, and there were no U.N. forces to protect the country, the only alternative was to keep U.S. forces in Japan after a treaty was agreed upon, which would not receive either Russian or Chinese approval. Therefore, a peace treaty would have to be signed between the U.S. and Japan alone, which would create problems at the United Nations unless something drastic occurred that convinced the world there was no acceptable alternative. Which the Korean War provided.[27]

As previously stated, John Foster Dulles visited MacArthur in Japan in June 1950, shortly before the Korean War began. To the surprise of the State Department, he supported MacArthur one hundred percent. He predicted "positive action" would be initiated by the United States to preserve peace in the Far East, which would also "preserve international peace, security, and justice in the world—and that includes this part of the world as well as the so-called Western world." Meanwhile, General Eichelberger said a peace treaty with Japan "would be disastrous to the United States in the Far East at this time." MacArthur and the military agreed. At the proper time, the treaty would come when the Truman administration had no choice but to agree to maintain a military presence in the Land of the Rising Sun. But how to make that happen was the question.[28]

Around the same time, elections in Japan created an unwelcome state of instability. The pro-American party in Japan, which favored a separate treaty with the

U.S., did not constitute a majority and garnered only thirty-six percent of the vote in the election. The Socialists, who emerged as the second-largest party, opposed a treaty that excluded the Chinese and the Russians and allowed the U.S. to keep its bases in Japan. According to *London Times* Tokyo correspondent Frank Hawley, General MacArthur's Headquarters and Mr. Yoshida (the Liberal Prime Minster) were trying to "convince the world of the pro-American feelings of the present Japanese government, [so that a separate peace treaty could be signed] and quickly pushed through." But a quick peace treaty was not what MacArthur wanted, for it would require U.S. military troops to leave Japan. To counter, MacArthur continued to press for the outlawing of communism altogether, despite the "free" constitution imposed in Japan. Two days after the election, MacArthur ordered the twenty-four members of the Central Committee of the Communist Party purged from public office, which brought a protest from the Russian representative on the Allied Council in Tokyo but to no avail.

Meanwhile, the U.S. and British military seemed to be planning for war, holding top-level conferences just before fighting broke out in Korea. Perhaps this was a coincidence, perhaps not. Korea was at a critical crossroads, and Japan feared the military threat that would arise if either the Chinese or Russians took control of South Korea. The Truman administration was playing with fire in the first six months of 1950. They were willing to abandon Formosa and South Korea to the Communists and sign a peace treaty with Japan, leaving them essentially defenseless. If this happened, it would only be a matter of time before Japan fell as well. From the military's perspective, this could not occur, for if Japan were lost, another world war was inevitable. Regardless of what Washington politicians wanted, the military would not abandon South Korea.

Richard Hughes of the *London Times* was one of the best-informed British correspondents in Tokyo. According to Hughes, MacArthur's position was that "American armed forces must be retained in Japan for the duration of the cold war at no less than their present occupation strength . . . whatever the decision on a theoretical 'separate peace treaty.'" For the U.S. needed Japan if hostilities took place. Existing occupation bases were essential "for American interception of Soviet bombers flying over the roof of the world to attack American cities, and for [an] effective counterattack on Soviet air bases in the Vladivostok area." MacArthur, meanwhile, insisted that "sober military necessity must override political arguments for the withdrawal of American forces." Okinawa was 1,000 miles away. North Honshu was only 500 miles from Vladivostok. The closer to the Soviet Union, the better.[29]

* * *

The time had come to commence the war between North and South Korea. Within two days after fighting began, U.S. protection was given to Chiang on Formosa against a potential invasion by Red China, when the official U.S. position had been to abandon him if that were to occur. In South Korea, U.S. and U.N. support was provided to Rhee, even though recent elections indicated his days as President were coming to an end, and the U.S. was resigned to accept a united Communist Korea. In Japan, the United States government no longer wanted to sign a quick peace treaty. Japanese bomber bases near Vladivostok, which were to be closed as soon as a peace treaty was signed, remained in place. NSC-68, which Truman thought was too costly, was approved. The U.S. military budget ballooned threefold. And finally, the Japanese economy received the shot in the arm it desperately needed via a massive $2.3 billion inflow of U.S. military dollars during the Korean War. "A gift from the gods," said Prime Minister Shigeru Yoshida.[30]

The evidence is overwhelming that the Korean War came at the perfect time for those who did not want to abandon South Korea and Formosa and wanted to maintain a military presence in Japan. MacArthur and the U.S. military purposely started the war to prevent this from happening is indisputable and supported by facts. And as the next chapter will demonstrate, how the U.S. military did this, the lies that they perpetrated, what they did to the Korean people, and how many Americans died in the process of carrying out their operation was a national disgrace.

- 6 -

How Do You Solve a Problem Like Korea?

"... we now have at our command a weapon that can really dish out some severe destruction, and let us go to work on burning five major cities in North Korea to the ground ... they better have their wives and children and bedrolls ... with them because there is not going to be anything left up in North Korea to return to."

—Major General Emmett O'Donnell, Jr.,
Air Force Bomber Commander

The immediate hours after President Kennedy's assassination were the tensest peacetime moments in the United States during the Twentieth Century, followed by the Cuban Missile Crisis. The third was the period right before the Korean War, for so much hung in the balance. The future of South Korea, Formosa, and Japan was at stake, and the Joint Chiefs would not let them fall to the Communists. So, the military fabricated one story after another, beginning by stating that North Korea was the aggressor that started the war, followed by a series of lies by the Joint Chiefs and MacArthur, as they tried to goad Truman into approving the use of nuclear weapons. American bombs obliterated Korean cities because the best interest of the Korean people was never a consideration. In the age of eugenics, they were expendable. It is a troubling story, the Korean War. Like the Warren Commission, it demonstrates how authorities can cover up evidence and history can be distorted to create a narrative that never occurred, so that what happened disappears forever, unless one is willing to dig for the truth. The military drew the blueprint for treason during the Korean War, for it was the first example in post-world War II America that showed the Deep State ran the country. There were many other similar examples to follow, culminating in the assassination of JFK, but it all began with the Korean War.

* * *

The story begins on June 1, 1950, when President Harry Truman told a press conference that the world was closer to peace than in 1945. He was cutting military spending, even though Secretary of State Dean Acheson had urged Congress to do the opposite, which is likely why Truman said what he did. It was a curious time. CIA analysts were reporting increased Soviet risk-taking around the world. The Russians were testing how far they could push the U.S. What worried the CIA most was that Moscow might go too far and cause "an issue out of proportion to its actual merits and thus precipitate war."

Meanwhile, the Pentagon was surprisingly not advocating for the passage of NSC-68 and only requested token additions, such as another division here or there, which made little sense. They were severely short of troops in Europe and Asia, limiting their ability to counter Soviet aggression in either area. Acquiescence was not in the military's DNA, and they were usually willing to fight to get what they wanted. Why the hesitation here? Did they know something was in the works?[1]

In May and June 1950, NSA Sigint (Signals Intelligence) intercepted communications which showed that significant elements of the Chinese Fourth Field Army had moved from Central China to Manchuria. In mid-July, an intercepted Shanghai message identified General Lin Piao as the commander of Chinese forces that would intervene in Korea if the Chinese elected to get involved.[2] And around the same time, there were several engagements between North and South Korean troops along the 38th parallel, with thousands of people dying in "political disturbances, guerilla warfare and border clashes."[3] "There is constant fighting between the South Korean Army and bands that infiltrate the country from the North, wrote "Ambassador-at-large" Philip Jessup, legitimate "battles involving perhaps one or two thousand men." [4]

The Joint Chiefs of Staff and MacArthur were fully aware of the Sigint intelligence reports and fighting along the 38th parallel, but they remained quiet. In fact, in early May, the Joint Chiefs continued to reject offers of additional military aid, and on the eve of the war, MacArthur was silent regarding any potential hostilities. However, eighteen months after the war began, in a December 1951 *Cosmopolitan* article entitled *The Truth About Korea*, MacArthur's intelligence chief General Charles Willoughby told a different story. According to Willoughby, MacArthur advised the Truman administration that their intelligence people "unmistakably traced the North Korean buildup for war," and "the entire South Korean army had been alerted for weeks and was in position along the 38th Parallel." Dean Acheson confirmed the North Korean mobilization. MacArthur sent him a cable on March 10 stating that the North Korean army "will invade South Korea in June 1950." There was "armed-force expansion and major troop movements at critical thirty-eighth parallel areas." However, another cable on March 25 told a different story and reported: "there will be no civil war in Korea this spring or summer." Why the confusion and contradictory messages? Was Washington being given a false sense of security by the military, even though they knew a North Korean invasion of South Korea was imminent? Or were conditions in Korea relatively peaceful, but the military wanted to mislead Washington into believing that the country was on the verge of going to war? It could not be both.

After May 11, the South Korean government also went silent and arranged their army into a defensive position so observers sent to the Parallel by the United Nations could attest to this after hostilities had started. War finally did come on June 25, 1950, and two days later, President Rhee fled Seoul in an apparent panic, his army offering no resistance to halt the invaders. The South Korean military destroyed the Han Bridge the following day, which prevented thousands of citizens from fleeing the capital. On June 28th, North Korean soldiers entered Seoul, virtually unopposed. With South Korea entirely at the mercy of the invading Communist horde, a potential humanitarian crisis loomed, one that the United States could not ignore. Was this all a staged event?[5]

When newspapermen called the Pentagon, "an aide said privately they [had] expected the attack . . . ships were ready to evacuate the families of American officers and others in South Korea as evidence that the invasion was not a surprise." These same newspapermen approached CIA Director Rear Admiral Roscoe H. Hillenkoetter looking for confirmation. Hillenkoetter told the reporters that the CIA had been aware that "conditions existed in Korea that could have meant an invasion this week or next." The *New York Times* reported "a marked buildup by the North Korean People's Army along the 38th Parallel . . . [had] begun] in the early days of June." Intelligence reports confirmed that "light and medium tanks . . . and other heavy equipment were assembled at the front, and troop concentrations became noticeable." In *The Riddle of MacArthur—Japan, Korea, and the Far East*, John Gunther stated that the North Korean attack consisted of 70,000 men and about 70 tanks at four different points. "Ask any military man what all this means," Gunther wrote. "To assemble such a force, arm and equip it, and have it ready to wheel into precalculated action over a wide front . . . must have taken at least a month. Yet South Koreans and Americans in Korea, to say nothing of [MacArthur] in Tokyo, were taken utterly by surprise. It was more disgraceful than Pearl Harbor. Our eyes were shut . . ."[6] Were their eyes really shut, or just waiting for an attack to occur that they could exploit?

Consider that the U.N. observers mentioned above issued their report on June 24 and called specific attention to the South Korean defensive troop placements they had seen along the border. Perhaps by coincidence, perhaps by design, the very next day, hostilities began. Rhee announced it was an unprovoked invasion from the North. On the other hand, North Korea claimed that South Korean forces crossed the Parallel at three different locations and the North Koreans forced them back. Subsequently, North Korean troops went on the offensive. Someone was not telling the truth.

Why did the U.S. Ambassador in Seoul advise that South Korean reports on how the war began could only be "partly confirmed" by Americans serving with South Korean forces? If the North Korean's had instigated hostilities by crossing to the South, shouldn't South Korean troops have quickly confirmed this, without question? Was this diplomatic double-talk to camouflage the possibility that the South Koreans had provoked the North Koreans?

According to John Gunther, he was in Tokyo at the time with "two important members of the occupation" when one took a telephone call. He came back and whispered, "A big story has just broken. The South Koreans have attacked North Korea." It was eight hours after the fighting had begun.[7]

The Yugoslav delegate to the U.N. Security Council insisted "there seemed to be lack of precise information that could enable the Council to pin responsibility." He urged for a cease-fire but would not name an aggressor.

The night the war began, Truman met with the Secretaries of State and Defense and the Joint Chiefs. He then issued a statement the following morning. The U.S. would "vigorously support" the effort of the UN Security Council "to terminate this serious breach of peace," and that Korea could expect "the cooperative action of American personnel in Korea . . ." Truman's statement did not mention U.S. military intervention.

As the *New York Times* reported the next day, the American plan was to "keep South Korea supplied with all the arms that General MacArthur could rush to the beleaguered country . . . but to avoid any semblance of direct military intervention . . ." Senator Eugene D. Millikin, speaking for the Senate Republican Policy Committee, echoed the *New York Times*, saying they were "unanimous that the incident should not be used as a provocation for war." The *New York Times* chief U.N. correspondent did report that the U.S. was "studying the possibility of asking the Security Council to authorize the use of United States troops . . . [but it would not] go this far because of the increasing deterioration of the situation in Southern Korea." In other words, the South Korean army was on the run, the South Korean government had abandoned Seoul, and the government was on the verge of collapse. South Korea would fall by all appearances, which the Truman administration said they were willing to live with, so why needlessly sacrifice American troops into a hopeless situation?

But by the night of the 26th, the day after fighting began, things were different. At noon the next day, Truman issued a statement that reflected a policy change, one that Chiang and MacArthur had been urging for months, which pledged U.S. military intervention against any further expansion in the Pacific arena against Communist aggression. It promised more military aid to Indochina and the Philippines and "ordered the United States air and sea forces to give the Korean Government troops cover and support." And Truman did not stop there. He instructed the Seventh Fleet to "prevent any attack on Formosa," which his administration previously was willing to abandon, and Formosa's future "must await the restoration of security in the Pacific, a peace settlement with Japan, or consideration by the United Nations." But there still was no mention of the U.S. Army sending combat troops to Korea, and it appeared Truman was going to let Communists take control of that country.[8] However, when he finished reading his statement, Truman said: "The Soviet Union very obviously inspired this act. If we let Korea down, the Soviets will keep right on going and swallow up one piece of Asia after another . . . If we were to let Asia go, the Near East would collapse, and [there was] no telling what would happen in Europe. Therefore, I have ordered our forces to support Korea as long as we can—or as long as the Koreans put up a fight and give us something we can support."[9]

What made Truman change from total noninvolvement to taking an aggressive military position in the entire region and that the free world's future became dependent on America saving Korea? According to John Gunther, "After the Communist attack on Korea, the word was that it was solely MacArthur's vigorous intervention in Washington which led Mr. Truman to announce that the United States would give military assistance to the South Korean government." And that "MacArthur got his instructions from the Joint Chiefs . . . in a long conversation held just before the Truman announcement." And it was Formosa, more so than Korea, that was the primary area of concern.[10]

Was it just a coincidence that only days before the Korean attack, MacArthur met in Tokyo with Secretary of War Louis Johnson and Chairman of the Joint Chiefs Omar Bradley to discuss the defense of Asia? Consider that MacArthur handed them a memo dated June 14, which assessed the situation in the Far East, and focused almost exclusively on Formosa. "The strategic interests of the United States will be in serious jeopardy if Formosa is allowed to be dominated by a power hostile to the United States," MacArthur asserted. "Formosa in the hands of the Communists," MacArthur continued, "can be compared to an unsinkable aircraft carrier and submarine tender ideally located to accomplish Soviet offensive strategy and at the same time checkmate counteroffensive operations by United States Forces based on Okinawa and the Philippines." "Historically, Formosa has been used as a springboard for military aggression directed against areas to the south." Losing Formosa, MacArthur said, would inevitably lead to other Asia countries falling to the Communists as well, which is what Truman said he feared might happen. "The future status of Formosa," MacArthur continued, "can well be an important factor in determining the political alignment of those national groups who have or who must soon make a choice between Communism and the West."[11]

MacArthur was expecting a more aggressive intervention in Korea from Truman, and he pushed to ensure that would happen. On June 25, the Chief of Staff of the United States Army, Lawton Collins, reported that MacArthur, without Washington's authorization, had already shipping military equipment to South Korea and made F-51s available for South Korean pilots to fly from Japan back to South Korea. What happened next suggests that MacArthur, most likely with the approval of the Joint Chiefs, was intent on leaving the President no choice but to introduce U.S. military troops into Korea. For he did something unprecedented—he visited Korea, went to the front, and witnessed Korean soldiers streaming away from the fighting. "It is a strange thing to me that all these men have their rifles and ammunition, they all know how to salute, they all seem to be more or less happy, but I haven't seen a wounded man yet."

On his way back to Japan, MacArthur told a reporter, "The moment I reach Tokyo, I shall send President Truman my recommendation for the immediate dispatch of American divisions to Korea," which he did on June 30. "The Korean army and coastal forces are in confusion . . . and lack leadership through their own means," he wrote, and ". . . are incapable of gaining the initiative over such a force as that embodied in the North Korean army . . . It is essential that the army advance be held, or its impetus will threaten the overrunning of all Korea . . . The Korean army is entirely incapable of counteraction, and there is grave danger of a further breakthrough. If the enemy advance continues much further, it will seriously threaten the fall of the Republic." "The only assurance for the holding of the present line, and the ability to regain later the lost ground, is through the introduction of U.S. ground combat forces into the Korean battle area."[12]

In compliance with Truman's directive, Secretary of War Johnson cut military spending to levels that many believed placed the nation in danger just before the Korean War. The future Chairman of the Joint Chiefs, General Lemnitzer, recalled that Johnson was trying to trim another two billion dollars from the thirteen-billion-dollar defense budget and "did some horrible things. He was closing hospitals, closing stations, cutting back the forces, stretching our procurement programs, and so forth. And he got his two billion dollars."[13]

MacArthur's reports from the field, coupled with potential Soviet and Chinese aggression elsewhere, resulted in a dramatic change in President Truman. There was now virtually no limit to what he was willing to spend on defense. On July 19, he asked Congress for an additional $10 billion, followed by another request for $4 billion on August 1, $1.6 billion on August 4, and $16.8 billion more on December 1. The total amount approved for 1951 came to $48.2 billion, a 257 percent increase over the original White House request of $13.5 billion. Projections made at the end of 1950 by the Council of Economic Advisers showed that if the proposed military buildup continued, yearly defense expenditures would be around $70 billion within a year. If the military's objective were to create a situation in Korea that would light a fire under the President, they accomplished what they had set out to do.[14]

However, the State Department still wanted to write off Korea and Formosa and spend the money to concentrate military strength in Europe, regardless of what happened in the Far East. It was why at the end of July, Acheson told the Senate Foreign Relations Committee that they might have to cede additional areas to the Russians if the U.S. did not want to find itself "hopelessly committed all over the world." On August 25, the NSC concurred and went even further. Stating that should hostilities in Korea end quickly, "the increased military stature and preparedness of the U.S. should proceed without regard to [a] possible temporary relaxation of international tension . . ." Europe was still the focus of the non-military segment of the government.[15]

The reference to "possible temporary relaxation of international tension" pertained to continued attempts by the U.N. to put an end to hostilities. On July 27, Jacob Malik, the Russian representative to the U.N., announced that the Soviets would return to the Security Council on August 1. It was a source of optimism, for, before this, Russia said they would not return until Chiang's representative was expelled and replaced by someone from Red China. The Soviet peace gesture was not something the military had anticipated. It was at that moment when peace was a possibility that MacArthur made another trip. This time to Formosa, where he declared that an agreement had been reached "for effective coordination between the American forces under my command and . . . [Chiang's] Chinese government to better to meet any attack." He praised Chiang's "indomitable determination to resist Communist domination." He asserted that this "parallels the common interest and purpose of Americans that all peoples in the Pacific area shall be free—not slaves." It implied an alliance with Chiang against the mainland, which countered the voices at the U.N. calling for peace. Truman sent Averell Harriman to Tokyo to tell MacArthur that U.S. policy on Formosa had not changed. The general had to state on August 10 that his assertion that the U.S. provided political support to Chiang was untrue. Regardless, he had accomplished what he had set out to do, which was to tell Harriman upon his arrival that "The United States ought to take a vigorous position against Communism everywhere in Asia, and Korea ought not to be an isolated case."[16]

* * *

Syngman Rhee had the Hangang Bridge destroyed on June 28 following the evacuation of Seoul the day before. In addition to civilians, the North Korean advance trapped many of his troops, and they could not leave. In only five days, his army had dwindled from 95,000 to 22,000. As North Korean troops entered Seoul, he ordered the massacre of suspected political opponents. South Korean National Assemblymen were left behind, and forty-eight subsequently pledged allegiance to the North. Those in Washington were shocked by the turn of events. Republican Senator H. Alexander Smith had visited Tokyo and Seoul before the war began. He believed that the South was "thoroughly capable of taking care of . . . any possible conflict with the North." And John Gunther was told by "a high American intelligence officer" that "if an outbreak did occur, South Korean forces . . . could wipe out the North Koreans with no difficulty." But they were routed in five days. The whole affair gives credence to the possibility that this was a staged event by MacArthur and Rhee to drag the U.S. into a war with the Communists.[17]

The first combat action for U.S. troops occurred on July 5 at the Battle of Osan. The North Koreans thoroughly defeated the joint U.S./South Korean force, and the rout continued throughout August. With the superior troop numbers and weaponry possessed by North Korea, it was an outcome that was not unexpected, and maybe that was the idea, for the defeats served a purpose. Recall that it was during this time that Truman repeatedly allocated more and more funding for the military, which he undoubtedly did in response to the American failures on the battlefield. And since the Russians had returned to the Security Council, it was advantageous to keep hostilities going in Korea. If nothing else, it delayed a United Nations decision on Formosa and Japan.

Despite the string of defeats experienced by American troops, it appears that MacArthur was trying to goad the Soviets and Chinese into entering the war. On August 17, a flight of American B-29s made a 500-ton bombing raid on Rashin, a North Korean seaport only seventeen miles from the Siberian border and 110 miles from Vladivostok. Shortly after that, a series of attacks took place along the border between Korea and Manchuria. Peking (Beijing today) protested to the U.N. on August 29 that American planes had strafed airfields and railways on the Chinese side of the Yahu River near Antung, which the U.S. denied. When a second border raid occurred, resulting in another Chinese protest, the U.S. had no choice but to concede that the Chinese were right but that it had all been a mistake. Mistake or not, the fact was that MacArthur, and likely the Joint Chiefs, were trying to push the Chinese into entering the war.

On August 26, Truman learned that MacArthur had sent a message to the Veterans of Foreign Wars convention and made matters worse. He attacked Truman's policies on Formosa, referring to "the threadbare argument by those who advocate appeasement and defeatism in the Pacific that if we defend Formosa, we alienate continental Asia." On the contrary, MacArthur argued that if they held Formosa, the U.S. could "dominate with air power every Asiatic port from Vladivostok to Singapore."[18]

In September, the President finally passed NSC-68. It created an almost 2 to 1 advantage in the number of troops the U.S. had over the North, not to mention the arrival of an influx of artillery and tanks, with naval and air support. United Nations troops retook Seoul on September 25, and the North Korean army had all but disintegrated. Yet, despite the victory, there were problems. "The coolness of the welcome received by the liberators," reported a *United Press* dispatch from Seoul, "is understandable in the light of the millions of dollars worth of damage . . . Despite communiqués that Seoul was spared, there is evidence everywhere of the pummeling it took from United States planes and artillery." The *United Press* reported that "an Army officer attributed the city's destruction to 'international politics.'" A lieutenant colonel said, "A triumphal entry into the city was needed as soon as possible, and we gave it to them, but it cost us and the Koreans plenty."

Some believed that a siege around Seoul would have led to the North Koreans surrendering eventually. They failed to understand that the city had to be quickly taken, regardless of the casualties and destruction of property. A prolonged stalemate increased the possibility that a peace treaty would be signed, which the military had to prevent from happening. Soviet diplomats in Moscow said they wanted to see a peaceful settlement with general elections "in both North and South Korea to elect a single government as soon as possible." The original June 25 U.N. resolution called for a cease-fire and withdrawal of North Korean troops above the 38th Parallel. The time was ripe for a potential agreement, which the U.S. military wanted to avoid. The *New York Times reported,* "there is a strong probability of an overall Communist majority if the election [happen] before . . ." the North Koreans withdrew. Furthermore, the South Koreans were doomed if elections occurred "before a U.N. reconstruction program had assuaged the bitterness of North and South Korea against the destruction of their homes during their liberation by U.N. forces. In that case, communism would win by an election what it failed to obtain by an invasion."

Rhee knew he would lose a nationwide election, and "the only terms acceptable [to Rhee] were unconditional northern surrender," something he knew the Chinese and Soviets would not accept. Meanwhile, the South Korean delegation to the U.N. General Assembly called for their jurisdiction to include North Korea. Elections should be held only in the North to decide who would fill the one hundred seats made available for Northern representatives and still left vacant in the Southern legislature. That MacArthur would cross the Parallel and enter the North "to obtain peace for the world" was also expected.

The *New York Times* reported that the United States "does not intend to impose Dr. Syngman Rhee and his government upon the North Koreans." However, regardless of what Washington wanted, in a public ceremony in Seoul, MacArthur installed Rhee. It made a quick treaty between North and South Korea impossible.[19]

Conservative Japanese wanted the U.S. to stay on the offensive, cross "the 38th Parallel, and put a definite end to the Communist state in the North . . ." On September 27, Truman instructed MacArthur that this was acceptable only if "at the time of such operation there was no entry into North Korea by major Soviet or Chinese Communist forces, no announcements of intended entry, nor a threat to counter our operations militarily." Three days later, a defiant Secretary of Defense, George Marshall, told MacArthur he could cross the border and that he could ignore the restrictions imposed by Truman: "We want you to feel unhampered tactically and strategically to proceed north of the 38th parallel."[20] The military was looking to confront China directly, for Chinese troops were on the move.

That Marshall told MacArthur to ignore the President was treasonous and should come as no surprise. Marshall was highly close to Major General George Van Horn Moseley, who, as described in the Introduction, was an anti-Semite Fascist whom anti-FDR plotters planned to install as a dictator in 1940 after they removed Roosevelt from power. "I know you will leave behind a host of younger men who have a loyal devotion to you for what you have stood for," Marshall wrote. "I am one of that company, and it makes me very sad to think that I cannot serve with you and under you again."[21]

* * *

Three weeks earlier, the *New York Times* had reported that "The Chinese Communists are making troop dispositions that will enable them to intervene militarily in Korea if they wish." From Hong Kong on September 8 came news of "the transfer of Chinese Communist troops from South and even West China northward to Manchuria." That month, the NSA identified six field armies in Manchuria near the Korean border.[22]

On September 29, the *Associated Press* reported from Moscow that the Soviet Union "would unquestionably take a grave view of any effort by the United States or Allied forces to push up beyond the 38th Parallel." They also said that Chinese Premier Chou En-lai warned that his country would not "supinely tolerate" an invasion of North Korea. But South Korean troops were already at the Parallel, waiting for the U.N. to advise what they should do. The next day they crossed the parallel without U.N. approval and did so, according to a *New York Times* dispatch from Tokyo, "under orders of the United States Eighth Army." The same report advised "that United States warships, as well as the Air Force, were supporting the South Korean advance north of the Parallel along the east coastal road, where cruisers and destroyers were lying offshore." By October 3, South Korean forces had moved more than fifty miles north of the Parallel, supported by U.S. air and naval power, without U.N. authorization. These were the same South Korean troops that had supposedly run scared from the North Korean army that had invaded the south just a few months ago. On October 7, U.S. troops crossed the Parallel for the first time, the day before the U.N. finally approved the resolution defining acceptable military conduct.

Meanwhile, MacArthur tried again to expand the conflict. Two American fighter planes attacked a Soviet airport forty miles south of Vladivostok, prompting a protest from the Soviet government. Two days later, a concerned Truman flew to meet MacArthur somewhere in the Pacific to instill in him the administration's contention "that Communism, especially in China, cannot be overcome by armed force." His concerns fell on deaf ears.[23]

On October 20, U.S. armed forces captured the North Korean capital of Pyongyang, and around the same time, the First Marine Division moved into the port city of Wonsan. As a *New York Times* report stated, "There are increasing [pieces of] evidence[ ] that the Russians have cut their losses in Korea and are pulling out altogether." On October 24, a Peking radio broadcast said Chou En-lai intended for a delegation to attend Security Council talks on Formosa, which, the *United Press* would report from Tokyo, "was a complete about-face for General Chou."

Still, the *New York Times* report warned there possibly were 250,000 Chinese Communist troops near the border, as well as another 200,000 elsewhere in Manchuria. It was probably why a spokesman for the U.S. First Corps in Korea announced on October 24 that "foreign troops [non-South Korean] would halt forty miles south of the Manchurian border in their pursuit of the shattered North Korean Communist army." Two days later, Truman told a press conference that "only South Korean troops would occupy the north frontier of Korea in the final drive of the war there," only to be defied by MacArthur from Tokyo once again. The *New York Times* reported that "MacArthur's headquarters for the first time formally denied repeated reports that United Nations forces would halt south of the Chinese Communist line . . . A spokesman told correspondents, 'The mission of the United Nations is to clear Korea.'"[24]

Meanwhile, as reported from the battlefield, a large, well-armed enemy force resisted the American advance. The Army called it "a token force." And on October 30, MacArthur's people still insisted that "hardening resistance" and "Soviet-made armor, in somewhat larger numbers than a week ago" did not mean that Communist China had received "any large-scale reinforcements."

MacArthur was purposely deceptive, hoping to draw the Russians or Chinese into a major military confrontation that would leave Washington no choice but to expand the war.

However, on November 1 came "the first official confirmation that a large force of Chinese . . . was fighting against the UN forces in Korea." And on November 2: "The South Koreans feel certain that the whole corps [42nd Corps of the Chinese Communist Eighth Route Army] has been assigned to duty in Northern Korea" by China. Despite this, American forces attacked Changjin's reservoir on November 3, another deliberate attempt to fight with the Chinese. Control of the Changjin's primary source of water was not necessary to complete the victory in Korea.

Despite the increased fighting, MacArthur would still not admit that Chinese intervention in North Korea had occurred, perhaps fearing Washington would instruct him to back off. It was probably why, on October 30, a Tokyo spokesman for MacArthur said the North Korean army had suffered 460,000 casualties in dead, wounded, and captured and had only 37,000 men left. However, by November 4, Tokyo reported that the North Koreans "now had at least elements of twelve divisions and five independent brigades in the northern area." The following day, the U.S. government was ". . . considering telling Communist China that power plants on the North Korean-Manchurian border would be attacked and destroyed if more Red troops were sent against the United Nations forces in Korea." When MacArthur finally admitted the Chinese had joined the fight, he accused them of committing "one of the most offensive acts of international lawlessness . . ." by intervening in Korea from their "privileged sanctuary" across the border, which, he warned, ". . . might not forever command immunity." MacArthur wanted to expand the war into China, and his spokesman now said 300,000 Chinese Communist troops were in Manchuria and another 300,000 were "either in Manchuria or North China." With the Red Chinese involved, calls for Chiang's troops to join the fight with South Korea resounded once again, which the military wanted from the beginning. Both Peking and Washington, fearful that things could quickly escalate into World War III, publicly made statements to defuse the situation before things got out of control.

On November 8, the day after Chinese and North Korean troops withdrew from their defensive line at Anju, in an apparent effort to allow the U.N. to broker a peace, The United Nations invited Red China to discuss a potential treaty at the Security Council. It was not what the U.S. military wanted, which prompted MacArthur's forces to search for the Chinese. The next day, as Chinese troops retreated, Tokyo reported the opposite, that ". . . for the first time . . . strong forces of the Chinese Communist Army, estimated at 60,000 men, had entered the Korean War, with an equal number of reinforcements believed to be on the way." Mao Tse-Tung had "as many as 500,000 men . . . capable of reinforcing the Communist forces in Korea . . . immune from attack on the Manchurian side." In Washington, an Air Force spokesman announced the lifting of "an earlier ban against flights within three miles of Manchuria." "United States pilots in Korea are operating right up to the Chinese border along the Yalu River."

That same day, seventy-nine B-29 bombers and three hundred fighter planes dropped 630 tons of bombs on the North Korean city of Sinuiju and ". . . destroyed ninety percent of the city." The U.S. tried to misrepresent Chinese intentions, force the Chinese military to engage, and destroy the UN peace talks.

A November 10 newspaper headline said there were "60,000 REDS IN WAR." On November 15, papers reported that "about two-thirds of three Chinese Communist armies—estimated at 75,000 men—now had reached Korea from Manchurian bases." By November 18, MacArthur's headquarters in Tokyo estimated 100,000 men in front of U.N. forces with 40,000 guerrillas in the rear. Finally, they lamented "the concentration of perhaps 250,000 Chinese Communist soldiers in Manchuria and what might happen if Mao Tse-Tung decided to throw the forces into Korea."[25]

Peace talks and peace rumors created optimism for some, trepidation for others. The Chinese released one hundred U.S. prisoners with a message that they did not want war with America. To underscore the point, they offered to release one thousand more. The United States ignored the offer.

On November 24, U.S. and South Korean forces advanced in northwest Korea, while the US X Corps attacked along the Korean east coast, but opposition forces were waiting in ambush at both locations. By November 28, the U.N. line had "sagged back" due to heavy attacks, and in the east, trapped Marines were dramatically evacuated by sea from Hungnam under naval and air power cover. In the west, where the principal action took place, the Eighth Army Corps was pushed back from the Manchurian border and retreated to Seoul but had to evacuate from there as well.

MacArthur now seemed in a great hurry to withdraw, despite that Communist forces seemed in no hurry to attack. It appeared to be a rout, and Truman, at last, threatened to use the atomic bomb against China, which made a peace agreement virtually impossible. Meanwhile, in Europe, German rearmament, which had faced strong resistance from NATO countries, particularly in France, was finally agreed to among the western countries. Rearming Germany was what the radical right had wanted ever since the European war ended, and it took the Korean conflict to make it happen. One could argue that was all part of the plan.

By December 21, the *New York Times* reported that the only "contact" with the enemy was an encounter between a U.S. patrol and "a small group of North Koreans." "As for the last three weeks, there again was no contact with the Chinese Communists . . . in central Korea with a wide no man's land between them and the United Nations forces." Three weeks took one back to December 1, only seven days after the American and South Korean offensive had begun. Where were the Chinese? And why was MacArthur in such a rush to retreat if he could not locate them?

The *London Sunday Observer* reported on December 10 that the Eighth Army, after retreating about a hundred miles in a week, was given "a good chance to re-form and reorganize" by the "leisurely pace of the Chinese advance." That same day the *London Sunday Times* Tokyo correspondent cabled that Chinese forces were "apparently in no hurry to resume battle." Press reports started to contain a degree of cynicism. On December 10: "The regiments concerned in the rearguard action have yet to fire a shot in anger. None of them has yet seen a Chinese Communist." Eight days later, the report was the same. Where did the Chinese go? U.N. forces, wrote Hanson Baldwin of the *New York Times* on December 24, had violated "one of the first rules of war—never to lose contact with the enemy." He said that "we did so for days on end, and high commanders had to insist last week upon large-scale aggressive patrolling along the Eighth Army front to try to determine where the enemy was and how strong he was."[26]

The Chinese seemed to have disappeared, but MacArthur had to look like he was running from someone, so he resurrected the North Korean army, even though on November 6, he had claimed to have virtually destroyed them. On December 19, MacArthur's people reported that the North Korean military now had six divisions more than what they had at the peak of their power, an incredible turnaround if it were true. On top of that, China was training more North Koreans in Manchuria, "and . . . another 50,000 conscripts and recruits are probably available, even though they are not actually in North Korea at the moment." And on December 24, Tokyo said: "that the Chinese assault would come soon . . ."

Christmas morning headlines continued the deception: "Chinese Sweep South Over 38th Parallel—First Wave Heads For Seoul; 100,000 Troops Massed In Support. Government Flees From Southern Capital," reported the *London Daily Mail* from Tokyo, but nothing happened. On the following day, the *Daily Mail* correspondent from Tokyo wrote, "The big Communist push into South Korea—regarded as a certainty for Christmas Day—has failed to materialize." And "no new reports of Communist drives south of the Parallel, and statements yesterday that the Reds had crossed the parallel are now denied officially."[27]

In Seoul, with the U.S. army in full retreat and a massive Chinese army allegedly heading towards the city, Rhee must have known something was amiss, for the *United Press* quoted him as saying he "has no intention of leaving its capital." He told an interviewer he was calling a mass meeting to tell the people "it would be unwise to flee Seoul this time."

On December 28, MacArthur's intelligence service reported that enemy forces numbered an amazing 1,350,406 men, 906,000 still in China and on their way to Korea. According to a spokesman, the figures were "partly based on the interrogation of several hundred prisoners." Now, how would a prisoner of war know the number of Chinese troops who were still in China or, for that matter, the total number of troops in Korea? MacArthur was inflating the size of the enemy, but the Truman administration, undoubtedly by now aware of MacArthur's deceptions, was not fooled. As stated by the *New York Times* reporter in Tokyo, ". . . reports from Washington [state] that no reliable intelligence assessment thus far had been received . . . to substantiate General MacArthur's estimate of the overwhelming Communist strength arrayed against his forces in Korea."

On December 29, a MacArthur spokesman reported that the Communists would attack the U.S. Eighth Army in Korea by January 1, based upon "time-distance factors and last-known Chinese positions." Yet, a lengthy December 28 report from headquarters had contradicted this, stating that the "last positive . . . identification as of December 12 placed the Chinese Communist forces generally . . . in the vicinity of Pyongyang," which U.N. forces had abandoned on December 4. We can assume it was a reconnaissance plane that last spotted Communists forces there on December 12, seventy miles north of the Parallel. Yet, on December 29, without seeing the enemy for seventeen days, headquarters knew they would attack in three days in South Korea. The whole thing was an embarrassingly transparent fabrication.

U.S. forces could not locate the massive Communist offensive anywhere. As a result, they changed the expected time when the offensive would occur until after New Year's Day. A spokesman for the South Korean government said they would not leave the capital because they thought "the defense line north of the city would be held" by U.S. forces. Yet the American army was still planning to evacuate, per a December 30 dispatch that Seoul would probably be abandoned "within a short time after the enemy's attack." But there would not be an attack, for neither China nor Russia wanted to fight the U.S. and start World War III. If they did, they could have driven U.N. forces from Korea at any time.[28]

So, what was the rationale behind this blatant deception? What was coming out of Tokyo at the time provides the answer. As MacArthur wrote in December 1950, the Truman administration "just will not recognize that it is Asia [where] the test of Communist power [will happen,] and that if all Asia falls Europe would not have a chance—either with or without American assistance." He wanted the U.S. to remove restrictions on military action in the Far East, utilize Chiang's troops in Korea and elsewhere, bomb industrial targets inside China, and force a withdrawal from Korea in preparation for a massive offensive, which didn't necessarily have to occur in Korea. To reject this scenario would involve the U.S. in "an indecisive campaign with the cost of holding a position in Korea becoming . . . infinitely greater than were we to fight back along conventional lines."[29]

Consider that potential Republican presidential candidate Harold Stassen told the press in Tokyo as early as December 6 that after meeting with MacArthur, he realized that limitations placed on the general made it "impossible" to thwart the massive Chinese attack forthcoming. Stassen suggested an unconditional cease-fire to take effect in forty-eight hours. If the Chinese agreed, there would be mediation, but based on what had transpired thus far, it is safe to assume that MacArthur would do something to ensure the Chinese would reject the offer. And if the Chinese did not agree, Stassen said, MacArthur should be permitted to retaliate "by striking in any manner any objects of military significance either in Korea or China." When asked whether this included the atom bomb, he replied, "I say any manner and any objects of military significance; that includes everything." Stassen also said the timing of the bombing should occur after MacArthur was allowed ". . . to withdraw land forces from Korea in as orderly a manner as possible . . . ," which explains the hasty retreat down the peninsula.[30]

Atomic warfare was what the military wanted, and MacArthur lamented that "This small [UN] command actually under present conditions is facing the entire Chinese nation in an undeclared war." He cautioned that his army was facing destruction "unless some positive and immediate action [atomic bombs]" were to occur. Without it, "hope for success cannot be justified, and steady attrition leading to final destruction can reasonably be contemplated."

Once again, MacArthur wanted to escalate the war by instituting the following measures:

1. Blockade the coast of China.

2. Destroy China's industrial capacity to wage war through naval gunfire and air bombardment.

3. Secure reinforcements from the Nationalist garrison on Formosa to strengthen our position in Korea if we decide to continue the fight for that peninsula.

4. Release existing restrictions upon the Formosan garrison for diversionary action (possibly leading to counter-invasion) against vulnerable areas of the Chinese Mainland.

"I believe," he said, that by implementing these measures, "we could severely cripple and largely neutralize China's capability to wage aggressive war and thus save Asia from the engulfment otherwise facing it." "Evacuation of our forces from Korea . . . would at once release the bulk of the Chinese forces now absorbed by that campaign for action elsewhere."[31]

Washington responded immediately that the U.N. would evacuate its military forces from Korea unless Chinese forces compelled them to do so, and the U.S. denied MacArthur permission to bomb China. Truman also said an escalation of the war was not going to happen. "There is little possibility of policy change or other external eventuality justifying strengthening of our effort in Korea," Truman said. And attacks "in Communist China probably can be authorized only if the Chinese Communists attack the United States forces outside of Korea."

Left with no alternative, on January 1, Tokyo announced that the Chinese offensive had finally begun. On January 4, U.S. troops abandoned Seoul. As they retreated, MacArthur's troops burned and destroyed Seoul following "the United Nations Command's 'scorched earth' policy," which "has been to leave no facility standing which the enemy might use." The next day they pulled out of Inchon, the key South Korean seaport adjoining the capital. Based on reports from Tokyo, the situation looked grim. January 1: "The Communists, who have an estimated 1,250,000 men at their disposal, were rushing division after division to the break-through points." January 2: "Unofficial reports said three Chinese corps, plus nine reconstituted North Korean divisions, were advancing abreast in a total force estimated at more than 100,000 men." January 3: "Red hordes, supported by tanks, swarmed southward under a deadly hail of rockets and machine-gun bullets fired by low-flying United Nations planes." January 4: "The Red attack has been a series of hammer blows that have overwhelmed the U.N. troops by sheer weight of numbers." "The pathos of this retreat," said General Ridgway, "ought to wake up the people at home like nothing else."[32]

Washington's radical right responded with a call to bomb China and open a second front with Chiang's troops as quickly as possible. The ominous reports created an atmosphere of panicked desperation. But once again, news of the pending disaster had been exaggerated. On January 9, villages on both sides of the Parallel "continue to be raided by armed bands in search of manpower." Why look to empress local villagers if the Chinese and North Koreans had such a massive force. If U.S. Military Headquarters could observe this around the Parallel, they would have been aware that no huge opposing military party was near Seoul. January 13: "From end to end on the Eighth Army front . . . the enemy was either out of contact or contained. At certain points, Eighth Army troops were ranging farther north than at any time since . . ." the evacuation of Seoul.

The truth was evident to anyone willing to take the time to investigate. The *London Daily Mirror* spoke of "FAIRY TALES FROM KOREA." The *Sunday Pictorial* asked in large red type, "IS THIS A PRIVATE WAR?" On January 9, Tokyo imposed censorship restrictions on the press, to which the *London Daily Express* responded: "There has been no sign of any Chinese Communist 'hordes' in the front-line fighting." The *Washington Post* reported that "something fishy is going on."[33]

President Truman told MacArthur to stay in Korea and fight and that the general retreat from an army that did not exist, which the nuclear bombing of the Chinese would have followed, was not going to happen. At the same time, Major General Emmett O'Donnell, commander of the Far East Air Force's Bomber Command, was relieved of his post. O'Donnell responded by saying, "We have never been permitted to bomb what are the real strategic targets, the enemy's real source of supply." Three days later, back in California, he said the strategic bombing had been "designed to deliver the atomic offensive to the heart of the enemy," which should have occurred.[34]

MacArthur could not fool Washington any longer. He stopped withdrawing his troops and began searching for the enemy so he could resume fighting to forestall the peace talks he desperately wanted to prevent from occurring. The about-face started in January 1951. It continued through the second crossing of the Parallel, which occurred in early April of that year. It was to keep the war going despite an apparent desire by the opposition to end hostilities.

On January 11, the U.N.'s cease-fire negotiating committee declared: "When cease-fire occurs . . . [we should] pursue consideration of further steps to be taken for the restoration of peace." It was a potential problem for those not prepared for peace. The U.S. military did not want the U.N. to finalize peace negotiations regarding Japan, Formosa, and Korea until hostilities in Korea favored them. It was why MacArthur now began to search for a Chinese army that appeared more than happy to remain hidden. And the embellishment of events about the war continued. In February, based on information received from Tokyo, the *New York Times* reported that "UN patrols have been probing for the main body of the Chinese army." Last week they "finally found it stretching from just south of Seoul on the west, along the southern bank of the Han River, up to the central mountain spine." However, six days later, U.S. troops entered an industrial suburb of Seoul unopposed by Chinese soldiers who were supposed to be there. As the *New York Times* described, the Americans walked "through silent empty streets past bomb-wrecked factories and shrapnel-pocked houses." U.S. troops entered Seoul with "no enemy contact." Yet, reports from Army Headquarters stated U.N. forces were inflicting heavy casualties. "Enemy troops in almost full division strength [6,000 men] fell before the U.N. onslaught each day this week," said a report from Eighth Army Headquarters on February 10, which also claimed to have killed or wounded 69,500 of the enemy from January 25 to February 9. Tokyo said they had killed or captured 134,616 Chinese since mid-October, about 36,000 a month, which the *New York Times* found questionable.[35]

The truth is, it appeared the Chinese had left South Korea entirely, which prompted those who wanted an expeditious peace to pursue that avenue. To prevent this from happening, MacArthur once again considered crossing the Parallel to keep the war going. From Washington, a *Reuters* dispatch reported that he had asked again to bomb Manchurian bases and to use Chiang Kai-shek's troops. At the same time, South Korean Marines, protected by Allied naval units, established a beachhead at Wonsan ninety miles north of the Parallel. Rear Admiral Allen E. Smith told a press conference that a U.N. maritime task force had been bombarding Wonsan for forty-one "straight days and nights . . . the longest sustained naval or air bombardment of a city in history . . ." It was so severe that "you cannot walk in the streets. You cannot sleep anywhere in the twenty-four hours unless it is the sleep of death."

The military was still trying to provoke the Chinese into retaliating to keep the war going, and excessive force was necessary to accomplish this. Simultaneously, the sixteen nations fighting under MacArthur drafted a statement calling for a cease-fire that "would open the door to negotiations for a general settlement of Far Eastern problems." It insinuated that a final armistice also had to include issues related to Formosa and Japan. The U.S. military did not want this, which was why MacArthur publicly announced on March 24 that he wanted to meet the enemy commander to discuss a truce. He did so without authorization from Washington. An agreement was possible, he said, "if the issues are resolved on their own merits without being burdened by extraneous issues . . . such as Formosa and China's seat in the United Nations." "The enemy . . . must by now be painfully aware," he said, "that a decision of the United Nations to depart from its tolerant effort to contain the war to the area of Korea through expansion of our military operations to his coastal areas and interior bases would doom Red China to the risk of imminent military collapse." He was telling the Chinese, accept a peace that pertained to Korea only, with terms favorable to the United States, or risk the U.S. bombing China into oblivion. By April 7, nine separate divisions, including six American divisions, had crossed the Parallel.

Joseph W. Martin, Jr., the Republican leader of the House of Representatives, wrote MacArthur that he should use Chiang's forces on Formosa to open a second front. MacArthur replied that he agreed. He added, "It seems strangely difficult for some to realize that here in Asia is where . . . we fight Europe's battle with arms while the diplomats there still fight with words . . . if we lose the war to Communism in Asia, the fall of Europe is inevitable." It was a challenge to the President's policies and the Constitutional principle of civilian authority in times of war. Five days later, Martin would read the general's letter to the House and April 11, 1951. Truman replaced MacArthur, and General Mathew Ridgeway was now in charge.

Ridgeway's ascendency did not change things, for he was a MacArthur disciple. In response to a cease-fire offer from the Soviets, on June 26, the *United Press* reported from Tokyo that the "State Department suspects Russia's cease-fire mi just an attempt to dupe the Allies . . ." And the *Associated Press* said that a State Department memorandum, made available to the press in Tokyo, "virtually branded" the Russian offer "a cover . . . to place the enemy in a better position militarily." Why did the military in Japan think it was their responsibility to provide the press with State Department memos if, in fact, they indeed came from the State Department? The only explanation is that the military made another attempt to delay peace negotiations with an enemy they believed would not abide by any agreement. Others concurred.

Thomas Dewey opined, "Every time the Soviets make a peace move, I get scared . . . Every time the Soviet's Stalin smiles, beware." Senator Taft agreed, saying we are not prepared to recognize the "Chinese aggressors." George Marshall said, "I'm worried . . . whether we'll relax after the Korean action," and the military, as a group, agreed.[36]

Talk of bombing China still resonated. "The Chinese," the *Washington Post* reported, "should also understand that if they put forth no genuine effort to bring about a cessation of hostilities . . . the resumption of the war would not be on the limited scale that has characterized it to date . . ." Senators Smith and Taft declared on August 18 that if the cease-fire talks broke down, the U.S. would widen the war and bomb Manchurian bases. If the Chinese and Russians thought they could buy time to strengthen their military, atomic weapons would be the American response.

On August 19, with peace finally a real possibility, U.N. troops "behind one of the most devastating artillery bombardments of the Korean War" launched "the heaviest attack since the . . . armistice talks began." The next day the *United Press* reported that "a third of the Korean battlefront was aflame."[37] In response, the Communists broke off peace talks on August 23. The U.S. military's intent to disrupt the peace talks had succeeded.

Meanwhile, the CIA asked William Pawley to visit the Far East in August 1951, another example of his close relationship with U.S. intelligence. He visited Hong Kong, Formosa, Japan, Burma, and Siam to appraise CIA activities and discuss the possibility of furnishing Formosa with military supplies from Japan and Korea. Pawley still supported Chiang, not understanding why ". . . it is necessary to sacrifice large numbers of American and other allied troops . . . when there are millions of Asiatics who are willing and anxious to fight Communism in defense of their own freedom." The military and CIA were on the same page, equally dissatisfied with Washington's bumbling effort. It would not be the last time they would join forces against politicians who, in their collective mind, placed the country's welfare at risk.[38]

Just days after truce talks came to an end, the *Wall Street Journal's* Washington bureau reported, "Military men and diplomats are discussing General Douglas MacArthur's old proposals for winning the Korean war in a hurry . . . ," which meant using atomic weapons. The military's position was clear and unified. Earlier, on June 25, 1951, Major General O'Donnell, who, as previously described, had been relieved of duty, testified before a Senate inquiry into MacArthur's management of the war and said something similar. According to O'Donnell, "It was [their] intention and hope . . . that by putting a severe blow on the North Koreans, with advanced warning, perhaps, telling them that they had gone too far in what we all recognized as being a case of aggression . . . and we now have at our command a weapon that can really dish out some severe destruction, and let us go to work on burning five major cities in North Korea to the ground, and to destroy completely every one of about 18 major strategic targets."

The Senate inquiry questioned O'Donnell about giving an advanced warning. Never was it more on display that the Koreans were considered subhuman and worth sacrificing for the greater good. "I thought that would take care of the humane aspect of the problem, he answered. "They should stop the aggression . . . or they better have their wives and children and bedrolls to go down with them because there is not going to be anything left up in North Korea to return to."[39]

* * *

The United States and Japan signed a peace treaty in San Francisco on September 8, 1951. It was only made possible by the Korean War. It included that the United States had the right to maintain a military presence in Japan to deter potential armed attacks. It prohibited Japan from providing any other foreign power bases or military-related rights without the consent of the United States. It gave Japan the right to rearm to defend itself. It was what the military wanted.

The United States did not consult China regarding the treaty with Japan, which drew objections. The Soviet Union, India, and Asian and Pacific countries that were plundered by the Japanese during World War II opposed it because their claims for war reparations would go unheeded.

As for Korea, armistice negotiations continued for two years until North and South Korea signed an agreement on July 27, 1953, which ended the fighting, but solved nothing. It was the treaty with Japan that made this armistice possible. The country remained divided, and a Demilitarized Zone separating the two countries was established along the 38th Parallel, which remains in place to this day.

Nothing officially was done regarding Formosa, but the U.S. Pacific Rim policy abandoning the island would never reappear. The United States now vowed to protect Formosa from any Red Chinese aggression. During the Eisenhower administration, they would have to honor that commitment.

Regarding the assassination of JFK, the Korean War has an unquestionable relevance. The military and CIA believed the policies of the Truman administration jeopardized American security. If left unchecked, it would have resulted in South Korea, Formosa, and Japan becoming part of the Communist sphere. Inevitably, the potential existed that all Southeast Asia could have become Communist. The United States goaded North Korea into invading South Korea to prevent this from happening. The U.S. military misrepresented the entire war effort to force the administration to expand into China and destroy that country with atomic weapons. Even when peace was within reach, lies kept the war going at the expense of countless American lives. Their deaths were a necessary evil as far as the military was concerned. In the fight against communism, they had a duty to protect the United States from politicians who, in their opinion, placed the nation in danger.

With Truman, it was relatively simple, for MacArthur's deceptions easily manipulated him. It was nothing short of treason by MacArthur, his subordinate generals, and the Joint Chiefs. CIA, to a certain extent, was also guilty. It would establish a precedent for how the military and the CIA should handle a President they believed was ill-equipped to lead. Truman's successor, Dwight Eisenhower, was also accused of appeasing Communists and violating the sacrosanct policy of containment. He would fall victim to similar deceptions by the military and the CIA.

Under Eisenhower, the CIA conducted foreign policy independent of the government and was answerable to no one. The Agency sabotaged Ike's plan to sign a nuclear test ban treaty with the Soviets and thwarted a potential overthrow of Castro in Cuba because they believed the government in exile to replace him leaned too far to the left. And the military repeatedly hounded him to use nuclear weapons against China and Russia.

But no one felt the wrath of the military and CIA, as would JFK, for he pursued an agenda that was against everything they stood for and attempted to take the country down multiple paths of Communist appeasement. As previously mentioned, the test-ban treaty with the Soviets, the sale of wheat to the Russians, negotiations with Castro to ease tensions, the pull out of Vietnam, his failure to attack Cuba during the Cuban Missile Crisis, and his threat to destroy CIA all threatened Communist containment. JFK was also looking to create a new world order, but not based on white, racist, Anglo-Saxon Christian, anti-Communist fascism. Appeasement was what he proposed during his second term, which left assassination as the only alternative for those who believed the failure to contain the spread of communism threatened America's very existence. For whether it was the needless death of American servicemen in Korea, the destruction of every city in that country by a scorched-earth policy, or the forcible removal of an American president from office, the rationale was always the same. In the war against communism, anything was acceptable, even treason, to maintain the American way of life.

The Korea War was the first of many examples of outright treason by the military and CIA. But the war caused one other thing, which went a long way in sealing Kennedy's fate. It ensured peacetime military spending would increase year after year, resulting in the Military-Industrial Complex Eisenhower warned the nation about during his farewell address. Before long, big business, the military, and the CIA would become woven together into a singular fabric that thought they were entitled to dictate foreign policy. Coupled with the new world order sought by the Deep State proponents, it created a powerful block that considered themselves better suited than any President who resisted what they thought was best for the country. And any President who tried to stop it had to suffer the consequences.

In 1932, World War I veterans marched on Washington D.C. and created a "bonus army" camp to protest the government not providing them money they were entitled to receive.

In 1933, Marine Major General Smedley Butler was approached by a right-wing group of wealthy industrialists to organize a military march on Washington and forcibly remove President Franklin Roosevelt from office.

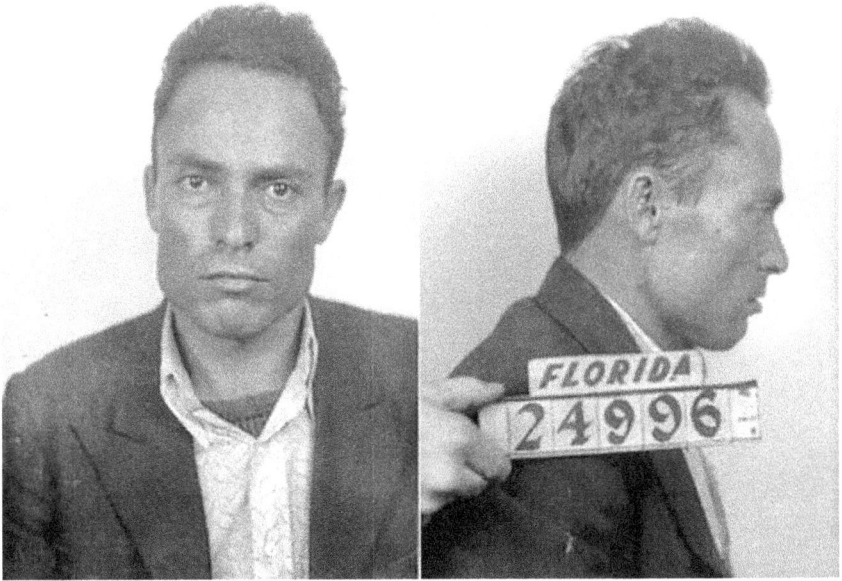

Giuseppe Zangara attempted to assassinate President-elect Franklin Roosevelt on February 15, 1933. In a little over a month, he would be tried, convicted, and executed for the crime.

Cornelius Vanderbilt, IV claimed there was a plot by a wealthy right-wing cabal to assassinate FDR.

In 1938, U.S. ambassador to Germany, William Dodd, wrote that a group of wealthy elites opposed FDR and wanted to "bring fascism to America."

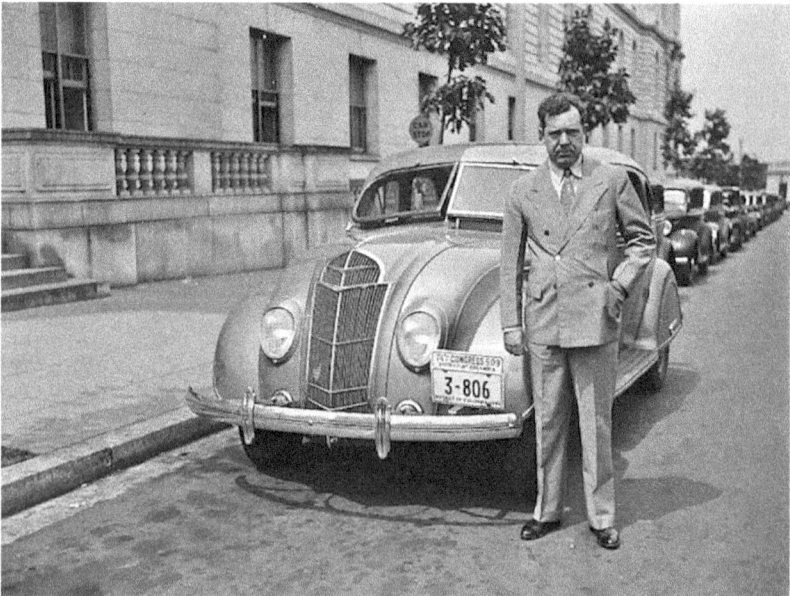

U.S. Senator Huey Long intended to run for President in 1936 but was assassinated on September 10, 1935, by Dr. Carl Weiss. Weiss may have been part of the Square Dealers, a radical right-wing group that opposed New Deal social programs and thought FDR was a Communist.

Charles Lindbergh, shown receiving a medal in Germany from Nazi Hermann Goering in 1936. Lindbergh was a proponent of eugenics and America First. Like so many of his class, he thought the U.S. should stay out of World War II and support Nazi Germany.

Henry Luce, the radical right-wing publisher of Life magazine, hated FDR's New Deal with a passion and wanted him removed from office. After the JFK assassination, Luce would purchase the Zapruder film and locked it away so no one could see it.

A 1920s typical eugenics booth. After World War I, this pseudoscience gained popularity and looked to advance the Nordic, Anglo-Saxon northern European bloodline in America long before the Nazis promoted the same thing. Congress would change immigration laws to ensure only "acceptable" people were allowed to enter the U.S.

The English Mitford Sisters, seen here in 1935. Unity (far left) and Diana (center) were ardent Nazis who were close to Hitler. Like many right-wing aristocrats in pre-war Europe and the U.S., they blamed the Jews for the rise of communism and did not object to the Nazi attempt to exterminate them.

Pope Pius XI blamed Jews for the Bolshevik takeover of Russia and supported Mussolini and fascism to ensure the same did not happen in Italy.

Pope Pius XII worked to suppress the rise of communism in Italy. His secret network of spies during World War II tried to assassinate Hitler. After the war, he joined with U.S. intelligence to fight communism throughout western Europe and used the Vatican Bank to launder drug money as part of the stay-behind army operation.

Along with his brother John Foster, the future Secretary of
State under Eisenhower, Allen Dulles had strong business
ties to Nazi Germany. They considered the Soviet Union the
greatest threat to the Western World. Allen, who would become
the legendary head of the CIA during the Cold War, was an
intelligence agent stationed in Switzerland and tried to broker
peace with the Nazis to curtail the advance of the Red Army.

Frank Wisner brought an anything-goes mentality to the CIA and engaged in risky covert intelligence
operations against Communists. Much of what he authorized the CIA to do was kept hidden from Presidents
Truman and Eisenhower.

"Wild Bill" Donovan was the head of the OSS during World War II and advocated for a central intelligence group. He started a private intelligence agency when the war ended, and along with Allen Dulles, created the anti-Communist stay-behind armies in Europe.

While in prison, Mafia boss Lucky Luciano ordered his minions to help the U.S. fight the Nazis in Italy. After the war, he funded the stay-behind armies fighting communism in Europe organized by James Donovan and Allen Dullen with narcotics sold in African American neighborhoods in the U.S.

Meyer Lansky assisted Lucky Luciano in the stay-behind army drug operation. He would later be instrumental in bringing the Mafia to Cuba.

Lyndon Johnson typified crooked Texas politicians during the late 1940s and throughout the 1950s. He won rigged elections, conducted shady business deals with fellow Texans, and had strong ties to the Mafia in Texas, to whom he was beholden.

The New Orleans Mafia boss Carlos Marcello, shown testifying before the McLellan Committee and Robert Kennedy in 1959. He ran New Orleans, was connected to Jack Ruby, and reportedly "owned" Lyndon Johnson.

Tampa Mafia boss Santo Trafficante was employed by the CIA to assassinate Castro. The evidence shows he was working undercover for Castro at the time, keeping the Cuban leader informed of what the CIA was doing. A year before the assassination, he would threaten the life of JFK.

Jack Ruby, in the 1950s, was part of the Marcello crime family. He associated with gunrunners to Cuba, drug traffickers, and wealthy Dallas elites, who knew him well. He was also an informant for the FBI when he traveled to Cuba in 1959 to help get Santo Trafficante out of prison

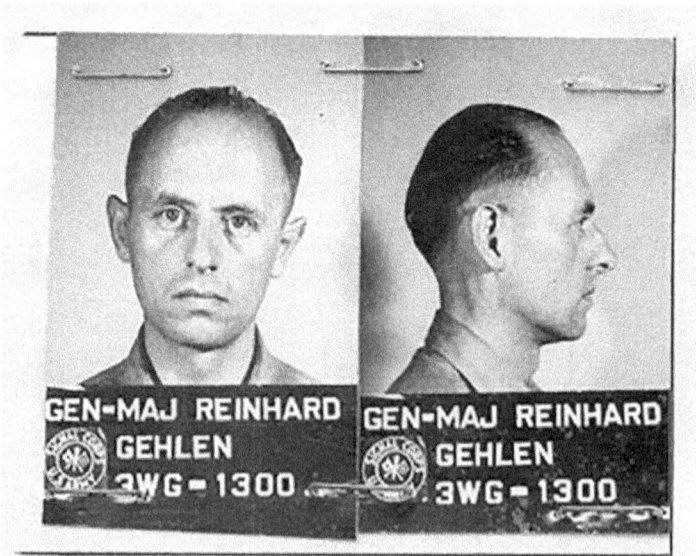

The Nazi head of military intelligence on the Eastern Front, Reinhard Gehlen, was responsible for countless innocent deaths. After the war, he worked with U.S. intelligence to create the stay-behind armies in Eastern Europe and brought ex-Nazi killers into the operation

Shown standing wearing a suit, Werner von Braun was one of many Nazi scientists, including war criminals, brought to the United States as part of Operation Paperclip

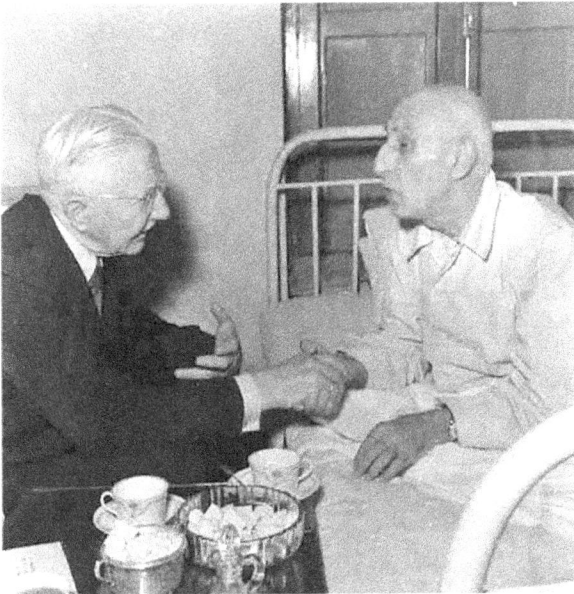

Hitler's former finance minister, Hjalmar Schacht, in the 1950s worked with Otto Skorzeny and the ex-Nazis operating out of Madrid. This group was close to the World Commerce Corporation (WCC) and the stay-behind armies fighting communism.

Ex-Nazi Otto Skorzeny worked with Victor Oswald, the World Commerce Corporation, and the ex-Nazis operating out of Madrid. The group also associated with Thomas Eli Davis, the American mercenary who put together a paramilitary force to invade Haiti when the JFK assassination took place. Skorzeny's work with the CIA included assassinations.

George Kennan's policy of containment defined U.S. foreign policy throughout the Cold War. When his Pacific Rim Strategy was willing to sacrifice Japan, South Korea, and Formosa to Communist China and Russia, it turned the right-wing and the Joint Chiefs against the Truman administration.

Harry Dexter Whiter (shown on the left) was a high-level U.S. Treasury Department official accused of passing information to the Soviet Union. White, along with several other suspected Communists in the Truman administration, died mysteriously in the late 1940s. The CIA may have been responsible.

James Forrestal was the first United States Secretary of Defense. On May 22, 1949, he fell from the sixteenth floor of the National Naval Medical Center in Bethesda, Maryland, under suspicious circumstances. His death was ruled a suicide by the coroner, but evidence suggests he was pushed to his death.

John McCloy was probably the least know important person of the twentieth century. An American diplomat, Presidential advisor, and Warren Commission member, he was also High Commissioner in Germany after World War II. He secretly pardoned many Nazi war criminals who then worked for the U.S. during the Cold War.

General Douglas MacArthur believed his allegiance was to the Constitution and the American people, not Presidents. His conduct was treasonous.

As shown here with MacArthur, South Korean President Syngman Rhee was a willing participant in the U.S. Army's successful attempt to lure North Korea into attacking the South, starting the Korean War.

Chiang Kai-shek, the leader of China, was forced to seek refuge in Formosa when the Communists took over the mainland. He was a darling of the radical right in the U.S., but President Truman was willing to abandon him to the Communists until General MacArthur took drastic action.

General Omar Bradley (right) was the first Chairman of the Joint Chiefs of Staff. He supported MacArthur's desire to fight the Red Chinese in Asia and publicly criticized Truman for being too passive. His public criticisms of the President, wrote Hansen Baldwin of the New York Times, "helped put General Bradley and the Joint Chiefs of Staff into the political hustings where they have no business to be."

Pricilla Johnson, shown here with Marina Oswald after JFK's assassination. A one-time supporter of Soviet communism, in the 1950s, she was a CIA asset involved in Oswald's defection to the Soviet Union. After the assassination, she "babysat" Marina to ensure her story remained untold.

Rebels barricades in Algiers in 1960 during the Algerian war for independence from France. When France agreed to grant Algeria independence, it spawned a military uprising to take over the French government.

French General Raoul Salan was the founder of the OAS, the military group that rebelled against France. They attempted to assassinate French President Charles de Gaulle on several occasions after France granted Algeria its independence. The CIA and members of the military, similarly dissatisfied with their government, supported the OAS.

The destruction of Port Said during the Suez Crisis of 1956, when England, France, and Israel tried to take control of the Suez Canal from Egypt.

As shown here, Hungarian rebels marching in Budapest during the ant-Soviet Hungarian revolt in 1956. After promising to support the rebels, the CIA was nowhere to be found and offered no assistance, leading to their massacre.

Indonesian President Sukarno with Fidel Castro in Havana in 1960. The CIA tried to assassinate Sukarno in the mid-1950s and instigated a military coup to overthrow him in 1957. Both efforts failed, but the CIA eventually succeeded and removed Sukarno in 1965.

- 7 -

The War Machine

"Someday there is going to be a man sitting in my present chair who has not been raised in the military services and . . . if that should happen while we still have a state of tension that now exists in the world, I shudder to think what could happen in this country."

—President Dwight David Eisenhower

During the Cold War, the radical right seized upon an abnormal fear of communism to create an atmosphere of hysteria. It was a time when what the U.S. was willing to spend on nuclear weapons was limitless. The military and their radical right-wing supporters, realizing they had a numerical advantage in this area, wanted to use them in an unprovoked first strike against the Soviet Union and China to eliminate communism once and for all. They repeatedly demanded that Eisenhower allow them to do so. Greed was also a factor. Defense contractors hired generals and admirals after they retired at lucrative salaries, which told those still serving in the military that a high-paying job was waiting for them as long as they continued to perpetuate the ever-increasing war machine.

Meanwhile, business leaders were appointed to important positions in government, creating a bloc whose sole desire was to constantly push the nation towards war. Eisenhower recognized that these men were Fascists who wanted to control the government themselves, which was why, as his presidency neared its end, in his Farewell Address, he warned the American people about the danger the country faced from the Military-Industrial Complex. Ike's warning went unheeded, and less than three years later, the assassination of John F. Kennedy happened. The young President should never have tried to curtail what these militarists wanted to do.

* * *

The fear that Communists had infiltrated the U.S. government characterized the immediate post-World War II era. In 1946, Congress gave the Secretary of State authority to remove an employee if deemed "necessary or advisable in the United States' interests." Congressman Bartel Jonkman was even stricter, stating that hearsay evidence should be sufficient cause for removal. Conservative Republicans, who for decades had claimed that the Socialist welfare programs instituted by Democrats had threatened self-determination and the American way of life, now warned that "alien-minded radicals" were running the Democratic Party, which included subversives "high up in government." David Niles, Harry Hopkins, and Harry Dexter White all served FDR and Truman in high-level capacities. All were accused publicly of being Communist spies.[1] The midterm elections of 1946 made domestic security a primary issue, calling it a fight "between communism and republicanism." The rhetoric resonated with voters as Republicans won control of Congress for the first time in sixteen years. Congressman Karl Mundt, a member of the House Un-American Activities Committee (HUAC), summed up the radical right-wing position. He said the country "for eighteen years had been run by New Dealers, Fair Dealers, Mis-dealers . . . who have shuttled back and forth between Freedom and Red Fascism like a pendulum on a cuckoo clock."[2]

Given little choice with the country's mood, President Truman established a federal loyalty program on March 22, 1947. It stated an employee could be removed from government employment if there were "reasonable grounds . . . for [a] belief that the person involved is disloyal to the Government of the United States." And it defined disloyalty as serving "the interests of another government," or a group "designated by the Attorney General as totalitarian, fascist, communist, or subversive."[3]

Truman was aware of the rumors about his administration. In 1946 he received a report from J. Edgar Hoover regarding Harry Dexter White, which described him as "a valuable adjunct to an underground Soviet espionage organization operating in Washington D.C. Material which came into his [White's] possession . . . was made available . . . to the Soviet Union." Hoover added that the Canadian government was also concerned. They had been fed information about White by a Soviet military intelligence defector. Secretary of State James F. Byrnes was shocked by the report and thought the President should fire White, but Truman did nothing. It was a mid-term election year, and he did not want to give the Republicans proof that Communists were working in his administration. So, a suspected Communist in a high government position remained in place for political reasons. White would resign the following year. Testifying before the HUAC in 1948, he denied all charges. He would die of a heart attack at his home in August of that year.[4]

Truman had good reason to bury the Harry Dexter White story because the American people wanted Communists removed from government. In July 1946, 36 percent polled thought they should be either killed or imprisoned.[5] By 1949,

68 percent would outlaw Communist Party membership, 83 percent would make Communists register with the government, and 73 percent would ban them from college teaching. As a result, the Eighty-First Congressional class of 1948 initiated twenty-four investigations into communism; the Eighty-Second, thirty-four; and the Eight-Third, fifty-one. By 1953, 185 of the 221 Republican Congressmen asked to serve on the House Un-American Activities Commission.[6]

As the 1952 election approached, Republicans continued to attack the Democrats, as the party platform accused Democrats of shielding "traitors to the Nation in high places . . ."[7] Meanwhile, the Truman administration tried to change the perception that Democrats were soft on communism. By January 1952, the FBI had conducted over 18,000 loyalty inquiries of federal employees. It resulted in over 4,000 resignations by those who did not want to deal with the scrutiny suspected Communists had to endure. The State Department fired, or forced the resignation of over four hundred people who were not heterosexual. Ruth Shipley of the Passport Office, who ruled with an iron fist, prevented travel outside the country of Communists or anyone suspected of being one.[8] But Democrats could not change the consensus opinion that Communists permeated the Truman administration from top to bottom.

Anti-Communist fears did not diminish with Eisenhower's election in 1952. Almost everyone wanted public schools to teach a course about the evils of communism, and seventy-five percent wanted Communists and ex-Communists prohibited from teaching in colleges. A VFW post in Connecticut sent the FBI the names of people thought to be "Communistic." Twenty-six states put into effect laws prohibiting Communists from running for public office; the Constitution be damned. Thirty-two states required teachers to take a loyalty oath. And the Communist Control Act of 1954 declared that anyone who advocated the violent overthrow of the government could have their citizenship revoked.[9]

It was this anti-Communist hysteria that made it possible for Senator Joseph McCarthy to become a national figure. It began with a February 9, 1950, Wheeling, West Virginia speech, while Truman was still President, where McCarthy spoke about "a serious problem of Communist infiltration at the State Department . . . ," which was followed by a telegram to Truman claiming that, ". . . we have been able to compile a list of fifty-seven Communists in the State Department . . . you can get a much longer list by ordering Secretary Acheson to give you a list of those whom your own board listed as being disloyal and who are still working in the State Department."[10]

Domestic communism had put the fear of God into the heart of almost every red-blooded American. Alger Hiss of the State Department had been found guilty of spying for the Russians and sentenced to prison for five years. The Soviets had successfully tested the atomic bomb, McCarthy was going strong, so it was not surprising that the Republican convention that summer seized upon the nation's anxiety. Herbert Hoover told delegates that Roosevelt and Truman had ignored self-determination when they forced citizens to finance social programs without their consent, which "distorted and violated" the Constitution, a right-wing mantra. McCarthy stated, "We cannot fight Communists . . . [by] hitting them with a perfumed silk handkerchief at the front door while they batter our friends with brass knuckles and blackjacks at the back door." And General MacArthur charged Democrats with setting "the national course . . . toward the socialistic regimentation of a totalitarian state."[11]

As the Republican candidate for President, Eisenhower continued the party's onslaught against the "Red Menace." In an October speech, he sounded a lot like McCarthy, saying communism "insinuated itself into our schools, our public forums, some of our news channels, some of our labor unions, and—most terrifyingly—into our Government itself." He said there was subversion in "virtually every department, every agency, every bureau, every section of our Government." Men ran the government, he said, who "condoned the surrender of whole nations to an implacable enemy [an obvious reference to Truman's Pacific Rim strategy]," who were "infiltrating our most secret counsels." Those who had allowed this to happen, in his opinion, were guilty of "treason itself."[12]

On another occasion, Eisenhower told a Montana crowd, "We will find the pinks; we will find the Communists; we will find the disloyal." He spoke of running for President as a moral obligation that it was his destiny directed by God to destroy a "godless enemy."[13]

* * *

During these turbulent times, the military began to insert itself into the political discourse, a place where military men dared not tread in the past. General Omar Bradley made numerous speeches which, wrote Hansen Baldwin of the *New York Times*, "helped put General Bradley and the Joint Chiefs of Staff into the political hustings where they have no business to be." Meanwhile, perhaps the most ardent right-winger in the Senate and a presidential candidate himself, Senator Taft excused the generals, saying they were only offering expert advice. MacArthur supported Taft, as did General Albert Wedemeyer, and General Bonner Fellers was on the Republican National Committee. But MacArthur was the most vocal, and in direct violation of Army regulations, he publicly attacked current administration policies.[14]

Only one year after Truman had removed MacArthur, the Korean War was still ongoing, and the military wanted the freedom to do as they pleased, which was to bomb China. In April 1952, Navy Secretary Dan Kimball told a reporter that the Seventh fleet would "cheer" from the "sidelines" if Chiang invaded the mainland. By July, one hundred jets from a U.S. carrier task force flew just outside mainland China's territorial limits, just to give them something "to think about." Asked the next day in Manila about the jets, a grinning navy chief William Fechteler said if he could add "baby atom bombs" to their arsenal, he could hit Korea too. On July 24, in Chicago and supposedly off the record, Kimball said the navy would fly over Chinese cities the next time. The military never stopped trying to instigate a war with China, probably believing that they would have that opportunity with a soon-to-be-elected President who was an ex-military general. [15] It was also in July 1952 when General Omar Bradley stated that since Washington had spent "billions" on atomic bombs, it seemed a shame to leave them "in storage."[16]

The military position remained clear—appeasement of Communists was not an option. Bombing China was what the military wanted. Whenever Eisenhower looked to improve relations with the Soviets during his presidency, such as signing a nuclear test ban treaty, the military and the CIA took action to stop him. Kennedy would face even more resistance, for he was a junior naval officer who could never garner the respect of the military or the radical right. Before the Korean war, the extreme right-wing planted anti-Communist seeds of discontent. The war served to exacerbate these anti-Communist feelings as treason became an acceptable option to curtail a President thought to be naive. These feelings were nurtured under Eisenhower and were in full bloom while JFK was in charge. But it was not just anti-Communist ideology that was the motivation behind assassinating a President. There was greed involved, as Kennedy threatened to end the gravy train of ever-increasing military spending. To understand how this came to be, a review of conditions under Eisenhower is in order.

* * *

The record is clear that candidate Eisenhower was not a darling of the radical right. During the primary campaign, his most militant opponents recalled Ike's friendship with Russian General Zhukov during World War II, his failure to take Berlin before the Soviets could get there, and his accommodating postwar talk about the Russians. When John Wayne saw an ex-GI waving an Eisenhower banner, he yelled, "Why don't you get a red flag?"[17]

Despite his hardline speeches, there was another side to Eisenhower that did not support bombing China. After retiring from the military, he became a proponent of psychological warfare as a less dangerous alternative to conventional war. He stayed in close contact with the early leaders of U.S. intelligence who felt the same way, including C.D. Jackson, Walter Bedell Smith, Allen Dulles, Bill Donovan, and Frank Wisner. He had no illusions about communism, and in 1950 Truman named him NATO commander. He subsequently wrote Truman that they faced an enemy who relied upon "deceit, propaganda, and subversion . . . ." The U.S. should respond in kind. During the campaign, despite his anti-Communist rhetoric, Eisenhower emphasized that "the struggle between communism and freedom is a struggle of ideas." The U.S. "must fully develop . . . every psychological weapon that is available to us," which included "diplomacy, the spreading of ideas through every medium of communication, mutual economic assistance, trade and barter, friendly contacts through travel and correspondence and sports."[18]

Diplomacy, economic assistance, trade, and barter sounded like appeasement, and during the Cold War, any President was called a Communist who thought this way. But this did not concern Eisenhower. He wanted to ensure that the presidency stayed out of the hands of those like Senator Robert Taft, who was too eager to drop bombs on China. Conversely, Ike believed the social programs that Roosevelt and Truman had thrust upon the country were evaporating the self-determination of the American people. So, he decided to run as what many would call a liberal-minded Republican. But make no mistake—he did not underestimate the danger posed by Communists and what it would take to defeat them.

One hardline Republican Eisenhower did not object to was John Foster Dulles. Dulles called for the "liberation" of Soviet satellite countries and the need to "roll back" the Soviet Union's sphere of influence. Eisenhower agreed. Both men supported the Republican platform condemning the "negative, futile and immoral policy of 'containment' which abandoned countless human beings to despotism and godless terrorism." Two years later, Ike proposed the Domino Theory, that if one nation in an area turned toward communism, the rest would follow. "Where in hell can you let the Communists chip away any more," he asked Congressional leaders in April 1954. "We just can't stand [for] it."[19]

Dulles agreed. "Already one-third of the world is dominated by an imperialist brand of communism," he warned in 1952, "already the free world has been so shrunk that no further substantial parts of it can be lost without danger to the whole that remains." Dulles was aware that his brother Allen and Bill Donovan were involved in covert operations involving stay-behind guerilla armies throughout Europe, which was likely why Foster called for an escalation of the underground war against Russia and a commitment to psychological warfare. "We should be dynamic, we should use ideas as weapons, and these ideas should conform to moral principles . . ." Despite some reservations, Ike chose Dulles as his Secretary of State because he shared his interest in psychological warfare. He wanted to satisfy the right-wing element of the Republican Party that called for a hardliner in that position.[20]

The Republican sweep of 1952 increased McCarthy's influence, forcing Eisenhower to institute a stricter loyalty program beyond what Truman had done. Now, federal employees could be considered security risks for "personal habits or actions," which included alcoholics, philanderers, "blabbermouths," and non-heterosexual sexual orientations, because all were considered candidates for potential blackmail. Attorney General Herbert Brownell proudly reported that "fourteen hundred fifty-six persons . . . [were] ejected from government service . . . [who were] found to be security risks." Eisenhower boasted that "more than 2,200 employees have been separated from the Federal Government." He called membership in the Communist Party "treason" and proposed that the government deprive guilty persons of their U.S. citizenship. By 1954, Brownell proudly reported that "thirty-six active Communist leaders have been convicted and sentenced to jail for conspiring to advocate the overthrow of our Government by force and violence."[21]

Ike favored ridding the State Department of liberals who were perceived to be soft on communism. He complained to Dulles that top-level posts in the previous administration had obtained their jobs "through a process of selection based upon their devotion to the socialistic doctrine and bureaucratic controls practiced over two decades." Amazingly, considering the war with Nazi Germany had ended only eight years before, the State Department burned books related to communism. Books in overseas State Department libraries that contained "the works of all Communist authors" were banned. Voice of America sent eight hundred suspected Communists packing. Eisenhower responded to the madness by saying: "If the State Department is burning a book which is an open appeal to everybody in those foreign countries to be a Communist . . . they can do as they please to get rid of them."[22]

*　*　*

The radical right approved of the hardline Eisenhower took against domestic communism, but there was a level of concern in other areas. He proposed cutting military spending by five billion dollars, with further cuts to come, until the government could achieve an annual defense budget of thirty-three billion dollars by 1957. His first budget came with a force reduction of 250,000 military personnel. Military and defense industry leaders tried to stop it, with high-ranking officers leaking classified information to the press, an unconscionable offense. There developed a desire to restrain the President, which was not the military's place to do. Ike's Defense Secretary, Charles Wilson, considered it treason and told Congress the military violated the Consitution. The "authority, direction, and control" of the armed services were in civilian hands, and those in the armed forces arguing against the budget were threatening that principle. The ensuing years, especially while Kennedy was President, would demonstrate how right Wilson was to be concerned.[23]

On March 6, 1953, a little over a month after Eisenhower became President, Joseph Stalin died unexpectedly, causing tremendous upheaval and unrest behind the Iron Curtain. In May, thousands of Czech workers marched on city hall in Plzen, occupied the building, burned Soviet flags, and threw busts of Lenin and Stalin out the window. Strikes spread among tobacco workers in Bulgaria, one of the most obedient countries in the Soviet bloc. The Politburo found this particularly disturbing—if hitherto loyal Bulgarian workers were restless, then the rest of the region must be even more unstable. In East Berlin, people continued to flee to the West—160,000 in 1952 and another 120,000 in the first four months of 1953.[24]

There was considerable agreement among Ike's psychological warfare strategists and intelligence analysts that a great opportunity had arrived. According to William Morgan, acting head of the Psychological Strategy Board, their objective "should be to do everything to encourage and promote chaos within the USSR." C.D. Jackson, Eisenhower's special assistant for Cold War operations, agreed. He wanted the President to deliver a speech promoting American democratic values. "It is fundamental," he believed, that the initiative should be to "strike the Russian peoples and the peoples of the Communist bloc, at a moment of emotional indecision and even bewilderment, with a new vision of possibilities." "I am interested in the future," Eisenhower said. "Both their government and ours have new men in them. The slate is clean. Now let us begin talking to each other. And let us say what we have got to say so that every person on earth can understand it." Ike was talking appeasement and normalizing relations with the Soviets, a language most around him vehemently opposed.[25]

On April 16, Eisenhower delivered the speech suggested by C.D. Jackson to the American Society of Newspaper Editors and shocked the radical right by extending an olive branch to the Soviet Union. "A nation's hope of lasting peace," he stated, "cannot be firmly based upon a race in armaments . . ." He said that "Every gun . . . every warship launched, every rocket fired," constituted "a theft from those who hunger . . . , those who are cold and are not clothed." He spoke, he said, "without ulterior purpose or political passion, from our calm conviction that the hunger for peace is in the hearts of all peoples—those of Russia and [ ] China no less than our own country."[26]

The speech was well-received internationally, but two days later, John Foster Dulles defused the temporary euphoria when he brazenly spoke before the same Society of Newspaper Editors. Instead of promoting coexistence, he said the U.S. was acting from a position of strength and should seize the opportunity. "The Russians were suggesting changes were in the wind but could never be trusted . . . so long as vast power is possessed by men who accept no guidance from the moral law." Dulles ruined any chance there was for a lasting peace was ruined.[27]

Meanwhile, the unrest behind the Iron Curtain continued, with a strike by construction workers in East Berlin on June 16, followed by a general revolt the next day that involved over one million people. The uprising was quickly suppressed by the introduction of tanks and Russian troops, demonstrating to the world the oppressive nature of the Soviet Union, with or without Stalin. It presented an opportunity for the U.S., and they worked with the West German government to distribute food to East Berliners and East Germans. By mid-August, 865,000 East Germans had flocked to centers in West Berlin to pick up food; by early October, the number of people receiving aid increased to more than 5.5 million packages. The East German and Soviet governments were embarrassed and angry and did all they could to stop the food program, but it was a major international propaganda coup for the United States. It was psychological warfare in action.

With unrest behind the Iron Curtain, stay-behind units in place throughout Europe, and propaganda-driven psychological warfare working, the administration thought the time might be suitable to give "rollback" a chance. However, American diplomats in Eastern Europe cautioned that the U.S. should tread slowly, for "stirring up resistance elements or incitements to revolt might have the long-range effect of retarding a Soviet military withdrawal." There was even concern that the food distribution program could provoke a Soviet advance against West Berlin. As a result, C.D. Jackson submitted a detailed plan of psychological warfare initiatives to exploit unrest in satellite states and undermine puppet regimes without inciting rebellion. But there remained questions as to how to proceed in the post-Stalin era.[28]

John Foster Dulles thought he knew what the administration should do. The "present course we are following is a fatal one . . . we are always worrying about what the Soviets will take next. Unless we change this policy or get some break, we will lose bit by bit the free world, and break ourselves financially . . ." He had numerous options in mind, such as telling the Chinese that if another country fell to communism, the U.S. would retaliate with measures of its choosing, clearly alluding to the employment of atomic bombs. Another possibility was to win back one or more areas that had turned Communist—for example, all of Korea. Or to incite subversion within the Soviet empire, especially in eastern Europe. The goal was to "disturb the Kremlin; make it think more of holding what it has . . . turn the Soviet bloc into a loose alliance, without aggressive capacities, far different from Stalin's monolith."[29]

Early on in his Presidency, Eisenhower was determined to make covert action the focus of his foreign policy, for, in his opinion, it was "just about the only way to win World War III without having to fight it." C.D. Jackson wrote in his diary that year, "He [Ike] is convinced that psychological warfare should not be the pet mystery of one or more Departments of the Government, but should be the entire posture of the entire Government to the entire world."[30]

The logic was that a conventional war would include atomic bombs, which had to be avoided at all costs, even though America had an advantage in this area in the early 1950s. So Ike preferred to pursue a policy of psychological warfare and covert intelligence operations. John Kennedy would feel the same way, but his reliance on covert operations and psychological warfare proved unsuccessful. So, with employing the military an option he refused to entertain and psychological warfare not working, he turned to the only choice he had left—appeasement and détente. Normalization of relations with Cuba, the Soviet Union, and treaties to reduce nuclear weapons with an adversary the United States could not trust to honor their agreements were now on the table, and this radical shift sealed Kennedy's fate, for, by 1963, the tolerance for this had run thin. And it all began with Eisenhower's decision not to use the military and atomic weapons when America had a distinct superiority in these areas and could have rolled back communism had they chosen that path.

In June 1953, the (C.D.) Jackson Committee, whose function was to determine how to employ psychological warfare for the Ike administration, emphasized that "the greatest danger of Soviet expansion lies in political warfare and local communist armed action." The Soviets intended to pursue its goal of "world domination" by "political warfare methods" and "will avoid initiatives involving serious risks of general war, especially since it may hope to make additional gains by political warfare methods without such risk." Eisenhower agreed, but unlike Jackson, he did not expect the Soviet Union to implode anytime soon. The United States had to maintain a between psychological warfare, conventional armed forces, and atomic weaponry that was economically feasible. How Eisenhower planned to achieve that balance was a question that had to be determined.[31]

The President asked the National Security Council to investigate. What they decided upon was code-named Project Solarium. It would guide the administration's foreign policy over the next eight years. Three task forces were brought together at the White House, with each investigating a different alternative. Under the direction of George Kennan, Task Force A considered unifying the free world while instigating subversion within the Soviet Union and its satellite countries without the risk of initiating a significant war. Major General James McCormack headed Task Force B, which drew an imaginary line around the existing Soviet bloc which, were the Soviets to cross it, the U.S. would act to counter their offensive and risk global war. Under Admiral Richard L. Conolly, Task Force C assumed the U.S. "cannot continue to live with the Soviet threat. So long as the Soviet Union exists, it will not fall apart, but must and can be shaken apart." The U.S. would consider aggressive action under this scenario, even if it required a preventative first strike to destroy their adversary.[32]

As discussions proceeded, it became evident that the cost of all three options was prohibitive. To obtain a fresh perspective, Eisenhower instructed the heads of the military branches to develop alternative solutions that would not bankrupt the budget. At an NSC meeting, the Joint Chiefs stated that the nation should cut its overseas troop deployments. The primary focus should be on strategic airpower (i.e., atomic weapons, which the military had been promoting since the Korean War) and defense of the continental U.S in the event of a Soviet attack. JCS chairman Radford said this would cost more in the short term but would produce significant savings as time went by. The NSC embraced the new proposal.

John Foster Dulles was the only dissenting voice. He feared European allies would feel abandoned with the removal of U.S. troops from the continent. He presented a new view, which was a total reversal from what he had previously supported, which included "the possibility of . . . mutual withdrawals of Red Army forces and . . . U.S. forces . . . [and] limitation of armament and control of weapons of mass destruction." As would be expected, Ike agreed. So, with a newfound willingness to pursue peace, at the expense of being accused of appeasement by the radical right at home, Eisenhower and Dulles attempted to explore détente with the Soviets. However, the effort was futile, for they realized they could not trust the Russians. And while nuclear war remained a possibility, the defense budget would have to be increased dramatically. The clash of ideologies made peace impossible.

With peace negotiations off the table, all three task force proposals from Operation Solarium, and the Joint Chiefs' recommendation, were combined into one overall strategy based upon nuclear superiority and containment, with the possibility of rollback under the right circumstances. A strong military was a priority, "with emphasis on the capability of inflicting massive retaliatory damage by offensive striking power," while maintaining the "cooperation of our allies" and a need to "seek to win the friendship and cooperation of . . . uncommitted areas of the world, and thereby strengthen the cohesion of the free world." Operation Solarium said psychological and covert warfare was critical. It should be "designed to create and exploit troublesome problem[s] for the USSR, impair Soviet relations with Communist China, complicate control in the satellites, and retard the growth of the military and economic potential of the Soviet bloc."[33]

John Foster Dulles told the NSC that the United States had to stop Soviet expansion, "even at the risk of war." The New Look Strategy was based on nuclear superiority and "massive retaliation." The reasoning was for the Soviets to consider any attempt by them at military aggressiveness or territorial expansion to be suicidal, and they would back down. It was the culmination of what NSC-68 had, under Truman, attempted to introduce.

The new policy was part of NSC 162-2 and relied on nuclear weapons instead of overseas troops. It resulted in the Army losing a half-million soldiers, as they saw their share of the shrinking defense budget fall from 33 percent to 25 percent. The Air Force's allotment rose from 39 percent to 47 percent, resulting from the additional aircraft needed to deliver an atomic attack.[34]

The U.S. buildup of atomic weapons created concern around the world. On December 8, 1953, Eisenhower spoke at the United Nations and gave what came to be known as the "Atoms for Peace" speech. It was to calm nerves around the world. He said, ". . . the miraculous inventiveness of man shall not be dedicated to his death, but consecrated to his life." He received a standing ovation, even from the Soviet delegation. However, all hope for a thaw in the Cold War ended when John Foster Dulles spoke before the Council on Foreign Relations a month later. He warned the world that the U.S. would use nuclear weapons to stop Communist aggression wherever it occurred, and it would be unrestricted "massive retaliatory power . . . by means and at places of our own choosing."[35]

Dulles' "Massive Retaliation" speech would govern U.S. defense policy throughout Eisenhower's Presidency, but the military was equally responsible for the massive shift toward atomic weapons. Joint Chiefs Chairman Admiral Arthur Radford said it was "high time" the administration publicly declared its willingness to use nuclear weapons. According to General Alfred M. Gruenther, the NATO Supreme Commander in 1954, "simply because atomic bombs do create casualties—and very heavy casualties against women and children—is no reason why we should become sentimental . . . The chore is to make war itself impossible." Even Eisenhower said early in 1955, "I see no reason why they [atomic weapons] shouldn't be used just exactly as you would use a bullet or anything else."[36]

* * *

There were two ideological camps under Eisenhower—proponents of psychological warfare and advocates of massive retaliation. Both wanted to wage war against communism, albeit from different directions. In theory, psychological warfare would contain communism without a military conflict, while massive retaliation relied upon nuclear superiority and the willingness to use nuclear weapons if necessary. But there was one other aspect of enormous nuclear retaliation that its proponents found appealing. There was a great deal of money to be made in weapons production, which brought big business into the mix. The result was the Military-Industrial Complex that Eisenhower warned about at the end of his Presidency, for this two-headed alliance of big business and the military would jeopardize the nation's stability throughout the Cold War.

The government awarded seventy-four percent of defense contracts without competitive bidding during World War II. Harry Truman chaired the Senate Special Committee to Investigate the National Defense Program from 1941 to 1944. There were definite abuses, Truman said, as contractors were able "to earn, on a three-month job at government risk, three or four times as much as they had formerly been able to make at their own risk in an entire year of work." Large companies monopolized defense contracts, with three-fourths of defense spending going to only fifty-six companies. In comparison, only six companies were awarded a third of the agreements, with Bethlehem Steel, General Motors, and Du Pont leading the way.[37]

Like FDR's vice president Henry Wallace, New Dealers said it was "American Fascism," a shadow government of elites that parceled out contracts "to control production, prices, distribution, and the very lifeblood of world industry." Treasury Secretary Henry Morgenthau called these people Fascists. In *The New Dealers' War, FDR and the War Within World War II,* Thomas Fleming states that FDR "was 'gravely concerned' about the way the army's generals were forming alliances with . . . businessmen through their ability to determine where and how weapons and other war material would be produced."[38]

The modernization of warfare during World War II forced the military to get involved directly with defense contractors. Wright Mills wrote *The Power Elite*, an insightful 1956 book about the rise of the "Deep State" during the 1950s. According to Mills, "unless the military sat in on corporate decisions, they could not be sure that their programs would be carried out; and unless the corporation chieftains knew something of the war plans, they could not plan war production. Thus, generals advised corporation presidents, and corporate presidents advised generals."[39]

Under Eisenhower, industry executives and military leaders shared common values, which resulted in the private sector hiring an influx of retired officers. It was when the relationship between the military and big business began to flourish. As described by Mills, there were General Lucius D. Clay (board chairman of the Continental Can Company) and General James H. Doolittle (vice president of Shell Oil). "General Omar Bradley . . . board chairman of Bulova Research Laboratories. General Douglas MacArthur . . . chairman of the board at Remington Rand, Inc. General Albert C. Wedemeyer . . . vice president of AVCO Corporation. Admiral Ben Moreell . . . chairman of Jones & Laughlin Steel Corp. General Jacob Evers . . . technical adviser to Fairchild Aircraft Corp. General Ira Eaker is vice president of Hughes Tool Co. General Brehon Somervell . . . chairman and president of Koppers Co. Admiral Alan G. Kirk . . . chairman of the board and chief executive officer of Mercast, Inc. . . . General Leslie R. Groves . . . vice president of Remington Rand . . . General E.R. Quesada . . . vice president of Lockheed Aircraft Corporation; General Walter Bedell Smith . . . vice chairman of American Machine and Foundry Company's board of directors; Army Chief of Staff General Mathew B. Ridgway . . . chairman of the board of the Mellon Institute of Industrial Research."[40]

The departure of military officers into the private sector would continue under JFK. By 1962, a House Subcommittee investigation revealed that ". . . 262 generals and admirals and 485 retirees above the rank of colonel . . . were employed by companies with 80 percent of the [defense] contracts. General Dynamics had 186 retirees, including a four-star general, a lieutenant general, five brigadier generals, one vice admiral, and nineteen rear admirals."[41]

The practice of large defense contractors hiring ex-military officers created a scenario where it was in the best interest of military officers to increase military spending as much as possible because it guaranteed them high-paying jobs in the private sector once they retired. Obviously, this was not in the best interest of the country. Worse yet, it was conceivable that an overzealous military leader could initiate a nuclear war because of the future payday which waited over the horizon. Such a scenario was not beyond what military generals, who did not trust politicians and were willing to take matters into their own hands, might do. The danger was genuine because to keep defense spending on the rise, the constant threat of war existed. Referring to Korea, in 1953 *New York Times* Washington reporter and bureau chief Arthur Krock wrote that, "What officials fear more than dateless war . . . is peace . . . which could lure the free world into letting down its guard . . . while the Soviets maintained and increased their military power . . ."[42]

The military buildup required a weapons development program that ensured there was always something bigger and better on the horizon throughout the decade. By 1954, the government was spending about $2 billion on research per year, which was twenty times greater than what they had spent in the period leading up to World War II. Eighty-five percent of research was for "national security" purposes, a veiled reference to the defense industry, which dominated the research budgets of both the private sector and large universities. Some colleges received three or four times as much money from the military as all other combined sources. It is not surprising that retired military leaders were also offered high-level positions at these schools. Dwight Eisenhower was head of Columbia University before becoming President. Rear Admiral Herbert J. Grassie was Chancellor of Lewis College of Science and Technology; Admiral Chester Nimitz, regent of the University of California at Berkeley; Major General Frank Keating, a member of the Ithica College board of trustees; Rear Admiral Oswald Colcough; dean of George Washington University Law School; Colonel Melvin A. Casburg, dean of St. Louis School of Medicine; and Admiral Charles M. Cook, Jr., a member of the California State Board of Education.[43]

The military found itself deeply entrenched in leadership roles at major defense contractors and universities. Meanwhile, many of those working within the government promoted nuclear war with an almost delusional disregard for the consequences. One of the most egregious examples of this occurred just three weeks after the reelection of Eisenhower. On November 25, 1956, science adviser George Kistiakowsky briefed the President on the Single Integrated Operational Plan (SIOP), a title that sounded innocent. However, the plan was anything but and described the steps necessary for the United States to destroy the Soviet Union, Red China, and the Soviet satellite states in a single all-out attack. Under SIOP, nothing would be left behind. The U.S. would fire off its entire strategic arsenal of 3,500 weapons. The plan was an exercise in "overkill," said Kistiakowsky, and "kill four or five times over." Eisenhower's reaction was to tell a naval aide, this SIOP "frightens the devil out of me."[44]

There was good reason to be frightened. As the military infiltrated the defense industry at the highest levels, corporate leaders increasingly found themselves, at the same time, holding positions of importance within government. Many of these were people connected to the defense industry, or at the very least, supported increased spending in that sector for national security reasons. There was a crossover between ex-military officers and defense-related contractors, and over time those who wanted to limit defense spending were no longer relevant.

Consider that the Secretaries of State, Treasury, and Defense, the three most important policy-making positions in government, were held by business leaders. Ex-Sullivan & Cromwell lawyer John Foster Dulles ran the State Department. George M. Humphrey, the president of steel manufacturer M.A. Hanna Company who, after World War II, advised on the rebuilding of Germany with General Lucius Clay, was close to Eisenhower during the war, ran the Treasury Department. And finally, the Defense Department was run by Charles E. Wilson, the ex-president of General Motors, a company that made a fortune during World War II under Wilson. The following people comprised the rest of the cabinet:

Attorney General: Herbert Brownell accused Harry Dexter White of being a Communist spy. He drafted a proposal that eventually became the Civil Rights Act of 1957. He had to step down that year when he blamed Little Rock, Arkansas, for obeying the Supreme Court order to desegregate their schools.

Postmaster General: Arthur Sommerfield owned of one of the largest General Motor dealerships in Michigan and was Republican National Committee Chairman between 1952 and 1953.

Secretary of the Interior: Douglas McKay was governor of Oregon in 1948 and promoted fiscal conservatism and a balanced budget. Eisenhower asked him to resign in 1956 because he leaned too far to the right.

Secretary of Agriculture: Ezra Taft Benson was a Mormon Church's Quorum of the Twelve Apostles member. As late as 1967, he spoke of "how the Communists are using the Negros to . . . foment trouble in the United States." Under Eisenhower, Benson opposed price support for farmers, calling it socialism, and supported the John Birch Society, which he referred to as "the most effective non-church organization in our fight against creeping socialism and Godless Communism." He told his congregation to read Gary Allen's "New World Order" book *None Dare Call It a Conspiracy*. The book claimed that elites in developed countries like the U.S. used income tax to extort money from its citizens and created a central bank to finance wars and pay for defense spending.

Secretary of Commerce: Sinclair Weeks was a past U.S. Senator from Massachusetts involved with the First National Bank of Boston, the United Carr Fastener Corporation, and Reed & Barton Silversmiths president.

Secretary of Labor: Democrat Martin P. Durkin was president of the Plumber's and Pipe Fitter's Union (Eisenhower's cabinet was derisively called "Nine Millionaires and a Plumber"), then Illinois State Director of Labor. After only eight months, Ike asked him to resign because he wanted to revise the Taft-Hartley Act in favor of organized labor.

Secretary of Health, Education and Welfare: Oveta Culp Hobby was married to a former governor of Texas who became the *Houston Post* owner. Both were Southern Democrats who opposed FDR's social programs. She attempted to restructure

Social Security payroll taxes during her tenure as HEW Secretary and resigned in 1955 due to opposition against this effort.

In summation, in the Cabinet, four members of the corporate rich were from General Motors, one leading financier and director of New England's largest bank, and a millionaire publisher from Texas. The Secretaries of Agriculture and Labor were professional outsiders, and the Attorney General was the only one who was a political insider.[45]

The lower levels of government were no different, and according to Mills, ". . . predominately Ivy Leaguers . . . from wealthy families." There was one Rockefeller and a former financial adviser to the Rockefellers. Thus, the men of the President's inner circle come from [Thomas] Dewey's inner circle, from Henry Luce's, or the higher levels of the Pentagon. Eisenhower received advice from a small cadre of men. Of these, Mills continued, "Three quarters are political outsiders, [and] most of these outsiders—thirty of the thirty-nine—are quite closely linked, financially or professionally, or both, with the corporate world, and thus make up slightly over half of all the political directors . . ."[46]

The result was an Eisenhower administration with critical positions filled by people with limited or no political experience, with many connections to the defense industry and other major corporations. Meanwhile, retired military leaders continued to join significant defense contractors and were equally unqualified to hold the high-level positions they were appointed to. It did not happen by accident. The objective was to create a permanent war economy. It was essential to establish a crossover between government and defense contractors so that everyone was on the same page, perpetuating the war machine. And as the military ascended into prominent private industrial positions, they obtained political relevance and became part of the political establishment, where they certainly did not belong. But an alternative did not exist because while "massive retaliation" was official government policy, a permanent military threat remained. As a result, the stature of the military grew in importance. Virtually all political and economic decisions were now based upon the military's definition of what was required to maintain a military advantage over the Communist adversaries of the United States.

And it is not surprising that war zealots within the government repeatedly tried to push Eisenhower into making an unprovoked nuclear first strike against the Soviet Union. ". . . For the next few years," said Admiral Radford, ". . . the military posture of the Free nations is strong . . . compared to that of the Soviet," which was why many believed the time was right to eliminate communism with a first strike while the U.S. had a distinct advantage.[47]

Those that supported the first strike scenario brazenly disrespected their Commander-in-Chief. "By God, this has got to stop," Eisenhower said. "These fellows . . . don't yet realize that they . . . have a boss."[48] On another occasion, Ike lamented the insubordination of his top military leaders. "All these fellows in the

Pentagon," he said, "think they have some responsibility I can't see. I hate to use the word, but this business is damn near treason."[49]

When General Robert Cutler, Eisenhower's Special Assistant for National Security Affairs, told the President that the NSC was considering using nuclear weapons if the U.S. intervened in Vietnam, an exasperated Ike replied: "You boys must be crazy." The U.S. couldn't use atomic weapons "against Asians for the second time in less than ten years. My God."[50] Undeterred, Cutler reported: "U.S. power should be directed at the source of the peril, which was . . . China, and that in this connection, atomic weapons should be used."[51] Five times in a single year, Ike's advisers urged him to use nuclear weapons against China. Even John Foster Dulles said, "we'll have to use nuclear weapons."[52]

Such talk frightened Eisenhower, but the military did not share his concern. According to General Curtis LeMay, he "did not see the ultimate horror predicted by arms controllers. One or both sides would stop before we have an Armageddon."[53] He never explained the policy if he were wrong, and neither side was willing to stop.

Eisenhower understood the need for a large nuclear arsenal so that the threat of "massive retaliation" would be a deterrent to reduce the chance of nuclear war. However, what concerned him was "an all-out effort on military buildup, military technology, and tremendous attempts at secrecy," and he desperately tried to convince his critics that the arms race had gone far enough. He complained that the military had gotten "themselves into an incredible position of having enough to destroy every conceivable target all over the world, plus a threefold reserve."[54]

Then there was the quality-of-life issue. Ike warned at a December 8, 1955, NSC meeting that a significant price would have to be paid by the American people for the continued increases in military spending. They were defending a way of life over a prolonged period, and the "economy could stand it for a while; but you cannot do it for the long pull without destroying incentives, inflating the currency, and increasing government controls. It would require an authoritarian system of government and destroy the health of our free society."[55]

A few weeks later, Eisenhower was irate because NSC members believed a nuclear war would be over in thirty to sixty days. Some thought they could save money by cutting back on maintaining a five-year stockpile of raw materials to sustain the country. With American ports "in ruins," Ike told them, it might be "three or four years" before the nation could be able to import anything, raw materials or otherwise.

On January 23, 1956, Lieutenant General Harold George, NSC staff director of the Net Evaluation Subcommittee, presented a damage assessment report resulting from a nuclear war with the Soviet Union. It predicted "practically [a] total economic collapse" for the U.S., lasting six months to a year." All government leaders would be dead, and "a new government would have to be put together by the states, and international commerce would halt for months. Sixty-five percent of the population would be killed or badly injured, and medical attention would be virtually nonexistent. The American damage inflicted on the Soviet Union would be roughly three times greater, but this was a small consolation for what the U.S. would have to endure.[56]

During a February 27 National Security Council meeting, it became apparent to Eisenhower that the Joint Chiefs were blind to the gravity of what the Net Evaluation Subcommittee had reported. Their only concern was what roles the Army and Navy would have in a nuclear war. Ike bluntly told them the Army's chief task "would be to preserve order in the United States," for chaos would ensue, and "God only knew what the Navy would be doing in a nuclear attack."[57]

The President began to question if the enormous price the country had to pay to keep the war machine going was necessary and if the nation "must face national bankruptcy and the prospect of a totalitarian control as the only means to deal with an implacable enemy." He told the Joint Chiefs "that they must behave as statesmen as well as military leaders," but the warning fell on deaf ears, and he was livid. "Any person who doesn't clearly understand that national security and national solvency are mutually dependent," Ike lectured, does not understand that the "crushing weight of military power would eventually produce dictatorship." Such people "should not be entrusted with any . . . responsibility in our country."[58] It was clear he had lost faith in his military leadership. "If you go to any [American] military installation in the world . . . and tell the commander that Ike says he'll give him an extra star for his shoulder if he cuts his budget, there'll be such a rush to cut costs that you'll have to get out of the way." And: "God help the nation when it has a President who doesn't know as much about the military as I do."[59]

Eisenhower did not realize he was describing the man who would come after him. On another occasion, he went even further. "Someday there is going to be a man sitting in my present chair . . . who will have little understanding of where the slashes in their estimates can be made with little or no damage," he wrote. "If that should happen while we still have a state of tension that now exists in the world, I shudder to think what could happen in this country."[60]

Eisenhower understood there was too much money to be made by defense contractors and military officers. As a result, the defense budget would increase as much yearly as possible. It was why that during his farewell address to the nation, Ike warned that they had created a "permanent armaments industry of vast proportions." Also, he continued, "three and a half million men and women are directly engaged in the defense establishment." The President lamented that "we annually spend on military security more than the net income of all United States corporations."[61] The union "of an immense military establishment and a large arms industry is new in the American experience . . . , " he continued, and "*we must guard against the acquisition of unwarranted influence, whether sought or unsought, by the military-industrial complex.*" In conclusion, he said that the joining of military and industry should not be allowed to *"endanger our liberties or democratic process. We should take nothing for granted."*[62] (Author's Italics)

The Encyclopedia Britannica website defines fascism as a political ideology. It includes "extreme militaristic nationalism, contempt for electoral democracy and political and cultural liberalism, a belief in [a] natural social hierarchy and the rule of elites, and the desire to create a Volksgemeinschaft (German for 'people's community'), in which individual interests would be subordinated to the good of the nation."[63]

The Military-Industrial Complex and their radical right, Christian, racist, White Nationalist supporters perfectly fit the definition of fascism. Extreme military nationalism defined them. They believed in American superiority and had contempt for those who disagreed with their anti-Communist philosophy; they believed in racial segregation and eugenics. A social class system was part of their core values, including the purging of undesirables from society. The subordination of individual interests for the nation's good was another way of saying self-determination was their God-given right guaranteed by the Constitution. And advocates of self-determination thought the American people should have a choice in whether or not to support social programs. They believed communism was so evil that it had to be removed from the face of the earth, even if that meant starting a worldwide nuclear war. These people were beyond right-wing, as we would define it today. They were Fascists in every sense of the word who were willing to fight and die to preserve their American way of life in the 1950s. Eisenhower had good reason to publicly warn the nation because these Fascists thought it was their Constitutional duty to protect the people from politicians who could irreparably harm the country. It is not a coincidence that around the same time, there was concern in many quarters that the military might be planning a coup to take over the government around the same time. Recall that General MacArthur said it was a ". . . dangerous concept that the members of our armed forces owe primary allegiance . . . to those who temporarily exercise the authority of the Executive Branch of the Government rather than to the country and to the Constitution which they are sworn to defend . . ."[64] It was treason. In less than three years after Eisenhower's farewell address, John Kennedy would be dead because, by that time, they embraced their Fascist beliefs with an almost religious devotion that had become a Crusade to rid the government of undesirables who threatened the nation's existence.

Recall that during his interview with the Warren Commission, Jack Ruby said, ". . . a whole new form of government is going to take over our country, and I know I won't live to see you another time . . ."[65] Two years later, Ruby would write: "[There] is only one kind of people that would do such a thing, that would have to be the Nazis, and that is who is in power in this country right now . . . There is only one kind of people that would go to such extremes, and that would be the Master Race . . ."[66]

Jack Ruby had inside information into the assassination plot, and we should not dismiss the fact that he blamed right-wing Fascists for JFK's murder. And if Ruby were involved, there is no doubt that organized crime was as well. The Mafia had been in bed with the military and U.S. intelligence since World War II. They had a motive for wanting Kennedy killed, so their involvement in the assassination plot would be logical. Therefore, they require a closer look to determine what their role might have been.

- 8 -

Organized Crime—Don't Dance with the Devil

"William Harvey, the CIA man in charge of assassination . . . was directly involved with us [in illegal drug experimentation]. He was White's compatriot. Harvey was very much interested in it . . ."

—Federal Bureau of Narcotics agent Ira Feldman

In the early 1950s, George Hunter White of the Federal Bureau of Narcotics was loaned to the CIA and became part of a program that secretly supplied drugs such as LSD to unsuspecting Americans without their consent. White was a logical choice because of his strong connection to organized crime and their many joint operations with the CIA. Involved with White in this drug program was the head of CIA's assassination squad, William Harvey. Another key person was FBN agent Jean Pierre Lafitte, who strongly ties to the Corsican Mafia, the American Mafia, and the CIA. Lafitte used several aliases, which make him a person of interest in the JFK assassination. Among the names he used were John Martino, who later admitted involvement in Kennedy's murder, and Hidell, a disclosure with tremendous import because it was the same alias Lee Oswald used in New Orleans in the summer of 1963. Lafitte also used the alias Jack Martin, the name of a man who worked out of Guy Banister's office in New Orleans, which Oswald frequented. These men were all connected. Including Jack Ruby, an informant for George Hunter White during the Kefauver Hearings into organized crime in 1950. The mysterious deaths of many mobsters before they had a chance to testify characterized the hearings. The CIA may have been responsible for each murder to ensure they could not disclose the Agency's relationship with the Mafia. How these agents and mobsters came together over a decade before Kennedy's murder is an integral part of the JFK assassination saga. Lee Harvey Oswald would cross paths with many of them in the years to come.

* * *

As previously described, Frank Costello became the acting boss of the Luciano crime family after Vito Genovese had to flee to Italy to escape a potential murder wrap. He worked with other mob families to expand organized crime's influence throughout the country. Costello managed gambling operations and casinos with Meyer Lansky, his brother Jake, and Carlos Marcello.[1]

Another old-time gangster was Thomas Lucchese, whose relationship with Luciano went back to the 1920s when they formed the 107th Street Gang in New York. In 1931, Lucchese organized a Mafia hit squad, including Vito Genovese, Albert Anastasia, Joe Adonis, and Bugsy Siegel. The 107th Street Gang was involved in the drug trade by the early 1940s. They smugged opium from Mexico into Texas, then processed it into heroin in New York. The operation suffered a setback in 1943 with "the arrest of 106 smugglers in Mexico, including several Germans, and the conviction of seventeen Mafia smugglers in the US."[2]

The head of the Federal Bureau of Narcotics, Harry Anslinger, could not connect top Mafia leaders to the drug smuggling bust, and Costello, Lansky, and Lucchese remained free. Undoubtedly, Luciano's relationship with the U.S. military at the time had something to do with this. For as long as the Mafia supported the war effort, they were immune from prosecution.

Meyer Lansky remained in charge of the family's financial interests, a significant portion of which was the distribution of heroin. The Caribbean, particularly Cuba, made up a large part of the syndicate's drug trade and gambling operations and suited Lansky just fine. He was aware of the benefits this tropical vacation paradise had to offer. During the 1930s, he had invested lucrative illegal gambling profits in the Caribbean on behalf of several northeastern organized crime bosses. By 1933, Lansky was living in the Miami Beach area, and on his own, he took control of the illegal off-track betting network and numerous hotels and casinos. With the intent of building on this success, he moved to Havana for three years. By the beginning of World War II, he owned the Hotel Nacional de Cuba's casino and leased the municipal racetrack from a reputable New York bank.

The scope of Lansky's operations became too much for one man to handle. So he began to delegate day-to-day management to local mobsters. Lansky chose Santo Trafficante, Sr. to run his Florida operations. Lansky was so impressed with Trafficante that he added Havana to Trafficante's responsibilities when he returned from Cuba. Cuba embraced the arrival of organized crime and the money their illegal operations brought to the small island nation, as Havana became the most important transit point in Luciano's European heroin network.[3]

As described in Chapter Four, the United States deported Lucky Luciano to Italy. Still, he needed to meet with his underlings in Cuba to discuss the details of the Helliwell/WCC/ Corsican drug operation the Mafia was entering into with U.S. intelligence. It violated his parole agreement, but we can assume the CIA was aware of what he was up to and conveniently looked the other way.[4] Luciano secretly entered Cuba on October 29, 1946. With the help of Meyer Lansky, Frank Costello, and Bugsy Siegel, he began paying off local officials so he could remain in the country. He intended to stay in Cuba indefinitely, or at least long enough to complete the business behind his trip. It was not long before his presence became known to the FBN, who was aware that members of the New York mob had brought money to Havana to finance Luciano and that Lansky pulled ". . . all the strings he could to keep his friend in Cuba." Lansky reportedly met with ex-President Batista to remind the dictator of the "enormous bribes they had been paying him over the years and demanding his cooperation."[5]

Corruption in Cuba had been a concern for quite some time. The U.S. ambassador to Cuba, Spruille Braden, had reported in 1942 that "Illicit dealings and corruption . . . are fully operative in Cuba . . . Even those in the president's immediate circle, and some members of the cabinet . . . have a direct interest in the profits realized from such practices."[6]

Luciano's arrival concerned the FBN's Anslinger. "I had received a preliminary report [that] stated that Luciano had already become friendly with . . . high Cuban officials," Anslinger reported. "Luciano had developed a full-fledged plan which envisioned the Caribbean as his center of operations . . . [and] Cuba was to be . . . the center of all international narcotics operations."[7]

Anslinger's information was correct, and in December 1946, Luciano met with the prominent Mafia families in Havana to discuss the mob's involvement in the international heroin trade and Cuban gambling. Lamar Waldron reported in *The Hidden History of the JFK Assassination*, ". . . that [the heroin] network originally extended 'from Marseilles, France, through Cuba to Florida,' and from its Tampa base, the Trafficante family helped supply heroin to cities ranging from New York to Chicago. In the 1950s [Carlos] Marcello's organization was part of that network, bringing in heroin through ports in Louisiana and Texas, as well as across the border from Mexico."[8]

The timing of the meeting coincided with the onset of the Helliwell/WCC/ Corsican operation, which was the real reason Luciano wanted the see the mobsters in Havana. With an international drug operation already in existence, it made sense that Luciano would involve the major players he already had in place, and he needed to explain how they would handle the new setup. In the future, Helliwell would reportedly engage in other business dealings with Meyer Lansky, which confirmed this was true.[9] In any event, after some discussion, the operation was approved.

In charge of the American portion of the French Connection heroin network would be Trafficante Sr.

With so many leading mobsters in Havana, it became impossible for Luciano to keep his presence hidden from U.S. authorities. As a result, the U.S. pressured the Cuban government to deport him to Italy, and the FBN placed an embargo on the export of all medicinal drugs to Cuba while Luciano remained there. By

February 1947, Luciano was labeled an "undesirable" by the Cuban government. The Cubans returned Luciano to Italy on March 19, where he was arrested and put in prison. The Italian government set him free a month later, and he resumed his involvement with the American Mafia, albeit from overseas. In about four months, Luciano had secretly traveled to Cuba, had hastily called a meeting of Mafia bosses, and the Cubans deported him to Italy shortly after that. He was then imprisoned for a month and then quietly released. The speed by which all this occurred suggests it was preplanned, with the blessing of U.S. intelligence, and Luciano accomplished what he had set out to do. It was to obtain the approval of the Helliwell plan from all the mob families so the operation could move forward. The relationship between the American mob and U.S. intelligence remained intact. More importantly, the protection from prosecution, which the mobsters received by prolonging this unholy alliance, continued as well.[10]

* * *

Ex-OSS officer George Hunter White first met mobster Johnny Roselli while working as a newspaper reporter in the Los Angeles area in the early 1930s. A leading organized crime figure in the post-World War II era, Roselli's relevance to our narrative comes from the relationship he maintained with the CIA throughout the years, from the beginning of the Cold War to well past the assassination of JFK. Among other things, Roselli reportedly took part in a CIA-backed coup in Guatemala in 1954. Along with Santo Trafficante, Jr. and Sam Giancana, he was one of the mobsters involved in CIA attempts to assassinate Fidel Castro. Roselli was somewhat of a fixture around the CIA station in Florida that waged a secret war against Castro, referred to as "Colonel Roselli."

Most importantly, Roselli was extremely close to William Harvey, the legendary head of the CIA's assassination program, ZR/Rifle. They would remain close until their deaths, which occurred around the same time by coincidence or design. Harvey died of an apparent heart attack on June 9, 1976, but this does not eliminate murder as the probable cause of death. As for Roselli, his decomposed, dismembered body was discovered floating in Dumfounding Bay, near Miami, on August 9, 1976 (The exact date of his death is unknown). By the time of his death, Roselli had testified three times before congressional investigators regarding his involvement with the CIA the last April. Before he went missing, he reportedly had dinner with Santo Trafficante Jr., which, considering the timing, probably sealed his fate.

Also curious is that in June of the previous year, right before he was to testify before the Senate Intelligence Committee, Sam Giancana was shot to death in the basement of his home. A month later, Jimmy Hoffa disappeared.[11] Both were close to Roselli and may have had a connection to the JFK assassination. Just two more in a series of seemingly endless coincidences.

George White got to know Johnny Roselli and other organized crime figures early on, and as the years went by, they frequently worked together. "I don't dislike criminals," White said in 1971. "When I used to hang around with gangster types, I had very good times in their company." [12]

White eventually became an agent for the U.S. Immigration Service's Border Patrol, where he worked undercover in towns along the Mexican border. He frequently crossed paths with federal narcotics agents in his work, which led him to join the FBN in 1936. Before long, the FBN transferred him to Manhattan, where he served under Garland Williams, whose job was to destroy the numerous international drug cartels operating in New York City. [13]

When the United States entered World War II, White joined the OSS, as did FBN agents Charles Siragusa and Jean-Pierre Lafitte. The OSS sent White to Camp X for training in guerilla warfare, covert action, assassination, and eventually trained future CIA notables such as Richard Helms, Frank Wisner, James Angleton, Lyman Kirkpatrick, Thomas Karamessines, and William Colby.

Reportedly, White, and other ex-FBN OSS agents, were involved in Operation Underworld. This top-secret project involved Lucky Luciano, including his extradition from prison and deportation to Italy, confirmed by ex-OSS agent Ira Feldman. [14] "In the OSS, he [White] made a lot of connections," Feldman said. "White's supposedly the guy who got Luciano out of the can . . ." If true, he had to have been aware that Luciano worked with the military for the remainder of the war. [15]

George White became FBN branch chief in Chicago after World War II. He immediately met with numerous Mafia leaders across the country, culminating in a meeting with Santo Trafficante Sr. on September 3, 1945. Why they met is unknown, but White's diary reported that drugs were being supplied "by Mafia agents in Tampa, Florida, who received the smuggled drugs from Marseilles, via Havana." Since Anslinger already knew that Luciano, Costello, and Lansky were in bed with U.S. intelligence and were essentially untouchable, White must have been aware of this. Trafficante probably told White that a Mafia/ Marseilles/Havana drug operation involving U.S. intelligence was being put together (the Havana meeting with Luciano would occur the following year). Since White's past association with Luciano may have been why he and Trafficante met, it made sense. Recall from Chapter Two, that while a member of OSS in the summer of 1943, White "attended several Mafia Plan meetings, including an August excursion into Chinatown [New York City] with James J. Angleton, who was soon to become chief of OSS's X-2 operations in Rome . . ." The OSS was recruiting organized crime figures to perform assassinations on behalf of Division 19. [16]

The Chinatown meeting occurred when Anslinger tried to connect Frank Costello to the 107th Street Gang drug bust in Mexico. And according to Douglas Valentine in *The Strength of the Wolf,* "through March 1943, White and Ulius Amoss, [the OSS officer in charge of Mideast operations], investigated 'the frequent tie-up' between smuggling and spying, until the OSS fired Amoss for importing 'an ex-convict from the United States for the purposes of expert assassination.'" If anyone knew assassins, it was White, but OSS security officer Robert Delaney cleared him of any wrongdoing. Amoss was expendable, but White's underworld connections may have protected him. In April, he met again with Delaney to discuss what he termed in his diary the "Mafia Plan," which was the Luciano/Helliwell/WCC operation to import drugs into the U.S.[17]

Rome played an essential role in executing the Luciano/Helliwell plan. The OSS had located Angleton there, and he undoubtedly was aware of what the project entailed. And as stated above, Angleton already had a relationship with George White, while Trafficante worked closely with Meyer Lansky in Havana and elsewhere. It seemed to confirm that the meeting between White and Trafficante was related to this operation.[18]

An FBI memo supports this possibility. It referred to a *New York Mirror* article on March 15, 1951, which stated that White had been "conferring with [CIA agent] Newbold Morris . . ." and "that White was being loaned by the Treasury Department [FBN] to work as an investigator for Morris on a special phase of corruption. White, it was said, would attempt to uncover the links between the underworld and the government officials . . ."[19]

Consider also that by this time, Santo Trafficante, Sr., who died in 1954, had his organized crime responsibilities taken over by his son Santo Trafficante, Jr. White would also meet with the younger Santo numerous times throughout the 1950s. Each Trafficante developed a relationship with White adds credence to the idea that the mobsters kept White up to date on what was transpiring with the so-called "Mafia Plan."[20]

White's association with the mob in the Mafia Plan led to an increased involvement between himself and the CIA, primarily the testing of illegal drugs on unsuspecting victims. A letter to J. Edgar Hoover dated July 2, 1953, stated that "A confidential informant of this office advised . . . that his former supervisor in the Bureau of Narcotics, George White . . . has become associated with CIA in an 'ultra-secret' assignment as a consultant. White and CIA have rented dual apartments at 81 Bedford Street, New York City." The apartment "is being used by CIA . . . [to take] motion pictures through an x-ray mirror of the activities in the former apartment." The letter continued that, "White indicated to the informant that no one in the Bureau of Narcotics or CIA is aware of this apartment . . . , except Commissioner Anslinger of the Narcotics Bureau and top officials of CIA."[21]

A follow-up FBI memorandum dated August 5, 1953, reported that "George White, under the name Morgan Hall, leased two adjoining apartments . . . at 81 Bedford Street . . . Informant is of the opinion . . . that the setting up of these quarters . . . could very well be that the individuals meeting Hall might be compromised, through the medium of the installed equipment and bedroom facilities to the extent that they would become sources of information . . . the informant's opinion is partially based on the fact that CIA has been experimenting with drugs, such as 'knock-out drops' and a type of 'truth serum [sic] capsule' designed to 'loosen one's tongue.'"[22]

Then, another FBI Memorandum dated August 14, 1953, reported that ". . . two samples of the drugs . . . were secured and turned over to the NYO [New York office] by [redacted] with which CIA and White are experimenting. The larger of the vials is believed to be 'knock-out' drops, and the smaller glass sealed container allegedly holds 'truth serum [sic].'"[23]

Considering White's close ties to organized crime, it all suggests a relationship throughout the 1950s involving White, CIA, Trafficante Jr., and likely other mobsters, which means the relationship between the Mafia and CIA, in existence since World War II, continued to expand. And the FBI had become aware of this and knew what White was up to, which involved CIA experimenting with illegal drugs within the continental U.S., which was supposed to be off-limits.

White's interest in illicit drugs began during his OSS days when the spy organization was trying to develope a "Truth Drug" derived from marijuana, which White experimented with on unsuspecting human subjects. In New York in May 1943, around the time he was in the city with James Angleton, White tested "Truth Drugs" on August del Grazio, the manager of a heroin factory in Istanbul, whose connection to Corsican and Mafia drug smugglers was well known. According to author John Marks, Del Grazio revealed that "the ins and outs of the drug trade" were "so sensitive that the CIA deleted it from OSS documents it released thirty-four years later." It adds credibility to the possibility that White became aware of a potential Luciano/ Helliwell operation as early as 1943, possibly from Angleton, then approached Trafficante two years later after leaving OSS to continue his investigation. An FBI internal memo dated February 28, 1952, provided confirmation. It reported that "On June 2, 1943, E.P. Coffey of the [FBI's] Bureau Laboratory attended a meeting . . . of the National Academy of Sciences." The group was "looking into the possibility of using a truth serum [sic] saturated in cigarettes on a narcotics gangster who called at his apartment in New York City the past week. He described the effects of the drug, indicating it removed any apparent restraint on the gangster who spoke freely in his presence."[24]

Meanwhile, in 1950 several U.S. soldiers captured during the Korean War claimed they were members of a secret bacterial warfare unit. Investigators would determine the Chinese probably brainwashed the soldiers during their incarceration. It created a sense of urgency, for the U.S. feared they were way behind the Communists in mind-control experimentation. It prompted the CIA to research various psychiatric hospitals, universities, and pharmaceutical companies with whom the Agency had a relationship to close the gap in this potentially critical area. Within a year, the investigation also involved the FBN. They began providing the CIA with different drugs to be used on unsuspecting American citizens.[25]

Considering White's previous OSS involvement in drug experimentation, joining the CIA in the mind control endeavors described above was natural. OSS veteran Ira Feldman was interviewed by author Dick Russell. Russell wrote that after the war, "Feldman was involved in covert testing of drugs, primarily LSD, posing as a racketeer to get prostitutes to lure unsuspecting clients to a CIA safe house, where their drinks were laced with strange concoctions. It had begun during a conversation with [George] White, which Feldman had described this way to journalist [Richard] Stratton [*of Spin Magazine*]: 'I said, 'Why the hell do you want to test mind-bending?' He [White] said, 'Have you heard of *The Manchurian Candidate* [a movie about the brainwashing of an unsuspecting individual to murder an American politician]?' I know about *The Manchurian Candidate*. In fact, I read the book. 'Well,' White said, 'that's why we have to test these drugs, to find out if they . . . brainwash people.' He says, 'If we can find out just how good this stuff works, you'll be doing a great deal for your country.'"[26]

William Harvey, the CIA man in charge of assassination, was another Feldman contact. "He was directly involved with us, yes," said Feldman. "He was White's compatriot. I met him through White, who must have told him what we were involved in. Harvey was very much interested in it . . ."[27]

George White was involved with Ulius Amoss to bring a mob assassin to the Middle East. With James Angleton, he recruited Mafia assassins for OSS through Division 19. The CIA then used White in drug experimentation operations with William Harvey, the head of ZR/RIFLE, CIA's assassination program. To say White was well connected to "murder and mayhem," as he called it, would be an understatement.

Then there was mobster and CIA asset John Roselli, whom the Agency involved in the Castro assassination plots. According to Feldman, he was also one of White's informants. "More than once, White sent me to the airport to pick up Roselli and bring him into the office." Without question, the relationship between organized crime and the CIA was strong. White, Harvey, and Roselli were in the middle of everything, including ties to anyone remotely associated with an assassination operation. And this started at least ten years before Kennedy's assassination.

White first met Dr. Sidney Gottlieb, the research scientist in charge of CIA's LSD-testing program, in May 1952 (They would work together until White's retirement in 1965).[28] They met again in Boston later that month, and on June 9 in New Haven, Connecticut. For the New Haven trip, White's "special employee," Jean-Pierre Lafitte, picked up Gottleib at Idlewild Airport (Kennedy Airport today). The three men would discuss LSD for the first time, and Gottlieb was surprised that White was already familiar with it. According to White's diary, they met again on October 20 in Washington D.C. to "prepare cigs," laced with a drug to test on unsuspecting individuals. Ten days later, White was back in Washington to brief numerous CIA officials, including James Angleton, on what he and Gottlieb were doing.[29]

The CIA formally designated White's safe house as MKULTRA Subproject 3 on May 21, 1953. According to an Agency memo, the operation "will involve the realistic testing of certain research and development items of interest . . . not suited to ordinary laboratory conditions . . . The [safe house will] provide facilities to fill this intermediate requirement." Morgan Hall, an alias often used by White, was the person who rented the apartment. The CIA memo continued that, ". . . White, of course, is interested in narcotics and reputed to have contacts in the underworld and among seamen who are in or on the fringe of the narcotics business . . . he [can] get these people to his apartment at 81 Bedford Street where he tries to elicit information." CIA then admitted they were aware of what White was doing. "White gives drugs to these unaware individuals . . ." to facilitate the gathering of information. He then reports on "what drug was administered [by him] and gives his judgment as to success attained."[30]

Jean-Pierre Lafitte was another person of interest. Along with George White, Lafitte served in the OSS during World War II. After the war, their first known interaction came in 1951 when White needed help regarding Frenchman Joseph Orsini, an ex-acquaintance of Lafitte's from Marseilles, arrested in New York City for dealing heroin. They would often cross paths following that, for Lafitte also had associates in the mob, including Santo Trafficante, Jr. and Meyer Lansky. Still, it was to the Corsican Mafia to whom he was most closely connected. According to H.P Albarelli, Jr., in *A Terrible Mistake, The Murder of Frank Olson and the CIA's Secret Cold War Experiments*:

> Lafitte was well acquainted with Amleto Battisti y Lora, a wealthy Corsican who had come to Cuba via Uruguay. He was referred to as a Mafia kingpin. He was a member of Cuba's House of Representatives and operated Havana's luxurious Hotel Sevilla Biltmore . . . within which . . . Meyer Lansky held a silent partnership . . . He also operated two casinos in Cuba and several bolita gaming operations in Florida, in partnership with Santo Trafficante, Jr . . . Lafitte had known and worked with Battisti in France, where the two had teamed up with [Corsican mobster] Francois Spirito to operate an extensive white slavery and prostitution ring . . .[31]

"Battisti was also very much involved in drug trafficking," Albarelli continued, and "it was Battisti who convinced Lucky Luciano . . . that Cuba was the ideal location from which to establish his main heroin distribution route into North America . . ."

Corsican Paul Mondoloni was another Lafitte contact who, along with fellow Corsican Jean Jehan, was behind the French Connection international heroin operation. The CIA thought Jehan was the owner of the Bedford Street building where the George White safe house was located, according to an Agency document released in 1976. Mondoloni and another Corsican drug dealer named Antoine D'Agostino supplied Lansky with heroin, and Lafitte brokered many deals involving shipments to Lansky's dealers.[32]

Lafitte was playing both sides of the fence at the time, acting as a government informant and undercover operative while simultaneously dealing drugs throughout the world. It was typical behavior for many mobsters, and at times it is hard to differentiate between the good guys and the bad guys, including George White, Jean-Pierre Lafitte, CIA, FBN, and a host of others. And that is the point. By the early 1950s, mobsters, intelligence agents, and law enforcement officers were increasingly coming together because they needed each other—agents needed the Mafia so they could maintain plausible deniability; mobsters required the agents to protect them from prosecution.

John Martino's name is in multiple George White address and datebooks and Lafitte's notes concerning his many trips to Florida and Cuba. It is potentially significant since Martino was a mob-connected courier who delivered money on the mob's behalf and later claimed to be involved in the assassination of JFK. He had CIA connections, worked with anti-Castro Cubans, William Pawley and Santo Trafficante, Jr., electronically fixing machines for Trafficante at the Cuban casinos the mobster managed to maximize profits. Martino was arrested in Havana in July 1959 after Castro came to power, and by then, Lafitte had known him for at least seven years.

Using the alias Jean Pierre Martin, Lafitte visited Martino in a Cuban prison on at least one occasion in 1961. A George White notation found in an address book tracking Lafitte's activities provided this information. According to another item in White's diary, mob-connected FBN agent Charles Siragusa visited Martino in the same Cuban prison. The notation read: "Siragusa re Martino Cuba." What makes this interesting is that the year before, the CIA had approached Siragusa about contacting mobsters who could be employed to assassinate Fidel Castro. Two of those were John Roselli and Santo Trafficante, Jr.; Castro also imprisoned the latter simultaneous to Martino. Another person who visited Trafficante while behind bars was none other than Jack Ruby (We will discuss Ruby's role in detail in Volume Two).[33]

In 1969 Lafitte was arrested by the FBI in New Orleans but was quietly released within weeks, for the FBI also had a relationship with Lafitte that they preferred to keep hidden. And according to FBI documents, during their six-year "search" for Lafitte before his arrest, he used dozens of aliases, including Louis Romano, Frank Maceo, Paul Maceo, Jean Martin, Peter Martin, John Martin, Jack Martin, Paul Martino, Paul Mertz, Jean Mondoloni, Louis Hidell, Paul Jehan, Jean Jehan, Louis Mancuso, Jacques Montaine, Peter Orsini, and Louis Tabet.

Some of these names are familiar to us and were people with whom Lafitte interacted and knew. People such as Martino, Mondoloni, Jehan, and Orsini, and considering John Martino's claim that he was involved in the JFK assassination, Lafitte's use of his name was especially significant. We can safely deduce that all the people on the list were related to illicit activity and operations with which Lafitte was involved. They are all revealing, but the name Hidell causes alarm bells to go off because this is also the alias Lee Harvey Oswald used in the year leading up to the assassination. The rifle found in the Texas School Book Depository, the alleged murder weapon, was ordered by someone using the name A. Hidell and delivered to Oswald's Post Office box. After his arresr, Alek James Hidell's name was on a false military Selective Service Notice of Classification card found in Oswald's wallet. And in New Orleans, where Oswald established a branch of the pro-Castro Fair Place for Cuba Committee in 1963, the name Hidell was on membership cards he handed out.

There was also one other person who claimed to have used the alias Hidell. That was Richard Case Nagell, the U.S. intelligence officer who knew Oswald was involved in the assassination plot before it happened. Nagell had himself arrested by shooting a gun into the ceiling of a bank in El Paso, Texas, two months before the assassination so that he would be behind bars with an airtight alibi when the assassination occurred. It is relevant that when arrested, Nagell had a copy of Oswald's forged Selective Service Notice of Classification card described above in his possession, most likely because he wanted authorities to know who he was involved with and why he had himself arrested.

In July 1979, while trying to obtain his past CIA files through the Freedom of Information Act, Nagell received a letter from the CIA asking for any aliases he may have used to assist them in their search. On July 18, Nagell replied with a notarized affidavit that stated that "among other fictitious names ". . . Alex Hidell [and] Aleksei Hidell . . ." were aliases he had used in the past.[34]

In the 1970s, an officer with the 112th Military Intelligence Group in San Antonio, Lieutenant Colonel Robert Jones, testified before the House Select Committee on Assassination (HSCA) that on the afternoon of the assassination, he received a call from Dallas "advising that an A.J. Hidell had been arrested." The caller did not mention the name Oswald. Jones located the name Hidell in his files, which cross-referenced with a different file on Lee Harvey Oswald. Years later, the 112th Military Intelligence Group told the HSCA that the Oswald/Hidell files were destroyed as a matter of routine. How convenient.[35]

When New Orleans District Attorney Jim Garrison investigated the Kennedy assassination in 1968, he spoke to Richard Case Nagell. Garrison notes about his conversations with Nagel included the following: "A number of people were using the name Hidel[l]," which seemed to have been an accurate assessment.[36]

There were other oddities. New Orleans police arrested Lafitte at the Plimsoll Club, where he worked as the manager chef in the World Trade Mart building, where Clay Shaw was the director. Shaw was the man who Garrison tried in court for conspiracy in the JFK assassination. And according to author Albarelli, Lafitte worked at William B. Reily Coffee Company in New Orleans. Lee Harvey Oswald also worked at Reily from May to July 1963, simultaneously as Lafitte. Since both men used the same Hidell alias, it is logical to assume that they were working together on some operation at that time, around when they had the FPCC handbills printed FPCC, just months before the JFK assassination.[37]

It also makes sense that Lafitte's other aliases had a connection to his drug and intelligence network of associates. These were all Corsicans, America Mafioso, and CIA-connected agents and traveled in the same circles as Lafitte. They were all connected to the Helliwell/CIA/Mafia/Corsican drug operation, which suggests that what Lafitte was doing with Oswald was also connected to this operation. Perhaps Oswald was not aware of what he had become involved with, for his activities centered around New Orleans and the connections he had made there.

Oswald's connection to New Orleans brings us to Lafitte's other aliases, namely, John and Jack Martin. It is an essential piece of Oswald's puzzle because a detective worked out of Guy Banister's office at 544 Camp Street, named Jack Martin, who associated with Banister, assassination suspect David Ferrie, and Lee Harvey Oswald in the summer of 1963. Banister pistol-whipped Martin on the night of the assassination, prompting Martin to publicly accuse Banister and Ferrie of involvement in the assassination plot. But there was more to Jack Martin. As Joan Mellon described in *A Farewell to Justice*, during Jim Garrison's investigation, there was a report which involved "' the most Reverend Christopher Maria Stanley' of Louisville . . . who was once wrapped in the cloak of a marginal religious sect, as were Ferrie and Jack Martin . . . reported to the FBI that 'John J. Martin' had been associated with Ferrie, and that Martin claimed ' . . . to have worked for CIA.'" CIA quickly responded "that Jack Martin of New Orleans, also known as 'John J. Martin of Louisville,' was not their acknowledged former employee, 'Joseph H. Martin.'" Why the confusion over so many Martins?

As Mellon writes, "Then something strange happened. In the course of their denial that Joseph and Jack were the same person, CIA stopped investigating the identity of the New Orleans Jack Martin. 'OS [Office of Security] does NOT believe identical nor do I,' writes CIA's Scott Miler, following up on a request from one J.L. of Counter Intelligence's Research and Analysis . . . 'Have agreed with OS no further action and think this proper.'"

According to Mellon, "Like the Jack of New Orleans, Joseph was given to engaging in 'rambling talk.' Joseph made habitual unwelcome telephone calls to the CIA Watch Office. Once he even called the Director of Central Intelligence . . . Even as in New Orleans Jack Martin experienced a stint at the psychiatric ward of Charity Hospital, Joseph was described by CIA as being of 'unsound mind.'" "These two Martins were . . . interchangeable . . . Joseph was alcoholic; Jack was alcoholic. A Roman Catholic, Joseph sneered that he 'wouldn't vote for Kennedy.'"

Jack was linked to several people involved in the assassination, among them Oswald, David Ferrie . . . and Guy Banister. Jack and Joseph even looked alike. They shared a puny physique and a small mustache."[38]

When the Church Committee investigated the JFK assassination in the 1970s, the CIA's Office of Security (OS) denied them access to certain documents about Oswald. There was also a second group of records that the OS denied them access to, which referred to "Jack Martin" or "John G. Martin" or "Joseph James Martin." Of all the potential assassination suspects, the CIA denied information to the Church Committee pertaining only to Lee Harvey Oswald and Jack Martin. There was something about the Agency's relationship to these two men that they dared not disclose, and it makes Lafitte's use of Martin's name as an alias that much more suspicious.

Regarding the Hidell alias, many people may have shared the same phony name, as Nagell told Garrison, and in 1998, the CIA released a document that confirmed this was typical. It reported there were CIA operations where several people used the name "Jack Martin." CIA revealed there were three 201 (personnel) files on different people with variations "Jack Martin," but none of them was the actual active CIA employee, "Joseph James Martin," or so they said.

"These same three Jack Martins," Mellon continued, "all bearing different middle initials, were listed on another CIA document, along with their AINS numbers or Internal CIA File Subject Identification Numbers. AINS were 'Agency Identification Numbers,' CIA explained, 'not necessarily suggesting an employee relationship . . . '" "In contrast was the EIN or 'Employee Identification Number.' On the list of those with AINS in the security files were: Jack Martin; Jack M. Martin; Jack S. Martin (reflecting in the New Orleans' Jack's 'real name,' Edward Stewart Suggs); and a Lawrence J. Martin."

Mellon writes: "While the Agency might not have technically classified them as 'employees,' those with AINS numbers . . . might have been [CIA] 'assets' or 'contacts.' Among those listed on the same 'smoking gun' document with AINS numbers were such known CIA-connected figures as Richard Case Nagell, Frank Fiorini [aka Frank Sturgis]; Cesar Diosdado; who, while working for Customs was paid by CIA; and George de Mohrenschildt. Another of those to use the Martin alias was Watergate burglar and CIA operative Virgilio R. Gonzalez."[39]

The names of Nagell, Fiorini, and de Mohrenschildt, three potentially prominent people in the Lee Harvey Oswald saga, all listed in the same CIA document, are critical. All three having an association with the CIA, and the document also pertained to Jack Martin, which speaks volumes. There had to have been a connection here. We have Richard Case Nagell, Jean Lafitte, and Lee Harvey Oswald using the alias Hidell. Lafitte and Oswald worked together at Reily in the summer of 1963 in New Orleans. Oswald associated with Jack Martin at the same time in New Orleans, out of Guy Banister's office.

Meanwhile, Lafitte also used the alias Jack Martin, at the same time he was working with Oswald at Reily. Recall that Nagell had Oswald's phony identification card in his possession when he fired shots in the bank in El Paso. When the police arrested Oswald in Dallas, he had the same bogus I.D. card in his wallet. Meanwhile, Nagell and de Mohrenschildt were close to Oswald, and the CIA admits to having a relationship with each man. As we will see, there is also evidence that future Watergate burglar and CIA operative Fiorini/Sturgis had contact with Oswald in the fall of 1963, right before the assassination. It is all explosive information that seems to expose the intelligence network with whom Oswald was involved.

It is also worth noting that the FBI made a concerted effort after the assassination to conceal a relationship between Oswald and the activities associated with 544 Camp Street in New Orleans, the address of Banister's office, and where Martin would get to know Oswald. In the summer of 1963, the police arrested Oswald because of an altercation that occurred while he handed out pro-Castro leaflets on the streets of New Orleans. While in custody, Oswald covertly let authorities know he was associated with the radical-right wing Banister's group. He gave an FBI agent a booklet entitled *The Crime Against Cuba,* which had Banister's 544 Camp Street address stamped on its inside cover. The FBI knew that Banister used people such as Oswald to infiltrate pro-Castro and Communists groups. And Oswald knew that the FBI would have concluded he was handing out pro-Castro leaflets on Banister's behalf at the time of his arrest. However, the FBI deceived the Warren Commission when they provided them with Guy Banister's address. The FBI said Banister's business was 531 Lafayette Street, which was around the corner and provided an alternate entrance to the same 544 Camp Street building. However, it was not the address Banister used, and the Commission was unaware that both the Camp Street and Lafayette Street addresses pertained to the same building. However, they did know about the stamped, pro-Castro booklet and would have connected Oswald to Banister had the FBI provided them with the correct 544 Camp Street address of Banister's office. It was a purposeful deception to protect the anonymity of Banister and anyone else associated with his office, which included Jack Martin. Consider that the FBI also admitted knowing Jack Martin, calling him a "nut." The FBI went to great lengths to prevent the Warren Commission from learning the truth.[40]

Albarelli writes in *A Terrible Mistake* that Lafitte knew Frank Sturgis and William Morgan. He mentions them regarding Cuba. Lafitte's opening line in his notebook about the men and the Cuban revolution states: "Never was there a more brave and fascinating (some would argue foolhardy and opportunistic) band of men than those I encountered in Cuba during the budding revolution there."[41]

Lafitte's connection to Sturgis and the affairs in Cuba involved him with many CIA figures during the late 1950s who later admitted, or are suspected of, having a link to, JFK's assassination. At the time, the CIA operatives in Cuba, including

Sturgis and Morgan, were involved in attempts to overthrow Castro. The author will discuss this in detail in Volume Two. However, it is important to mention now because Lafitte's trail of contacts left in his wake is worth considering at this point in our discussion. In summary, in 1959/1960, he associated with a CIA and paramilitary team in Cuba that may have later participated in JFK's murder. In 1963 he was in New Orleans and appeared to have had a relationship with Lee Oswald and Jack Martin, out of Guy Banister's office. A CIA document lists him and Richard Case Nagell, John Martino, and George de Mohrenschildt, all connected to Oswald. Nagell, Lafitte and Oswald all used the Hidell alias. Lafitte was also involved in illicit drug experimentation and OSS and OPC assassination teams with George White. To say Lafitte is a person of interest would be an understatement.

Finally, let us consider the name Mertz, another Lafitte alias. The real Michael Mertz was a French Resistance leader in World War II, a former French intelligence agent, and a drug smuggler with the Corsican Mafia. He associated with Joseph Orsini (another Lafitte alias), and the two men, along with Santo Trafficante Jr. and Carlos Marcello, were involved in a drug bust at Fort Benning, Georgia. A Mertz partner in his heroin network was Paul Mondoloni (also a Lafitte alias), who, along with Trafficante, was connected to the Luciano/Helliwell/WCC operation.[42]

Ever since a declassified CIA document titled "Jean SOUETRE aka Michel ROUX aka Michael MERTZ" was released in 1977, Michael Mertz has been a Kennedy assassination person of interest. "On 5 March [deleted] the FBI advised that the French had [deleted] the Legal Attaché in Paris and also the [redacted] had queried the Bureau in New York City concerning subject stating that he had been expelled from the U.S. at Fort Worth or Dallas 48 hours after the assassination. He was in Fort Worth on [the] morning of 22 November and in Dallas in the afternoon. The French believe that he was expelled to either Mexico or Canada . . ."[43]

Souetre was a member of the OAS, a group of French generals and soldiers that rebelled against France after de Gaulle granted Algeria its independence (to be discussed in Chapter Twelve). The OAS tried to assassinate de Gaulle multiple times, and on one occasion, Mertz, who had infiltrated OAS, thwarted the plot. Authorities do not know if Souetre was in Dallas at the time of the assassination or if it was Mertz impersonating him, as some allege. The latter is a possibility, for Mertz may have used Souetre as an alias to deflect attention away from the actual assassins. Or, maybe it was Lafitte, using the name Mertz, which he was known to do. Whoever it was, the U.S. did not want it known that he was in Dallas on the day the Kennedy assassination took place. Whoever the Frenchman was, he was quickly taken out of harm's way by military aircraft, no less, before his presence became known. The fact that Lafitte used the Mertz alias only adds to the intrigue.

They say where there's smoke; there's fire. We have here a potential inferno, for there is too much going on with multiple aliases and connections to Oswald for it all to be just a coincidence. We will revisit many of these names as our narrative moves forward.

* * *

With their relationship to U.S. intelligence ever increasing as the decade of the 1950s began, organized crime had a right to feel protected from public scrutiny and prosecution. Unfortunately for them, not everyone got the memo. In 1950, the Senate Special Committee to Investigate Organized Crime in Interstate Commerce, chaired by Democratic Senator Ester Kefauver, targeted national crime figures like Frank Costello and Carlos Marcello, whom Kefauver called "the evil genius of organized crime in New Orleans." Networks televised the Senate hearings held in fourteen cities, with over six hundred witnesses called to testify. It was a noteworthy event, as the nation received its first glimpse of the Mafia being questioned under oath by an investigative committee.[44]

The FBI did not offer to help Kefauver's committee, primarily because J. Edgar Hoover was indebted to the mob. The Mafia paid for Hoover's annual vacations, various business arrangements, gambling debts, and other amenities for years. They also knew about Hoover's homosexuality, and there were reports they had compromising photos of Hoover involved with another man. So, it is not surprising that an investigation into organized crime, which threatened to destroy Hoover potentially, went forward without FBI support. Hoover, who still publicly professed that organized crime did not exist, claimed the Bureau was too busy saving the country from Communists to get involved with Kefauver. As a result, the committee turned to the FBN for help, and George White and Charles Siragusa became the committee's sole investigators. Their mandate was to show the extent of Mafia infiltration into American life and prove to Congress that organized crime existed. For like Hoover, many politicians still refused to admit this was the case.

George White quickly dispelled any doubts that an organized Mafia existed, as described by Douglas Valentine in *The Strength of the Wolf.* White connected ". . . [Vincent] Mangano warlord Joe Adonis to Frank Costello. . . . produced documents linking gambling czar Frank Erickson to the Democratic Party, legal gambling establishments, and politicians in Florida, thus paving the way for the Committee's hearings in the Sunshine State. Santo Trafficante in Tampa was linked to fourteen murders over twenty years, including the June 1950 murder of James Lumia . . . [a] potential witness the Committee intended to hear from. Tampa's police chief told the Committee that the Mafia had a standard operating procedure for murder, which included the importation of hired killers from out of town and setting up patsies to take the fall."[45]

James Lumia was not the only potential witness to suffer an untimely death. Phil Mangano was murdered in April 1951, shot multiple times. A woman found his body while she was fishing in Jamaica Bay, Brooklyn. Around the same time, his brother rother Vincent disappeared. They were not the only ones prevented from testifying:

- Kansas City enforcer Charles Binaggio was shot and killed on April 5, 1950.
- A Chicago Police Department detective turned mob reporter, William Drury was shot and killed in his garage on September 25, 1950.
- Willie Moretti was shot and killed on October 4, 1951, in a Cliffside Park, NJ restaurant.[46]

There is no doubt someone killed these men to prevent them from testifying, but it may not have been the Mafia that was responsible. For U.S. intelligence was equally motivated to silence these mobsters to ensure the ongoing relationship between the intelligence community and organized crime remained hidden. Douglas Valentine wondered, "were crime's new patrons in the U.S. intelligence . . . weeding out troublesome Mafiosi? The master spies certainly had the capability; they even had their own hit team under Colonel Boris Pash [See Chapter Four] . . . Is it possible that Pash's hit team murdered Moretti, and perhaps other alumni of the Luciano Project, to prevent the Kefauver Committee from uncovering the Mafia's ties to the espionage establishment—to people like Kefauver's close friend William Donovan, whose law firm provided the Committee with several staff members? Though not widely disseminated, this theory has a lot to recommend it: as Salvatore Vizzini—an FBN agent with solid CIA connections—says so succinctly, 'Starting around 1947, a lot of Mafia hits weren't.'"[47]

Moretti's murder was maybe the most suspicious. At a public hearing held on December 13, 1950, he told the committee, "Yeah, sure, I know George White for a long time. George is a swell fellow. He all but admitted he was White's source into the inner workings of the Mafia the committee was looking to investigate. White had already stated he had a 'pipeline' to the 'inner circle' of four Mafia bosses 'who passed on murder requests from the underworld and occasionally commissioned a Mafia enforcement ring to do the killing.'"[48]

New Orleans crime boss Carlos Marcello testified on January 25, 1951. He appeared at the hearings accompanied by his attorney, G. Wray Gill, who also had a working relationship with Guy Banister and David Ferrie. Marcello took the Fifth so many times he was charged with contempt of Congress. The hearings showed that there was a connection between Marcello, Trafficante, and Costello.[49]

Marcello paid off enough local authorities in the corrupt city of New Orleans to ensure he was virtually untouchable. His only brush with the law was a 1938 arrest and conviction for selling marijuana, for which he served only ten months due to an arrangement he made at the time with Huey Long. When Marcello's prison term came to an end, Sam Carolla was the New Orleans crime boss. He had just closed a deal to put a thousand of Frank Costello's slot machines in New

Orleans (Mayor Fiorello La Guardia had banned the machines in New York City and Costello needed another location). Carolla gave Marcello ownership of a percentage of the slot machines to ensure that the operation was a profitable one for all. His ruthless approach to business and the money he was able to generate caught the attention of Costello. In 1945, when Costello and Meyer Lansky built an upscale gambling casino near New Orleans, called the Beverly Country Club, they made Marcello a 12.5 percent partner. And two years later, when authorities deported Sam Carolla to Sicily for a narcotics violation, Marcello was chosen to take over the Mafia in Louisiana. He continued to impress, prompting Costello and Lansky to establish a national underworld communications center and a clearinghouse for underworld money laundering in New Orleans.[50]

During the hearings, Kefauver recommended that Marcello's 1938 drug conviction warranted deportation. The Justice Department would hound Marcello for years. Things reached a breaking point in 1961 when a directive issued by Robert Kennedy, then the Attorney General, resulted in Marcello essentially being kidnapped. He was put on a plane and unceremoniously dropped in Guatemala shortly before the Bay of Pigs. Marcello survived the ordeal, but it was clear that his future was in jeopardy while Robert Kennedy was in charge.

Considering that Costello and Lansky were promoting Marcello's advancement, it is not surprising that Marcello also became involved with Santo Trafficante, Jr., since New Orleans was part of the heroin network that Trafficante ran through Havana and Mexico. Marcello was also involved in mob business in Havana, even though his lack of a passport and U.S. citizenship made this problematic. While in prison near the end of his life, Marcello befriended fellow prisoner Jack Van Laningham. Unknown to Marcello, Laningham was wearing a wire and working for the FBI. The FBI learned that "he [Marcello] was partners with a man that ran the Mafia in Florida, Trafficante, [and] they were [also] partners in a casino in Cuba, and made millions before Castro took over and shut them down." Long before the assassination, these two mob bosses were a lot closer than the official record suggests.[51]

The Kefauver Hearings put a dent in organized crime. In Chicago, they established a connection between the Mafia, Cook County Sheriff Dan Gilbert, and Democratic politicians. In general, it proved "that local law enforcement officials . . . were more important in setting [illegal] policy than the gamblers" and that the federal government was powerless to stop it. In New York, testimony linked Frank Costello to former New York City mayor William O'Dwyer, the same man involved with the Mafia in Italy during World War II, as described in Chapter Two. Costello was "linked to Luciano in Italy, Lansky in Las Vegas, Adonis in Florida, Fischetti in Chicago, dubious Texas oil deals, gambling joints in New Orleans, Tammany intrigues, and bookies everywhere," resulting in an eighteen-month prison sentence for contempt of the Senate for walking out of the hearings. Adonis was also convicted, Lansky and many of his associates received indictments, and Lucchese went into hiding.[52]

Meyer Lansky's clubs in Florida were closed after the Kefauver Committee came to an end. He logically turned to Havana, where he opened the Cabaret Montmartre gambling casino in partnership with President Batista. His expanded Cuban presence allowed Trafficante to increase the smuggling of narcotics into Havana and on to Miami.[53]

Marcello and Trafficante were left essentially unscathed in the wake of the Kefauver Committee investigation, probably because they were involved with U.S. intelligence on the Luciano/WCC/Corsican drug operation. In any event, their relationship would flourish as the years progressed and grew even more profitable with the addition of Jimmy Hoffa to this sinister triumvirate.

Hoffa started smuggling drugs in the 1940s, "receiving narcotics from Santo Trafficante in Tampa, via New Orleans . . . ," which involved Marcello, Costello, and Lansky. From Hoffa's Detroit headquarters, the Teamsters distributed drugs throughout the country for the Mafia. "Hoffa . . . worked with the mob," said former Teamster vice president Allen Friedman, finding "ways to exchange favors, to gain mob influence" while "protecting organized crime members wherever he could." Friedman wrote that "French Connection . . . drug dealers were connected with Hoffa in legitimate business activities." Hoffa "understood the economic importance of narcotics to organized crime members who were friends of his. By helping the men . . . he was winning their gratitude . . ."[54]

So as early as 1945, these three men, Hoffa, Trafficante, and Marcello, who informants would later claim threatened President Kennedy's life a year before the assassination, were working together smuggling narcotics throughout the U.S. and involved with U.S. intelligence in the same endeavor. At the time, they believed this protected them from prosecution. However, when Bobby Kennedy became Attorney General and brought his quest to destroy the mob with him, they would learn that this assumption was incorrect.

* * *

At the start of the Kefauver Committee's investigation, George White and Rudolph Haley, the Commission's chief counsel, met privately with an unknown, small-time gangster. His name was Jack Ruby, and he was there to provide information on the mob's operations in Chicago. Haley later informed Kefauver that "Ruby is a syndicate lieutenant who has been sent to Dallas to serve as a liaison for the Chicago mobsters" and "was the payoff man for the Dallas Police Department." Milton Viorst confirmed Ruby's story in 1975. Writing for the *Washingtonian*, Viorst said that "Louis Kutner, a Chicago attorney who had worked for the Kefauver Committee, said Ruby had appeared before Kefauver's staff in 1950 . . . [He] was a syndicate lieutenant who had been sent to Dallas to serve as a liaison for Chicago mobsters."[55]

There was a family history that explains how the FBN became aware of Jack Ruby. In 1947, his older brother, Hyman Rubenstein, was an FBN informant in Chicago who ratted out Paul Roland Jones, an associate. According to George White's diary, Hyman had been his informant since 1946, when Jones attempted to bribe Steve Guthrie. Guthrie was to take office as the new sheriff in Dallas County in January 1947. Jones was aware that outgoing Sheriff Smoot Schmid engaged in such practices with the help of various members of the Dallas Police Department, so in late October 1946, Jones allegedly contacted Dallas detective George Butler. Jones would claim that Butler made the initial contact, telling Jones that Guthrie wanted to see him, and the three did meet at Guthrie's home on November 1, 1946, but who made the first contact is unimportant. For either way, Butler was aware of the payoffs made while the previous sheriff was in office, for how else would Jones have known to contact him. And it is known that Butler was a suspicious character.

Who's Who in the JFK Assassination describes Butler as a "former head of the Dallas Policeman's Union; associate of Dallas oil billionaire H.L. Hunt; member of the Ku Klux Klan." Butler also claimed that half the Dallas Police Department belonged to the Klan, which would not be unexpected in the southern city of Dallas in 1963. The Warren Commission, perhaps fearful of what they might uncover, never called Butler to testify.[56]

Butler was part of the department's Juvenile Bureau. On the weekend of the assassination, reporter Thayer Waldo of *The Star-Telegram* used him as a source of information regarding Oswald. Waldo told the Warren Commission he found Butler to be a man of "almost stoic poise." However, when Waldo approached Butler in the police department basement shortly before Ruby killed Oswald, Butler's poise "appeared to have deserted him completely . . . He was an extremely nervous man, so nervous that . . . I noticed his lips trembling."[57]

Investigators have suspected Butler of being one of the officers who helped Ruby enter the basement where he shot Oswald. It does not imply that Butler was involved in the JFK assassination. The murder of Oswald was a separate issue, deemed necessary to silence the accused assassin before he could talk or stand trial. Policemen like Butler, who for years were catered to by Ruby and had ties to the Dallas Mafia and local racist hate groups, were powerless to stop the killing, even if they wanted to. Just like Jack Ruby, they had no choice but to comply.

Local law enforcement tape-recorded Jones, Guthrie, and Butler when they met again. According to the House Select Committee on Assassinations, "An FBI report states that at the November 7 meeting: Arrangements were perfected . . . for the Chicago syndicate to move into Dallas, take over all gambling activities in the county, and set up their slot machines and other gambling devices." The transcript also reported that Guthrie thought "four men should be run out of town because they could jeopardize the takeover . . . they are de Lois Green, Johnnie Grizzaffi, Junior Thomas, and Mac Barnes . . ." But according to Jones, one person they could rely on was Bill Decker, who Jones said "was an 'old-time bootlegger here and he's rather a popular sort of fellow, and he's been the undersheriff all of the time.'"[58]

"Jones spoke of setting up a gambling club in Dallas County. He told Guthrie, 'Here is my proposition to you. You pick a man, a local man; we will put him in business. We will rent him a building . . . We will furnish him all the slot machines, marble tables, punch boards, etc. . . . We will operate, and there will be only one gambling house in the county.'—Guthrie stated that, 'We all know Bill Decker is a payoff man with Bennie Binion' and Butler agreed with Guthrie . . ."[59]

Bill Decker would be present when the Warren Commission interviewed Jack Ruby in Dallas in 1964. Reluctant to talk at first, Ruby eventually told Earl Warren that his life "is in danger here," and he referred to the right-wing John Birch Society. And it was the same Bill Decker who urged Ruby to talk, telling him, "be a man and say it." Now, we know from the 1946 exchange with Jones that Decker had Mafia connections, and we can assume he would not have prompted Ruby to talk if it was organized crime that concerned Ruby. And according to Ruby, it was not—it was the radical right that frightened him, which may indicate who it was that forced him to kill Oswald.[60]

It is also curious that the same Paul Roland Jones made a surprise visit to Dallas to see Jack Ruby on November 12, 1963, ten days before the assassination, at a time when Ruby was making phone calls to mobsters across the country. At the time, Jones lived in Birmingham, Alabama, and he told the FBI he "stopped at Ruby's club and spoke to him briefly and generally." A trip from Alabama to Texas was quite a distance for an encounter that Jones said was not for any specific purpose. The mob up to something at the end of November 1963, and it involved Jack Ruby. The question is, was it the assassination of JFK or something else?[61]

Paul Roland Jones was arrested on December 18, 1946, for the bribery of elected officials and convicted on January 9, 1947, but was released. On October 24, 1947, the FBN arrested Jones for smuggling opium into Texas from Mexico. Hyman Rubenstein allegedly informed the FBI about Jones, which was how Jack Ruby came to be interviewed by FBN agents that same October. Ruby told them he had known Jones for the past few months and was introduced to him by his sister Eva Grant in Dallas. In 1947, Ruby moved to Dallas to help Eva run the Singapore Club, which she managed, and when he changed his name from Rubenstein to Ruby. Shortly after that, Eva left for California, leaving the club entirely in her brother's hands.[62]

The FBI was concerned that Ruby might have played a role in the bribery operation that involved Jones. According to the HSCA, "Ruby's name came up on numerous occasions, according to Guthrie, as being the person who would take over a very fabulous restaurant at Industrial and Commerce Streets in Dallas—Ruby was to run the club. Jack Ruby never in person talked with Guthrie . . . However, according to Guthrie, Ruby's name constantly came up as being the person who would run the restaurant, and Guthrie said if the records can still be heard, Ruby's name will be heard on numerous occasions."[63] Frank Kiernan, special assistant to the U.S. attorney in Chicago, confirmed this was true. He was told by Jack Wilner, a crime reporter for the *Chicago Daily News*, "that Ruby was reportedly involved in 1947 with . . . Jones . . . to take over gambling in the Texas area." *Chicago Daily News* reporter Morton William Newman "stated he had heard from George Butler that Ruby was involved in an attempt to bribe Steve Guthrie." So, the evidence is compelling that Ruby was to run the gambling operation in Dallas for the Chicago syndicate, but the sting operation that put Jones in jail put an end to that.[64]

According to Ruby, he had to stay in Dallas, which people who knew him confirmed. One associate claimed Ruby "would sit at the table where I was seated and discuss how he was sent down here by them. He always complained that if he had to be exiled, why couldn't it have been to Florida or California."[65] Another claimed it was a "common story [that] Ruby been run out of Chicago by the mob."[66]

In 1946, Dallas was not under the control of any Mafia family. The failed attempt by the Chicago Mafia to take over the city opened the door for Carlos Marcello and his New Orleans crime family. They took advantage and made Dallas part of their empire in 1947. Considering the level of corruption in Dallas, one wonders if Marcello was behind the sting that thwarted the Chicago mob's plan. There was a reason that the names of the same corrupt law enforcement officials from 1947 would resurface again in 1963 with the assassination of JFK.

Jack Ruby was not a prominent organized crime figure at the time Marcello took over Dallas. Still, the evidence suggests that on a lower level, he maintained a position of importance. According to one Warren Commission document, in 1956, "Jack Ruby of Dallas" gave "the okay to operate" locally for a "large narcotics set-up operating between Mexico, Texas, and the East." To have such authority meant that Ruby was part of the Trafficante and Marcello drug network that brought heroin into the U.S. through Mexico. As we will see, there is sufficient evidence to conclude that Ruby worked for both mob bosses at a low level.[67]

Not long after arriving in Dallas, Ruby became manager and part-owner of the Silver Spur Club. During an interview after his arrest for shooting Oswald, Ruby said the following: "You had to know this place to know what went on. You could get exonerated for murder easier than you could for burglary." It was a not-so-subtle indictment of Dallas's homicide squad and perhaps a hint at who had assisted Ruby in making the murder of Oswald possible.[68]

Ruby eventually became part owner of the Vegas Club, which was around the time he began a relationship with Joseph Civello, the Mafia boss in Dallas during the 1950s and 1960s. Civello was originally from Louisiana and was the liaison between Ruby and the man Civello worked for, Carlos Marcello. Civello was also close to Sergeant Patrick Dean of the Dallas Police Department. Dean was responsible for security in the police department basement on the day Ruby shot

Oswald. Dean would fail a lie detector test regarding how Ruby had entered the police station basement, despite being the fact he was allowed to write the questions they would ask him. Like Butler, Dean's past mob connections left him little choice but to do what the mob asked of him.[69]

The Civello/Ruby relationship was elaborated upon by Bobby Gene Moore, who, between 1952 and 1956, played piano at the Vegas Club. As David E. Scheim writes in *Contract on America,* after Ruby killed Oswald, "Moore told the FBI of deals involving Ruby, two Dallas policemen, and local underworld figures; several of his allegations were verified years later by arrests for the activities he described . . . [There was an] Italian importing company at 3400 Ross Avenue in Dallas, where Moore [worked] during the early 1950s. Moore . . . told the FBI he suspected that his employers, Joseph 'Cirello' and Frank LaMonte, might have been importing narcotics . . . [and] the Dallas directory listed the store at 3400 Ross Avenue to a brother of Mafia boss Joseph Civello. The Joseph 'Cirello' transcribed by the FBI was thus Joseph Civello, whose business fronts included import-export, olive oil and cheese, and whose criminal activities did in fact include narcotics dealings." Moore also told the FBI that Jack Ruby was "a frequent visitor of Cirello and LaMonte." Interviewed after the assassination by the FBI, LaMonte admitted having known Ruby since the early 1950s, and Civello would state: "Yeah, I knew Jack—we were friends, and I used to go to his club."[70]

That Ruby worked for Marcello was confirmed by Marcello's recorded prison admission to Jack Van Laningham. The mob boss stated that he controlled the Carousel Club, the strip joint Ruby operated at the time of the assassination. According to Marcello, mobster Joe Campisi in Dallas funneled money to Ruby associate Ralph Paul, who then laundered the funds for the Carousel Club. It was why Marcello said Ruby worked for him and would visit him in New Orleans on occasion. It also explains why HSCA investigators were confused when Campisi stated that "Ralph Paul [was] his partner" in an FBI interview.[71] The HSCA would uncover that Paul repeatedly loaned Jack Ruby money for numerous failed business ventures, which Paul could not afford. He owned the Bull Pen Drive-In, a small restaurant that did not generate sufficient profits to support Ruby financially. But it was possible if Paul was acting as a middleman for Marcello.[72]

Perhaps significant is that Ralph Paul and Ruby had dinner at Campisi's restaurant the night before the assassination. Campisi would also visit Ruby in jail on November 30, six days after Ruby shot Oswald. It was also just days after the FBI interviewed Joseph Civello, and implies there was early concern at the FBI that the Mafia may have been responsible for Oswald's murder. It is safe to assume that Campisi's visit to see Ruby was not a social call and that Campisi instructed Ruby to remain quiet and not mention Marcello by name.[73]

By the assassination, Jack Ruby was not a big-time mobster, but he was known to Carlos Marcello and part of the New Orleans crime family. Meanwhile, Jean

Lafitte was using aliases of Oswald and others familiar to the Marcello crime family. Lafitte and George White knew Jack Ruby as early as 1947, which means Lafitte knew Ruby and Oswald long before they would become household names. Lafitte had intelligence and Mafia connections, as did Jack Ruby, which is critical in determining how all the pieces fit together. Organized crime, U.S. intelligence operatives, and the Corsican Mafia were busy smuggling drugs to provide financing for the stay-behind armies in Europe. Jack Ruby, involved in drug smuggling through Marcello, was part of this operation, albeit a small cog. When the time was right, the man who for years had ingratiated himself with the Dallas police would serve a purpose, and he could not say no.

But we are getting ahead of ourselves, for it was in the 1950s when various groups came together that would eventually lead to the assassination of JFK. There was a right-wing storm brewing, which grew in ferocity as the years went by, and Dallas was in the eye of the hurricane. For in no other place did disgruntled groups come together with more urgency than they did in Dallas. Big business, especially oil interests, radical right-wingers, paramilitary groups (including retired military generals), the Ku Klux Klan and other racist groups, corrupt politicians, organized crime figures, police officers on the take, and intelligence operatives all found a home in this Texas city. And the self-serving Jack Ruby managed to ingratiate himself with all of them.

Robert Kennedy was attempting to destroy the Mafia while U.S. intelligence was simultaneously employing their services. One should not underestimate the importance of this. For not only was the future of organized crime at stake, but the arrest of mobsters could have also brought down U.S. intelligence, corrupt politicians, and radical right-wing Texas oilmen. Hence, there was a common interest in preventing this from occurring. And Texas was where it all came together in the 1950s.

- 9 -

Deep in the Heart of Texas

"Isn't it strange that Oswald, who hasn't worked a lick most of his life, should be fortunate enough to get a job at the Book Bldg . . . now where would a jerk like Oswald get the information . . . that man was [Lyndon] Johnson."

—Jack Ruby

There was a history of lawlessness in Texas at the time of the JFK assassination. One could blame it on the pride of frontier-minded people who believed the government wouldn't tell Texans how to solve their problems. A Lone Star State mentality of independence and self-determination existed, a "Remember the Alamo" approach to life where a person had to avenge unrighteous wrongs perpetrated against them. Texans in the early 1960s were an independent breed. Unfortunately, this above-the-law approach also gave rise to the bribing of corrupt politicians, fraudulent elections, Southern racism, and an aversion to Northerners trying to change the Southern way of life. There was distrust for foreigners or anyone who thought differently, a hatred for Communists, and anyone they disagreed with. An elite class of Texans evolved who disrespected Northern politicians and would not let anyone tell them what to do. For more than any other state, Texas was where big business not only embraced a right-wing agenda but actively tried to overturn policies construed to be detrimental to the American way of life. And it was clear there were those in Texas who would go to any length to keep Socialist programs out of the country.

* * *

On November 8, 1954, President Eisenhower wrote a letter to his brother Edgar.

He was concerned by the unrest demonstrated by the elites in Texas. Ike wrote, "Should any political party attempt to abolish social security, unemployment insurance, and eliminate labor laws and farm programs, you would not hear of that party again in our political history . . . there is a tiny splinter group, of course, that believes you can do these things. Among them are H.L. Hunt . . . a few other Texas millionaires, and an occasional politician or businessman from other areas. Their number is negligible, and they are stupid." [1]

The President was wrong, for their numbers were not negligible, and they were far from stupid. And perhaps unknown to Eisenhower, many were in bed with the CIA and the U.S. military, for they all shared the same anti-Communist plan, which drew them to each other. It was a relationship that would exist for decades to come. As *San Francisco Chronicle* reporter Terry Leonard wrote as late as 1982, "Nowhere but in Texas is the relationship between government and business so purposely close."[2]

The discontent in Texas began in the 1930s, as the attempted coup against FDR was occurring up north. For the same reasons, New Deal social programs created deep resentment among the wealthiest Texans, particularly the oilmen. Determined to do something about it, they formed the Suite 8F Group, named for the room at the Lamar Hotel in Houston, where they held the meetings. One of their main concerns was to protect the interests of the Texas oil industry, and by the 1950s, that industry was well represented.

Notable Suite 8F members included George and Herman Brown of Brown & Root, former Texas Governor and owner of the *Houston Post*, William Hobby (the husband of Oveta Culp Hobby, Eisenhower's Secretary of Health, Education and Welfare), and oilmen Clint Murchison, Sid Richardson, H.L. Hunt, David Harold Byrd, Hugh Roy Cullen, Billy Byars, and Thomas Corcoran.

Herman Brown was a "hater" who "hated Negroes and . . . unions," wrote Robert Caro in *The Years of Lyndon Johnson: The Path to Power*. "He believed that Negroes were lazy and that unions encouraged laziness in white men . . ." And he also hated FDR, "that man in the White House" who was responsible for programs designed to help "unions and Negroes."[3]

Hugh Roy Cullen had similar opinions. He said FDR was a Communist because of the social programs he created. But it did not end with Roosevelt. According to the author of *Red Scare*, Don E. Carleton. "Truman . . . was just an extension of the New Deal and even more dangerous than FDR." He was "more susceptible to control and influence by the labor unionists, 'fellow travelers' [Communists]," and one-world proponents that supported the United Nations.[4]

Cullen ". . . despised liberals as much as he hated Communists," Carlton continued. He "believed the federal government was rotten with Socialists [and he] demanded that President Truman and Secretary of State Dean Acheson be arrested and tried for treason . . . Cullen was an isolationist who equated internationalism with 'one world' Communism. This view extended to the United Nations, which Cullen believed was 'gradually usurping our national sovereignty.' His idea of a foreign policy was to obliterate with nuclear weapons any nation foolish enough to oppose the United States with military arms. Alliances were 'un-American.'"[5]

In a televised speech in October 1952, ex-Governor Hobby stated that Eisenhower would "save our country from . . . the dictatorship that goes with communism, a dictatorship that can easily result from an administration too long in power," a clear allusion to the long reign of the Democratic party.[6] These 8F men did not mince words, and one knew where each one stood. They were anti-Communist racists who were strong advocates of self-determination.

Thomas Corcoran was an isolationist and Fascist sympathizer who had provided arms to Chiang Kai-shek during World War II. He was involved in forming the Flying Tigers with Claire Chennault and William Pawley, which eventually led to the WCC/Helliwell/Mafia drug operation and the CIA's creation of Civil Air Transport. A Lyndon Johnson supporter and United Fruit Company lobbyist who actively promoted the 1954 Guatemala coup by the CIA, his right-wing credentials typified the other group members.

Eugene B. Germany belonged to the Texas Regulars, a group of Democratic Party right-wingers who wanted to remove FDR from office in the 1940s. William Pawley was well-connected to anti-Castro Cubans, CIA, Mafia figures, and virtually any radically anti-Communist group. Edward Clark, the legal counsel to both Lyndon Johnson and Clint Murchison. In 2003, Clark's former legal partner Barr McClellan, in his book *Blood, Money & Power: How LBJ Killed JFK*, accused Clark and Johnson of involvement and coverup in the JFK assassination.

White supremacists dominated the Suite 8F Group. There was avid LBJ supporter, Florida Congressman George Smathers, linked to Mafia figures and the Bobby Baker scandal. Senator Richard Russell, who would serve on the Warren Commission. Chairman of the Judiciary Committee, Senator James Eastland, who fought desegregation with all his might. Senator Benjamin Everett Jordan would survive a 1972 sniper attacked that killed three people (He was shot at because he had decided to oppose the Vietnam War). It almost seemed like being a white supremacist was a prerequisite for membership in the Suite 8F Group.

Texas Congressman Albert Thomas, an LBJ supporter, was caught on camera smirking and winking at Johnson aboard Air Force One immediately after LBJ became President following the assassination. Lyndon Johnson was also a member, as was John Connally. Legal counsel to oilman Sid Richardson during the 1950s, Connally was a right-wing member of the Democratic Party, Secretary of the Navy under JFK, and Texas Governor at the time of the assassination, who would be shot by the so-called magic bullet while riding in the limousine with JFK.

There were also corrupt Suite 8F members. Congressman Homer Thornberry was involved in the Bobby Baker scandal and had to resign in December 1963. Billie Sol Estes, LBJ's close business associate, was found guilty of mortgage fraud. It also involved Johnson and could have put him in jail had JFK not been murdered. Fred Korth was president of Continental National Bank and Navy Secretary under JFK. He had to resign in October 1963 on corruption charges related to awarding questionable defense contracts to Texas contractors. Fred Black established the Serve-U Corporation, which was at the center of the Bobby Baker scandal. In 1964, he would be convicted and sent to prison for tax evasion. And Bobby Baker himself, political lobbyist, and Lyndon Johnson protégé. He was also connected to oilman Clint Murchison and would be at the center of the Serve-U Corporation scandal.[7]

The Houston Chamber of Commerce acted as the "unofficial spokesperson" for the Suite 8F Group during the 1950s. Through its magazine, *Houston*, the chamber warned that Communist infiltration was everywhere, including "newspapers, magazines, books, radio . . . churches, schools, colleges, and even fraternal orders . . ." "Americans, patriots, stand up and be counted," the magazine declared. "Assert yourselves . . . [or] you may find it too late," because America was "fast becoming socialistic." There was no limit to how far these people would go to defend the Constitution, segregation, and self-determination.

We can assume that Suite 8F Group members did not shed a tear when they learned JFK was dead. They despised the young President and what he stood for. These men did not want JFK reelected in 1964 and had the connections and power to have Kennedy killed if any were inclined to do so. Their discontent was well known to outside associates who shared their desire to remove Kennedy from office. For over a decade before the assassination, these individuals shared their vision for the country with each other. They knew something had to change to preserve the American way of life, as they defined it. Many Suite 8F members had a relationship with the CIA, which put them in bed with a group that shared their discontent and could carry out a political assassination.

Herman and George Brown allowed the CIA to use their company, Brown & Root, as a front. The company offered the perfect cover by placing agents in responsible corporate positions in foreign nations of interest. As Joan Mellon writes in *A Farewell to Justice*: "As a result of George Brown's name surfacing in the [Jim] Garrison investigation . . . CIA generated documents that attested to its long history with Herman and George Brown, as well as with a group of lesser Brown & Root executives. At the same time, CIA admitted to a congressional probe that they used the Brown Foundation as a cover for its illegal domestic operations . . . George had been granted a Covert Security Clearance on 23 October 1953 . . ."[8]

Other companies that had a relationship with the CIA were Bechtel Corporation, Hughes Aircraft, Dillon Read, Exxon, Gulf Oil, Hughes Tool, Pan American Airways, to name a few. And just like the departure of military officers to major defense contractors, there were numerous examples of retired CIA leaders joining companies with whom the Agency worked. CIA Director Richard Helms would become an "international consultant" for Bechtel. Theodore Roosevelt's grandson

Kermit, who served CIA throughout most of the 1950s, would join Northrop Corporation upon his retirement in 1958. They were not the only ones to engage in this legal but unethical practice.[9]

H.L. Hunt and Clint Murchison's right-wing credentials were never in doubt. When Douglas MacArthur returned to the U.S. after being dismissed from Korea, the two oilmen chartered a plane and brought him to Texas. MacArthur told the crowd that "If this country is ever destroyed it will be from within, not from without," from U.S. leaders operating under a Marxist philosophy. As described by William Manchester in *American Caesar*, MacArthur

> . . . praised "that small band of Texans who stood and died rather than yield the precious concepts of liberty," concepts which, he evidently believed, were now extolled by another small band of Texans led by H.L. Hunt and Clint Murchison. He urged [for the pursuit of self-determination and the] removals of "the burden of taxation" from enterprising industrialists who would otherwise become "stultified and inert," burdens imposed by "those who seek to convert us to a form of socialistic endeavor, leading directly to the path of Communist slavery."[10]

Hunt and Murchison shared this view and supported MacArthur's presidential run in 1952, the thought of which so disturbed Truman that, according to his 1947 diary, he offered to serve as Eisenhower's vice president on the 1948 Democratic ticket if MacArthur were to win the Republican nomination.[11] Truman knew how dangerous a MacArthur Presidency would be.

H.L. Hunt was a radical-right crusader. A member of the John Birch Society, he supported General Edwin Walker, had a right-wing radio show called *Life Line*, provided funding to the Cuban Revolutionary Council (CRC), the anti-Castro Cuban group operating out of New Orleans, and generally actively supported radical right-wing and racist groups. Frank Ellsworth was a Bureau of Alcohol Tobacco and Firearms agent in Dallas in 1963. He told Warren Commission counsel Burt Griffin that Walker and Hunt were the leaders of the Minutemen in Dallas who, Ellsworth said, was "the Right-Wing group in Dallas most likely to have associated with any effort to assassinate the president." The group was certainly capable of such violence. Ex-Minutemen member Jerry Brooks was tape-recorded, saying that the Minutemen's mission was to "overthrow the government by violence and force." More about them later.[12]

There were reports that Hunt had a connection to Jack Ruby through high-stakes gambling, which the oilman was known to enjoy. In addition, H.L. Hunt's son Lamar's name appeared in one of Ruby's notebooks. There was an association between the Hunts and Jack Ruby, which placed the small-time mobster at the heart of the radical-right movement in Dallas.

Madeleine Brown was LBJ's mistress from 1948 through 1969, which handwriting experts who analyzed various correspondence sent to Brown have confirmed. And through LBJ, she got to know some interesting people in Dallas, including Jack Ruby, whom she claimed to have seen frequently. "I used to go to his club, gambling and playing cards in the afternoon before the strip part opened at night," she said. "A bunch of us would see him around town. Lots of people in town knew him, especially people in the downtown area like H.L. Hunt, [District Attorney] Henry Wade, [Mayor] Earl Cabell, they all knew him . . ."[13]

Ann Marsh, a former Ruby employee who dated him at one time, confirmed that what Brown alleged was true. Ruby took her to the homes of some of Dallas' most prominent citizens, "including District Attorney Henry Wade . . . Once we got there, I never saw Jack. He would be off gambling." And according to one gambler present at these gatherings, he once won a large sum of money from H.L. Hunt after Ruby introduced the two.[14]

Henry Wade was Dallas District Attorney at the time of the assassination. In 1959, Lyndon Johnson had begun his campaign to seek the Democratic Party nomination for President in the 1960 election. Powerful Dallas officials supported LBJ, like Judge Sarah Hughes (for whom Johnson kept Air Force One waiting on the runway at Love Field in Dallas so she could swear him in). She was an avid gambler and favorite of the Dallas Mafia. Then three was Henry Wade.[15]

Wade was a conservative, and he and Johnson were one hundred percent for each other, as they liked to tell people. During his first year as D.A., Wade made numerous trips to Washington to meet privately with Johnson and attend political parties at LBJ's house. J. Edgar Hoover lived virtually across the street and was a regular at Johnson's home. It was there that Wade, a former FBI agent, got to spend quality time with the FBI director.

Wade became involved in Johnson's political career in 1948 and traveled throughout Texas on his behalf, conducting surveillance on political opponents. As early as 1955, he began urging LBJ to run for president, and by 1959 Wade decided to tie his political future to Johnson's. He wrote to LBJ that, "I have thought some about running for Attorney General of the State next year, but now feel I will remain here and do what I can on your behalf towards your nomination and whatever assistance I could be in your election. If there is anything that you would like for me to do, please call me. Your devoted friend."[16]

When LBJ lost the party's nomination to JFK, Johnson thanked an embittered Wade for his dedication, telling him, "I am deeply grateful to you for all your help and support. It is most rewarding for a man in public life to be able to count on friends like you."

Wade was also close to the Dallas crime organization known as the Pearl Street Mafia. In early May 1951, the vice squad raided Joseph Civello's primary bookmaking operation, which resulted in the arrest of John Eli Stone, Isadore Miller, and

Louie Ferrantello, close criminal associates of Jack Ruby. Yet, Wade failed to act appropriately. Stone and the others remained in business and would develop the largest bookmaking operation in Dallas by the end of the decade.[17]

On the night of the assassination, Wade brought Oswald before reporters during a late-night impromptu press conference. He told the crowd that Oswald was a member of "Free Cuba," an anti-Castro organization. It was an obvious mistake, for this did not fit the narrative that Oswald was a Communist supporter of Fidel Castro. So, Jack Ruby, who had secretly managed to sneak his way into the gathering, immediately shouted out that Oswald belonged to the Fair Play for Cuba Committee, a pro-Castro group. It was not Free Cuba, as Wade had said. Wade knew Ruby well but did not question why he was there posing as a reporter or how he knew so much about Lee Harvey Oswald. For it was far too early in the investigation for people to understand the significance of the mistake Wade had made, and none of the reporters realized it, but somehow Jack Ruby did. Unless Ruby knew Oswald, how was that possible was familiar with his connection to the FPCC and understood the importance of Wade's error. Ruby set the record straight before Oswald could be connected to an anti-Castro group. Perhaps Wade was right, and he had evidence that Oswald was a member of Free Cuba. It did not matter. Wade simply accepted the correction and moved on.[18]

During Ruby's trial for shooting Oswald, his defense counsel Tom Howard reminded the local press that "District Attorney [Wade] has known Jack Ruby on a first name basis for many years." One reporter expanded on this, stating that Ruby "knew most of the officers who questioned him . . . When Assistant Dist. Atty . . . [Bill] Alexander entered the room . . . , Rubenstein looked up and said, 'Hi Bill.'" When the FBI interviewed Alexander in late December 1963, he denied a connection between Ruby and the local Mafia. However, shortly after Ruby's arrest, the police searched his car and found Carousel Club membership cards in the names of mobsters Sam Campisi and John Grizzaffi. Even though Alexander knew this before his FBI interview, he still found it necessary to reject a Ruby/Mafia connection. Also, in his first statement to investigators on December 13, Sam Campisi admitted knowing Ruby "for approximately ten years." And as previously mentioned, one of the first people Ruby called from jail after his arrest was Sam Campisi's brother Joe.[19]

Alexander had to deny that a Mafia connection to Ruby existed, for the truth would have compromised many of Dallas's leading citizens and revealed their relationship to the local Mafia. It seemed every politician and law enforcement official in Dallas was on the take, and everyone knew Jack Ruby, the payoff man for the mob. And according to David Scheim in *Contract on America*, Campisi and Grizzaffi were not the only names found in Ruby's car after his apprehension:

Among the items found in Ruby's possession were the business cards of
the chief of the Narcotics Division in Austin, Texas and of the captain
of the Traffic Division in El Paso . . . ; permanent passes to the Carousel
Club, issued to and signed by the recipients, Dallas Assistant District
Attorney Bill Alexander, Garland Deputy J.T. Ivey, and City Hall officials
Ray Hawkins and John D. Bailey; five bail bond cards, and various lists
with the notations "Rosemary Allen . . . Deputy Sheriff Decker's secretary," "Buddy Walthers . . . Deputy Sheriff," "Travis Hall . . . County
Clerk Deputy" and "Clint Lewis . . . Deputy Sheriff." Also found was
a card bearing Ruby's name and the Dallas County official seal, signed
by Justice of the Peace Glen W. Byrd. It read: "To all public officials:
kindly extend to the individual whose signature appears above any and
all assistance which may be properly given in keeping with your official
duties . . ."[20]

Another contact of H.L. Hunt's was Guy Banister, the ultra-right, racist, rabid anti-Communist associate of the previously mentioned CRC. David Ferrie,
Lee Harvey Oswald, and Jack Martin frequented Banister's New Orleans detective
agency in 1963. In the mid-1950s, Banister had been Chief of Police in New Orleans, and Joseph Oster was a young police officer who served under him. When
the police dismissed Banister in 1957 for brandishing a gun at a waiter at a local
restaurant, Oster joined him as a partner in the detective agency. Jeffrey H. Caufield, M.D., the author of *General Walker and the Murder of President Kennedy,
The Extensive New Evidence of a Radical-Right Conspiracy*, interviewed Oster. When
asked if Banister knew H.L. Hunt, Oster replied, "Oh yes. We met with Hunt
a number of times at the Petroleum Club [in Dallas]." Hunt's oil operations in
Louisiana had been the target of continuous thefts of drilling equipment, which is
why Hunt hired Banister and Oster. Oster showed Caufield letters on *Guy Banister
and Associates* stationery that referred to Banister's work for Hunt. He also said that
Banister did security work for Sun Oil, owned by J. Howard Pew of the American
Liberty League and the Sentinels of the Republic (see Chapter One), and Texas oilmen Murchison and Richardson.[21] Recall that Sun Oil was where Ilya Mamantov
worked, the Russian émigré who acted as a translator for Marina Oswald after the
assassination. That the ultra-right Banister knew these conservative Texas oilmen
is significant, for it demonstrates that the right-wing was widespread and not just
isolated to local pockets of resistance. Instead, there was a working relationship
between like-minded groups that transcended state lines. The war against communism and racial desegregation brought these people together to pursue a common
cause. And it also was not a coincidence that Dallas and New Orleans, the two
major centers of resistance, were the cities where Lee Oswald involved himself in
matters related to political discontent.

Minutemen member Jerry Brooks reported that Banister, and two Banister associates, Hugh Ward and Maurice Gatlin, were Minutemen. Gatlin was also general counsel for the Anti-Communist League of the Caribbean. Jim Garrison would uncover that in 1962, Gatlin secretly sent $100,000 to a right-wing group in France that was plotting to assassinate Charles de Gaulle, which suggests the right-wing connection between Dallas and New Orleans extended internationally.[22] Ward was a business associate of Banister. Paul Rothermel, who worked for H.L. Hunt, said that Hunt and General Walker were friends and that Frank Ellsworth stated that Walker and Hunt were also members of the Minutemen. So, it is likely that Banister knew Walker.[23]

Ward and Gatlin would both die under suspicious circumstances. The plane Ward was flying crashed on May 23, 1964, just before the Warren Commission concluded its hearings. New Orleans Mayor DeLesseps Morrison was also on board and died as well. Gatlin would die that same year after falling from the sixth-floor window of a hotel in Panama.[24] The official cause of death was a heart attack. However, foul play was a possibility. Consider that the 1952 CIA Assassination Manual instructed that the best way to kill someone was as follows: "The most efficient accident, in simple assassination, is a fall of 75 feet or more onto a hard surface. Elevator shafts, stairwells, unscreened windows, and bridges will serve."[25] As the following chapters will show, an excessive amount of relevant people similarly fell to their death.

Ruby and Banister were not the only assassination figures to whom Clint Murchison and H.L. Hunt were connected. In 1960, American aid to Haiti was $21.4 million, despite that Haitian President Duvalier's heroes were Marx, Lenin, and Mao Tse-Tung. Duvalier consistently voted with the U.S. at the United Nations, including the Cuban Missile Crisis. So, the United States tolerated his left-wing politics for a while. And according to Joan Mellen, "Eighty percent of all American aid disappeared into the pockets of Duvalier, and his minions . . . Foremost among the entrepreneurs rooted in Haiti was Clint Murchison, Jr. To be safe, he was registered in Washington as a lobbyist for Duvalier."[26]

The FBI interviewed George de Mohrenschildt's Texas associates after the assassination. An offshore oil engineer named George Kitchel (incidentally, a close friend of George H.W. Bush) reported that de Mohrenschildt was an intimate acquaintance of H.L. Hunt, Clint Murchison, and Sid Richardson. In support of this, there were three Murchison family names in de Mohrenschildt's address book from 1954-1955.[27]

De Mohrenschildt knew a lot of people in Dallas. He was a member of the Dallas Petroleum Club (where Banister and Hunt would meet) and the Dallas Council on World Affairs. He also belonged to the right-wing Texas Crusade for Freedom, whose members included Dallas Mayor Earle Cabell and conservative oilman Harold Byrd.[28]

As described in Chapter Four, de Mohrenschildt knew the CIA branch chief of the Soviet Russian division Nicholas Anikeeff. The two met in Washington during the spring of 1963 when de Mohrenschildt stopped there before going to Haiti on business. However, according to a CIA-connected New York attorney named Herbert Itkin, the CIA was interested in assassinating Papa Doc Duvalier to use the country as a jumping-off point to harass Cuba. The mobsters were willing to murder on behalf of the CIA in exchange for Haitian gambling rights once the Agency removed Duvalier from power. One of Itkin's CIA contacts in Haiti identified himself as Philip Harbin, who Itkin described as a man who "could have been of Polish or Russian family background." He was a man who "had an affluent, professional air." The description matched de Mohrenschildt, and he may have been passing himself off as Philip Harbin, for de Mohrenschildt's wife Jeanne was born in Harbin, China, which suggests this may have been the case. If true, it confirms that de Mohrenschildt did work on behalf of the CIA.[29]

An attempted assassination of Papa Doc was the likely reason why de Mohrenschildt was in Haiti, which only adds to the intrigue. Recall that Anikeef may have been part of the Gehlen operation after the war. Both Anikeef and de Mohrenschildt were likely involved in the stay-behind army operation established by William Donovan and Allen Dulles throughout eastern Europe. It further supports the idea that a connection existed between anti-Communist Monarchists in Europe and the right-wing in the U.S. Included in this were U.S. intelligence and the military. The many left-wing international governments that were overthrown by the United States around the time of Kennedy's death, as described in this book's Introduction, is possible confirmation that this was true. And as previously mentioned, Maurice Gatlin sent money to Europe for the assassination of Charles de Gaulle. It all implies that the resistance movement in America was not a disorganized coalition blindly pursuing a right-wing agenda. Still, they were also part of an international right-wing Fascist group removing leftist foreign leaders from power. And a group such as this had the means and connections to forcibly remove a President and orchestrate a violent government overthrow in the United States if they were so inclined.

* * *

Murchison and de Mohrenschildt were not the only suspicious Texans involved in Haitian activities. According to a memo sent by J. Edgar Hoover to the State Department, Thomas Eli Davis was a soldier of fortune who, around June 1963, was attempting to recruit "men for an invasion of Haiti."[30] What makes this so compelling is that, in addition to de Mohrenschildt's interest in Haiti, in the late 1950s, Jack Ruby was involved in running guns to Cuba with none other than Thomas Eli Davis. It is known because after shooting Oswald, Ruby told his first attorney that despite his mob connections, the only information he feared coming out during his trial was his relationship to Davis and their joint effort in running guns to Cuba. Davis's connections were with the CIA and right-wing paramilitary types. Since Ruby did not want his relationship with Davis publicized, the only conclusion one can draw is that Ruby worked with right-wing groups himself. Perhaps this occurred in conjunction with his organized crime connections, which would mean paramilitary groups and the Mafia worked together, possibly as part of the JFK assassination group.

The plot thickens even further. Sixteen days after the assassination, Davis was arrested in Tangiers, Morocco, allegedly "trying to sell two Walter pistols." However, there was more to the story. According to a cable subsequently forwarded to the CIA and the Office of Naval Intelligence, which was sent from the U.S. State Department in Tangiers the previous day, Davis was detained in Tangiers because he had in his possession an unsigned letter that referred to "Oswald" and the "Kennedy assassination." Davis was supposed to forward the letter to an attorney named Thomas G. Proctor. Proctor had CIA connections and was associated with two CIA assets in Mexico, June Cobb and Warren Broglie, two prominent figures in the Oswald saga and JFK assassination. For now, the question is, how did Jack Ruby get involved with a man like Davis, years before the assassination, who had an interest in Haitian affairs at the same time as George De Mohrenschildt? And how could Davis associate with so many intelligence assets and not be connected to U.S. intelligence himself? Did this imply that U.S. intelligence was responsible for Ruby killing Oswald to silence him, either because of the assassination or something unrelated to the President's murder?

It turns out that the "Oswald" in Davis' letter referred to a Madrid businessman named Victor Oswald. And according to a December 30, 1963 cable to Secretary of State Rusk, "Victor Oswald . . . came to Madrid approximately six weeks ago with a letter of business introduction to Oswald from a friend of Oswald's, the New York lawyer Thomas Proctor . . ."[31] This should have put the matter to rest. Still, as might be expected, it did not.

Victor Oswald came from a wealthy family from Lucerne, Switzerland. During World War II, he was an intelligence operative for both the OSS and the British. By the 1950s, he was a representative of the Chase National Bank in Spain, and in that capacity, worked for John McCloy, who was Chairman of Chase Manhattan Bank at the time. And according to the author of *The Skorzeny Papers*, Major Ralph P. Gains, "Victor Oswald was also an original member of the SOE/OSS group that established the British-American-Canadian-Corporation (BACC) and the World Commerce Corporation (WCC)."[32] Like de Mohrenschildt, this placed Thomas Eli Davis, through Thomas Proctor and Victor Oswald, in direct contact with the Donovan/Dulles group that organized and funded the stay behind guerilla armies in Europe after the war. It was at a time when Davis was recruiting an army to invade Haiti. And if Davis was involved, through Proctor and Victor Oswald, to the

Donovan and Dulles WCC operation, it may connect his gunrunning partner Jack Ruby to this group as well. And finally, Thomas Davis was released from custody in Morocco through the intervention of QJ/WIN, a CIA assassin who worked for William Harvey as part of the CIA's ZR/RIFLE assassination operation, which connected Davis directly to the CIA.

There is also a possible connection between Davis and Jean Pierre Lafitte, which brings everything full circle if true. While working for the CIA covertly in New Orleans during 1961, Lafitte traveled to Europe, the Middle East, and Africa on numerous occasions as part of an assassination team, which was likely part of ZR/RIFLE. At the time, Davis was an informant for the FBN and was known to Charles Siragusa and George White, both associates of Lafitte. According to a letter Siragusa sent to White, he referred to Davis as "a galloping clod whose testicles are larger than his home state of Texas, but who lacks the adjoining brains . . ." Davis did meet once with drug traffickers in Algiers, including Jean Souetre. Recall it was Souetre, or Michael Mertz secretly posing as him, who U.S. intelligence secretly removed from Dallas on the night of the assassination.[33] And according to Mark North in *Betrayal in Dallas*, Michael Mertz was associated with significant players in the Mafia's international heroin trafficking operation. Lamar Waldron and Tom Hartmann wrote in *Ultimate Sacrifice* that, "Two of Mertz's partners in this heroin network, Lucien Rivard and Paul Mondoloni, had ties to Trafficante and to associates of Jack Ruby."[34]

Consider how all these people came together. Jean-Pierre Lafitte was involved with George Hunter White in the CIA's drug experimentation program involving unsuspecting civilians. CIA Counterintelligence chief James Angleton was part of this as well, as was CIA assassination chief William Harvey who, along with George White, was connected to John Roselli. Lafitte was close to Santos Trafficante Jr., Paul Mondoloni, and the Corsican Mafia, which put him in contact with the Mafia/WCC/Corsican drug operation, which funded the stay-behind armies started by Donovan and Allen Dulles. Lafitte visited Trafficante in a Cuban prison, as did Charles Siragusa of the FBN, who also had organized crime connections. Jack Ruby also visited Trafficante in the Cuban jail. Assassination suspect John Martino was incarcerated in the same Cuban detention facility as Trafficante, and Lafitte also used his name as an alias. Like Lee Oswald, Lafitte used the Hidell alias and worked at the same establishment in New Orleans as Oswald did. He also used the Martin alias, which connected him to Guy Banister's office, to which Lee Oswald was also connected. Richard Case Nagell used the Hidell alias, was close to Lee Oswald, and had himself arrested to have an air-tight alibi when the JFK assassination occurred, the details of which he was intricately familiar.

Lafitte also uses Michael Mertz as an alias, and it was either Mertz or Jean Souetre who was in Dallas on the day of the assassination. Souetre was a member of OAS, the French military group that tried to assassinate de Gaulle and wanted to take over the French government. Mertz also had a connection to Corsican Paul Mondolini.

Thomas Eli Davis had a connection to Souetre and was involved with Victor Oswald and Thomas Proctor, which connected him to the Mafia/WCC/Corsican drug operation. He was also involved with George Hunter White and Charles Siragusa and was a gun runner with Jack Ruby, which logically connected all three to the international drug operation. William Harvey and ZR/RIFLE also were aware of Thomas Davis, for why else would QJ/WIN have traveled to Morocco to get Davis out of jail. Harvey was close to John Roselli, who, along with Santos Trafficante and Sam Giancana, would try to kill Castro on behalf of the CIA around 1959/1960. Harvey would eventually separate the CIA from Trafficante and Giancana because they may have been working for Castro and keeping him apprised of the assassination plots against him, but he kept Roselli on.

While Davis was putting a mercenary army together to invade Haiti, Clint Murchison and George de Mohrenschildt were there at the same time. De Mohrenschildt's interest in Haiti may have been part of a CIA operation to kill Papa Doc Duvalier, which again brings us back to William Harvey and ZR/RIFLE. De Mohrenschildt knew H.L. Hunt and Sid Richardson, and likely most of the Suite 8F Group, the oilmen especially. Hunt and Murchison also knew Guy Banister. De Mohrenschildt was involved with Nicholas Anikeeff, who connected to Gehlen and the stay-behind armies in Europe, which meant de Mohrenschildt might have been involved with this group.

Proctor was a contact of June Cobb, who became involved in a CIA-connected group in Havana that attempted to remove Castro from power and take over the Cuban government after Castro came to power. Frank Sturgis/Fiorini was also involved in the Havana group that included Cobb. Lafitte was aware of this, and based on his correspondence, knew Sturgis and William Morgan. Morgan was also involved in the Havana operation. Meanwhile, a CIA document that listed CIA-connected figures included George de Mohrenschildt, Frank Fiorini, and Richard Case Nagell.

The connection of critical individuals is too strong to ignore. A private international intelligence group was funding their operations with drug money furnished by organized crime, with ties to Texas oilmen and wealthy radical right-wingers in Texas, while working with various operatives associated with the CIA's assassination group. Meanwhile, a network in Dallas was close to Lyndon Johnson and recognized the benefits they could reap if he were President instead of Kennedy. Without question, something sinister was happening with this group, and their tentacles spread far and wide. Were they directly involved in JFK's assassination, or is there a presumption of guilt by association? It is key to unraveling the answer to the assassination riddle.

* * *

There were other vital individuals from Texas worth examining. Clint Murchison owned the Haitian-American Meat and Products Company (HAMPCO), a meatpacking plant in Port-au-Prince, Haiti. When it failed to pass the sanitary requirements of the Department of Agriculture, it prevented HAMPCO from exporting meat to Puerto Rico. The government reversed its ruling through the intervention of Bobby Baker in Washington, also known as "Little Lyndon." The well-connected Johnson must have helped Baker obtained this reversal.[35] In fact, according to Michel-Rolph Trouillot in *Haiti, State Against Nation* Haiti, Lady Bird Johnson had an interest in the Texas firm that controlled HAMPCO.[36]

Via the intervention of Irving Davidson, an arms dealer for the CIA and a registered lobbyist for both Clint Murchison and the Haitian government, the tainted meat was eventually sent to Chicago instead of Puerto Rico. Baker and his law partner, Ernest Tucker, were paid ten percent of the net profits for bringing this deal to fruition. Into 1963, the two men received kickbacks from the Chicago Packing and Provision Company, HAMPCO, and Clint Murchison.[37]

Robert Kennedy was investigating Baker for several shady deals as the day of JFK's assassination approached, including HAMPCO and the Quorum Club. The Quorum Club was a social establishment where D.C. lawmakers and other men of influence could eat, drink, and meet call girls. Baker had a financial interest in many questionable business ventures. He was able to buy a family home near LBJ's for $124,500, which was why the November 8, 1963 issue of *Life* magazine asked, "How had a simple, hardworking majority secretary, earning $19,612 a year, struck it so rich in so short a time?"[38] The U.S. Senate was asking the same question.

Baker's world began to unravel due to the financial problems of Alfred Novak, a Washington D.C. builder who had lent Baker money around 1960-61 to build the Carousel Motel on Novak's property, and Novak was afraid he was going to lose his shirt. On March 23, 1962, the forty-four-year-old Novak was found dead in his car, parked in his garage with the engine running. The coroner ruled his death a suicide. However, a large bruise on his head some found suspicious. Washington D.C.'s *Daily News* called it a "mystery death." Baker subsequently told Mrs. Novak he had a buyer for the Carousel, Serv-U company, which provided vending machines made by a company partly owned by mobster Sam Giancana. The involvement of Serv-U was made possible by Ed Levinson. Along with an associate named Benjamin Seigelbaum, he arranged for a $400,000 loan from an Oklahoma City bank that put Serv-U into operation.[39]

The relationship connected Bobby Baker to the mob, for Levinson owned the Fremont Hotel in Las Vegas and was close to Meyer Lansky and Sam Giancana. Baker used his influence to try and obtain gambling rights for Levinson in Latin America, as the mob continued to look for an alternative to the Cuban casinos they had lost when Castro came to power. In November 1962, an FBI wiretap of Levinson's Las Vegas office picked up a reference to Baker, which led to allegations

of a conflict of interest and corruption after a disgruntled former government contractor sued Baker. In September 1963, two months before the assassination, the
Senate Rules Committee began investigating Baker on potential bribery charges for
illegally using money allocated by Congress and arranging sexual favors in exchange
for votes and government contracts. Under pressure, Baker had to resign as Secretary to the Majority Leader, LBJ, the following month.[40]

The allegations against Baker were not the only scandal making headlines in
1963. Billy Sol Estes was a businessman who also had close ties to LBJ. In the late
1950s, Estes got involved in the ammonia business with Texas farmers and land
deals with cotton growers, and both turned out to be scams. The Justice Department began an investigation into Estes in 1962 for paying off four Agricultural
officials for grain storage contracts. In 1963 Estes was tried and convicted.[41]

The Bobby Baker and Billy Sol Estes scandals threatened to put LBJ in prison,
for the investigation would eventually expand to include him. The JFK assassination
saved him, but these were not the only LBJ relationships that caused concern for
those afraid of what an investigation into the vice president might uncover. Lyndon
Johnson, for decades, had been involved in unsavory deals in Texas that could have
destroyed many influential people if the details about them ever saw the light of day.
It does prove Johnson was involved in JFK's assassination. But those who murdered
Kennedy knew someone was waiting in the wings who would not investigate the
assassination properly because to do so would open an investigation into himself.

One need only look at the financial record of Lyndon Johnson to understand
that he was a dishonest politician. In 1934 he entered politics as a man of modest
means, but he was worth an estimated $20 million by the time of his death, an
impossible sum to accumulate on a public servant's salary. Consider what occurred
in the early 1940s while Johnson was still in the House of Representatives. At
the time, television was in its infancy. In 1943 Johnson purchased KTBC, a radio
station that operated in the Austin area. It was not a coincidence that the Federal
Communications Commission had suspended the station's right to broadcast just
before the purchase, making it possible for Johnson to buy the station at ten percent
of its original value. Then, a month later, the FCC granted Johnson the right to
resume broadcasting, thanks in no small part to the intervention of the nephew
of Texas Congressman and LBJ mentor Sam Rayburn, who was a member of the
FCC. In addition, Johnson received permission to broadcast at 1,000 watts, four
times the power granted to the original owner. Shortly after that, Johnson's company, the Texas Broadcasting Corporation, entered the world of television, and it
became one of the first companies to receive a license to broadcast nationwide. The
FCC prohibited anyone from competing with Johnson in the Austin area for a
decade, preserving his monopoly.[42]

In 1948, Johnson won the Democratic nomination for the U.S. Senate with
a mere 87 votes out of 988,295 votes cast. Thanks to a suspiciously late ballot

count in the town of Alice in Duval County on the Mexican border, Johnson's total increased by 202 votes, and he was named the winner. His opponent, Coke Stevenson, thought it was a fraud. He appealed the ruling in federal court, claiming the vote count correction only occurred after Johnson phoned George Parr, an influential South Texas political boss known as the "Duke of Duval County." The final total included votes from the graveyard and Mexico, but the court still disregarded Stevenson's protest.[43]

After Parr committed suicide in 1975, Luis Salas, the local election judge in 1948, admitted to the *Dallas Morning News* that Parr ordered him to certify fictitious ballots in favor of Johnson. Worse yet, newsman Bill Mason, who had investigated possible fraud in the election, was murdered by Sam Smithwick, an associate of Parr. After he agreed to talk, the police found Swithwick hanging from his prison cell. It was how a person got ahead in Texas politics.[44]

When Earl Warren was District Attorney in California, an associate of his was executed gangland-style after attempting to expose Johnson's theft of the 1948 Texas U.S. Senate election. The man's son tried to investigate his father's death but was attacked and nearly beaten to death. Warren undoubtedly had suspicions of what transpired in Dallas. He knew Johnson and his cohorts were capable of anything, which was why he initially turned down Johnson's request for him to head the investigation into JFK's assassination. He finally relented and left his meeting with Johnson with tears in his eyes.[45]

As previously mentioned, George and Herman Brown were strong backers of Lyndon Johnson when he was a Congressman. The Federal Corrupt Practices Act prevented corporations from making political contributions in the 1940s, and personal donations were limited to $5,000. Undeterred, the Brown brothers had their employees each make a $5,000 contribution. When the IRS investigated, they discovered that each employee received a $5,000 cash payment from the Browns around the same time.[46]

Future Texas Governor John Connally served briefly as Congressman Lyndon Johnson's administrative assistant in Washington, but he soon tired of it and returned to Texas to practice law. Initially a liberal Democrat, Connally refused to join Hunt and Murchison in San Antonio to hear MacArthur's speech in 1952. He eventually became associated with Sid Richardson, and this relationship changed his life. After Richardson died in 1959, Connally became executor of his estate and a rich man in the process. He also became more conservative, shedding party loyalties to vote for Eisenhower. Johnson underwent a similar shift, changing from a liberal to a conservative Democrat. The reason behind Connally and Johnson's decision was apparent—the oil industry leaned heavily to the right, and it behooved them to stay in their good graces.[47]

* * *

Carlos Marcello's Mafia control over Texas began when Johnson's political career began to flourish, which was not a coincidence. Jack Halfen was a bagman for Marcello in Texas who made payments to local politicians, which provided Marcello the protection he required. The Marcello crime family paid a percentage of the profits generated from illegal activities in Texas to Congressman Albert Thomas and others. Still, according to author John H. Davis in *Mafia Kingfish*, Lyndon Johnson benefited the most. According to Davis, "Of all the Texas politicians the Marcello-Halfen interests supported, the most powerful was Senator Lyndon B. Johnson. It has been estimated the Marcello-Halfen group funneled at least $50,000 a year of Marcello's gambling profits alone to Lyndon Johnson, and in return, Johnson helped kill in committee all anti-rackets legislation that could have harmed the interests of Carlos Marcello and Jack Halfen. It was safe to say that Carlos Marcello was able to operate freely in Dallas in 1963."[48]

As previously mentioned, Bobby Baker was associated with Johnson and Murchison, but the previously mentioned Irv Davidson tied all these nefarious characters together. A lobbyist who was a fixture in Washington in the mid-1950s, Davidson was also an arms dealer who represented, in addition to Duvalier in Haiti, the dictator Trujillo from the Dominican Republic and the Somoza government in Nicaragua, to whom he sold a shipment of Israeli weapons.[49] "My specialty," he told an FBI source in 1955, "is to furnish anyone, anywhere, whatever armaments and other equipment they need as long as no questions are asked." Reports during the 1950s connected him to the Murchison family and Jimmy Hoffa. Davidson was the middleman for several loans from the Teamsters' Central States Pension Fund. While this was happening, he stayed on good terms with the CIA and FBI. In November 1958, working with Cuban leader Batista, the FBI learned that Davidson had received a $260,000 letter of credit from the Cuban government to purchase more arms from Israel.[50]

One person whom Davidson was very close to was Carlos Marcello. When Robert Kennedy had Marcello deported to Guatemala in 1961, Davidson was the only person in Washington who had the mobster's phone number. According to Edward Partin, an informant whose testimony would send Hoffa to prison years later, he was present at a secret meeting in late 1960 where Hoffa and Marcello contributed $500,000 to Richard Nixon's election campaign.

Years later. Marcello solicited Davidson's help to get Hoffa out of prison, resulting in a pardon being granted for Hoffa by President Nixon, another well-connected associate of Davidson.[51]

Jimmy Hoffa did business with Murchison through Davidson, arranging a massive Teamster Pension Fund loan for the Texas oilman. The Davidson/Murchison connection was secretive and only surfaced during the Bobby Baker investigation. So, as an investigation into Baker's affairs deepened, his ties to mobsters and unscrupulous Texas oil barons became apparent, much to the chagrin of Lyndon Johnson.

In 1963, associates of Baker's vending machine company filed a lawsuit against him. What intrigued Senate investigators most was that they were all members of organized crime. And one of these associates, the previously mentioned Edward Levinson, was also a lieutenant of Meyer Lansky. It was Davidson who initially put Baker in touch with Clint Murchison.

On November 9, 1963, the *New York Times* reported that Baker ". . . had made a special trip to California last May . . . to protect a racetrack monopoly in San Diego. Governor Brown said Mr. Baker had spoken to him in opposition to legislation requiring competitive bidding for a lease at the Del Mar racetrack. The track . . . has been leased to a charitable organization headed by the wealthy Murchison family of Texas . . . Mr. Baker was intervening on behalf of the Murchisons because of the financial support the family had given the Democratic Party. Governor Brown noted that Mr. Baker had said the appointment was setup by Vice President Johnson . . ."[52]

Meanwhile, the *New York Times* reported the details of Baker's involvement with the meatpacking company HAMPCO in Haiti, and that "Clint W. Murchison, Jr., the Texas industrialist, who has an interest in a flour monopoly in Haiti, also had an interest in the slaughterhouse and packing plant."[53] Thus, in the early part of 1963, Marcello, Murchison, Hoffa, and Lyndon Johnson were all connected. Hoffa dealt directly with Levinson, Davidson, and Murchison, who was associated with LBJ through Bobby Baker. And to this group of nefarious characters, add one more name, who also relied on Irv Davidson—FBI Director J. Edgar Hoover.

It was an aide to Clint Murchison who introduced Hoover to Davidson. In later years, Bobby Baker stated that "Murchison owned a piece of Hoover. Rich people always try to put their money with the sheriff because they're looking for protection. Hoover was the personification of law and order and officially against gangsters and everything, so it was a plus for a rich man to be identified with him. That's why men like Murchison made it their business to let everyone know Hoover was their friend. You can do a lot of illegal things if the head lawman is your buddy."[54]

The relationship between Hoover and Murchison began in the late 1940s when, along with Sid Richardson, Murchison entertained Hoover regularly by taking him on hunting trips, among other things. It was all free of charge—Hoover did not pay for anything. From 1953 until his death, Hoover and his companion, Clyde Tolsen, stayed every year at the Murchison-owned Del Carro hotel in La Jolla, California, situated close to the Del Mar racetrack. The La Jolla was a small hotel that catered to those who could afford the exorbitant nightly rate. Murchison picked up the tab for Hoover every year, despite that his stays sometimes lasted two months. "Hoover made no attempt to pay the bill," recalled the hotel manager years later.[55]

And that was not all. "Hoover did have oil ventures with Clint Murchison," recalled John Dowd, the head of a Justice Department investigation into possible illegal FBI activity initiated after Hoover's death. "If the drilling company hit a dry hole, he'd [Hoover] get his money back. Everything was a sure thing . . . It was extraordinary." William Sullivan, Hoover's Assistant FBI Director, confirmed what Dowd had said. He recalled that Hoover ". . . had a deal with Murchison where he invested in oil wells and if they hit oil, [Hoover] got his share of the profits, but if they didn't hit oil, he didn't share in the costs . . . One time, he got into severe trouble on his income tax manipulations, and we had to send an accountant from New York to Houston, Texas, where apparently the operation existed."[56]

The Del Carro was a favorite hangout for the mob. Dub McClanahan, a business partner of Carlos Marcello, was a yearly companion of Hoover's there. John Roselli claimed, "I knew Hoover. I'd buy him drinks, and we'd talk. It was fun to be with the Director of the FBI like that."[57]

In 1954, Clint Murchison and Sid Richardson purchased the Del Mar racetrack and immediately established Boys Inc., a fraudulent fund designed to take profits from the racetrack and donate them to underprivileged boys. It was a tax shelter. "This dodge is as old as the hills," charged ex-President Herbert Hoover. Despite this, J. Edgar Hoover did not find fault with what his old friends were doing. "I know Clint Murchison," Hoover said, "and I think he would be the last person in the country to use such a plan as a clever tax on business subterfuge . . ."[58]

It was clear that if wealthy Texans and Mafia figures were involved in the assassination of JFK in any capacity, there was nothing for them to fear from a potential FBI investigation into the crime. The incriminating information they had on Hoover made that a certainty.

* * *

Clint Murchison's ties to Mafia figures extended beyond Carlos Marcello. The Vito Genovese crime family owned twenty percent of the Murchison oil lease company.[59] Recall Genovese's relationship with Lucky Luciano and his involvement in the Mafia/WCC/Corsican drug operation that funded the Donovan/Dulles stay-behind armies in Europe. Murchison was a bridge between the radical right in Texas and leaders of organized crime like Genovese and Marcello.

In 1962, an ex-employee of Jack Ruby's from the Carousel Club, Nancy Perrin Rich, became involved in gun smuggling to Cuba with her husband. A meeting at a Dallas motel room included a U.S. military colonel, but a lack of financing threatened to cancel the operation. Until, to her surprise, Jack Ruby entered with the necessary money. Then, at a subsequent meeting, Nancy Perrin Rich claimed that the son of Vito Genovese was also in attendance. If she intended to lie to connect Ruby to organized crime, why would Perrin Rich pick Genovese's name? Marcello, Trafficante, Civello—maybe, but a connection of the Genovese family to the JFK assassination or Jack Ruby was never publicly reported. Perrin Rich likely told the truth that the Genovese family was involved in a Cuban gun smuggling operation with Jack Ruby. However, it is unknown if this gathering had anything to do with the assassination of JFK. It was probably unrelated, but its importance is that Ruby was involved in an operation that made him known to people who could have been behind JFK's murder. And this made him vulnerable.

Ruby knew what was happening in Dallas in the early 1960s. It makes what he had to say after his arrest so interesting. In 1964, he wrote a letter to a fellow inmate about to leave prison, which the ex-convict subsequently sold to an assassination researcher. In it, Ruby wrote, ". . . isn't it strange that Oswald who hasn't worked a lick most of his life, should be fortunate enough to get a job at the Book Bldg. two wks. [*sic*] before the president himself didn't know . . . when he was to visit Dallas, now where would a jerk like Oswald get the information that the president was coming to Dallas. Only one person could have had that information, and that man was Johnson . . ."[60]

Ruby's question regarding Oswald's employment at the Texas School Book Depository could be considered the mindless rambling of a desperate man. That is, were it not for the fact that oilman David Harold Byrd owned the building. This Suite 8F Group member was also closely associated with Clint Murchison, Sid Richardson, and H.L. Hunt. Along with George de Mohrenschildt, Byrd belonged to both the right-wing Texas Crusade for Freedom and the Dallas Petroleum Club. He knew de Mohrenschildt well enough that the good Baron put Byrd's wife on the board of the cystic fibrosis charity he had established. Byrd was also close friends with Lyndon Johnson, Sam Rayburn, and John Connally. His cousin was U.S. Senator Harry Byrd of Virginia, a white supremacist and a leader in the conservative movement.[61]

The Dallas Petroleum Club membership also included Murchison, Richardson, H.L. Hunt, and Dallas Mayor Earl Cabell (whose brother was Allen Dulles' CIA deputy). Future President George H.W. Bush, who was well acquainted with Byrd and de Mohrenschildt, was also a member.

It was an elite group, and Byrd's contacts were impressive. If there was one thing that characterized them all, it was a hatred for JFK. The fact that the Texas oilman owned the Texas School Book Depository building is, by itself, no reason to view Byrd with suspicion. However, Byrd's conduct was puzzling. He had the eight-panel sniper's nest window, from which Oswald allegedly fired at Kennedy, removed, then hung in his Dallas mansion as a macabre kind of trophy, a gesture that gives one pause. In addition, at the beginning of November 1963, just a couple of weeks before the assassination, Byrd left Dallas for a two-month African safari.[62]

In 1948, Byrd founded Byrd Oil Corporation and B-H Drilling Corporation, followed by Three States Natural Gas Company in 1952. He eventually sold Byrd Oil and Three States and used the money to establish Temco, Inc., an aircraft company. In the early 1960s, Byrd merged Temco with his friend James Ling's electronics company and an aircraft manufacturer named Chance Vought Corporation to form Ling-Temco-Vought (LTV). Byrd purchased 132,000 shares of LTV in early

November 1963, even though the company was struggling at the time. It was most fortuitous, for a couple of weeks later, Byrd's good friend LBJ became President, and in early 1964, as the Vietnam War began, the U.S. military bought 1,500 new A7 aircraft from LTV. By 1968 the company was worth $3.8 billion.[63] Did Byrd purchase all those shares in LTV because he knew the war was about to escalate or was this another lucky coincidence?

In October 1950, a man named Mac Wallace went to work for the United States Department of Agriculture (perhaps involved in the shady dealings of Billy Sol Estes described above) as a political operative for Lyndon Johnson. At the time, Johnson was under scrutiny because of the election he had stolen from Coke Stevenson two years before. Meanwhile, Wallace was also having an affair with LBJ's sister, Josefa; at the same time, she was seeing an Austin miniature golf course owner named John Douglas Kinser. When Kinser asked Josefa to arrange for LBJ to lend him money, the Senator took it as a blackmail threat. On October 22, 1951, Mac Wallace shot and killed Kisner at his miniature golf course. A witness took down Wallace's license plate number as he tried to escape, and in short order, the police apprehended the accused murderer.

Out on bail, Wallace immediately resigned from his job at Agriculture to protect Lyndon Johnson. His murder trial began in February 1952, and his lawyer admitted Wallace's guilt but justified the shooting of Kinser because he was sleeping with Wallace's girlfriend. The defense's position fell on deaf ears, for the jury found Wallace guilty of "murder with malice aforethought." Eleven jurors voted for the death penalty, with one opting for life imprisonment. None of it mattered because Judge Charles O. Betts overruled the jury and gave Wallace a five-year suspended sentence.[64]

Five months after the trial was over, Wallace went to work for Tempco, the aircraft company owned by David Harold Byrd. He remained there until he relocated to LTV's office in Anaheim, California, in February 1961. Around the same time, USDA Inspector Henry Marshall was investigating the shady dealings of Billy Sol Estes, which would lead directly to LBJ when exposed. In January 1961, two days before he became vice president, Johnson met with Estes and an LBJ underling, Clifton Carter. Five months later, on June 3, 1961, Henry Marshall was dead, shot five times with a rifle owned by Marshall. And in fine Texas tradition, the County Sheriff ruled the death a suicide. But by the following year, the Estes investigation was heating up. The coroner exhumed Marshall's body, and murder was the cause of death.[65]

A closer look at the case raised serious questions. How did a convicted murderer like Wallace obtain a security clearance to work for a defense contractor, even though the job transfer required a background check by the Navy? Some have alleged this could only have happened with the intervention of the vice president, but there is no concrete evidence proving that this occurred.

Madeleine Brown called Wallace a "hatchet man" for Lyndon Johnson, and the evidence supports this. Josefa Johnson, employed at a local brothel, had become a liability to LBJ and was murdered on Christmas Eve, 1961. No autopsy was performed on the body, even though state law required it. George Krutilek was Estes' business associate and accountant. On April 4, 1962, seven days after the arrest of Estes on fraud charges and five days after the FBI interrogated him regarding Estes, Krutilek was found dead in his car. Just like Henry Marshall, his death was ruled a suicide, though by carbon-monoxide poisoning. In 1964, two other Estes associates, Harold Eugene Orr and Howard Pratt, were found dead of carbon monoxide poisoning.[66] The message was clear. Cross Lyndon Johnson, and you might wind up dead. JFK should have paid more attention to what his running mate was capable of doing.

* * *

Another associate of David Harold Boyd was Dallas oilman Jack Crichton. Recall from Chapter Four that Crichton was also a former OSS officer who had served in Europe, and by 1956 had organized the 488th Military Intelligence Detachment, a U.S. Army Reserve unit operating out of Dallas. Crichton asked White Russian Ilya Mamantov to be Marina Oswald's interpreter after the assassination, whom de Mohrenschildt called the one "excessive rightist" among the Russian émigré community in Dallas. Mamantov was also a Republican precinct boss, and Crichton was the Republican candidate for governor of Texas in 1964.[67]

Crichton was president of Nafco Oil and Gas, and both Crichton and Byrd were directors of Dorchester Gas Producing. According to author Russ Baker in *Family of Secrets*, Clint Murchison was a director of one of Crichton's companies. Crichton also served as President of the Dallas Petroleum Engineers Club, so he was part of Dallas's "Big Oil" network and well connected without question.

According to an ex-Cuban intelligence officer under Fidel Castro, Fabian Escalante, CIA's "Tracy Barnes . . . called a meeting on January 18, 1960 . . ." to discuss a possible invasion of Cuba to get rid of Fidel Castro. Invited to the meeting, said Escalante, was an "important group of businessmen headed by George Bush [Sr.] and Jack Crichton, both Texas oilmen, to gather the necessary funds for Operation 40."[68]

If true, over three years before Kennedy's assassination, Crichton was at the heart of U.S. intelligence when the CIA was trying to kill Castro. Also noteworthy is that in 1963, Tracy Barnes was head of CIA's Domestic Contacts Division. It was a local Dallas agent from this division who, according to George de Mohrenschildt, asked him to contact Oswald when he returned to Texas from the Soviet Union. The reference to Operation 40 is equally significant, for it was the CIA group responsible for assassination during the Bay of Pigs invasion.

The relationship between Crichton and George H.W. Bush is also a matter of record. In the 1964 election, George Bush and Jack Crichton stumped together;

the former was running for the U.S. Senate, the latter for Texas Governor. Crichton would later state that they "spoke from the same podiums." Considering Mamantov was a local precinct boss, George Bush knew him as well.

Crichton maintained a relationship with U.S. intelligence from his time with the OSS through the Kennedy assassination. In August 1953, he joined Empire Trust Company and eventually became vice president. Empire had a worldwide network of associates, a private version of the CIA, which could also describe Donovan and Dulles' WCC organization.[69]

In 1952, Crichton was part of a group, including Clint Murchison and the Du Ponts, that tried to negotiate oil drilling rights in Spain with Fascist dictator Francisco Franco.[70] It may have been part of something bigger, for, at the same time, the U.S. was negotiating with Spain for permission to build airbases there. One person heavily involved in that effort was the seemingly ever-present and Suite 8F Group member, William Pawley.

In 1948, Secretary of State George Marshall asked Pawley to accompany him to a United Nations General Assembly meeting in Paris. Still, his attendance there was likely a cover for something else. Shortly after arriving in Paris, Pawley left for Madrid to discuss the possibility of the U.S. building airbases in Spain. The trip was unofficial, and Pawley did not come as an accredited diplomat or carry papers that explained the purpose of his visit. He met with Franco on September 11, and the Spanish dictator approved the airbases in exchange for the repeal of a U.N. resolution that had called him "an enemy of world peace." Pawley reported the excellent news to Marshall, but Truman's surprise victory in the 1948 election delayed signing a treaty with Spain.[71]

By 1950, Dwight Eisenhower was appointed supreme allied commander, Europe (SACEUR) by Truman. Eisenhower and Pawley were close, and the future President wanted him appointed ambassador to Spain, which did not happen. However, in February 1951, Pawley was appointed special assistant to Secretary of State Acheson instead. The new U.S. ambassador to Spain was Stanton Griffis, and he asked Pawley to come to Madrid, which he did. But once again, the trip was shrouded in mystery. The State Department declined "to say what Mr. Pawley's assignment was or to divulge the nature of his position with Secretary Acheson." In any event, when Griffis made an official visit to Spain's Foreign Minister Alberto Martin-Artajo Alvarez, he was accompanied by Pawley, which suggests talks about U.S. airbases were the topic of discussion.

After the meeting, Pawley traveled to Paris and told Eisenhower that a change in U.S. foreign policy was needed. "Political obstacles" were blocking the Pentagon's desire to rearm Spain. Undeterred, Ike wanted confirmation that Spain was willing to join NATO and provide troops for Western Europe's defense. After another trip to Spain, Pawley submitted a report to U.S. Embassies in London, Paris, and Madrid, stating that "Franco does not object to the use of Spanish troops in Western

Europe . . . Franco is willing to make available to US air, naval and other bases . . . and he would have no objection to Spain's ultimate integration into NATO . . ." Eventually, due mainly to Pawley's efforts, the U.S. military ". . . acquired the Air Force bases at Torrejon, Zaragosa, and Moron; the Navy complex at Rota; and the pipeline across Spain from Seville to Madrid and Zaragoza."[72]

William Pawley knew how to get things done when dealing with right-wing dictators, and his presence in Spain is relevant to our narrative. While Pawley was there, the Clint Murchison and Jack Crichton group appeared in Spain around the same time. Amazingly, so did General Charles Willoughby, MacArthur's intelligence chief in Japan and Korea. He was also in Madrid to discuss potential U.S. military bases with Franco. For three months, Willoughby, the general whom MacArthur called "my little Fascist," remained in Spain, was provided government limousines, and was in constant contact with Franco's ministers. Spain under Franco was, in Willoughby's words, "a cradle of supermen."[73] Like Pawley, the public did not know why he was there. The *Portland Oregonian* reported that the "purpose of the retired general's visit was not learned, but he will confer with Spanish military men."[74]

Willoughby was a racist, anti-Semite Fascist whose heroes were Franco and Mussolini. In 1939, he wrote about the Italian Fascist leader: "Historical judgment, freed from the emotional haze of the moment, will credit Mussolini with wiping out a memory of defeat by re-establishing the traditional military supremacy of the white race." Willoughby believed that Communists, Russians, and Eastern Europeans were to be eliminated, for they represented "the historical continuity of 'Mongoloid-Pan Slavism,'" which threatened Western society.[75]

Willoughby had a relationship with both William Donovan and Allen Dulles. Before World War I, he chased Pancho Villa in Mexico with Donovan. And in the mid-1950s, he and Dulles maintained a back-and-forth correspondence, as Willoughby offered his services to the head of CIA, writing on one occasion, "I have an exceptional entrée in Spain." Dulles rejected Willoughby's request to join the CIA. Still, the two men likely had a behind-the-scenes professional relationship that they wanted to keep hidden. Willoughby had contacted Dulles regarding developing a "youth movement" within Germany between young American and German servicemen. "The new generation has less to remember—and to resent," he wrote. "I do not want to stand alone (though the Germans will take it up), and I suggest that you examine it, from the viewpoint of a 'discreet' penetration and the 'making of friends.'"

Dulles showed an interest, responding, "I trust we may soon get together for a personal account of your conversation with the German gentlemen. I have also had two very interesting meetings with them . . ." One of the two was General Hans Speidel, chief of staff for Rommel during World War II.[76] Since the ex-Nazi was not a Communist, working with him was acceptable, no matter what dastardly deeds he had perpetrated in the past.

The discussion between Willoughby and Dulles must have pertained to the stay-behind armies Dulles had established with Donovan, which was in full swing when they spoke. The German "youth movement" could be of service to that operation. Willoughby most likely did get involved in this, based on the path he would follow during the ensuing years. He eventually became a member of the radical right-wing Committee of Correspondence for the Anti-Communist Liaison. Retired Brigadier General and ex-MacArthur military secretary in Japan, Bonner Fellers, was also involved with this group. Fellers advocated a rollback of communism, but he was not a CIA supporter, calling the organization "a group of Marxist-Socialist Pro-Communists." It did not preclude dealings with Donovan and Dulles, for their private army operated outside the CIA. Fellers became a military attaché in Spain after Franco came to power and was part of Donovan's original OSS "planning group." With his right-wing credentials and background, it is plausible that Fellers was also involved with Willoughby in the negotiations to build military bases in Spain.[77]

Nazi Otto Skorzeny, who had once led a commando raid to rescue Mussolini, was an ex-SS colonel who also settled in Madrid in the early 1950s. Dick Russell wrote in *The Man Who Knew Too Much* that Skorzeny ". . . set up his "International Fascista" . . . [and] reportedly kept in close contact with Gehlen [which meant he was involved with the stay-behind armies]." As the years passed, Russell continued, "Skorzeny's name would be linked not only to CIA but also to Latin American death squads, global illegal arms deals, and assassination plots against de Gaulle and Castro."[78] Add to this that Skorzeny was associated with Victor Oswald, who worked with the WCC, which leads back to Dulles and Donovan. Recall that Victor Oswald had a relationship with Thomas Eli Davis, which led to Jack Ruby, George De Mohrenschildt, and the host of others mentioned earlier in this chapter. The various interconnecting relationships all point toward the possibility that an international Fascist organization was involved in the JFK assassination.[79] At the very least, it demonstrates that those in Dallas who are assassination suspects were working in concert with Donovan and Dulles's WCC organization in Europe for over a decade in the war against communism. And they knew that their relationship with J. Edgar Hoover and Lyndon Johnson, whose private behavior could never be made known to the public at large, guaranteed them immunity from prosecution. And in the middle of this was the CIA, the missing but most important piece of the puzzle. And what they were up to during the Cold War years was unconscionable, making them very suspect and worth investigating. For like those in Texas, they had skeletons in their close in 1963, and they would have done anything to keep their "Family Jewels" hidden from public scrutiny, even if it meant assassinating a U.S. President.

- 10 -

The Best Laid Plans of Mice and Men

"It is now clear that we are facing an implacable enemy whose avowed objective is world domination by whatever means and at whatever cost. There are no rules in such a game."

—General James Doolittle

On December 22, 1963, exactly one month after JFK's assassination, an article appeared in the Washington Post, written by Harry Truman. The ex-President must have had the assassination in mind when he wrote:

". . . [for] some time I have been disturbed by the way the CIA has been diverted from its original assignment. It has become an operational arm and . . . a policy-making arm of the Government . . . I never had any thoughts when I set up the CIA that it would be injected into peacetime cloak and dagger operations. Some of the complications and embarrassments that I think we have experienced are in part attributable to the fact that this quiet intelligence arm of the President has been so removed from its intended role that it is being interpreted as a symbol of sinister and mysterious foreign intrigue . . . There is something about the way the CIA has been functioning that is casting a shadow over our historical position, and I feel we need to correct it."[1]

* * *

Truman was right to be concerned, for covert operations were never in the Agency's job description. At its formation, the Truman administration gave the CIA five general assignments:

1. to advise the National Security Council in matters concerning such intelligence activities of the government departments and agencies as relating to national security;

2. to make recommendations to the National Security Council for the coordination of such intelligence activities;

3. to correlate and evaluate intelligence relating to the national security and provide for the appropriate dissemination of such intelligence within the government . . . Provided that the Agency shall have no police, subpoena, law-enforcement powers, or internal-security functions . . . ;

4. to perform, for the benefit of the existing intelligence agencies, such additional services of common concern as the National Security Council determines can be more efficiently accomplished centrally;

5. to perform such other functions and duties related to intelligence affecting the national security as the National Security Council may from time to time direct."[2]

Indeed, the creation of the Office of Policy Coordination (OPC) and the passage of NSC-10/2 provided the CIA with a mandate to do whatever it pleased when fighting communism; however, no one anticipated the extent to which the Agency would go. Allen Dulles would involve the CIA in secret stay-behind armies in Europe, funded by an international drug operation run by organized crime syndicates that encompassed three continents, employed the services of ex-Nazis and involved the Vatican in the execution of their operations. And they would use ex-Nazis in various other capacities. Very few people knew about this, or that PB/7 specialized in assassination, and that other nefarious covert operations, such as illicit drug experimentation, were conducted and kept hidden from Congress. Soon it became clear the Agency was somewhat of a loose cannon, and people began to notice.

As described in Chapter Seven, in 1954, there were two ideological camps in Eisenhower's young administration—psychological warfare and massive retaliation. The latter required maintaining nuclear weapon superiority over the Soviets. The former relied on staying out of a shooting war by focusing on U.S. intelligence and covert operations. Eisenhower cautiously supported psychological warfare, which meant a more substantial reliance on the CIA. However, the official U.S. position was a combination of both. Still, Ike had reservations. A CIA mission gone awry could provoke a retaliatory military response from the Soviets to escalate and start World War III just as quickly as a military general could. As a result, in 1954, Ike authorized two separate committees to investigate the CIA.

An innocent game of tennis between William Pawley and Phil Graham of the *Washington* Post was how the first investigation of the CIA came to be. Graham informed Pawley that he knew about a pending invasion of Guatemala by the CIA. "I might have been listening to a top-secret briefing at State," Pawley wrote. He was already involved in the invasion, having had discussions about it with Eisenhower and Allen Dulles and purchasing planes to support the Guatemalan rebels in their attempted coup. Graham's information came from a high-level CIA official who had leaked information to him, troubling Eisenhower and Pawley. In the end, Pawley turned down Eisenhower's request to investigate the CIA because of his close relationship with both Dulles brothers and did not want to betray their trust. Eisenhower then gave Lieutenant General James Doolittle the responsibility to "make any recommendations calculated to improve the conduct of these [CIA] operations."[3]

The Soviets had established the KGB in March 1954, which made Doolittle's investigation more urgent. Ex-CIA Director Walter Bedell Smith told the commission he had doubts about Allen Dulles, whom he believed "was too emotional to be in this critical spot." There were other areas of concern as well. They concluded that the CIA had "ballooned out into a vast and sprawling organization manned by a large number of people, some of whom were of doubtful competence." Frank Wisner was a potentially dangerous person. He surrounded himself with people "having little or no training for their jobs" and initiated projects without any oversight that were unknown to anyone outside the CIA.[4] It mirrored the concerns that others had about the Agency. Yet, the report must have surprised Eisenhower when Doolittle finally submitted it to him. It did not denounce the CIA and its leader, Allen Dulles. On the contrary, Doolittle reported that the CIA needed to improve and expand covert operations and categorically stated that the CIA had not gone far enough, as per the following:

"As long as it remains national policy, another important requirement is an aggressive covert psychological, political, and paramilitary organization more effective, more unique, and, if necessary, more ruthless than that employed by the enemy . . .

"It is now clear that we are facing an implacable enemy whose . . . objective is world domination . . . There are no rules in such a game. Hitherto acceptable norms of human conduct do not apply [and] long-standing American concepts of 'fair play' must be reconsidered. We must develop effective espionage and counter-espionage services and must learn to subvert, sabotage, and destroy our enemies by more clever, more sophisticated, and more effective methods than those used against us . . ."[5]

Instead of reigning in the Agency, the Doolittle Report provided a mandate for the CIA to do whatever it wanted, and in some cases, without Congressional oversight. The President soon received another report from David Bruce, who had been Donovan's personal assistant during World War II and was a close friend of Frank Wisner and Allen Dulles. The report, co-authored by former Secretary of Defense Robert Lovett, and former Deputy Chief of Naval Operations Richard Connolly, was more candid than Doolittle's analysis. "The supporters of the 1948 decision to launch this government on a positive psychological warfare and paramilitary program," the report stated, "could not possibly have foreseen the ramifications of the operations which have resulted from it." It continued that only "those in the CIA immediately concerned with their day to day operation, has any detailed knowledge of what is going on." A primary concern was that "almost any psychological warfare and paramilitary action can be . . . justified." "The CIA, busy, monied, and privileged, likes its 'kingmaking' responsibility. The intrigue is fascinating—considerable self-satisfaction, sometimes with applause, derives from 'successes'—no charge is made for 'failures'—and the whole business is very much simpler than collective covert intelligence on the USSR through the usual CIA methods."[6]

They referred to the CIA as a "rogue elephant" that "mingles in the affairs of other countries" and enjoyed "almost unilateral influence . . . on the actual formulation of our foreign policies." The Directorate of Plans was operating "on an autonomous and free-wheeling basis in highly critical areas," its actions "in direct conflict with the normal operations being carried out by the Department of State." "Congress had never intended to grant a United States Intelligence Agency authority to conduct operations all over the earth," the report continued, and they essentially accused CIA of treasonous conduct, operating in opposition to official U.S. foreign policy. It was why they called for "a total reassessment of our covert action policies."[7] They could not have been more critical of what the CIA was doing.

It was the beginning of the "Deep State" that Eisenhower faced in the early 1950s. The military perceived itself constitutionally mandated to protect the American people from politicians who were not qualified to make foreign policy decisions, so they sabotaged the Korean War. In addition, many generals wanted to initiate a first-strike, unprovoked nuclear attack against the Russians and Chinese, while the U.S. still had a nuclear superiority. Many influential right-wingers in the private sector supported this view. Meanwhile, the CIA was out of control. They created a foreign policy outside what Washington directed and was unknown to anyone but a select few inside the Agency.

In response to the Bruce/Lovett report, Eisenhower reportedly considered firing Allen Dulles, Deputy Director of Plans Richard Bissell, and Dulles' deputy, General Charles Cabell but decided not to. For despite the Agency's treasonous, rogue mentality and elitist attitude, Ike needed the CIA. Even though the CIA was prone to operate out of control, he understood that without a solid central intelligence agency conducting covert operations throughout the world, he would have to turn to the military if the CIA did not exist, which would have been a hundred times worse. There was no doubt. Leaving the military unchecked would inevitably lead to a worldwide nuclear holocaust. So, Eisenhower kept the CIA in place but with strict oversight over approved covert operations. Most importantly, plausible deniability had to be maintained, but he would soon learn that this was a losing proposition.

The Operations Coordinating Board (OCB) was formed on September 2, 1953, to report directly to the National Security Council and implement a national security policy. By the following March, Ike approved NSC 5412, which required the CIA to consult with OCB regarding any operations it wished to pursue. The problem was that OCB had no use for covert operations. "The cold war is . . . a contest between two antithetical ideologies," OCB reported, "that of the totalitarian Communists and that of the US and the rest of the Free World." The solution was to find "an ideological weapon which can be used offensively." They called for the "formulation of the Free World position in terms that will gain the adherence of the variety of cultural, economic, and social patterns which . . . make up the Free World."[8]

CIA did comply with OCB's winning of "hearts and minds" approach in Third World countries where the U.S. competed with the Soviets for widespread approval, but the President did not want to clip the wings of CIA entirely, just keep them under control. As a result, OCB became streamlined on March 12, 1955, with NSC 5412/1, which created the Planning Coordination Group (PCG) within OCB. Chaired by Nelson Rockefeller, PCG was responsible for approving all covert operations. Still, it was abolished within a year because the CIA was too secretive regarding what they were involved in worldwide. It led to the passage of NSC 5412/2 in December 1955, which stated that "Except as the President otherwise directs, designated representatives of the Secretary of State and of the Secretary of Defense . . . and a representative of the President designated for this purpose, shall hereafter be advised in advance of major covert programs initiated by CIA . . . and shall be the normal channel for giving policy approval for such programs as well as for securing coordination of support therefore among the Departments of State and Defense and the CIA."[9]

NSC 5412/2, known as the 5412 Committee, would remain in place for fifteen years. It offered successful oversight and input into CIA operations. That is, those operations CIA was willing to share with the 5412 Committee. For the most part, secrecy remained in place. The CIA continued to operate as an entity unto itself, conducting the most egregious covert operations without the President's knowledge or anyone else. With its ability to independently create the financing it needed for unsavory operations, there was no way to control the Agency. Eisenhower's attempt to reign them in, but the CIA became even more independent and more reckless.

* * *

During the Cold War, one of the CIA's main objectives was to overthrow leftist or Communist-led foreign regimes that did not serve the United States' best interests and replaced them with governments that did. And it usually involved a country with strategic importance due to its geographic location or an abundance of natural resources. They did this with Eisenhower's knowledge, for it was safer and more plausibly deniable to rely on the CIA than asking the military to get involved. By 1963, when the time came to remove an American President from power forcibly, the CIA was well-versed in pulling off such an operation and covering it up after the fact.

It all began for the CIA in 1952. Kermit Roosevelt Jr., a grandson of Theodore Roosevelt, was a CIA officer operating in Egypt, involved with a group known as the Free Officers Movement, whose objective was to overthrow King Farouk and control the Egyptian government. The coup succeeded. Shortly after that, additional CIA operatives arrived. They trained Egyptian forces in covert warfare, and they included 1,000 German military advisers, many of whom were former Nazi SS and Gestapo agents. As we have seen, the United States utilized the services of ex-Nazis in the early 1950s in a variety of areas, and that they would do so again in Egypt was not surprising. During World War II, Muslim countries sided with Germany, and on their behalf, recruited local forces to fight alongside the Axis powers. They did this mainly for two reasons—they saw Germany as a means of bringing British colonial rule in the Arab world to an end, and they opposed the Western desire to create a Jewish state in Palestine. Kermit Roosevelt's intention in Egypt was to protect American and European oil interests and to keep Egypt out of the Soviet Union's sphere of influence, which he did. Inserting ex-Nazis into Egypt was understandable, considering the anything-was-acceptable mentality that existed during the war against communism. It is unknown if Eisenhower knew about this, but it did not matter. By the following year, Roosevelt was in Iran attempting to overthrow the government there as well.

The Iranian situation began in the 1920s when the United States was involved in Iran's opium business. A former advisor at the U.S. State Department's Office of Foreign Trade, Arthur Millspaugh was hired to reorganize the Finance Ministry of Iran to grant oil air transport contracts and various other commercial rights to American businesspeople. Millspaugh had numerous tours in Iran. By the time of his third "Millspaugh Mission" in 1943, his group was collecting opium revenues, managing the Pharmaceutical Institute, and directing the Royal opium factory. Critics referred to them simply as "drug sellers." The Iranian public viewed them as liberators from British and Russian control.[10]

Millspaugh defended his involvement in the drug trade, citing that the U.S. Army had provided Iranian narcotics to Kachin soldiers in Burma during World War II as justification. "Our long-term program looked to the eventual elimination of the opium business," he wrote, and he did strengthen the Iranian budget, which solidified the American position with the Iranian government. However, Reza Shah, who ruled Iran, terminated Millspaugh's services when he failed to comply with the Shah's request to increase military funding.

In 1949, Allen Dulles, ostensibly still employed at Sullivan and Cromwell, traveled to Iran to negotiate a lucrative deal with the Shah on behalf of Overseas Consultants, Inc. (OCI), a recently formed consortium consisting of eleven large American engineering firms. The Iranians were to pay OCI $650 million to modernize Iran, including significant infrastructure improvements, essentially transforming the country's major cities. Dulles eventually brought the Shah to the

U.S. in November 1949 and hosted a dinner for him at the Council on Foreign Relations. "My government and people are eager to welcome American capital, to give it all possible safeguards," the Shah stated as he addressed the distinguished members of the council, many of whom were oilmen and businessmen interested in investing in Iran. He made a point of clarifying that the Iranian government did not intend to nationalize industry.[11]

British colonialism had played a large part in Iran's history, ever since the Royal Navy switched from coal to oil during World War I, which prompted the British to install the Shah and control the country's oil reserves. However, because he was a Nazi sympathizer whom they feared would ally Iran with Germany, in the early 1940s, the British replaced the Shah with his son, Mohammed Reza Pahlavi.[12] A disdain for the British developed throughout the country. With the U.S. Millspaugh Mission gone from Iran, conditions were ripe in 1951 for Prime Minister Mohammad Mossadegh to seize control of the Anglo-Iranian Oil Company and effectively neutralize the Shah.[13]

The Mossadegh takeover did not end ex-Nazi involvement in Iran. According to German author and political scientist Matthias Kuntzel, "In 1952 the Mossadegh government chose as their economic adviser none other than Hitler's former finance minister, Hjalmar Schacht . . . who had been dispatched to Tehran in 1936 at Hitler's behest. In the same year [1952], Mossadegh sent his economic expert Ali Amini to Bonn with the task of recruiting hundreds of German oilmen to replace the British experts after the planned nationalization of the Iranian oil industry [that he envisioned would take place]."[14]

Although a former Reichsbank President and Minister of Economics under Hitler, Schacht never joined the Nazi Party. He was dismissed as Finance Minister in 1943 after his involvement in the failed attempt on Hitler's life in 1944. Charges were brought against him at the Nuremberg Trials after the war, but he was acquitted. He reportedly worked with U.S. intelligence and became a secret agent for Allen Dulles.[15]

Also, in 1952 Schacht developed a strong relationship with Otto Skorzeny in Madrid, around the time that the U.S. was negotiating with Spain to install military bases there. As described in *The Skorzeny Papers*, "Schacht . . . was a major financial backer of Skorzeny's many business ventures . . ." Their relationship involved a Spanish company named SOFINDUS, which acted as a cover for Nazi intelligence during World War II. Its operation extended into France, North Africa, and South America. SOFINDUS was still in existence after the war, and the group was associated with Victor Oswald, which is a critical connection. The Schacht-Skorzeny financial network would remain active until well into the 1960s," and numerous suspects had a relationship with these men and what was transpiring in Madrid. [16]

As we know, Victor Oswald was a Madrid businessman connected to the WCC, the Donovan/ Dulles stay-behind armies in Europe, Thomas Eli Davis, Jean

Pierre Lafitte, and all the others described in Chapter Four. An international anti-Communist group involved big business interests, CIA assassination operatives, and American far-right Fascists, who all worked together for over a decade before JFK's murder. And Schacht was connected to ex-SOFINDUS Nazis involved with the WCC and their Fascist collaborators that were part of this group. He may not have been a member of the Nazi Party, but he indeed approved of what the Nazis stood for and would have appealed to those in the U.S. who supported self-determination and opposed socialism. "Liberty is not synonymous with laziness," Schacht wrote in his diary. "Freedom is not given away: it must be earned daily . . . Whoever desires better housing, clothing, and food must work for it. That's God's law . . . The idea of a welfare state as a kind of public benefactor under official leadership is an assumption leading directly to totalitarian communism, but which has nothing whatever in common with the sense of responsibility to the individual."[17]

Returning to Iran, Mossadegh's coup was a threat to the British, who were still recovering from the effects of World War II and financially overextended, so they turned to the U.S. for help. At a National Security Council meeting on March 4, 1953, a little over a month after Eisenhower's inauguration, John Foster Dulles warned that "Communists might easily take over [in Iran]." If that occurred, "some sixty percent of the world's oil reserves would fall into Communist control." Oil was the key component behind the American interest in Iran. Still, Eisenhower's initial instinct was to prop up Prime Minister Mossadegh and win him over from the Kremlin with a $100 million loan. It did not work.

Mossadegh discarded the OCI deal that Allen Dulles had brokered, which only added to the Dulles brothers' desire to remove him. They turned to Kermit Roosevelt, who had been putting together an underground resistance network inside Iran for the past two years, hiding weapons in the desert to distribute to tribal warriors to resist a Soviet invasion. It was right out of the playbook derived from the stay-behind armies Dulles and Donovan had put together in Europe. That Hjalmar Schacht, an associate of Otto Skorzeny and Victor Oswald, and probably connected to Reinhard Gehlen, worked inside the Mossadegh government while the United States was considering his overthrow, may not have been a coincidence. Schacht may have already been undercover, working for U.S. intelligence.

Roosevelt hired bands of mercenaries and paid Iranian military leaders to overthrow Mossadegh. Key officials who remained loyal to Mossadegh were kidnapped and murdered. Hidden under a blanket on the floor of an unmarked car, Roosevelt was secreted into the Shah's palace in Tehran to convince him to stand up to Mossadegh. However, when riots broke out in the streets of Tehran, the Shah fled to Rome. Roosevelt refused to leave and responded by bribing army officers and distributing $10,000 to local goons to instigate riots supporting the Shah. Eventually, Mossadegh fled, and the Shah returned to power.[18]

With the Shah restored, American and British oil companies regained their properties in Iran. Roosevelt eventually became vice president of Gulf Oil. The CIA established itself in Iran and used it as a base from which they could launch operations inside the Soviet Union. Meanwhile, the young Shah continued trading opium on the international market, for oil and national security issues were more important than stemming the spread of drugs throughout the world.[19]

The coups in Egypt and Iran were just the beginning, and the following year CIA set its site on Guatemala. The story began in 1936, when John Foster Dulles, as an attorney with Sullivan and Cromwell, created a virtual monopoly in Guatemala for his client, United Fruit Company. On retainer for United Fruit was attorney and Suite 8F Group member "Tommy the Cork" Corcoran, the Fascist involved with William Pawley in China (see Chapter Nine).

Problems arose in 1951 when Jacobo Arbenz orchestrated a successful military coup and took over the country. His downfall began when he challenged United Fruit, Guatemala's largest employer, which enjoyed a controlling interest in railroads, utilities, communications, and other significant industry forms. When 225,000 acres of property owned by the company were taken by the Guatemalan government, followed by United Fruit workers unionizing and demanding a pay increase of almost 100 percent, people of importance in the U.S. began to notice.[20]

It was then that United Fruit hired Tommy Corcoran to lobby Washington to have Arbenz overthrown, and he had some powerful support. Both John and Allen Dulles had, at one time, sat on the board of United Fruit's partner in their Guatemalan monopoly, the Schroder Banking Corporation (which had financed Adolph Hitler during his rise to power). The assistant secretary of state for inter-American affairs, John Moors Cabot, owned stock in the company, and his brother Thomas had served as president of United Fruit. When U.N. Ambassador Henry Cabot Lodge was a U.S. senator, he was a stockholder and strong supporter of United Fruit. Ann Whitman, Ike's secretary, was the wife of Edmund Whitman, United Fruit's public relations director. And finally, Walter Bedell Smith, the head of CIA under Truman and future undersecretary of state under Eisenhower, would later sit on the board of United Fruit.[21]

Truman authorized the CIA to organize a coup early in 1952 to assist Colonel Castillo Armas in overthrowing Arbenz. However, when a ship loaded with arms was detained in New Orleans from leaving the United States, the State Department stepped in and stopped the operation according to a subsequent CIA report.[22]

It took the threat of a potential Communist intervention into South America to overcome the State Department's opposition to getting involved in Guatemala. In October 1953, a month after meeting with Arbenz, the U.S. Ambassador to Guatemala, Jack Peurifoy, reported to Washington that, "It seemed to me that the man [Arbenz] thought like a communist and talked like a communist, and if not actually one, would do until one came along."[23] Then, when a shipment of arms purchased from Czechoslovakia arrived in Guatemala, during a May 24, 1954 press conference, John Foster Dulles warned that it was proof of an international Communist conspiracy. "[T]his cargo of arms is like an atomic bomb planted in the rear of our backyard," said Speaker of the House, John McCormack. "The threat of Communist imperialism," reported the *Washington Post*, "is no longer academic; it has arrived."[24]

With talk of a Communist in power in the Western Hemisphere, there was no turning back. New CIA Director Allen Dulles brought Al Haney and Tracy Barnes in to run the operation. It was called Operation Success, and among the CIA field operatives involved were David Atlee Phillips, Howard Hunt, and David Morales, all destined to become legendary figures at CIA. Arbenz was removed from power on June 20, 1954, with the help of planes supplied by William Pawley,

Castillo Armas was the man who replaced Arbenz as president. In short order, American financial aid to Guatemala increased from $463,000 to $10.7 million per year, property Arbenz confiscated was returned to United Fruit, employees were no longer allowed to unionize, and opposition parties were banned. However, within three years, the U.S. would turn against Armas, and on July 26, 1957, a presidential guard with leftist sympathies allegedly assassinated him. However, his death occurred just four days after he tried to shut down a casino owned by an associate of mobster Johnny Roselli, at a time when Roselli and Carlos Marcello were trying to expand their presence in Guatemala.[25] Marcello, who was worried about being deported to Italy, had paid $100,000 to Armas' prime minister to obtain a fraudulent birth certificate stating he was born in Guatemala.

Meanwhile, Roselli's friend Ted Lewin, who was running the casino, was thrown in jail. Such activity meant things would not end well for Armas, especially when a young rebel named Fidel Castro was trying to overthrow the CIA-friendly Batista in Cuba. Of importance is that the relationship between U.S. intelligence and organized crime extended into Latin America, and they had interests in common.[26]

Interestingly, the names Barnes, Hunt, Phillips, Morales, Roselli, and Marcello would all surface again in the CIA's attempt to overthrow Fidel Castro after he came to power, as well as the JFK assassination. And if these men were involved in Kennedy's murder, it all began in Guatemala. Returning to the murder of Armas, the accused guard was a Communist named Vasquez Sanchez, whose story mirrored that of Lee Oswald. The Guatemalan government described him "as a 'Communist fanatic' . . . expelled from the Guatemalan Army six months ago for 'Communist ideology . . .'" Yet, "no evidence ever turned up that [he] was a member of the . . . Communist Party." He committed suicide with the same rifle he had used to kill Armas, and the police "produced some leftist propaganda that had supposedly been found in his pockets and a suspicious 'diary,' but few Guatemalans believed the official explanation." Setting up and blaming an assassination on a supposed Communist was already part of the CIA blueprint.[27]

Indonesia was where the next CIA attempt at nation-building took place. President Kusno Sukarno had headed the country since the Japanese surrender in 1945, whom the CIA intended to have forcibly removed from office.

In the mid-1950s, the Indonesian Communist Party (PKI) gained strength and influence, threatening the entire region. As a result, in 1955 CIA funneled millions of dollars to the Muslim-backed Masjumi Party to dispose of the PKI. That same year, Sukarno sponsored the Asian-African Conference, which intended to consolidate Third World nations that did not wish to align themselves with either the Soviet Union or the United States. Sukarno also wanted to create a financial institution like the World Bank, which would cater exclusively to non-aligned, third-world countries.[28]

In addition to Sukarno, present at the conference was the new leader of Egypt, Gamel Abdel Nasser, Prime Minister Nehru of India, and Foreign Minister Zhou Enlai of China. Nehru set the tone for the gathering, telling the assembled delegates, "We do not agree with the communist teachings, we do not agree with the anti-communist teachings, because they are both based on wrong principles." This display of independence and nationalism denouncing imperialism threatened to transform the Third World. It called for racial equality, respect for national sovereignty, and nonintervention in their internal affairs by the two great superpowers. At the time, such thinking alarmed the United States, for it rejected European colonialism, which made the U.S. guilty by its close association with Western Europe. The fear was that these countries would leave the West and turn toward the Soviet Union when they inevitably needed help. The preservation of self-determination only applied to the United States and its allies.[29]

The Asian-African Conference also marked the emergence of Communist China on the international stage. It could not be ignored by the U.S, for along with the potential consolidation of third world countries, many of which were rich in oil and raw minerals. CIA considered assassinating Sukarno but instead tried to embarrass him by making a pornographic film that showed a Sukarno look-alike engaged with a Russian spy. The effort failed, so on September 25, 1957, only two months after Armas was assassinated in Guatemala, Eisenhower approved a CIA-organized coup in Indonesia, like what the Agency had successfully carried out in Egypt, Iran, and Guatemala. However, this time things did not go as planned. The Indonesian army remained loyal to Sukarno, which was the first sign of trouble, for, without their support, a takeover was unlikely. Eisenhower was adamant that CIA personnel could not get involved to maintain plausible deniability. He considered using "soldiers of fortune" unattached to the U.S. government, for as the President said, ". . . every rebellion that I have ever heard of has its soldiers of fortune." Still, the CIA insisted that they should handle the situation themselves.

At the end of November, rebels threw hand grenades at Sukarno as he left a school fund-raiser in the company of children. Ten people died, and forty-eight children were injured, but Sukarno survived. It was another example of the unnecessary murder and wounding of innocents in the name of keeping the world free from communism. Meanwhile, the U.S. Navy kept vessels on alert in the area, including two submarines. They were going to force Eisenhower to intervene, if necessary.[30]

In the end, Ike agreed to permit the use of CIA proprietary personnel like Civil Air Transport pilots to assist the rebels, but this proved to be a disaster. By April 1958, the coup attempt came to an end. U.S. pilot Allen Lawrence Pope, who had flown in Korea and had helped the French in Indochina, which included fifty-seven missions to Dien Bien Phu, was shot down and captured after he bombed a church by mistake. It destroyed any pretext the U.S. had of maintaining plausible deniability. Pope had concealed papers aboard the aircraft, including CAT identification cards, his contract, and a post exchange privilege card for Clark Air Force Base. Eisenhower had lied in front of the world. For the past three weeks, he had steadfastly denied charges that the U.S. supported the rebellion against Sukarno.

The CIA may have done something to Pope's plane to aggressively set up Ike to increase the American military presence in Indonesia. There is no evidence that the Agency sabotaged Pope's plane. Still, it is a fact that Pope should not have been carrying identification with him on the flight and that the coup would not succeed without U.S. military intervention. And for those who wanted to initiate a major war with the Soviets and Chinese, while the U.S. held a nuclear weapon advantage, maintaining plausible deniability was never a concern. Regardless, it did not work, for Eisenhower aborted the operation as things began to unravel. The radical right would try to force Kennedy's hand to intervene with the U.S. military in Cuba three years later at the Bay of Pigs in the same fashion, also without success.[31]

It did not mean that the effort to oust Sukarno was over. By 1965 the CIA was able to gain the support of General Suharto and many right-wing junior army officers in Indonesia. The coup forced Sukarno to abdicate, Suharto was named president, and the United States established a pro-American military government. Over 750,000 Indonesians were arrested and placed in concentration camps, anti-Communists were encouraged to kill anyone suspected of being a sympathizer, and as many as 1,000,000 Indonesians died. It was just another example that anything was acceptable in the war against communism, and everyone was expendable. Especially those considered to be inferior to the white Anglo/Saxons who were behind these atrocities.[32]

In 1957 there was another CIA failure, this time in Syria. The plot involved paying off the commander of the Syrian armor school, who positioned his tanks around Damascus, which was supposed to entice others to support the rebels in their attempted overthrow. But Syria's security was aware of the plot from the beginning, and the CIA agents involved were apprehended and expelled from the country.[33]

The next victim was Iraq. In 1958 the monarchy was overthrown by a military coup believed to be pro-Soviet, which the CIA did not see coming. In April 1959, Eisenhower set up an interagency task force to investigate how to prevent a Communist takeover of Iraq covertly. Six months later, there was an attempted assassination of Iraqi leader Abdul Karim Qasim. CIA was behind the attempted murder, which involved a junior Iraqi officer named Saddam Hussein as one of the would-be assassins. Saddam fled for Egypt, only to return to Iraq years later.

Meanwhile, Iraqi exiles in Beirut bragged about their CIA connections. In 1960, another attempt at killing Quasim also failed, but a CIA-backed coup in 1963 removed him from power, eventually leading to Saddam Hussein taking control of the country. And the ramifications of this would be felt by the United States for decades to come.[34]

Egypt, Iran, Guatemala, Indonesia, Syria, and Iraq were not the only countries targeted for overthrow. British Guiana, Ecuador, Ghana, Chile, the Dominican Republic, Brazil, Bolivia, Cuba, and Vietnam were other nations where the CIA tried to replace a head of state accused of being a Communist with a right-wing, pro-American alternative. Most efforts were successful; some, like Cuba, were not. Regardless, there was a consistent theme for every coup attempt. First, accuse the leader who is to be removed of being a Communist, or at the very least, of being a leftist supporter. Second, without the military's help, the coup was destined to fail. Make sure they were involved and supported the coup. Third, to maintain plausible deniability, employ the services of American mercenaries should the operation go awry. Fourth, set up a Communist patsy to take the fall for the coup so that the people would blindly support the change in leadership. It was the perfect blueprint for instituting a changing of the guard.

One can't help but think about the JFK assassination in this context. The military questioned JFK's leadership as he abandoned the U.S. policy of containment and began normalizing relations with the Soviet Union and Cuba. The right-wing, which included big business and oilmen, called him a Communist. Paramilitary mercenaries were probably involved, and the government investigation falsely accused Oswald of being a Communist. If the CIA followed their blueprint for a coup, they would have first approached the military to see if they were interested in removing JFK. It is not out of the question, for the Joint Chiefs had made it abundantly clear how they felt about left-leaning politicians since the days of MacArthur. Is that how the plot began and did the rest then fall into place? We cannot say for sure, and to speculate without examining all the evidence would be irresponsible. However, there was a procedure in place for removing a left-leaning head of state. An American President was just as susceptible as anyone else to this misguided sense of patriotism.

* * *

When the CIA was trying to overthrow governments in Iran and Guatemala, trouble arose again in Italy. The Communists were once again a force in Italian politics, so Eisenhower approved NSC-5411 in 1953, which called "for all practicable means" to destroy the Italian Communist Party (PCI). In other words, nothing was off the table.

According to CIA estimates, the problem was the Soviets had inundated Italy with $50 million in 1953 to support the PCI to try and sway the upcoming national elections. Soviet and East European embassies and numerous front organizations provided the money. Future CIA Director of Central Intelligence William Colby, who spent most of the 1950s in Italy masquerading as a State Department employee, was instructed to counter what the Soviets were doing. Meanwhile, in 1953 the new American Ambassador to Italy, Clare Boothe Luce, arrived in Rome. It soon became apparent that the wife of the right-wing conservative publisher Henry Luce and Colby had different ideas about thwarting the Communists in Italy.

An ardent right-winger, Clare Booth Luce did not distinguish between Communist and Socialist groups and believed neither had a place in Italian politics. On the other hand, Colby thought the United States should support Socialists against the Communists, who were the real threat, and he provided funding to Socialists for propaganda purposes. Eventually, the right-wing at the CIA did not ask Colby to head the secret paramilitary army in Italy, which was part of the Dulles/Donovan operation to fight the Communists. He leaned too far enough to the left. It indicates that Colby's left-of-center approach to defeat the Communists did not gain traction in Washington.

Gerry Miller, an ex-OSS officer who ran the Jedburgh operation during the war (which included William Colby) and in the 1950s was CIA Station Chief in Rome, was the man chosen to be in charge of the stay-behind army. Miller was willing to make intelligence operatives out of former Mussolini supporters and Fascist Catholics, which was why the CIA gave him this assignment over Colby, who was not in lockstep with the Allen Dulles formula for battling communism. "A very deliberate and conscious policy was made both in Washington and in Rome that no help of any kind [should] go to Neo-Fascists or Monarchists," Colby wrote in his memoirs trying to justify his position. But the Eisenhower administration, as evidenced by the passage of NSC 5411/2, which pertained to Italy, declared that "an extremist rightist government," though "almost certainly authoritarian, probably ultra-nationalist," would be "far less dangerous than a Communist regime." It pleased the Fascists who wanted a far-right Italian government.[35]

The result was that ambassador Luce and CIA's William Colby repeatedly clashed. While Colby was willing to provide financing to any group that was not Communist, Luce wanted CIA funding withheld from all groups until they supported the anti-Communist plan put forth by the U.S. She envisioned a new right-wing ruling party consisting of the conservative wing of the Christian Democrats, the business-oriented portion of the Liberal party, neo-Fascists who supported the constitution, and Monarchists. Colby objected to this strategy, but Clare Boothe Luce received support from the right-wing faction within the CIA with her newfound success and far-right agenda. And that included James Angleton, who, as we have seen, was very interested in suppressing communism throughout Europe. Like Luce, Angleton thought the CIA should not support the Italian Socialist Party (PSI) because their goal was to help the Communists penetrate the ruling coalition. He did what he could to counteract what Colby was trying to do. In the end, Luce's approach proved to be successful.[36]

* * *

Two factions within the CIA with different ideas on combatting communism were clear from the Agency's beginning. Initially, Allen Dulles recruited agents from Ivy League schools, primarily Harvard, Yale, and Dulles' alma mater, Princeton. One-quarter of CIA's top officers came from Harvard. They considered themselves an elite group and included Frank Wisner, Richard Bissell, Tracy Barnes, Kermit Roosevelt, Archibald Roosevelt, the Bundy brothers, and Cord Meyer, to name a few. They socialized together with other like-minded people, such as Katherine and Phil Graham of the *Washington Post*. These men primarily came from the Office of Policy Coordination and were involved exclusively in covert operations under Wisner's leadership.

Their counterpart at the CIA was the Office of Special Operations (OSO), the old Strategic Services Unit (SSU) from the War Department, whose name was changed when it became part of the newly established Central Intelligence Group in 1946. The OSO specialized in classic intelligence gathering and counterintelligence and did not involve itself in covert operations.[37]

Eventually, OPC and OSO were combined into one unit within the CIA under the Directorate of Plans in 1951. Richard Bissell explained the relationship between the two groups as follows: "There always were two philosophies about clandestine operations, and they could be associated with OSO and OPC. OSO had an emphasis on high professionalism, with very tight security and the maintenance of espionage and counterespionage. OPC placed a great deal more emphasis on covert action and was probably less professional and less secure."[38]

Richard Helms, the antithesis of Frank Wisner, headed OSO. Helms had graduated from Williams College and was not a member of the Ivy League fraternity that characterized OPC. A colleague at the CIA described him as "the perfect model of the cool, well-informed professional manager of agent networks and case officers . . . Helms knew this arcane world, especially in Europe, better than anyone except Allen Dulles himself." He was opposed to covert action because of its publicity, which he believed the CIA should always avoid. "Let's do it right, let's do it quietly, let's do it correctly," was his general approach.[39]

When Senator McCarthy investigated suspected CIA loyalty breaches in the early 1950s, Dulles defended William Bundy and Cord Meyer against accusations of communism. It compelled Dulles to change the requirements for the type of agents he was willing to hire. The 1976 Church Committee investigation of the CIA concluded in its report that ". . . the effects of the new security standards were profound . . . [I]ndividuals who had been involved in . . . leftist ideological cause would find it difficult to obtain employment with the CIA . . . [a] like-minded manner of thinking began to evolve within the agency."[40] So as the decade moved forward, covert action still governed, sometimes recklessly, and the Agency's only plan was to defeat communism at all cost, with an increasingly right-wing approach.

* * *

In an attempt to disrupt the proceedings of the 1955 Bandung conference in Indonesia described previously in this chapter, the CIA recommended the assassination of an Asian leader before the gathering, according to a Senate investigative committee later assembled to look into the matter. The Senate's interest pertained to a flight from Hong Kong to Jakarta, which exploded shortly after take-off, killing sixteen passengers. A last-minute plane change saved China's Premier Zhou Enlai, who was supposed to be on the flight. Investigators found two bombs in the plane's wreckage, and it was believed that the CIA was complicit in the attack. CIA officials told Congress there had been rumblings about a potential assassination. They claimed they rejected the idea of killing an Asian leader, which is hard to believe considering their track record. Recall also that the CIA considered assassinating Sukarno around the same time. There is no doubt that an acceptable means of regime change for the CIA was the assassination of foreign leaders. The Agency proved time and again that they were not averse to taking such drastic measures because the ends always justified the means in the war against communism. This deadly logic also applied when it came to ridding the CIA of suspected Communists at home.

John C. Montgomery, a CIA employee who worked undercover at the State Department, was found dead at his Washington D.C. home on January 24, 1953. Tied tightly around the neck of his nude body was the cord from his bathrobe. Officially ruled a suicide by the D.C. police, many viewed the findings with skepticism, including Congressman Fred E. Busbey, who called for a full House investigation. "There are stories being bruited about that the police have been told not to talk," Busbey told the *Washington Post* six days after Montgomery's death.[41]

Montgomery's alleged suicide would have likely disappeared from the pages of history were it not for the death of James Kronthal two months later. Kronthal was a graduate of Yale and Harvard, one of the elites approved by Allen Dulles. He was with OSS during the war and joined the Central Intelligence Group on May

5, 1947. His first assignment, given to him by the head of OSO, Richard Helms, was to replace Allen Dulles as Chief of Station in Switzerland. After that assignment came to an end, Kronthal temporarily worked as a training instructor at CIA's Quasi Military Training Division in Washington D.C., and he was provided cover as a State Department employee. On March 31, 1953, Kronthal was found dead in his Georgetown residence. Only two days prior, the CIA deputy director of training had promoted him.

CIA security chief Sheffield Edwards reported that "an empty vial had been found near the body . . . with a personal note left for an acquaintance . . ." The cause of death was "an apparent suicide," but authorities never released the autopsy findings, contents of the vial, or any other pertinent information to the public.

Authorities revealed decades later that Kronthal had dinner with Allen Dulles alone at Dulles' Georgetown home on the night he died. He was unaware that while they dined, Sheffield Edwards' security officers secretly listened to their conversation from an adjoining room. A 1989 book written by three respected authors familiar with the intelligence community revealed the focus of their discussion. Kronthal was gay, a pedophile, blackmailed by the Nazis during World War II, and again by the Russians after the war. He was a liability.

Before his dinner with Kronthal, Allen Dulles had been warned by Sheffield Edwards that "six of the men you have brought over from OSS into the CIA are serious security risks." Dulles was stunned to learn that Kronthal was one of the six. Soon after, Dulles invited Kronthal to his home for dinner and confronted him with the allegations made against him.[42]

No one knows for sure what happened, but researchers suspect that Dulles gave Kronthal the vial containing poison, and Kronthal used it to kill himself, or perhaps he was murdered. Whatever the truth, it appears that Allen Dulles was complicit in his death, for he told Kronthal that the CIA was aware the Soviets were blackmailing him and the consequences he would face upon full disclosure of the facts.

If the deaths of Montgomery and Kronthal were not enough, on April 8, 1953, CIA security analyst Frederick E. Crockett was found in a semi-conscious state in his gas-filled Washington D.C. apartment, only eight days after Kronthal's death. A major with OSS during World War II, shortly after the war ended, Crockett headed to Java to take charge of Operation Iceberg, which involved the rescue of U.S. POWs from Japanese camps. Crockett also established a field station for espionage in what would become Indonesia, the home of Sukarno. He received his new assignment directly from Bill Donovan, who, along with Allen Dulles, was pushing for a post-war national intelligence agency. Part of his responsibility was to train behind-the-lines guerilla groups engaged in sabotage operations, a normal part of the CIA paramilitary approach to combatting Communists. When OSS finally disbanded, Crockett remained in Southeast Asia as part of the Strategic Services Unit (SSU). His mission ended when the British requested that the U.S. remove him because he was "uncooperative." Crockett disputed this, claiming the British and Dutch wanted to reestablish colonial rule and did not want the Americans there, which was likely the truth. An SSU report stated the Dutch "resent[ed] American neutrality in the present Indonesian situation and believe that the U.S. has failed to live up to its wartime agreements by not giving aid to the Dutch."

Crockett survived his brush with death in 1953. Interestingly, he left the CIA in 1954 and spent the last 24 years of his life as a commercial real estate broker, far removed from the intelligence community.[43]

The incidents involving Montgomery, Kronthal, and Crockett occurred a little more than three months apart, and it is hard to believe they were unrelated. Were all three men on the list of suspected security risks given to Allen Dulles by Sheffield Edwards? And if so, was the CIA tying up loose ends and willing to murder these men to keep their stories secret? Perhaps, because the Agency was still in its infancy and under intense scrutiny, as demonstrated by the investigations into their operations authorized by Eisenhower (see Chapter Nine). They remained a target of Joe McCarthy, and the military and FBI wanted control of intelligence taken away from the CIA and given back to them. Maybe that was why the CIA continued to operate in total secrecy, beyond what it was mandated to do, even after the blank check provided to the Agency by the Doolittle Report. If the public knew what the CIA did, could the Agency expect to survive such a disclosure? And suppose Allen Dulles and his cohorts believed the nation's security hinged on allowing the CIA to conduct covert operations unobstructed because the alternative would likely lead to nuclear war. In that case, it is conceivable that those within the Agency would have justified the death of a handful of insignificant traitors to maintain the plausible deniability they needed to exist. As it applied to assassinations, Richard Bissell's description of plausible deniability confirms that murder by the CIA could be rationalized and was acceptable.

"What is very difficult for anybody to understand," Bissell said, "is that if you say in however veiled or murky terms that you are going to do something, and if the terms aren't so murky that the listener doesn't know what you are going to do, and if you don't receive a negative and you think it will advance the cause, you go ahead and do it."[44]

There were more suspicious deaths. On November 28, 1953, which was the same year the murders of Montgomery and Kronthal occurred, and Crockett managed to survive barely; someone pushed Frank Olson to his death through the 10th-floor window of his New York City hotel room. Olson worked for the CIA at Camp Detrick, Maryland, where he was involved in the experimentation of LSD and other biological weapons such as anthrax. In the early 1950s, Olson had traveled to Camp King in Germany, which, as described in Chapter Four, was being used to detain Nazi prisoners, including Gehlen and Skorzeny. By 1953 it was part of the 513th Military Intelligence Brigade and was used as an interrogation center.

Camp King would have involved LSD and drug-enhanced interrogation of Nazi prisoners, for why else would Olson have been brought there. There were reports that he was troubled by what he witnessed. Olson began to have second thoughts about the work with which he was involved. At any rate, ten days before his death, Olson was given LSD by his own CIA group, without his knowledge, at a gathering just outside Camp Detrick in Maryland. Shortly after that, he allegedly had a nervous breakdown, asked to be removed from the bioweapons program, which led to his death in New York shortly after that.

Future Watergate burglar James McCord was the first to appear at Olson's hotel room five hours after his death. Interestingly, McCord's first assignment at the CIA was to conduct background investigations of CIA employees to weed out those who could embarrass the Agency, which Olson had the potential to do. Allen Dulles had given McCord this assignment to counter McCarthy's claims that Communists within the CIA essentially. Initially, he worked out of the Agency's Manhattan field office for the Office of Security. The CIA reassigned him in the summer of 1953 to the Security Research Staff (SRS) in Washington. The SRS's primary responsibility was to uncover efforts to penetrate the CIA and interrogate defectors and suspected spies, which the SRS accomplished by employing various behavior modification programs. It was with such a background that McCord showed up at Olson's hotel room.

Olson shared the room that night with his deputy, Robert Lashbrook, and Lashbrook let McCord into the hotel room upon his arrival. By that time, the NYPD had already interviewed Lashbrook at a local police station where. In addition to being questioned, the police asked Lashbrook to empty his pockets, which contained a slip of paper with none other than George Hunter White's name written on it. As described in Chapter Six, White worked for the CIA on loan from the FBN, was an associate of Jean-Pierre Lafitte, and would secretly slip LSD to unsuspecting victims at a safe house he operated. The paper found in Lashbrook's possession also listed White's alias, Morgan Hall, as well as the address of the safehouse in Greenwich Village that he had rented. In *A Terrible Mistake*, H.P. Albarelli Jr. writes that: "It is important to note . . . that a large portion of McCord's report pertaining to White remains completely redacted. A 1999 request . . . to the CIA to declassify the report was refused."[45]

New York's detectives were suspicious. They called the local FBI office and spoke to Special Agent Edward A. McShane, Jr. to learn more about Olson and Lashbrook. McShane had nothing of substance to add, but he may have known more than he let on because, for some reason, he thought it necessary to mention the "odd suicide of Forrestal" in discussing Olson's death. Four years earlier, on May 22, 1949, former Secretary of Defense James Forrestal had fallen to his death from the sixteenth floor of the U.S. Naval Hospital in Bethesda, Maryland. Not everyone believed the official verdict that his death was a suicide. His bathrobe cord had been tied tightly around his neck when he fell (just like Montgomery), an odd thing for someone jumping to his death to do.

And according to the *New York Times* May 23, 1949 account of his death, Forrestal was copying a poem written by Sophocles onto hospital memo paper in his hospital room, "but he had . . . been interrupted in his efforts. His copying stopped after he had written 'night' of the word 'nightingale' in the twenty-sixth line of the poem."[46] What makes this potentially relevant is that Nightingale was the name of an American intelligence program where former Nazi sympathizers were infiltrated into Ukraine after the war as part of the CIA's effort to place paramilitary groups behind the Iron Curtain.[47] Was it possible that Forrestal's death had something to do with this? Perhaps, but the real question is, why would McShane find it necessary to reference Forrestal, whose death occurred in Maryland four years earlier, to the New York detectives investigating Olson's death? And did Olson's work at Camp King have something to do with the Nightingales, and as a result, connect his death to Forrestal's? Did McShane provide a clue that Olson's death was part of a pattern?

It is also interesting that McCord and McShane had worked together at the FBI before joining the CIA. Why was this not mentioned in McCord's report about Olson's death? Why the secrecy?

Something suspicious was taking place. FBI documents uncovered in 1999 support this, the contents of which were eventually confirmed to be accurate by former FBI agents. Those documents revealed that McCord and McShane met to discussed Olson's death but did so in conjunction with the incidents involving Kronthal, Montgomery, and Crockett, which occurred earlier that year. They recognized a connection between all these cases. Even more concerning is that they included Forrestal's supposed suicide in their discussion, as well as another mysterious death, that of Laurence Duggan. There was a pattern here, the two agents recognized it, and in hindsight, it is clear these deaths were all somehow connected.

In December 1948, the year before Forrestal's death, forty-three-year-old State Department official Laurence Duggan, a father of four, "either jumped or accidentally fell through an opened window." The New York police closed the case within hours, but those who knew him doubted he had committed suicide. Congressmen Karl Mundt and Richard Nixon of the House Un-Americans Activities Committee told a press conference that Duggan and five other State Department officials were possible spies. It was investigated in a closed subcommittee hearing two weeks before Duggan died. The *New York Herald Tribune* reported that the man who advised the HUAC that Duggan was a Communist said his death "might have been another Masaryk affair . . ." Masaryk was a former Czech foreign minister who had fallen or been pushed to his death from a window in a government building in Prague nine months before Duggan.

Then there was the death of W. Marvin Smith on October 20, 1948. Someone discovered his body in the southwest stairwell of the seven-story Justice Building in Washington, D.C. Smith had testified before the HUAC regarding the Alger Hiss case. The HUAC wanted to determine if Smith had assisted the convicted Communist Hiss. Something unsettling was happening here, which the *Chicago Tribune* recognized and reported in their newspaper's April 1, 1951 issue. They listed the unusual number of suspicious deaths, not including the CIA deaths listed above, that occurred close to each other.

- August 1948: Harry Dexter White—A senior U.S. Treasury Department official who died of a heart attack after he was accused of spying for the Soviet Union.

- October 1948: W. Marvin Smith—See above

- December 1948: Laurence Duggan—See above

- May 1949: James Forrestal—See above

- Spring 1949: Morton Kent—A Russian-born State Department aide. Someone found his body floating in the Potomac River with his throat slashed. Top secret FBI documents read at the Judith Coplon espionage trial in April 1949 said that Kent was involved with the Soviet secret police.

- February 1950: Laird Shields Goldsborough—A senior editor at *Fortune* and *Time* magazines and former boss of Whittaker Chambers, the primary accuser of Alger Hiss. Goldsborough fell to his death from a nine-story building and left his estate to the Soviet government.

- April 1950: Francis Otto Matthiessen—A Harvard professor who fell to his death from the 12th floor of his Boston hotel. Matthiessen was a Socialist who anti-Communist groups were targeting.

- November 1952: Abraham Feller—The UN legal counsel and friend of Alger Hiss who jumped or was pushed from his high-story window after Adlai Stevenson lost the 1952 presidential election.[48]

How many people with alleged Communist connections had to fall from a tall building or be pushed down a stairwell before someone noticed? And were the above deaths and the Kronthal, Montgomery, Crockett, and Olson cases connected? McCord and McShane seemed to think so. And if this were true, does it suggest they were all spying against the United States? Or more likely, had these men, who were privy to secrets that were better kept hidden, compromised themselves by their behavior and became become potential targets of blackmail by foreign Communist agents, and did the CIA eliminate them as a result?

In the mid-1970s, Claire Booth Luce's old nemesis from Italy, William Colby, was Director of Central Intelligence when he testified before Congress and disclosed what was known as CIA's "family jewels." It included assassination plots against foreign leaders, coups to overthrow foreign governments, and mind-altering drug experimentation programs. The revelations split the intelligence community, with half regarding Colby as a traitor and the other half calling him a savior. Among the former was James Angleton, who thought Colby might be a Soviet mole for a long time. Colby had fired Angleton and the leadership at counterintelligence right before appearing in front of Congress. Another casualty was former Director Richard Helms, who pleaded no contest to having misled Congress regarding the CIA's role in the murder of Allende in Chile. The two men would not forget what the turncoat Colby had done to them.[49]

Roughly twenty years later, on April 28, 1996, William Colby's neighbor, Alice Stokes, phoned the local police from her Chesapeake Bay home to advise them that Colby's canoe was missing. His car was in the driveway, and she was concerned. Meanwhile, Kevin Akers, a local handyman in his boat on the water with his wife and two children, spotted a beached green canoe unattended. The police checked Colby's house and found the doors unlocked, the computer and radio on, and unwashed dishes and a half-eaten meal in the sink from the night before. A partially filled glass of wine was on the counter, as was a bottle of wine that was almost full. On the table were Colby's wallet containing $296 and his keys.[50]

The ensuing search uncovered nothing until nine days after anyone last saw Colby. On May 6, his body washed up on shore close to where Akers initially saw Colby's canoe. Of course, foul play was ruled out but wasn't that always the case. That someone was still tying up loose ends to protect the Agency was a more likely explanation.

On January 22, 1976, Colby's nemesis, James Angleton, also testified before the same Church Committee that Colby had appeared before. After his questioning was over, in response to a comment made by a reporter as he was leaving, Angleton said, "A mansion has many rooms. I was not privy to who struck John." Angleton was referring to JFK, a startling revelation, but he knew how to keep a secret, and he said no more. After the assassination, it had been Angleton's job to ensure that he buried forever any CIA's involvement in Kennedy's death was. Angleton could be trusted and would never place the integrity of the CIA in jeopardy.

On the other hand, Colby had demonstrated a willingness to talk, which probably cost him his life. Under the right circumstances, anyone who jeopardized American interests in the war against communism became a liability and could wind up dead. Unacceptable personal behavior, providing the Soviets and Chinese with information, or exposing Agency secrets were not tolerated. It was why many died mysteriously during the late 1940s and 1950s because the American way of life had to be protected. In so doing, assassination became an acceptable means to accomplish this. Even foreign leaders and an American president were not immune from this type of retribution. It was why many who eyewitnessed the assassination of JFK in Dallas, and people in possession of damaging information, would also die under mysterious circumstances. Maintaining that a Communist had killed the President also served to preserve the status quo. Those who could reveal what happened were subject to the same strict form of justice as anyone else capable of irreparably damaging the country. There was an anything-was-acceptable mentality in place, adhered to by those who believed in a cause that any rational person today would view as misguided. Still, one ardent Cold Warriors at that time embraced. And everyone was expendable in the pursuit of that cause, for there was no higher standard to aspire to, or so they believed.

During World War II, Phil Graham was an Army intelligence officer positioned close to MacArthur in the Pacific theater. He established long-term relationships with many who would become leading figures at the CIA. He married Katherine in 1940, whose family owned the *Washington Post*, and in 1946 Phil was named owner and editor in chief. A Harvard graduate, he was considered brilliant and deserving of the position. Meanwhile, he and his wife socialized with CIA Ivy League elites, which included Cord Meyer. At the time, Meyer ran Operation Mockingbird, which placed agents within media outlets to publicly promote policies that supported the CIA's point of view. The evidence is strong that Phil and Katherine Graham were initially brought into the CIA's disinformation operation by Phil's good friend, Frank Wisner.[51]

The problem was that Phil was also manic-depressive and was in and out of psychiatric institutions throughout the 1950s. By 1962, his marriage to Katherine had ended, but it did not stop Phil from partying with Washington's social elite, including the President of the United States, John F. Kennedy. "The pair of them were sleeping around with the same people," said Jean Friendly, the wife of *Washington Post* editor Al Friendly.

In mid-January 1963, Phil Graham was in Arizona and, in a drunken state, disrupted an *Associated Press* board of directors meeting at the Biltmore Hotel. He asked to address the audience but became unhinged and had awful things to say about those in attendance. Worst of all, he reportedly told the crowd that JFK was sleeping with Mary Meyer, Cord's ex-wife and a friend to Katherine Graham and James Angleton. Phil had crossed the line. He was sedated, taken from the hotel by ambulance, flown back to Washington the following day, and brought to Chestnut Lodge, a private sanitarium in Baltimore used by the CIA since 1952. He stayed there until August 3, when he was released on a weekend pass to visit Katherine at their estate in Warrenton, Virginia. Within three hours after arriving, while Katherine took a nap upstairs, Phil Graham was dead, the victim of a shotgun blast. The coroner ruled it a suicide, and there is no evidence to suggest otherwise, but the long list of murdered people who also allegedly killed themselves makes one wonder. Was the CIA still tying up loose ends? With JFK's assassination only months away, was Phil Graham a liability to those who would kill the President because Phil knew too much about the CIA's "family jewels"?[52]

Upon gaining control of the *Washington Post*, Katherine Graham continued the paper's support of CIA, which included, according to journalist Michael Hasty, "advancing the foreign policies and economic agenda of the nation's ruling elites." News analyst Norman Solomon went even further, alleging that Katherine's newspaper "mainly functioned as a helpmate to the war-makers in the White House, State Department and Pentagon."[53]

In 1988, Katherine Graham gave a speech at CIA's headquarters in Langley, Virginia. "We live in a dirty and dangerous world," she said. "There are some things the general public does not need to know and shouldn't. I believe democracy flourishes when the government can take legitimate steps to keep its secrets and when the press can decide whether to print what it knows."[54]

Graham spoke like the true elitist that she was; what she said should come as no surprise when put in the proper context of what we have already covered. A select few ran the country, and it was all about sustaining an American way of life that included a hierarchy separated by class, and no expense was too great to ensure that the status quo remained the same. It was why the CIA and the military kept secrets from the American public throughout the Cold War. For if truth be told, the American people were considered unimportant at best, subhuman at worst.

It was a shame they did not include the words from Katherine Graham's speech in the introduction to the Warren Report. It would have been so appropriate.

CIA and the Rule of Lawlessness

"We felt that it was our responsibility not to lag behind the Russians or the Chinese in this field [biological and chemical warfare], and the only way to find out what the risks were was to test things such as LSD and other drugs that could be used to control human behavior."

—Ex-CIA Director Richard Helms

During the 1950s, the United States never tired of embracing its Judeo-Christian values, even though the country involved itself in some of the most heinous activities in history. The U.S. justified such behavior because they claimed to be battling a Godless enemy without a moral compass that played by no rules. But not everything could be rationalized, for what the CIA and other government agencies did regarding drug experimentation on innocent people was particularly appalling. It was especially true when they experimented on children, and one fatherless teenager with a disinterested mother who likely suffered through such an ordeal was Lee Harvey Oswald. At the same time, he was convicted of truancy from school and sent to a detention center in New York. He was just another "undesirable," and the evidence is strong that U.S. intelligence subjected Oswald to mind-altering drug experimentation, and it continued later when he was in the Marines. The history of how he became involved in this is quite a story. The best place to start is at the beginning.

* * *

In the late 1930s, Japanese Dr. Shiro Ishii built Unit 731 in Pingfan, China, near Harbin, where George De Mohrenschildt's wife was born. Designed to research potential biological weapons, including the bubonic plague, which Ishii would use to attack Chinese cities, Unit 731 experimented on prisoners of war and civilians, resulting in over ten thousand deaths. Aware of what Ishii was up to, Chiang Kai-Shek sent word to FDR, which added to the President's concern because Japanese saboteurs had already tried to poison the Los Angeles water supply. Not wanting to cause a panic, Roosevelt kept quiet. Still, he warned, ". . . that if Japan persists in this inhuman form of warfare against China or any of the other United Nations, such action will be regarded by this government as though taken against the United States, and retaliation in kind and in full measure will be meted out." The warning fell on deaf ears, for Japan next launched balloons carrying anthrax over the United States, but the spores froze at high altitudes and were ineffective. Then, two years later, the Japanese launched 9,300 balloons with incendiary devices over the United States. Some 200 landed in Alaska, Hawaii, Vancouver, the Aleutian Islands, and Michigan. One of the balloons disabled power at the Hanford nuclear site in Washington state, causing a temporary delay in constructing the atom bomb that the U.S. would drop on Nagasaki. It was all kept hidden from the American public. The U.S. decided to pursue a biological warfare program of their own, and in 1943 the military built a research facility at Camp Detrick, Maryland.

After Japan's surrender and an intense search, Ishii turned himself in with an offer to work for the Americans. "My experience would be a useful advantage to the United States in the event of war with the Soviet Union," he told his captors. Camp Detrick's Dr. Edwin Hill agreed and reported that Ishii's information was "absolutely invaluable" because it "could never have been obtained in the United States because of scruples attached to experiments on humans." It would not be long before Dr. Hill was proven wrong. The United States conducted mind-altering drug experimentation on unsuspecting Americans, primarily those deemed expendable by those in charge.

Despite protests from the Soviet Union, the U.S. granted Ishii immunity for war crimes in exchange for what he knew, and his whereabouts remained unknown until 1958. He died of cancer the following year, and according to his daughter, he had converted to Catholicism by then. There is no evidence that the Catholic Church knighted him.[1]

* * *

The U.S. entry into the world of drug experimentation occurred on June 28, 1941, when, by executive order, FDR established the National Defense Research Committee's Office of Scientific Research and Development. Hidden within this department was Division 19, which included George White's secret OSS group that tried to develop a truth drug for use when interrogating prisoners and an "assassination and elimination" training program for OSS agents. Two years later, the U.S. Army established Camp Detrick to conduct intensive biological warfare research and development (What went on at Camp Detrick was not disclosed until 1956, when the army changed its name to Fort Detrick). In Maryland, they located the camp near Edgewood Arsenal, the primary location where scientists also conducted chemical research. But it was not until the war was over, and Operation Paperclip brought Nazi scientists experienced in biological warfare to the U.S., that America began to show a serious interest in this deadly means of war.[2]

The Camp Detrick program placed citizens at risk. As described in *A Secret Order*, "Two of the very first plans considered, according to once-classified Army, FBI, and CIA documents, were a covert spraying in the New York subway system in 1949 and a simulated spraying attack through the Pentagon's ventilation system, also in 1949. Indeed, at the request of the CIA's Technical Services Station, George Hunter White himself, in 1952, detonated a small aerosol device that released a cloud of vaporized LSD in a New York City subway car. The CIA destroyed the reported results of this experiment in 1973."[3]

There were similar tests conducted on unsuspecting U.S. civilians. In 1950, the Navy sprayed large quantities of the bacteria Serratia marcescens over San Francisco to simulate what would happen if the U.S. experienced a biological attack. Numerous people contracted pneumonia-like illnesses, and at least one person died.[4] The Army sprayed chemicals over six cities in the U.S. and Canada from 1950 through 1953. Records show that chemicals sprayed over Winnipeg included zinc cadmium sulfide.[5] The CIA conducted open-air biological warfare experiments in 1955 near Tampa and other Florida locations with whooping cough bacteria, which tripled infections in Florida to over one thousand cases and caused whooping cough deaths in the state to increase twelvefold from the previous year.[6]

Scientists at Edgewood Arsenal began conducting human experiments with a tabun nerve agent on soldiers as early as 1947. The men were all volunteers and unaware that the scientists were exposing them to harmful chemicals. As Annie Jacobsen wrote in *Operation Paperclip*, "Some of the tests took place in Utah . . . Other tests took place inside Edgewood's 'gassing chamber for human tests,' a 9 x 9-foot tile-and-brick cube with an airtight metal door . . . ," and involved Fritz Hoffmann. He was a "wartime organic chemist at the chemical warfare laboratories at the University of Wurzburg and the Luftwaffe. Under Operation Paperclip, he worked at Edgewood in the classified research and development division, the Technical Command, synthesizing tabun gas and later VX. For the CIA, he traveled the world in search of exotic poisons."[7]

CIA inherited many Division 19 programs after World War II, including assassination, better known as "health alteration" or "executive action." According to CIA's Sidney Gottlieb, who was associated with George Hunter White and Jean-Pierre Lafitte as early as 1952, as described in Chapter Eight, "CIA envisioned Detrick's SO [Special Operations] Division as a creation very much like the earlier Division 19. It was similarly compartmentalized, with the strict military security on top of ours . . . nothing was reduced to writing, except essential reports. The right hand never knew what the left was doing . . ."[8]

Experimentation in the use of dangerous drugs for assassination started with the Technical Services Division of CIA under Archibald Roosevelt, the fifth son of Theodore Roosevelt and the brother of CIA's Kermit Roosevelt, the previously mentioned overthrower of foreign Communist governments. Archibald was a highly decorated World War I veteran who later founded a successful brokerage house specializing in municipal bonds. A member of the John Birch Society and the founder of the Veritas Foundation, which sought to expose Socialist influences at Harvard and other major colleges and universities, he was very conservative. He was a racist and likely a eugenicist. As described by author Stephen Hess in *America's Political Dynasties*, "Archie Roosevelt . . . sent a letter to every U.S. Senator, stating 'modern technical civilization does not seem to be as well-handled by the black man as by the white man in the United States.' Present civil rights difficulties he blamed on 'socialist plotters.'"[9]" Socialists have infiltrated our schools, our law courts, our government," he wrote. "The Socialist movement is made up of a relatively small number of people who have developed the TECHNIQUE OF INFLUENCING large masses of people to a VERY HIGH DEGREE."[10] An affluent member of America's elite, Archibald was willing to do anything to preserve the American way of life, including using CIA drug experimentation programs to exploit society's less fortunate.

Sidney Gottlieb worked for Roosevelt in the Technical Services Division, experimenting with mind-control drugs and exotic poisons. According to CIA's Miles Copeland, in 1957, Gottlieb laced Egyptian leader Gamel Abdel Nasser's favorite cigarettes with a toxin that Nasser never smoked, much to Gottlieb's dismay. Allen Dulles reportedly approved the failed assassination attempt in advance.[11]

Returning to the ex-Nazi Fritz Hoffman, as the arena of drug testing expanded, he was at the forefront of a partnership between Edgewood's U.S. Army Chemical Corps and CIA, which further grew to include scientists from Camp Detrick. The SO was in charge of the collaborative effort, which was only possible through the expertise of Paperclip's ex-Nazi scientists.[12]

Harold Batchelor was a U.S. Army expert in the weaponized bubonic plague at Camp Detrick. A member of the SO Division, he and Frank Olson, the scientist thrown from a New York hotel window to his death (see Chapter Ten), conducted covert field tests across America. They used a pathogen, a microorganism that can cause disease, that simulated how bioweapons would disperse. The pathogen exposed unwitting Americans to bioweapon gases expelled into the atmosphere and proved once again that no life was safe.[13]

In 1947 Batchelor traveled to Germany and spoke with Dr. Kurt Blome, a Nazi scientist who the Nuremberg trials acquitted of war crimes. Blome had been "deputy surgeon general of the Reich, deputy chief of Reich's bioweapons facilities in Nesselstedt, Poland, and in Geraberg, Germany . . . was a lieutenant general in the SA (Storm Troopers)." The U.S. army ". . . tried but failed to bring him to America;

[so] he worked for the U.S. Army at Camp King, in Oberursel, Germany." He reportedly knew more about biological weapons than anyone in the world. Blome told Batchelor about areas the Nazis had been investigating, including biological weapons and poisons that could start epidemics or be used to "kill certain people." Without question, the CIA was interested. As Richard Helms described it years later, "We felt that it was our responsibility not to lag behind the Russians or the Chinese . . . , and the only way to find out what the risks were was to test things such as LSD and other drugs that could be used to control human behavior."[14]

The program, started by the CIA in 1949, was called Operation Bluebird. Information about it is limited because most of the official documents were destroyed by Richard Helms when the CIA was investigated CIA by Congress in the 1970s. We know it began as a defensive program "to apply special methods of interrogation for the purpose of evaluation of Russian practices." However, Allen Dulles expanded Bluebird in 1951. A secret memo Dulles sent to Helms and Wisner "outlined . . . the possibilities of augmenting the usual interrogation methods by the use of drugs, hypnosis, shock, etc., and emphasized the defensive aspects as well as the offensive opportunities in this field of applied medical science." Offensive meant drugs were not restricted for use in interrogating prisoners but could be used as a tool to infiltrate U.S. agents into Communist countries and for assassinations. Such work was to be conducted outside the U.S. since some foreign governments "permitted certain activities which were not permitted by the United States government (i.e., anthrax, etc.)."[15] Haiti, which attracted the attention of George de Mohrenschildt, Thomas Eli Davis, and a host of others, was used for drug experimentation because of their willingness to ignore what was taking place.

The defensive program was begun in 1949 when "special interrogation methods" were set up at Camp King in Germany. The CIA used drugs to interrogate Soviet spies caught by Gehlen's organization. Dr. Batchelor, who had already traveled there to consult with Dr. Blome, was a logical choice for inclusion in the program. Frank Olson worked with Batchelor. In April 1950, so that documents in his possession would not be subject to searches by customs officials, Olson was given a diplomatic passport for travel back and forth to Germany. At Camp King, he saw first-hand what his research in mind-altering drugs at Camp Detrick could do to a person. It was an issue of morality for Olson, and he began to doubt if what they were doing was justifiable. These pangs of consciousness would eventually cost him his life.

CIA also experimented with hypnotism and precisely defined what their objectives were, as per the following:

1. "Can we 'condition' by post-hypnotic suggestion, Agency employees (or persons of interest to this agency) to prevent them from giving information to any unauthorized source or for committing any act on behalf of a foreign or domestic enemy?"

2. "Can we . . . induce a hypnotized condition in an unwilling subject to such an extent that he will perform an act for our benefit?"

3. "Could we seize a subject and . . . by post-hypnotic control have him crash an airplane, wreck a train, etc.?

4. "Can we through post-hypnotic control induce a subject to commit violence against another individual, or induce a subject to murder another individual or group of individuals?"

5. "Can we, through post-hypnotic control, create a condition whereby a subject would forget any such induced act after the subject is brought out of his 'conditional' state?"[16]

In the 1970s, CIA released a memorandum which pertained to "Recent Discovery of Project ZR/ALERT Documents—A Study of the Use of Psychological Programming for Intelligence Purposes," which dealt with the "exploration and experimentation by the CI Staff of the use of hypnotism in certain operational situations." Counterintelligence was James Angleton, which should come as no surprise. Recall that Angleton was the person who cleared George White for Operation Bluebird and that Angleton and William Harvey were part of a select few who would receive top-secret reports on Bluebird. White was also closely associated with people in the CIA's drug testing and hypnosis programs, such as Lafitte and Dr. Gottlieb.

The military was conducting experiments simultaneously with the CIA, and what they were doing sometimes overlapped, as occurred in 1952 with Project MKNAOMI. Then in 1953, a memorandum was issued by Secretary of Defense Charles Wilson. It intended to govern the use of human subjects for all service branches and authorized the Army, Navy, and Air Force "to use human volunteers in experimental research conducted with the development of defenses of all types against atomic, biological, and/or chemical warfare agents." The critical word in the memo was "volunteer." The Army would later admit that between 1955 and 1958, they provided LSD to nearly 1,500 soldiers and civilians, often without their knowledge. And it would grow. In the early 1960s, the CIA's LSD conducted testing at eighty-six U.S. and Canadian hospitals, prisons, universities, and military installations.[17]

Nothing was off-limits. In 1952 the Army conducted experiments with bacillus globigii and serratia marcescens at Fort McClellan, Alabama, and the number of yearly pneumonia cases jumped from 4.6 to 12.3 percent. The following year, it dropped back to 4 percent. Two years later, they conducted experiments using tularemia on Ohio State Penitentiary inmates, who experienced high fever, severe headaches, chills, nausea, sweating, and weakness. In 1954, at Fort Sam Houston, Operation Whitecoat tested Seventh-Day Adventist conscientious objectors with viruses and bacteria prevalent during a biological attack.[18] It was a necessary evil in the war against communism that many innocent people would have to die for the United States to be victorious.

Bluebird would eventually evolve into Project Artichoke, which involved hypnosis and experimentation with drugs such as LSD. Its primary objective was to use drugs to program an individual to assassinate someone against their will. Project MKULTRA arrived in 1953, which expanded drug experimentation on unsuspecting subjects. Bluebird, Artichoke, and MKULTRA were all CIA programs designed to develop mind control and hypnotic techniques. The Agency hoped advancements in these areas would help interrogate prisoners, limit the information a U.S. agent might reveal if captured by the Communists, or plant information inside an agent's brain that the agent would purposely tell his Communist captors, whether he wanted to or not. According to Artichoke documents that have survived, the objective was ". . . ascertaining whether effective and practical techniques exist, or could be developed, which could be utilized to render an individual subservient to an imposed will or control, thereby posing a potential threat to National Security." In addition, the Artichoke document continued, "We need to also explore the 'subtle' means of making an individual say or do things he would normally not consider through the use of covertly administered drugs, 'Black Psychiatry,' hypnosis, and brain-damaging processes . . . these processes may [be] tried, but they are 'elaborate, impractical and unnecessary.'" As we will see in Volume Two, after becoming involved in such a drug experimentation program, an ex-Marine named Lee Harvey Oswald went to the Soviet Union as an alleged defector. At the time, he was just another innocent casualty in the war against the Red Menace.[19]

The CIA's Security Research Service (SRS), a typically innocent-sounding name, directed Project Artichoke and was part of the Office of Security, run by former Army Brigadier General Paul F. Gaynor. "It is imperative," Gaynor wrote in February 1953, "that we move forward more aggressively on identifying and securing a more reliable [group] of human research subjects for ongoing Artichoke experimentation . . ." By September 1953, Gaynor's deputy, Artichoke Project director and former naval intelligence officer Morse Allen, presented a potential solution.

He wrote that "four thousand (4,000) American military men . . . serving court-martial sentences in the federal prisons . . . [were] scattered through the federal institutions [and] the sentences of these men can be reduced by direction of the Adjutant General's office . . . [If] these men should be wanted for work on a dangerous research project, it might be possible to motivate their interest by promising . . . to have their sentences appropriately reduced if they co-operated in the experimentation."

Federal prisons "that have hospital setups with doctors on the permanent staff" were best suited for what they intended to do. "Such things as the size of the institution and current population would . . . be considered, but it is a fact that the federal prisons are not overcrowded as is the case with many state prisons. Thus, it would be much easier to obtain working space in a federal institution." Artichoke teams secretly working in the prisons could be passed off as "coming from nearby universities or research institutions."

Allen may or may not have been aware that what he was proposing was not new. As early as 1950, Camp Detrick's Special Operations Division had signed a multi-year contract with the New York State Psychiatric Institute (NYSPI) for the "psychological investigation of potential chemical warfare agents on human beings." NYSPI was chosen because, as early as 1945, the OSS and the FBN were already experimenting with "truth drugs" there (recall George White), which included hallucinogenic drugs like LSD. The SOD mandated NYSPI to "conduct studies of psychochemical agents on human beings to determine clinical effects on psychological behavior, including controls on normal human subjects necessary to evaluate the more profound changes expected in the behavior of psychiatrically liable subjects." The Institute would perform these dangerous tests on unsuspecting patients.

The Institute's Associate Research Medical Geneticist was Dr. Franz J. Kallmann. In Germany, Kallmann worked under Dr. Ernst Rudin at the Kaiser Wilhelm Institute of Psychiatric Research. Rudin was a proponent of eugenics and forced sterilization for the mentally unfit.

It was the age of eugenics. So, it is not surprising that the CIA and the military would justify drug experimentation as long as they restricted experiments to those who were a drain on society and offered nothing to the advancement of the American way of life. On the contrary, they sacrificed themselves for the greater good by being used as human guinea pigs, even if they were unaware that this was what they were doing.[20]

A case in point was the Addiction Research Center (ARC). Part of the federal Narcotics Prison Farm in Lexington, Kentucky, the ARC experimented on human subjects with nearly eight hundred different drugs. Run by Dr. Harris Isbell, the ARC worked with the Office of Naval Research throughout the 1950s, experimenting with "truth drugs" to assist U.S. intelligence during prisoner interrogation. It included research physicians from the University of Kentucky. A CIA front company, the Geschickter Fund for Medical Research, funded the project. The ARC also worked with the CIA on LSD research simultaneously, as attested to in a letter from Isbell to CIA Technical Services chief Willis Gibbons in April 1953. By August, Isbell was in contact with Sidney Gottlieb, writing that, ". . . we were able to begin our experiments with LSD-25 [in] July. We obtained five subjects . . . [who] were negro male patients, and all of them physically were in very excellent shape . . . Arrangements have been made with the Sandoz Company to obtain a supply of the drug."

Similarly, Dr. Robert Heath of Tulane University experimented on forty-two patients believed to have schizophrenia. They were all Louisiana State Penitentiary inmates, and the U.S. Army provided funding for the program. Heath gave the prisoners LSD and bulbocapnine and implanted electrodes into the septal area of the brain of these poor individuals.[21]

On June 23, 1953, James Angleton conducted his first MKULTRA briefing of George White in the middle of all this activity. Angleton was interested in how the Agency could use LSD to uncover moles inside the CIA and penetrate foreign intelligence services. As previously mentioned, White was already working with Gottlieb and Lafitte, and the timing could not have been coincidental. What makes this even more interesting is the potential that Lee Harvey Oswald may have been one of the unwitting subjects involved in one of the drug testing programs that interested the CIA and military intelligence so much.[22]

* * *

Thirty-eight-year-old Edward G. Gillin worked at Juvenile Court in New Orleans as an assistant district attorney in October 1963. It was two months before the JFK assassination. A young man approached his desk who "gave every indication of emotional disturbance and lack of personal conviction or sense of security." The visitor had a question regarding a book he had read, *Brave New World* by Aldous Huxley, which included a drug that the author stated would enable the reader to see into the future. The man wanted to know about the drug—if it were legal and its name, for he could not remember.

Gillin would later recall that part of the man's name was Oswald because it reminded him of a comedian on the Milton Berle radio show. After the assassination, looking at pictures of Oswald on television and listening to his voice, Gillin recognized him as the mysterious man who had come to his office. He thought authorities would be interested in his encounter, so he called the FBI. Years later, then a seated judge in Louisiana, Gillin would relate that he never received a reply from the Bureau. For some reason, they did not seem to care.

New Orleans library records confirm that Oswald checked out *Brave New World* on September 19, 1963, weeks before Gillin's encounter. Maybe Gillin was mistaken, but he was a credible witness, and the timing of the library book withdrawal adds credibility to his story. So does his assertion that a mind-altering drug interested Oswald. Consider that the general public was unaware of the heinous projects the CIA and the military were involved in, including drug experimentation, when Gillin met Oswald. There was evidence that Oswald may have been one of the unfortunate victims subjected to such tests. Gillin could not have been aware of this, so it is unlikely he would have fabricated such a story. The likely explanation is that Oswald approached Gillin searching for answers to something he was involved in but could not understand.

A CIA memo dated December 1, 1953, stated, "In summary, LSD material over which CIA has or had distributive responsibility is . . . in four places: (a) Dr.

[Willis] Gibbons' safe [one of Gottlieb's superiors], (b) Manila, (c) Atsugi [Japan], and (d) . . . George White . . ." The reference to Atsugi is of interest because Atsugi was where Oswald served as a U-2 radar operator in the Marines before defecting to the Soviet Union. And the evidence is strong that mind-altering drugs were given to him while stationed there, but this does not mean it had anything to do with the assassination of JFK. During the Cold War, the CIA and military intelligence experimented on specific vulnerable service members with drugs and hypnosis to see how they would perform as part of a covert mission that sent them behind the Iron Curtain. Could they be programmed to provide misleading information, resist interrogation, or commit an act against their will without knowing it? Oswald was as likely a participant in such a program as any other enlisted man, maybe more so, considering all the evidence revealed in the following pages.

And with the assassination in mind, drug experimentation on innocent victims was one family jewel the CIA could not reveal in 1963. The public response to this would have been devastating.

In addition, if a group wanted to guarantee that an investigation into a crime would result in a whitewash coverup, such as the JFK assassination, setting up an ex-Marine to take the blame, one who was tested with mind-altering drugs while in the military was the perfect way to do it. There is no proof that this scenario applied to Oswald, but it is worth considering as our narrative moves forward. And it should also not be forgotten that if this did happen to Oswald, it was unrelated to the assassination. It had to do with his defection only. However, after Oswald returned to the U.S., it is not illogical to believe that a group who knew Oswald's experience with drug experimentation before his defection would take advantage of it. They would be aware that those behind Oswald's previous drug experimentation would have to whitewash a post-assassination investigation to keep what happened to Oswald hidden in the name of preserving national security. In other words, by using Oswald and possibly setting him up, the perpetrators could get away with murder. It is why, even though it had nothing directly with the JFK assassination, Oswald's illicit drug ordeal is an integral part of our narrative.[23]

Volume Two covers Oswald's military experience. For now, we shall focus on his formative years, for amazingly, it is also possible that Oswald was given mind-altering drugs without his consent while he was still a boy growing up in the U.S. Some readers may find this difficult to believe, but anything was possible in the age of eugenics when coupled with the war against communism. It appears that Oswald was experimented upon as a youth, as well as a Marine. It is essential to understand this before investigating the JFK assassination itself. The road to Dallas and what Oswald was involved in during 1963, and the relevant relationships he developed during that year, are better understood once the facts surrounding Oswald's troubled childhood and Marine tour of duty are known.

* * *

The assertion that the military and U.S. intelligence conducted experiments on unsuspecting children is believable, considering what was happening at the time. As early as 1939, at the Iowa Soldiers' Orphans' Home in Davenport, Iowa, twenty-two children were victims of the so-called "monster" experiment, which attempted to use psychological abuse to induce stuttering in children who did not have trouble speaking. Conducted by one of the nation's leading speech pathologists, Dr. Wendell Johnson, the testing was done to determine what caused the stuttering.[24]

Dr. Lauretta Bender, a highly respected pediatric neuropsychiatrist, performed electroshock experiments on at least 100 children between three and twelve. At Bellevue Hospital in New York City, She engaged in this unacceptable conduct from early 1940 until 1953. Around the same time, the hospital applied electroconvulsive treatment on more than 500 children, including Bender's experiments. Bender would sometimes shock children who had schizophrenia twice per day for 20 consecutive days. Several of the children became violent and suicidal after receiving treatment. She publicly reported that the results from the experiments were positive, but in private memos, she expressed frustration over mental health issues caused by the treatments.[25]

University of California Department of Pediatrics researchers performed experiments on 113 newborns ranging in age from one hour to three days to study blood pressure and blood flow changes. They inserted a catheter through the babies' umbilical arteries and into their aortas and submerged their feet in ice water. In another study, researchers strapped fifty newborns to a circumcision board and then turned them upside down so that their blood rushed into their heads.[88]

With all the heinous things CIA and military intelligence did during the Cold War, nothing was more despicable than the experimentation done on children. But it is not surprising that this was considered acceptable by the mainstream medical community. These were children whom eugenics suggested would grow up to be a burden on society, and they were just as expendable as the adults who fit that description. The United States Aryan/Nordic community, which ran the government, benefited from experimentation conducted on such children. They did what they did in the name of science, and the children were expendable, which was how they rationalized the destruction of countless innocent lives. And a poor fatherless boy with an indifferent mother named Lee Harvey Oswald, may have been one of the children considered expendable.

* * *

Lee Harvey Oswald was born in New Orleans on October 18, 1939. His father, Robert E. Lee Oswald, named for the Civil War general, died of a heart attack two months before Lee was born. His two older brothers, Robert and John Pic, were temporarily placed in a boarding school. Within a year, they were out, but by 1941 they were placed in an orphan's asylum, and the following year Lee joined them there. Marguerite, Lee's mother, remarried in 1944, and the family moved to Fort Worth, Texas. The older boys were placed in a military academy until the marriage ended in divorce in 1948, and Marguerite had no choice but to remove her two sons from school. By 1952, both Robert and John Pic had enlisted in the military. John Pic was with the Coast Guard on Ellis Island in New York, which was why Marguerite took Lee in August of that year and headed north.[26]

They moved in with John Pic and his wife, but family tensions forced Marguerite and Lee to find a separate apartment. Lee went to school at P.S. 117 in the Bronx and was reportedly absent about half the time, and in January 1953, he transferred to P.S. 44, but truancy was a problem there as well. He was picked up at the Bronx Zoo by an attendance officer for truancy in the spring of 1953, and a court remanded Oswald to the New York City Youth House for a six-week observation period. He called the arresting officer a "damned Yankee," betraying the bias he was accustomed to using, having lived in the South.

The psychiatrist who examined Oswald for Youth House was Dr. Renatus Hartogs. Hertogs was also reportedly involved in mind-altering drug experimentation on unsuspecting patients at the New York Psychiatric Institute. His report at the time regarding Oswald stated that:

> This 13-year-old, well-built boy has superior mental resources and functions only slightly below his capacity level in spite of chronic truancy from school—which brought him into Youth House. No finding of neurological impairment or psychotic mental changes could be made.
>
> Lee has to be diagnosed as "personality pattern disturbance with schizoid features and passive-aggressive tendencies. Lee . . . [is] an emotionally, quite disturbed youngster who suffers under the impact of . . . emotional isolation and deprivation: a lack of affection, absence of family life and rejection by a self-involved and conflicted mother . . ." [We recommend] "that *he should be placed on probation* under the condition that he seek help and guidance through contact with a child guidance clinic, where he should be treated preferably by a male psychiatrist who could substitute, to a certain degree at least, for the lack of a father figure." (Author's italics)

Oswald's probation officer's report supported Hartogs' diagnosis. It stated that Lee was a "friendly and likeable [sic] boy, who portrays very little emotion . . . much of Lee's difficulties seem to stem from his inability to adapt himself to the change of environment and the change of economic status of his family."[27]

The FBI questioned Hartogs after the assassination on December 2, 1963, which should have been a straightforward interview. However, it was not, for there was an overall strangeness to what Hartogs had to say. First, he claimed that he learned from reading a New York newspaper story that a psychiatric interview was conducted of Lee Harvey Oswald when he was a boy. And key words in the report suggested to Hartogs that he was the one who had interviewed him. Phrases like "potentially dangerous" and "incipient schizophrenia" were "peculiar to his type [of] analysis, and he knows of no other psychiatrist who uses them," he told the FBI. It was a ridiculous claim to make. "Potentially dangerous" was a phrase no other psychiatrist used in 1953? Even worse, the terms "potentially dangerous" and "incipient schizophrenia" did not appear in Hartogs' Youth House report. He lied to provide a plausible explanation for why he could remember in 1963, ten years after the fact, that he was the one who had interviewed Lee Oswald. It begs the question, what was so special about that young truant named Oswald from 1953 that caused Hartogs to claim he could remember him ten years later?

When questioned by the Warren Commission, Hartogs was asked, "Do you remember the names of the other psychiatrists who were on the staff at the time Oswald was in the Youth House? "No, no," responded Hartogs. "They are continuously changing. Sometimes they were just for a few weeks there." At the same time, Hartogs admitted that he would spend "somewhere between 2 and 3 hours [per week] with each child . . ." But then he corrected what he said. "No, I mean not with the child itself. The child is seen for about half an hour to an hour." Interesting that he would refer to a child as "itself."[28]

So, according to Hartogs, for two months, which he told the Warren Commission was the average time a boy would be at Youth House, he spent only "about half an hour to an hour" each week with Oswald. Still, he had no trouble remembering the thirteen-year-old insignificant boy who was one of the countless youths Hartogs encountered over the years. Yet, he could not recall who his fellow psychiatrists were at the same time.

"This is tough," Hartogs responded when the Warren Commission asked him about his interview with Oswald. "I remember that . . . I reconstructed this from the seminar. We gave a seminar on this boy [Oswald] in which we discussed him because he came to us on a charge of truancy from school, and yet when I examined him, I found him to have definite traits of dangerousness. In other words, this child had a potential for explosive, aggressive, assaulting acting out, which was rather unusual to find in a child who was sent to Youth House on such a mild charge as truancy from school. It is the reason why I remember this particular child, and that is the reason why we discussed him in the seminar."

What made Oswald so unique that the psychiatric staff discussed his case at a seminar devoted to him alone? And how did he suddenly become so dangerous when Hartogs' original report said nothing of the kind. Hartogs also told the

Warren Commission that, ". . . every Monday afternoon, at 1:30 until 3 o'clock, the professional Youth House staff gets together . . . to discuss an interesting or unusual child. At that time, we selected Oswald because . . . [of] the discrepancy between the charge and the seriousness of his personality disturbance . . ." The Warren Commission asked Hartogs what recommendations he made to the court regarding Oswald. "If I can recall correctly," Hartogs replied, "I recommended that this youngster should be committed to an institution . . . I found him to have definite traits of dangerousness. In other words, this child had a potential for explosive, aggressive, assaulting acting out . . ."[29]

Hartogs was lying, for his actual report did not say this. As noted above, Hartogs initially recommended that probation be Oswald's sentence, which he would not have done if he thought the youngster was dangerous. Hartogs lied to the FBI and Warren Commission because something about the thirteen-year-old Oswald needed to be kept hidden. Hartogs needed to get out front with a false narrative to camouflage what happened to that young boy before someone uncovered the truth for themselves. The logical explanation is that Oswald, that interesting thirteen-year-old who warranted an entire seminar devoted to him alone, was placed in an institution even though the official psychiatric report said this was unnecessary. And Hartogs lied about it after the assassination to protect himself.

In *A Secret Order*, author H.P. Albarelli, Jr. writes that the Bordentown Reformatory in New Jersey was where Youth House psychiatrists would send troubled boys. Bordentown was an institution for what was called at the time "juvenile delinquents." During World War II, and from 1951 to 1964, the CIA and Army conducted behavior modification and mind control experiments at Bordentown. Although Albarelli admits "there is no known evidence," Oswald may have been one of their victims. The boys experimented on offered no redeeming value to society and were expendable, a description that fit Oswald. He was a poor Southern boy in New York with an overbearing mother and no father, who rarely attended school. He was stable enough to have warranted probation, and institutionalizing Oswald was excessive. Dr. Carl Pfeiffer conducted mind-control for the CIA, including testing young males at the New Jersey Reformatory at Bordentown. Pfeiffer gave LSD and amphetamines to each child to test the ability of the drugs to induce psychosis.[30]

In the 1950s, Dr. Sidney Malitz was a psychiatrist at the New York State Psychiatric Institute. Camp Detrick scientists worked with NYSPI, and what they did was unconscionable. In 1952, professional tennis player Harold Blauer died when he was unnecessarily given multiple injections of a mescaline derivative at NYSPI. The Defense Department provided funds for the program. Doctors administered drugs and claimed they were unaware of what the DOD had given them to inject into the veins of their patients. For twenty-three years, the Department of Defense, Department of Justice, and the New York State Attorney General conspired to conceal evidence of the testing done at the Institute.[31]

At NYSPI, Malitz worked under a eugenicist, Research Director Dr. Paul Hoch, one of the doctors involved in the killing of Harold Blauer. Born in Germany, Hoch emigrated to the U.S. in 1933 with the help of none other than the Dulles family. In the early 1950s, he also conducted experiments at the Bordentown Reformatory, and as early as 1948, he cited his Bordentown work in a book he edited, *Failures in Psychiatric Treatment*. While working under Hoch, Malitz became involved in "a number of covert contracts with the CIA and US Army to perform experiments with psychosurgery, electroconvulsive therapy, LSD, mescaline, and other drugs."

Malitz also worked with Camp Detrick's Special Operations Division, the unit Frank Olson headed at that time. According to former Camp Detrick scientists, the work involved experimentation on children and teenage patients without their consent. Malitz also worked with other physicians, most notably Drs. Bernard Wilkens, Harold Esecover, and Harold A. Abramson. Wilkens conducted tests on children during the years Oswald lived in New York. Abramson experimented on children with LSD as early as 1953 in New York City and at a small hospital on Long Island through 1963. Funding came from the CIA, the Army through Fort Detrick, Edgewood Arsenal, and the Office of Naval Intelligence.[32]

There is sufficient evidence proving that U.S. intelligence and the military funded mind-altering drug experimentation of children during the 1950s, much of which was associated with NYSPI and Bordentown, associated with Youth House. Oswald spent six weeks there undergoing intensive psychiatric examinations. And if Oswald was at Bordentown as well, there is a strong possibility mind-altering drugs were used on him, for he was a perfect candidate. Amazingly, the OSS had also used Bordentown Reformatory for truth-drug experiments. It involved the ever-present George Hunter White and Dr. Lawrence Kubie. Kubie would write to White in the late 1950s, saying how much he enjoyed working with him at Bordentown and a state prison in Baltimore. "I look back fondly on those days," wrote Kubie. "What great fun we had." It is doubtful the children they experimented on would have characterized the experience in the same way.

Was there a connection between George White and Oswald? Albarelli writes that "George White frequently used Central Park and the Bronx Zoo as rendezvous points for his meetings with criminals, confidential informers, intelligence agents, and drug traffickers." White use the alias "Morgan Hall" when doing business with the CIA. It is also a section of the American Museum of Natural History. According to the Warren Commission Report, this museum was one of the first places John Pic took Lee when he came to New York. And as reported by Albarelli, "In 1953 the Museum of Natural History "was a favorite rendezvous point for White. Several of White's date book notations cite a person referred to only as 'Lee,' but this Lee was thought to be much older than Oswald, and a close acquaintance of White's."

Whether or not the story connects White to Oswald, or this was just a coincidence, the fact remains that White was involved in drug testing at Bordentown.

So were the CIA and the Army, at a time when Oswald may have been one of their Bordentown subjects. Questioned about these experiments in 1981, the CIA's Dr. Sidney Gottlieb said, "The Agency learned that a person's psyche could be very disturbed by those means."[33]

* * *

Additional evidence related to Oswald, involving drug testing, adds to the mysteriousness of his story. Charles William Thomas worked for the State Department in Mexico in 1964, one year after Oswald had visited there. In 1969, Thomas stumbled upon a story in Mexico, which put Oswald's guilt in the JFK assassination in doubt. It prompted him to write a letter to Secretary of State William Rogers regarding Oswald's Mexico City visit. Thomas wrote it "threatened to reopen the debate about the true nature of the Kennedy assassination and [would] damage the credibility of the Warren Report . . ." He believed there had been a plot to kill JFK. He provided documentation to support his accusation. It involved a gathering in Mexico attended by critically acclaimed writer Elena Garro de Paz, the wife of Nobel Prize-winning writer Octavio Paz. Thomas believed her impressive credentials suggested she was someone he could trust. She revealed details of the party to Thomas, that Oswald was there, as were numerous Mexican Communists sympathetic to Fidel Castro. A Cuban diplomate named Eusebio Azcue, who had previously had a confrontation with Oswald at the Cuban embassy, and another Cuban diplomat, Silvia Duran, with whom Oswald allegedly had an affair, were both in attendance as well.

On July 31, 1969, only six days after he sent his letter to Secretary Rogers, Williams was inexplicably fired. Officially he had been arbitrarily "selected out" for removal, but the timing was suspicious. On August 29, the State Department forwarded Thomas' allegations about an assassination conspiracy to the CIA, who rejected the story in just three weeks. The CIA's Counterintelligence chief James Angleton and his deputy Raymond Rocca were assigned to look into Thomas's account. However, their sole purpose after the assassination was to discredit all reports that a conspiracy had taken place.

Thomas could not find a job after leaving the State Department, and the belief was he had been blackballed. On April 12, 1971, he committed suicide, which his death certificate said was due to a single gunshot wound to his right temple. But foul play should not have been ruled out if it were a legitimate inquiry, considering what we have already discussed. Thomas's family pushed for answers, and eventually, the State Department told them he had lost his job due to a clerical error. How convenient.[34]

Thomas's story is relevant to this chapter because of information he came across while serving in Haiti as the Political Officer in Port-au-Prince from January 1961 to August 1963. Purely by accident, he encountered a team of three physicians working as part of CIA's MK/NAOMI project. Both CIA and the U.S. Army, working independently and together, used Haiti to conduct drug experiments because of that government's willingness to ignore what they were doing. According to one report, Thomas "expressed innocent surprise and perhaps dismay" at these doctors' experiments.

There is circumstantial evidence confirming that drug experimentation took place in Haiti. Albarelli cites ". . . investigative journalists Dr. Jeffrey Kaye and Jason Leopold, [who reported that] the US Army and CIA, under MK/ULTRA, MK/NAOMI, AND MK/DELTS conducted extensive covert experiments with many 'incapacitating agents' during the 1950s through to about 1970. Haiti was a favored location for some experiment."[35]

Amazingly, before leaving for Mexico City, Thomas was invited to invest his own money in private ventures in Haiti by a then-unknown businessman, George de Mohrenschildt, which also "involved another CIA operative . . ." named Charles R. Norberg." Worth noting is that while serving as an Army Air Force intelligence officer during World War II, Norberg encountered George Hunter White in Burma and India. After the war, Norberg worked for the CIA and the State Department, joined a prestigious law firm, and eventually opened a private practice in 1956, where he became de Mohrenschildt's attorney.

Norberg represented de Mohrenschildt "in a series of complex Haiti-based oil and geological business ventures, some of which, according to at least two former US State Department officials, involved the 'technical, in-country [Haiti] services of Thomas Eli Davis III, [as well as] two or three other soldier-of-fortune types who were in and out of Haiti, Guatemala, Panama, and the Dominican Republic.'" From Chapters Nine and Ten, we know that Davis was trying to put together a paramilitary army to invade Haiti in 1963. He was then detained in Tangiers because of a letter in his possession referencing "Oswald" and the "Kennedy assassination." He was familiar with the CIA-connected Thomas Proctor, an associate of Victor Oswald in Madrid, connected to Otto Skorzeny and the World Commerce Corporation, which involved Allen Dulles and William Donovan. Davis was also an informant for George White (who had worked with Norberg and did work at Bordentown), dabbled in drug trafficking, and sold arms with Jack Ruby in the war against Castro. And if a de Mohrenschildt/Davis connection is genuine, a plan to assassinate Papa Doc Duvalier and take over the Haitian government must have involved the entire group. If so, the question then becomes, was what they were doing in Haiti related to Kennedy's assassination? Or did the connection of all these suspects, which included associations to Oswald and Ruby by some, create suspicion that they were guilty of killing JFK. Still, maybe they had nothing to do with it, and the operation in Haiti was unrelated to the events in Dallas. Perhaps the relationship some had with Oswald and Ruby made them assassination suspects after the fact. It is a mystery that must expose if one is to uncover who killed JFK.

Adding to the intrigue is evidence that Norberg was directly involved in the CIA's biological weapons testing during the 1950s. He was a member of the United States Psychological Strategy Board created in 1951 and served in the White House as the board's assistant director for several years. In the mid-1950s, he came to the attention of Allen Dulles. Dulles was impressed that Norberg thought biological warfare could be a psychological weapon in the war against communism. Norberg offered to place a psychological operations officer undercover in every U.S. embassy, which also attracted Dulles to him. And for over a decade, Norberg was a legal advisor for two CIA front companies, Morwede Associates and Mankind Research Unlimited. He was not your typical attorney, and George de Mohrenschildt may have been involved in drug experimentation in Haiti for U.S. intelligence through Norberg. If so, it adds a new dimension to de Mohrenschildt's relationship with Oswald. He may have been aware of the mind-altering drug experimentation program Oswald was part of before his defection. Then, after Oswald returned from the Soviet Union, the CIA asked de Mohrenschild to keep an eye on him.[36]

Returning to Charles Thomas, let us consider the timeline. While stationed in Haiti, he inadvertently comes across scientists involved in a CIA drug experimentation program. Also, while in Haiti, he had business meetings with de Mohrenschildt and Norberg, who allowed Thomas to invest his own money in their Haitian business ventures. Was the investment offer they made a veiled attempt at bribing Thomas so he would keep quiet about the CIA program upon which he had stumbled? It is impossible to know for sure, but we can assume that after details of the assassination became public, Thomas would have learned of de Mohrenschildt's connection to Oswald in the spring of 1963. That was right before de Mohrenschildt traveled to Haiti and interacted with Thomas. Considering the drug operation that Thomas learned about and his encounter with de Mohrenschildt and Norberg, a red flag must have gone up in Thomas's mind. He must have thought the coincidence was too outlandish not to have had some relevance to the assassination. It explains why the CIA fired him, and it makes one wonder if his death was by suicide.

In 1964 Thomas was then transferred to Mexico City and learned about the party Oswald attended. The second-hand information he received about the party could not have been sufficient for him to write the Secretary of State stating that the Warren Commission may have been wrong and there was a conspiracy in JFK's murder. It implies he must have connected the dots between his encounter with de Mohrenschildt in Haiti, de Mohrenschildt's connection to Oswald, and what he learned in Mexico City to reach this conclusion.

Summarizing what we know, de Mohrenschildt was close to Texas oilmen like H.L. Hunt, Clint Murchison, Sid Richardson, and Harold Boyd. Murchison was involved in a suspicious meatpacking plant in Haiti with LBJ protégé Bobby Baker while de Mohrenschildt was there. De Mohrenschildt met with the CIA branch chief of the Soviet Russian division Nicholas Anikeeff in Washington D.C. while he was on his way to Haiti. His role in monitoring Oswald was over, for he would never see Oswald again. Oswald had also left Dallas and gone to New Orleans, and it was now someone else's responsibility to keep an eye on him.

De Mohrenschildt supposedly went to Haiti on business when the CIA was interested in assassinating Papa Doc Duvalier. Thomas Davis was putting together an army to invade Haiti and take over the government. Mobsters were to be employed in exchange for Haitian gambling rights once Duvalier was gone.

We know that Anikeef was part of the Gehlen operation after World War II. Both Anikeef and de Mohrenschildt were likely involved with William Donovan, Allen Dulles, WCC, and an international anti-Communist network operating in Europe, including the radical right in the U.S. and U.S. intelligence. Guy Banister associate Maurice Gatlin sent money to Europe for the assassination of Charles de Gaulle, and the group in New Orleans was probably part of this international right-wing network. As described above, Thomas Eli Davis, Thomas Proctor, Victor Oswald, Victor Skorzeny, Jack Crichton, and Jack Ruby were also involved in this through the WCC and the international anti-Communist network.

Recall from Chapter Four that there was a connection between Tracy Barnes, Jack Crichton, and the group known as Operation 40. Barnes was head of CIA's Domestic Contacts Division, and de Mohrenschildt first contacted Oswald at the request of one of their agents. Operation 40 was a CIA assassination group that was part of the Bay of Pigs operation. Considering that de Mohrenschildt's reason for being in Haiti was to assassinate Duvalier, Operation 40 was likely involved in this well. The connection to the Bay of Pigs is interesting because, at the end of 1960, de Mohrenschildt and his wife embarked on a seven-thousand-mile "walking tour" along "primitive jungle trails" throughout Central America. They arrived in Guatemala City "by happenstance," a short time before the Bay of Pigs invasion, near where the CIA was training the Cuban exile force that invaded Cuba.[37]

We also know that in 1952, Jack Crichton was part of a group, which included Clint Murchison, to negotiate oil drilling rights in Spain with the Fascist dictator Francisco Franco. It may have connected to building military bases there.[38] Also involved in this effort was Suite 8F Group member William Pawley, Charles Willoughby, and Otto Skorzeny, as all roads seem to lead back to the WCC group. Then there was de Mohrenschildt's connection to Mamantov and Crichton and their involvement in translating Marina Oswald's testimony and Don Levine's interview of Marina for *Life* magazine on behalf of CIA, which was never published. Recall that Levine may have connected with the Dulles/Donovan stay-behind armies and WCC, as well as Harold Isaacs, which brings the MIT Center for International Studies and their involvement with Oswald's defection into the picture.

Thomas Eli Davis' attempt to recruit "men for an invasion of Haiti," when coupled with de Mohrenschildt's involvement in a plot to assassinate Haitian President Papa Doc, has all the ingredients necessary for the CIA's blueprint for toppling foreign governments. The only thing missing was a Haitian insider who could orchestrate the coup, and that person did exist. His name was Clemard Charles, the president of the Banque Commerciale d'Haiti. Charles and de Mohrenschildt were in Washington before going to Haiti. They met with U.S. Army Chief of Staff Dorothy Matlack, who served as the Pentagon liaison to the CIA. A follow-up meeting occurred, including CIA Domestic Contacts Division agent Tony Czaikowski, who worked under Tracy Barnes. The reason for these meetings was the alleged business ventures de Mohrenschildt and Charles were about to embark upon, but there must have been more to it since it involved the Army and CIA. The assassination of Papa Doc must have been the topic of discussion.

In *Our Man in Haiti*, Joan Mellen explained that in 1957, Papa Doc secured his election with a $400,000 bribe to the Haitian army via Clemard Charles, Duvalier's banker at the time. Papa Doc was very appreciative and awarded Charles the "Commander of the Order of Civil Merit," the "Order of Work," and the "Order of Agricultural Merit." Charles was even a godfather to one of Duvalier's children. In 1962, New York City gave Charles the key to the city when he visited as Duvalier's representative.[39]

However, not everything was going well for U.S. business was displeased with how Haiti was treating them. One American businessman called Duvalier "a terrorist and dictator worse than Batista," and the U.S. government had also become disenchanted. In 1959, they had sent Haiti a $4,300,000 loan to develop the Aretibonite Valley, along with a grant of $7,000,000. The following year American aid jumped to $21.4 million, while Haiti's sugar quota to the U.S. increased by twenty-five percent. But despite this, Duvalier's totalitarian rule and misappropriation of U.S. funds made him a liability, and it was not long before discussions were had, especially in U.S. intelligence and military circles, that it was in the best interest of the U.S. to have Duvalier replaced.

By the summer of 1962, Edwin Martin, the Assistant Secretary of State for Inter-American Affairs, advised JFK that they should consider "replacing him [Duvalier] with something we can live with." Richard Helms complained to the President about Duvalier's "shakedown of the business community," and General Maxwell Taylor advised he could have Marines in Haiti "within fifty-one hours." Still, Kennedy refused to consent to Duvalier's removal. Despite this, CIA and military intelligence pursued their agenda to remove the Haitian leader, which brought Clemard Charles to their attention. Both CIA and military intelligence placed him under surveillance, and as early as August 1962, the 902nd Military Intelligence Group, "90 Deuce," asked the FBI to check on Charles' business activities in Miami. By February 1963, Charles was aware of the interest in him, and he visited the U.S. Embassy in Port-au-Prince to enhance his possibility of being chosen Duvalier's successor. He let the embassy know that he had "favorable relations with well-placed Duvalier regime figures" and "a line into the palace."

By April 1963, Charles had aligned himself with de Mohrenschildt, looking to ingratiate himself with U.S. government officials and the CIA. It was a clear sign that De Mohrenschildt was part of U.S. intelligence, for why else would Charles have approached him? When meeting with the CIA in the U.S., Charles made his intentions clear. For the good of his country, he wanted the CIA to overthrow Duvalier and install him as the new President. Meanwhile, throughout 1963 CIA was "involved in discussions with an exile group which had the objective of overthrowing Duvalier," according to what William Colby told the Church Committee years later. There were "a couple of efforts to send people into Haiti . . . a paramilitary operation . . . sort of like the Bay of Pigs, that kind of invasion."[40]

It brings us back to Thomas Davis and that attempted CIA government overthrows always followed the same pattern. Remove the nation's leader with an internal coup, have someone in place ready to take over, get the nation's military on board with the operation, and invade the country with a small paramilitary force to preserve plausible deniability. It is what De Mohrenschildt, Charles, and Davis were doing in Haiti. There were two reasons why this makes sense. First is Haiti's proximity to Cuba, and once taken over, Haiti was likely to become a jumping-off point for another attempt to remove Castro from power. Second, the Mafia was looking for another Caribbean country to build their casinos. Haiti would have been the perfect location, which is why there were reports that the Mafia was to assassinate Duvalier.

Just before this, Oswald returned from the Soviet Union in 1962, and George de Mohrenschildt him at the request of the local CIA. He had control over Oswald, who seemed to listen to whatever the good Baron told him to do. He "babysits" the returned defector for a year, probably because of his familiarity with the mind-altering drug operation Oswald was involved with. In the summer of 1963, they part ways, never to see each other again. Haiti would become de Mohrenschildt's focus for the foreseeable future, and New Orleans Oswald's, which was probably the beginning of his entry into the JFK assassination conspiracy.

Regarding the JFK assassination, Oswald was the perfect patsy. Those attempting to assassinate Duvalier and take over the Haitian government knew all about Oswald's defection and knew what happened to Oswald before going to Russia. Because the Haitian affair was probably part of a more significant operation to take over Cuba and remove Castro from power, operatives from both the Haitian and Cuban operations were likely involved in the JFK assassination. The attempted takeover of governments simultaneously should not surprise us. It was also occurring overseas, as third-world nations were willing to fight to gain their freedom from European colonialism beginning in the mid-1950s.

Meanwhile, European countries were reluctant to let go. Progressives supported self-determination for every nation, while radical right-wingers feared this would draw third-world countries in Africa and Southeast Asia into the Communist camp. And nowhere was this more serious than in France, where leading members of the French military started a civil war against their government to keep colonialism alive. Their story is relevant to our discussion. As they looked to assassinate French President Charles de Gaulle, they became aligned with the right-wing of the CIA and American military generals who supported their cause. And their actions greatly impacted those in the U.S. who felt equally frustrated by their government. It included those who looked to overthrow Haiti and Cuba. As a result, a right-wing brotherhood of fascism developed between Europe and the United States that would end with blood on the streets of Dallas. The next chapter explains how that came to be.

- 12 -

Third World Unrest Threatens the New World Order

"We want to halt the decadence of the West [Capitalism] and the march of Communism. That is our duty, the real duty of the army. That is why we must win the war in Algeria. Indo-China taught us to see the truth . . ."

—French OAS Colonel Antoine Argoud

There are "two world systems, one twisted beyond recognition (communism) . . . the other decadent and dying (capitalism). A truly democratic system would combine the better qualities of the two upon an American foundation, opposed to both . . ."

—Lee Harvey Oswald

Like their counterparts in the United States, the French military could not understand why their government had abandoned them, resulting in their defeat in Vietnam. When Charles de Gaulle granted independence to the French colony of Algeria, French generals saw it as a betrayal of French nationalism. They formed the OAS to fight a civil war against their government, repeatedly tried to assassinate de Gaulle, and rejected socialism and capitalism. They were Fascists, supported by like-minded right-wing radicals in Europe and the United States, which resulted in an international Fascist movement whose goal was to create a new world order that rejected the American and Soviet forms of government. Based on his political writings, Lee Harvey Oswald embraced a similar creed and spent the last years of his life surrounded by American Fascists who thought the same way. And it was not a coincidence that both the U.S. military and CIA maintained a close relationship to the OAS, for each group wanted the same thing—to radically change the direction of their government, starting with the forcible removal of their President from office.

* * *

Before World War II, France controlled the opium trade in Indochina, using drug profits to finance their operations in the region, but this ended during the Japanese occupation. After the war, international pressure put an end to this. The U.S. had "extracted the agreement from its European allies" that they would abolish drug trafficking once the liberation of their colonies in Southeast Asia was complete. But there remained a much sought-after market for opium in Indochina in the early 1950s because the importation of Chinese and Iranian opium, which had supplied the region's addicts for almost one hundred years, was suspended. As a result, French intelligence and the French army stationed in Southeast Asia, who could not rely on their home country to provide the financing they needed, resumed their drug dealing. In what became known as Operation X, the French collected opium from Montagnard tribe members in Vietnam and transferred it to Saigon. The Binh Xuyen, Vietnamese gangsters who controlled the Saigon underworld, refined and sold opium through Chinese and Corsican operatives. And with the help of the Binh Xuyen, the French were able to keep the Communist Vietminh opposition force under control in Saigon. In addition, the police in Thailand, Chiang Kai Shek's Nationalist Chinese army, and CIA all established programs that allowed Southeast Asia's massive opium business to thrive.

Meanwhile, six months after China fell to the Communists, the Korean War began. It prompted President Truman, in November 1950, to approve an OPC and CIA plan to invade southern China using Chiang's KMT troops, who were now in Burma. By October 1951, Truman's executive order NSC 10/5 authorized an "intensification of covert action," basically "condoning and fostering activity without providing scrutiny and control." It resulted in an alliance between OPC, ex-Gestapo officers and Corsican gangsters in Western Europe, and opium warlords in Southeast Asia. The CIA also needed drug money to operate those programs they wished to keep hidden.[1]

U.S. intelligence already had a presence in Southeast Asia. The OSS battled the Japanese during the war, so the transition after hostilities had ended to the CIA was smooth. However, funding authorized by Congress was limited and required congressional oversight. The Agency was unwilling to publicize some of their more unscrupulous operations, so the CIA turned to drug dealing as another source of revenue to fund projects they knew Congress would never approve. They created alliances with local warlords and had CIA agents on the ground conduct covert operations far beyond what the U.S. government was capable of financing. They used the opium money to purchase arms, which increased the combat effectiveness of the locals in their employ, all independent of any oversight from Washington. Operating beyond the controls of bureaucracies in Paris and Washington, paramilitary CIA and French forces allied with local tribes and warlords, which enabled them to penetrate China on intelligence missions. It was similar to what was happening in Europe at the same time. As described in Chapter Four, the Service d'Ordre

Francais (RPF) and the World Commerce Corporation (WCC) worked independently of their respective intelligence agencies. Stay behind armies were created by Donovan and Dulles to battle the Soviets, financed by drug money, and operated without Paris and Washington's knowledge.[2]

* * *

Ho Chi Minh's story begins at the end of World War I. By that time, he had already visited India, Africa, the Middle East, Europe, and the United States, where he worked briefly as a pastry chef at the Parker House Hotel in Boston. He was in France, which ruled his native Vietnam, during the post-war peace conference, when President Wilson argued that no people should be "selfishly exploited" and that all must be "dominated and governed only by their own consent." It prompted Ho to publish a broadside demanding for Vietnam "the sacred right of all people for self-determination." However, in true eugenic fashion, Wilson only considered self-determination applicable to the remnants of the Ottoman and Austro-Hungarian empires in Europe. Sub-humans, whom Wilson believed inhabited Vietnam, were not included among the people he wanted to protect. Within a year, Ho Chi Minh joined the French Communist Party, traveled to Moscow, and became part of the Comintern, the international organization that advocated world communism. He eventually decided to wage war against the Western oppressors in Vietnam.[3]

World War II provided a temporary respite, as the United States supported Ho Chi Minh, furnishing him with military equipment and supplies to fight the Japanese. His army even received training from the OSS. When the war ended, U.S. Army commander Major Allison Thomas gave Ho a farewell dinner. A month later, Ho declared Vietnam independent of French rule and became the country's first leader. He signed a Declaration of Independence in Hanoi for the newly formed Democratic Republic of Vietnam, which stated that "All men are created equal. They are endowed by their Creator with certain inalienable rights . . . [such as] Life, Liberty, and the Pursuit of Happiness . . ."[4] The American influence was evident.

Ho intended to maintain good relations with the United States, but unexpected events made this impossible. The following month, French troops staged a coup d'état and installed a French-controlled government in Saigon, located in the southern part of Vietnam, which forced Ho and his Democratic Republic to seek refuge in the north. Ho Chi Minh wanted the U.S. to intervene and liberate his country. He wrote President Truman that "the French colonialists . . . are waging on us a murderous and pitiless war . . . to re-establish their domination . . . [Western nations] ought to keep their words . . . [and] show that they mean to carry out in peacetime the principles for which they fought in wartime . . ."[5]

Truman did not reply to the letter, for Ho was a Communist and, as a result, an enemy of the United States. On January 31, 1950, Secretary of State Dean Acheson said Ho was "the mortal enemy of native independence in Indochina" and the

United States, just four months after Mao Tse Tung founded the People's Republic of China, officially recognized the French government in Vietnam.[6] The previous October, the CIA had forecasted that the Chinese Communists would eventually involve themselves in Vietnam and assist Ho after destroying Chiang's forces. In January, three divisions of Mao's troops did enter Vietnam, prompting the response from Acheson described above. In February, both the Soviet Union and China recognized Ho's government in Vietnam. [7]

*　*　*

By 1954, the war in Vietnam was not going well for the French. The Montagnard, the indigenous peoples of the Central Highlands of Vietnam who supported them, had been virtually destroyed by the Vietminh. The French forces feared that the Vietminh could replenish their war chests with the Montagnard opium they now could access. It could not be allowed to happen, so the French decided to take a stand at Dien Bien Phu, but in March, the Vietminh destroyed the French airfield there, and within two months, they had overrun the French military bases. It was a resounding Vietminh victory and the decisive battle of the war. In July, the French government signed the Geneva Accords, ending the fighting in Vietnam.[8]

The United States was determined to ensure that they would not lose Vietnam to the Communists with the French departure. At a press conference, John Foster Dulles said that the U.S. objective was to ensure the Chinese did not "extend the political system of Communism to Southeast Asia."[9] Dulles and Eisenhower believed that if southern Vietnam turned Communist, all Southeast Asia would follow, and an area with vital raw materials would be China or the Soviet Union. Japan, which needed markets and raw materials from that region, would compromise with the Chinese Communists. We must not lose Japan, Ike wrote Churchill. "The moral, political and military consequences" would be a disaster.[10]

To keep the Communists out of southern Vietnam, the U.S. was willing to do whatever was necessary. If the Korean armistice collapsed, Dulles told Churchill, the U.S. was ready to attack directly at China, and the use of atomic weapons was a viable option. When the Geneva Accords mandated North and South Vietnam to hold elections so they could unite into one nation, Ike and Dulles were determined to "prevent a Communist victory . . ." Eisenhower's advisors were sure that Ho would likely win, so the newly installed president in the south, Ngo Dinh Diem, was instructed by the United States not to participate in the elections. He complied, and Vietnam remained two separate countries. There was no alternative, State Department policy planners concluded, but to destroy the organized armed forces of the Vietminh as "a precondition of achievement of US objectives in Indochina." The objective was a united, democratic Vietnam.[11]

Meanwhile, though defeated, 80,000 French troops remained in Indochina as permitted under the Geneva Agreement, while the United States increased its presence to ensure the Communists stayed out of the south. By early 1955, the French relinquished their control over the South Vietnamese army after General Edward Lansdale, the man Eisenhower and Dulles chose to battle the Vietminh, thwarted a coup by pro-French General Nguyen Van Hinh. When Lansdale eliminated the Binh Xuyen gangsters in Saigon and Cholon, upon whom French intelligence still relied, the fate of the French was inevitable. On May 11, 1955, French Premier Edgar Faure agreed to withdraw all French forces from Indochina. They left with anger for the United States, whom they believed had abandoned them in their time of need. They carried this animosity with them onto their next battlefield arena, which was Algeria.[12]

* * *

Algeria had become a French military colony in 1834 and officially part of France in 1848. Algerians fought for France during World War II. However, after the war, when anti-colonialism and self-determination began to take hold in third-world countries, rumblings about Algerian independence began to be heard. Hostilities began on November 1, 1954, with attacks on various French military and civilian targets, as bombs detonated simultaneously in numerous Algerian cities. The official French response was that Algeria would remain part of France.

Coming so soon after the debacle in Vietnam, the French military looked at Algeria as a chance for redemption. Alistair Horne wrote in *A Savage War of Peace* that Dien Bien Phu was "the most humiliating defeat suffered by any Western power since World War II . . . as humiliating as 1940 [when the Nazis marched into Paris] to French army sensibilities in that the victors had been despised 'colonials' and 'little yellow men.'" Those that defeated them were "subhuman," an inexcusable offense.

French General Henri Lorillot became the commander in Algeria. He said, "We were carted in Indochina . . . We were carted in Tunisia . . . We are being carted in Morocco. But they will never cart us in Algeria, I swear to you . . ." He was heard loud and clear in Paris[13]

The military blamed French politicians for the debacle in Vietnam and what was happening in Algeria, and Charles de Gaulle agreed with that assessment. He said the military took "upon itself not only the burden of the fighting . . . , [but were] haunted by [the] fear of another Indo-China . . . [and] felt a growing resentment against a political system which was the embodiment of irresolution."[14]

But there was more to it than just the military's dissatisfaction with French politicians. "We have not come here," declared Radio-Bigeard on the military's radio station, "to defend colonialism. We have nothing in common with the rich clons [short for colonists, the European population in Algeria] who exploit the Muslims. We are the defenders of liberty and . . . *a new order*. While we were fighting in Indo-China, while we were suffering in Viet-Minh prisons, men liberally paid betrayed us . . . [In Algeria] you will not be betrayed."[15] (Author's italics)

Once again, a "new order" is referenced. As described in previous chapters, the radical right in the United States also wanted to establish a new world order. Only this time, Frenchmen were looking to change the world. Also, the military in France and the United States both believed politicians were harming their respective countries. Some Americans embraced Socialist principles, while in France, colonialism was coming to an end. And each military thought it was more qualified to establish a foreign policy agenda than were the politicians they were supposed to serve. Insubordination was on the rise, and so was the concern that the military in either country might take it upon themselves to orchestrate a coup d'état before it was too late.

So, what was this new order that seemed to unite the military in these two western countries? In 1960, during the Barricades Trial, which involved the French military's attempt to take control of Algiers without the approval of the French government, Colonel Antoine Argoud explained what the military wanted to achieve. "We want to halt the decadence of the West and the march of Communism. That is our duty, the real duty of the army. That is why we must win the war in Algeria. Indo-China taught us to see the truth . . ."[16]

According to Argoud, the military was not just dissatisfied with communism. It was also capitalism. Their goal was to tear down both political systems and replace them with another. This disenchantment forced the French and American military elements to drift further toward the far-right in search of a political philosophy that supported their beliefs. Inevitably, fascism was the political system they embraced.

We should not dismiss the dissatisfaction the French and American military branches had with their respective governments, for the roots of their discontent ran deep. So much so that each threatened to take over their respective governments if conditions did not improve. They thought their way of life was in jeopardy, and each referred to a new world order, which was a return to what they believed their countries stood for. And that they each embraced such a belief simultaneously suggests they were acting in concert, not independent of one another. Like the Vatican and Fascists who supported the Church, the war against communism and the threat to Western self-determination bound them together.

Along with this, it is interesting to compare the words of Argoud to those of Lee Harvey Oswald, whose political philosophy he put forth in 1963, as previously mentioned in this book. According to Oswald, there were "two world systems, one twisted beyond recognition (communism) . . . the other decadent and dying (capitalism)." A system that was democratic "would combine the better qualities of the two upon an American foundation." After the final "conflict between the two world systems leaves the country without defense or foundation of government . . ." and the survivors would "seek an alternative to those systems which have brought them misery . . ." Oswald wrote of an "economic, political or military crisis, internal or external, [that] will bring about the final destruction of the capitalist system . . ."

He went on to note that ". . . only the intellectually fearless could even be remotely attracted too [sic] *our doctrine* . . ."[17] (Author's Italics)

Oswald continued that "*we* have no interest in violently opposing the U.S. government, or ". . . assuming the head of government." And a "separate, demo-cratic, pure communist society" was unacceptable. Oswald's group consisted of a small party of disenchanted radicals, socialists, and remnants of the Republican Party. Their goal was to *defend "the right of private personal property*, religious toler-ance, and freedom of travel."[18] (Author's italics)

Oswald's beliefs closely mirrored the words of Argoud, which suggests that he was aware of what the militaries in France and the U.S. wanted to achieve. How else did he develop a political philosophy that so resembled what these militaries stood for? It further supports the idea that an international anti-Communist, right-wing, Fascist alliance existed between Europe and the U.S., which tried multiple times to kill de Gaulle. The evidence suggests this was the impetus behind the assassination of JFK. It was a New World Order which these protagonists tried to bring about. Oswald was part of it. Oswald's and Argoud's writings indicate that the intent was to initiate a war between the U.S. and the Soviet Union, after which a new world order built upon the better parts of each political system would take control. Which raises the question: Was the assassination of JFK supposed to be the catalyst to bring this about? Was Oswald willingly prepared to take the blame because the intent was to get him out of the country, which would have left a dead American President assassinated by an American Communist who had previously "defected" to Russia? Was this supposed to be the spark that ignited hostilities? Is this why after Oswald was apprehended, they had to silence him quickly, and why the Warren Commission covered up the crime—to prevent World War III from occurring?

Those who were behind this New World Order and attempted government takeovers were Fascists. Another question is, could Oswald have been a Fascist, despite all the allegations that he was a Communist? The answer is a definitive yes. Recall Jack Ruby's ramblings after he killed Oswald that ". . . a whole new form of government is going to take over our country" and "there is only one kind of people that would go to such extremes, and that would be the Master Race . . . " Consider also that Oswald associated almost exclusively with ultra-right wingers, racists, and Fascists throughout his adult life. After his arrest for the assassination of JFK, the FBI discovered in Oswald's notebook the names of Lincoln Rockwell and Daniel Burros, one written right above the other. Rockwell was the founder of the American Nazi Party. On November 15, 1961, Burros left the American Nazi Party to found the American Nationalist Party.

Along with the names Rockwell and Burros, the notation "Hollis sec. of Queens NY" was also found in Oswald's notebook. The Hollis section of Queens was the home of Burros' organization. Burros cowrote *Kill!* magazine with fellow Nazi John Patler, which was "dedicated to the annihilation of the enemies of the white people." The back cover featured a hangman's noose and words: "Impeach the TRAITOR John F. Kennedy for giving aid and comfort to the enemies of the U.S.A." Why would Oswald have listed such people in his notebook unless he supported their point of view?[19]

Five days after the assassination, Rockwell wrote a letter to J. Edgar Hoover, similar to what Oswald had written. "We believe in the Constitution and government by law," Rockwell wrote. "We also believe that these things are under deadly attack by world Communism and that *it will take a more extreme political movement than "conservatism" to stop the red revolutionaries and killers. We thus believe that the only way to save our race and Nation is by a LEGAL counter-revolution, which is the open course of the American Nazi Party.*" (Author's italics) Rockwell went on to say in the same letter that his organization was "an extreme political movement [that] attracts irresponsible and lunatic elements . . . who force themselves upon the movement and are very hard to get rid of." He then provided Hoover the names of twenty-seven Nazi storm troopers he said were capable of similar acts of violence. Was this an admission that Oswald was part of the American Nazi Party? No one knows for sure, but the evidence suggests that Oswald belonged to this group and that Fascist elements, including Oswald, were behind the assassination to create a new form of government, a new world order, throughout the western world. Recall all the right-wing government overthrows which occurred around the time of JFK's assassination. From what we know of Lee Harvey Oswald, he would have found such international upheavals quite appealing.[20]

* * *

And there was a great deal of international upheaval happening at that time. While the Algerian war continued, France signed treaties of independence with Morocco and Tunisia in March 1956. Ghana achieved independence in 1957, and when sixteen states did so in 1960, the total number of newly independent states rose to twenty-seven. It was Africa where the drive to end colonialism was the strongest. The United States wanted to ensure that each country gained its independence and drifted into the American sphere of influence, not the Soviets. It was not a simple undertaking, as a U.S. study conducted at the time explained: "The African's mind is not made up, and he is being subjected to a number of contradictory forces: Xenophobic nationalism, Egyptian 'Islamic' propaganda, Pan-Africanism, Afro-Asian unity, tribal rivalry, federation, sectionalism, Communism, anti-economic imperialism, and Western appeals for orderly development," and "the demand for independence in Africa today over-shadows all other issues."[21]

One major uprising occurred in Egypt. In July 1952, a military junta, led by Gamal Abdel Nasser and Muhammad Naguib, seized power by dethroning King Farouk. The new government immediately called for the removal of British forces, who were in control of the Suez Canal. In less than two years, Nasser disposed of

Naguib and assumed the presidency himself, and his main area of interest became the building of the Aswan Dam. In October 1954, the British ceded control of the Suez Canal Zone to the Egyptians, but the British military remained to defend the canal against foreign aggression. June 18, 1956, was the date set for the withdrawal of all British troops from Suez. Meanwhile, the British and French still maintained a controlling interest in Suez Canal Company stock.

On September 27, 1955, Egypt announced it would procure Soviet-produced arms from Czechoslovakia for Egyptian cotton, which created tensions throughout the Middle East. Britain had to land troops in Saudi Arabia because of a dispute involving oil. Israel demanded that Egypt withdraw from the arms deal and that the U.S. sign a treaty with Israel that guaranteed their safety. Things got heated when Israel attacked Egyptian troops in an area classified as a demilitarized zone, resulting in the suspension of a U.S. arms sale to Israel. The following year riots broke out in Jordan, and Dulles was told: "There was evidence that the Communists were mixed up in it." On May 16, 1956, Nasser officially recognized the People's Republic of China, signifying that Egypt leaned toward the Communist camp. John Foster Dulles warned Nasser that he should "ponder carefully the consequences of the course you are now embarking upon." The threat was clear.[22]

The U.S. then canceled American financial aid for the Aswan Dam, which they had previously agreed to provide. When Nasser nationalized the Suez Canal in response, threatening Europe's oil supply, Britain, France, and Israel decided to wage war against Egypt behind closed doors. The objective was to take control of the canal and remove Nasser from power. The three allies kept their plans hidden from the United States and even lied directly to Eisenhower. On October 29, 1956, Israeli armed forces attacked the Sinai Peninsula, and two days later, claiming they needed to protect the Suez Canal, British and French troops began bombing Egyptian targets. By early November, British and French paratroopers and marines occupied strategic positions in the canal zone.[23]

The United Nations called for a cease-fire, and both the United States and the Soviet Union pressured Great Britain, France, and Israel to withdraw. The Russians said they would use nuclear weapons against Britain, while the U.S. privately threatened to implement economic sanctions against their allies. Eisenhower was upset because Britain, France, and Israel did not tell him ahead of time that they intended to attack Egypt, even though he had warned the Allies not to invade. As a result, the Allies threatened to undo the balance of power in the Middle East, and Ike argued that it could escalate into World War III if they did not remove their troops. As early as March 21, 1956, Eisenhower had told a news conference that "any outbreak of major hostilities in the region would be a catastrophe to the world." His fears were well-founded, for after the fighting started, 300,000 people rallied in Pakistan in support of Egypt, Syria blew up a major pipeline that allowed oil to reach tankers in the Mediterranean, and Saudi Arabia imposed a total oil embargo on Britain and France.

Due to pressure applied by the U.S., British and French troops departed Egypt in December 1956, Israel withdrew in March 1957, and Egypt eventually reopened the canal to commercial shipping. It was another sign that the age of colonialism was coming to an end.

The war had one other consequence that would affect relations between the Soviet Union and the Western Powers for the remainder of the Cold War. Amidst the hostilities, Soviet Premier Nicolai Bulganin warned the British and French that the conflict had the potential to escalate "into a third World War," and the Soviets were a "more powerful state possessing all types of modern weapons of destruction," including "rocket weapons." The Soviet threat to attack Britain and France with nuclear weapons could not have been clearer. The Russians believed this forced the Europeans to withdraw from Egypt, but they were unaware that economic pressure from the U.S. was the real reason Britain and France pulled out.[24]

The result was a change in the Soviet's public persona. Since the death of Stalin, they had tried to present themselves as more peace-loving than the U.S., and that the Americans were the ones responsible for bringing the world to the brink of nuclear destruction. In the wake of the Suez War, they changed to a hardline approach, believing that threatening an atomic attack was the only way the West would back down.

The United States did take the Soviet threats seriously. Even after a cease-fire in Egypt, Eisenhower ordered naval forces off the American East Coast should Soviet ships attack. They were authorized to "counter-attack using every available means to destroy." The U.S. Sixth fleet was shifted to an operating area southwest of Crete "in order [to] improve [a] readiness posture for [a] general emergency," and two aircraft carriers relocated to the eastern end of the Mediterranean. These maneuvers exacerbated an already tense situation, but the United States believed it was necessary, considering the Soviets' newfound bluster and what was occurring in Hungary around the same time.

* * *

The unrest in Czechoslovakia and East Berlin following Stalin's death in 1953 continued into the summer of 1956, when Poland was on the verge of exploding. In late June, a demonstration for "Bread and Freedom" in Poznan resulted in a clash with Polish troops, leaving fifty-six workers dead and more than three hundred wounded. Poland could not sustain itself, as the Soviet Union forced it to sell them coal at ten percent of the world's going rate. To keep the peace, the Kremlin stated it was willing to accept a higher coal price. A concerned Khrushchev believed Soviet troops would be necessary to keep Poland in the Warsaw Pact.[25]

The events in Poland encouraged the people of Hungary. On October 22, revolting Budapest students published a list of sixteen demands, which included "the withdrawal of all Soviet troops from Hungary, the nomination of Imre Nagy as Communist Party leader, . . . and the 'reconsideration' of the entire Soviet-Hungarian relationship." The next day, students tore down a massive statue of Stalin, and the revolt spread outside the capital.[26] Arrests by Hungarian secret police served to expand the uprising even further. In the village of Magyarovar, rebellious citizens murdered members of a security detachment. It did not take long for the Russians to take the necessary steps to restore order.[27]

The Soviets had already placed two armored divisions in Hungary on alert in preparation for a crackdown in Poland. Retaliation occurred on October 24, as Russia sent thousands of soldiers into Budapest and armored divisions from Romania and Ukraine, to maintain security outside the capital city. Soviet forces opened fire on demonstrators, killing at least seventy. Undeterred, the Hungarians began flying mourning flags. On October 26, a pitched battle broke out between Soviet troops and a large group of armed Hungarian freedom fighters in Budapest, including Soviet tanks. Hungarian casualties numbered six hundred dead and almost three thousand injured.[28]

The day the revolt began, CIA's Cord Meyer, who had been supervising Radio Free Europe since 1954, was awakened by a call from Allen Dulles, who told him, "All hell had broken loose in Budapest." Frank Wisner assembled a group in Paris, including Cord Meyer's deputy William Durkee and William E. Griffith, political director for Radio Free Europe. Wisner then traveled to Germany, where he found Tracy Barnes on the verge of a nervous breakdown.[29] According to Griffith, on October 27, Hungarian exiles working for Radio Free Europe aired a broadcast that "fairly clearly implies that foreign aid will be forthcoming if resistance forces succeed in establishing a central authority." The next day's broadcast was much the same: "Hungarians must continue to fight vigorously because this will have a great effect on the handling of the . . . question by the [UN] Security Council." On November 4, "In the Western capitals, a practical manifestation of Western sympathy is expected at any hour."[30]

John Foster Dulles had been calling for the "liberation" of Eastern Europe for years, while his CIA brother had guerilla armies planted in each country behind the Iron Curtain. However, despite the revolt in Hungary, U.S. support was not forthcoming, as was the case in East Berlin in 1953. Allen Dulles offered a humanitarian medical unit to be sent to Hungary, but the risk of military retaliation against Western Europe was too significant even for that. Even after Hungarians took to the airwaves appealing to the CIA for assistance, the United States did nothing.

By the end of October, the Russians withdrew from Hungary. They returned with a vengeance on November 4 with more than 200,000 troops and over 2,500 armored vehicles. They retook Budapest on November 8. By the end of the month, the rest of the country was once again under Soviet control.[31]

Frank Wisner arrived in Vienna on November 7, the day before Soviet tanks finished the job in Budapest. William Colby would recall Wisner being "totally out of control" during the rebellion. "He kept saying, all these people are getting killed, and we weren't doing anything; we were ignoring it."[32] Vice President Richard Nixon was there, asking Hungarian students who had fled across the border if Radio Free Europe and the Voice of America had encouraged them to rebel. They simply responded yes. Bill Donovan also traveled to Vienna, even though he no longer officially had anything to do with any U.S. intelligence branch. Wondering why the stay-behind armies he controlled with Dulles remained idle during the rebellion is the only explanation for his presence in the Austrian capital.[33]

Total Hungarian casualties due to the rebellion were 30,000 dead and 50,000 injured. The Soviets would later execute Nagy and his defense minister. Almost 200,000 Hungarian refugees escaped into Austria, while 30,000 made it to the United States. The latter wound up at Camp Kilmer in New Jersey, interrogated and debriefed by army intelligence. The person in charge of the interrogation was none other than Dorothy Matlack, the same person George de Mohrenschildt would meet in Washington in 1963 with Clemard Charles before departing for Haiti. That Dorothy Matlack debriefed Hungarian refugees in 1956 and then met with de Mohrenschildt in 1963 reinforces the possibility that de Mohrenschildt was a CIA operative connected to the Donovan/Dulles stay-behind armies in Europe, which consisted of local anti-Communists.

In addition, according to the U.S. Army website, Dorothy Matlack "played an instrumental role in establishing Department of Defense procedures for debriefing defectors, escapees, and refugees of intelligence interest . . ."[34] Did Matlack's 1963 meeting with de Mohrenschildt in Washington have something to do with the returned Soviet "defector" Lee Harvey Oswald, considering Matlack's responsibilities with Army Intelligence, and that de Mohrenschildt had just left Oswald in Dallas, never to see him again?

According to William Colby, Frank Wisner wanted to intervene in Hungary, for "this was exactly the end for which the Agency's paramilitary capability was designed [for]," but it was not to be. "Starkly," Colby observed, "we demonstrated that 'liberation' was not our policy when the chips were down in Eastern Europe as the price might have been World War III."[35]

After Hungary, Wisner wanted to involve the CIA's "liberation army" in a resistance movement in Czechoslovakia. Still, there was a concern about what might occur if the Agency's involvement were made public. Even Allen Dulles recognized that the risks involved outweighed the potential benefits. Before long, Eisenhower ordered General Lucien Truscott to dismantle the liberation force. The stay-behind army concept became a thing of the past, at least as part of official policy. The Soviet satellite country insurgents now knew they could not rely on the U.S. for help if they were to revolt, and their American radical right supporters felt betrayed.[36]

It does not mean the CIA considered what happened in Hungary unsuccessful. For in the wake of the Hungarian revolt, the international perception of the Soviet Union changed forever. The idea they were trying to sell to third-world countries, that communism was a more equitable form of government than capitalism that cared more about its people, no longer resonated. It was clear for all the world to see that Russia ruled its satellites with an iron fist. After Hungary, the French Communist Party fractured, the Italian Communist Party broke away from Moscow, and the British Communist Party lost two-thirds of its members.[37]

And perhaps the CIA's objective all along was not to roll back communism in Hungary but to reveal to the world what the Soviet Union was capable of doing. According to C.D. Jackson, whether it was East Berlin or Budapest, having the "blood of martyrs" spilled in the street was the perfect propaganda coup in the war against communism. That people in rebellion, who thought they could depend on the U.S. for support in their time of need, died needlessly in the streets did not matter. Like everyone else, they were expendable.[38]

* * *

Returning to Algeria, there was a dramatic increase in violence perpetrated by the FLN (Front de liberation nationale) in 1956, the nationalist party fighting against the French for independence. On June 20, a grenade was thrown into a cafe and killed nineteen civilians in Algiers. The following month there were 2,024 incidents of FLN terror, including eighty-one assassination attempts. By 1960, the FLN had assassinated no less than 148 municipal councilors.

The FLN also expanded its reign of terror directly into France. Between August 24 and September 28, 181 attacks on property and 242 attacks directed at people occurred, resulting in eighty-two deaths and 168 injuries. The increase in violence was in response to the SDECE's (France's counterpart to the CIA) own wave of terror against the FLN, which was doing anything it could to disrupt the sale of arms to revolutionaries, including hiring paid killers to murder those engaged in this illicit trade. Over two years, starting in September 1956, four separate bomb attempts were made against a third-generation arms manufacturer named Otto Schluter alone. He cut ties with the FLN after a car bomb killed his mother and injured him.

Ait Ahcene, the head of the FLN in West Germany, was killed in Bonn in November 1957 by a hired assassin simply known as "The Killer," who had once worked with Gehlen's intelligence organization in West Germany, as well as the SDECE. "The Killer" and his network, known as "The Red Hand," had gained notoriety in March 1957 when they received secret information on gunrunners from the Swiss Federal Attorney General, who then committed suicide after being publicly implicated. According to the book *La Legion! The French Foreign Legion and the Men Who Made It Glorious*, the Red Hand was "a commando [group] of Algerian Frenchmen whose job it was to roam Europe, assassinating arms dealers who supplied arms to the FLN . . . Their favorite tactic was to place a time bomb in the automobile of the victim . . ."[39]

In September 1958, a Swiss explosives expert named Marcel Leopold was killed in one of Geneva's best hotels by a poison dart shot by a blowpipe into his neck. Six months later, a car bomb in Frankfurt killed his collaborator, a German arms dealer named Georges Puchert in Frankfurt. "The Killer" was believed responsible for both murders.[40] Then there was Ahmed Ben Bella, a veteran of the French army in WWII, arranging arms deals for the FLN in Cairo, Tunis, and Rabat. Targeted by French intelligence, an attempted rifle assassination against Bella failed, as did a bomb left in front of Bella's Cairo office in 1956.[41]

By 1957 the violence continued to get worse as civilian casualties increased. French paratroopers cordoned off the Muslim area of Algiers known as the Kasbah, and many Algerians died or were taken prisoner by French troops. The French subjected those captured to torture, "including electrodes on genitals, dunking and drowning in bathtubs, brutal beatings, and executions."[42]

The French army, already enraged, reached the point of no return on May 9 of the following year, when the FLN summarily executed three French soldiers. The Fourth Republic, which ruled France, was blamed for allowing this to happen.

General Raoul Salan was a veteran of World War II and the Indochina War and France's most decorated soldier. In December 1956, Salan was named Commander-in-Chief of all French forces in Algeria. On the same day that the FLN executed the three French soldiers, Salan dispatched a long telegram to General Ely, Chief of the General Staff in Paris. "The army in Algeria is troubled," Salan wrote, "by recognition of its responsibility towards the men who are fighting and risking a useless sacrifice if the representatives of the nation are not determined to maintain *Algerie francaise* . . . [keep Algeria part of France]" "The French army, in its unanimity, would feel outraged by the abandonment of this national patrimony," Salan warned. "One cannot predict how it would react in its despair . . . only a government firmly determined to maintain our flag in Algeria can efface."[43]

It was an ultimatum from Salan to the government in Paris. For the first time since Napoleon's coup, a French army was about to intervene directly into national politics. And as previously described, it was not a coincidence that in the United States, at the very same time, MacArthur and many of his military subordinates were voicing similar treasonous threats against their government. It was clear that in the post-World War II era, the fear of communism encouraged the military in both France and the U.S. to threaten takeovers of their respective governments if those currently in power did not heed their warnings. The stakes were perceived to be too high for the military to stand down.

On May 13, prompted by a public ceremony honoring the three executed French soldiers, the military could no longer contain its disgust with the French government. The French army took control of Algiers. Pierre Lagillarde, a member of the "Group of Seven," who wanted to preserve Algerie francaise at any cost, announced that "from now on I consider myself an insurgent." "Are you going to let Algerie francaise be sold down the river," Lagillarde asked? "Will you allow traitors to govern us? Will you go to the end of the line to keep Algerie francaise?"

"[We] will show to the world that Algeria wants to remain French," Salan told a crowd in Algiers on May 15. "Our sincerity will carry us with all the Muslims." He concluded with a vibrant "Vive la France! Vive Algerie francaise!" He told the crowd that only de Gaulle could save both Algeria and France and that the army in Algeria was committed to carrying the coup forward. In Paris, de Gaulle responded by saying that he was "ready to assume the powers of the republic when asked."[44]

As de Gaulle sat on the sidelines, tensions mounted in Paris. Seventy American tourists refused to leave their plane at Orly airport because they feared the revolution might place them in danger. Meanwhile, Salan warned that if de Gaulle did not take power, the military leadership in Algeria might be unable to prevent a "military incursion" into France itself, an ominous warning. On the 21st of May, Salan once again addressed a crowd in Algiers, saying, "you must know that we are all now united and that thus we shall march together up the Champs-Elysees, and we shall be covered with flowers!" Preparations began for a military intervention into France, including a force of five thousand who would land at an airfield southwest of Paris. Other commandos would seize the Eifel Tower and critical points such as the Ministry of the Interior and the central offices of the Communist Party, while tanks rolled into Paris. Once the coup was successful, they would remove President Coty and install de Gaulle as his replacement. The military was deadly serious. On May 24, a stunned Paris learned Corsica had fallen to the rebels. De Gaulle began planning a new cabinet. For several days France was on the brink of civil war. On May 27, de Gaulle issued a communiqué announcing he had started forming a legitimate republican government. There was no alternative—on May 29, 1958, de Gaulle returned to power.[45]

De Gaulle visited Algiers on June 4 and told a cheering crowd: "I declare from this day forward, France considers that in the whole of Algeria there is only one category of inhabitants, that there are only Frenchmen in the full sense, with the same rights and the same duties." On October 3 he urged the FLN to stop fighting, promising a "future big enough for everybody . . . yourselves in particular . . ." However, the military became concerned when de Gaulle called for a cease-fire, which was considered tantamount to "capitulation." When he began to purge the army of the most extreme activists, including Salan, they felt betrayed. On October 25, Salan declared total war on de Gaulle and officially placed himself at the head of the Algerie francaise movement. Knowing little could be done in France, he left for Spain, a Fascist country where, as we have already discussed, many right-wing anti-Communists would support his quest to overthrow the French government.

By November, de Gaulle called for "an emancipated Algeria," independent of France, and Salan responded that "the time for evasions is over." When de Gaulle visited Algeria in December, four unsuccessful plots to assassinate him occurred, and the military was ready to revolt. In March 1961, posters bearing the initials OAS (Organisation Armee Secrete) appeared on the walls of Algiers for the first time, followed by multiple bombings and at least one plan to assassinate de Gaulle with a telescopic rifle. The OAS reign of terror had begun.[46]

Ruthless killers filled the rank and file of OAS, including the previously mentioned Red Hand. Many were Legionnaires who were drug dealers, bank robbers, and petty criminals when not serving France. As described in *Age of the Guerilla*, the OAS "had plenty of men to use, mainly deserters who were ready to assassinate for a price . . . plastic bombs were exploded nightly in Algiers. Arabs were killed indiscriminately, simply to frighten the Muslim population into submission." Their terror did not occur in Algeria alone. Though numbering only 600 in metropolitan France, after 1961, the OAS would be joined by 800,000 Algerian French that poured into the country.[47]

The main OAS objective was to keep Algeria part of France, but the revolt had another underlying cause. The fear was that once independent, Algeria would throw itself into the Soviet camp, and Soviet warships anchored in Algerian seaports would be free to roam the Mediterranean. The founders of the OAS were Fascist supporters of colonialism. They opposed their government as much as they did the Communists. Fascists in Europe and the United States supported the OAS, including their attempt to assassinate de Gaulle. It was all part of the radical right-wing new world order.

* * *

Throughout the Algerian War, there was talk of American involvement. However, once the OAS revolt began, there is no doubt that the Pentagon and CIA supported the overthrow of de Gaulle. General Challe, who had replaced Salan as the leader of OAS, had spent time with high-ranking U.S. generals in NATO, who made it clear they were against Algerian independence. There were reports that witnesses saw Challe accompanied by senior American officers in uniform. That the U.S. Military Attaché in Paris was seen in Algiers only supported the notion that the Americans backed the disgruntled French military. Tunis also reported that the CIA had promised Challe U.S. recognition if he removed de Gaulle from office.[48]

Possible confirmation of American involvement came from France's leading newspaper, *Le Monde*, which reported: "It now seems established that some American agents more or less encouraged Maurice Challe." Rumors circulated that John Philipsborn, a CIA operative working undercover as a State Department diplomat, met with Salan in Algeria in April 1961. In addition, James Reston wrote in the *New York Times* on April 29, 1961, that the CIA "was involved . . . with the anti-Gaullist officers who staged last week's insurrection in Algeria." *Time* magazine would also report, on May 12th· that Maurice Challe had been "encouraged by the CIA."[49]

Philippe de Vosjoli was a French SDECE agent who had served France during World War II and had gotten to know James Angleton in the years immediately after the war. It was probably why that in 1951, he arrived in the U.S. as a liaison between French intelligence and CIA's counterintelligence branch.[50] And when Vosjoli told the CIA after Castro came to power that Cuban diplomats were transporting FLN correspondence in their diplomatic pouches and had created FLN training camps in Cuba, his stock rose considerably. Any thought that the CIA would not back the OAS in their war with France was permanently gone.[51]

The FLN's alliance with Castro's Cuba created interest in France, which was why between 1959 and 1961, SDECE brought French intelligence officers to Washington, D.C., where they "met with their counterparts in CIA" to discuss the possible assassination of Fidel Castro. SDECE volunteered to carry out the assignment, but the CIA declined the offer. When de Vosjoli later learned that CIA turned to the Mafia to eliminate Castro, "he was appalled at the stupidity and amateurishness of it." The only way this was possible, he believed, "was if the CIA had 'other' dealings of a sinister nature with the same Mafia types which they were looking to conceal." Which, as we know, was the case. The importance of all this is that a couple of years before the assassination of JFK, French and U.S. intelligence discussed a possible joint effort to assassinate a world leader while the military in each country was looking to overthrow their governments. Did they, in 1963, just redirect their focus toward JFK?

Jacques Soustelle was Governor-General of Algeria who helped de Gaulle become president of the Fifth Republic. When de Gaulle announced Algerian independence, Soustelle joined the OAS in support of de Gaulle's overthrow, even if it took the assassination of the French leader to accomplish this. On December 7, 1960, de Vosjoli hosted a luncheon in Washington D.C. in honor of Jacques Soustelle. That CIA was honoring a French member of the OAS, who was interested in assassinating de Gaulle, demonstrated where their allegiance lay. CIA officer Paul Sakwa, who was sent home from France to become a special assistant to Richard Bissell, confirmed to author Douglas Valentine that the CIA supported the OAS. The luncheon was well represented by the CIA, with Richard Bissell and Richard Helms both attending, which naturally infuriated de Gaulle. But by this time, de Vosjoli, who undoubtedly supported Algerie francaise, was aligned with U.S. intelligence in their support of the OAS.

CIA secretly sent funds to the OAS through its front companies, including Permindex and the Centro Mondiale Comerciale, both based in Rome. The leader of Permindex was Ferenc Nagy (not to be confused with the executed Imre Nagy), a long-time CIA Hungarian asset who was close to Frank Wisner, and that Nagy was a generous supporter of the OAS.[52]

The most disturbing thing about the CIA's support of the OAS was that it directly contradicted official U.S. policy. During the spring of 1957, Senator John F. Kennedy spoke with Algerians seeking a hearing at the United Nations. He said on the Senate floor that "no amount of mutual politeness, wishful thinking, nostalgia, or regret should blind either France or the United States to the fact that, if France and the West at large are to have a continuing influence in North Africa . . . the essential first step is the independence of Algeria." He continued to support Algerian independence after becoming President.

Kennedy's position on Algeria made him an enemy of the OAS and anyone else opposed to Algerian independence, including all right-wing anti-Communists, French or otherwise, including those in the United States. From Chapter Eight, Jean Souetre of the OAS, or possibly de Gaulle supporter Michael Mertz impersonating Souetre, was in Dallas on the day of the assassination and was secretly flown out of the country on a U.S. military plane. And that Mertz, a drug smuggler who had ties to the Corsican Mafia and American gangsters, had infiltrated the OAS. We also know that Jean-Pierre Lafitte used the name Mertz as an alias. Hidell was also a Lafitte alias, also used by Lee Harvey Oswald and Richard Case Nagell. Lafitte and George White were involved in drug experimentation on unsuspecting individuals, which may have included Oswald. Lafitte had close Corsican connections, and that Corsican drug money funded the Dulles/Donovan stay-behind armies. The French military also relied on the Corsicans in Vietnam as did the CIA. Lucien Conein was another CIA asset who had Corsican connections. The ex-Jedburgh would be responsible for the assassination of the Diem brothers in Vietnam, three weeks before the assassination of JFK, resulting in a military takeover in South Vietnam.

Incredibly, Philippe de Vosjoli was also connected to what was going on in Haiti and would report that George de Mohrenschildt was involved in the JFK assassination. How did he know this, one might ask?

The same individuals keep showing up. They were all right-wing Fascists. To dismiss the possibility that an international right-wing Fascist network was behind all the right-wing military unrest worldwide would be foolish. It does not mean that if such a Fascist global network existed, the entire group was involved in JFK's murder. To think this would be equally irresponsible. But it makes sense that right-wing groups would support each other in a worldwide effort to contain the spread of communism. It was a right-wing world order based upon Christian values and the principles of eugenics, colonialism, anti-communism, and individual self-determination. And JFK gave them sufficient reasons to justify his assassination for the good of this Fascist new world order, including his position regarding Algerian independence.

- 13 -

Conclusion

As shown in the preceding pages, as John F. Kennedy's presidency approached, a right-wing element in the United States leaned toward fascism. It was especially true with the CIA, the military, and particular business and political leaders of influence. Franklin Roosevelt, Harry Truman, and Dwight Eisenhower found their presidencies undermined by those who opposed them with treasonous activity. The U.S. military sabotaged the Korean War and other incidents worldwide to maintain the anti-Communist foreign policy they wanted. A price would have to be paid by any President who violated the policy of containment. The Fascist right-wing would not tolerate the appeasement of Communists, and they required a continued increase in military spending to maintain superiority over their Communist opponents. It was especially true during the Cold War when maintaining dominance in the number of atomic weapons over the Soviet Union became almost a national religion in the United States. The right-wing military wanted to launch a first-strike nuclear attack against the Soviets, which they thought was inevitable. All they needed was a President who was willing to pull the trigger. Fortunately, that never happened.

As the presidency of John F. Kennedy drew near, other events would impact and play a role in his assassination. As our narrative continues in Volume Two, we will focus on this additional evidence that confirms why, in the collective mind of the right-wing, JFK's presidency had to come to an end by whatever means possible.

The saga of Lee Harvey Oswald will be covered, beginning with his teenage years in New Orleans in the mid-1950s, where he became involved with characters who would guide him to his eventual date with destiny in Dallas a few years later. We will discuss Oswald's military career—when he became involved with U.S. intelligence operatives and drug experimentation while stationed in Japan. We will also address Oswald's defection, but not just that he was part of a CIA operation to send supposedly disenchanted soldiers and Marines behind the Iron Curtain. The CIA created a false narrative that the Soviets had killed Oswald in Russia, and an impostor returned to the United States. The point was the CIA could set up this impostor to take the fall for any crime, with blame placed on the Soviets.

Volume Two will also discuss the rise of Fidel Castro, the Cuban revolution, and how a U.S. paramilitary/CIA group inside Cuba looked to create an internal uprising. Allen Dulles would sabotage this uprising because the Cuban government that would replace Castro leaned too far to the left for Dulles' liking. It will describe how an FBN/CIA operative named June Cobb was part of that group, how she joined the Fair Play for Cuba Committee, just like Oswald, and how she seemed to shadow Oswald for the remainder of his life. Also noteworthy was the right-wing faction with the CIA during the late 1950s. They looked to hire the Mafia to kill Castro and create a right-wing assassination squad to ensure that the Cuban government that would replace Castro was sufficiently anti-Communist.

Jack Ruby's story is also examined, including his Mafia activities during the 1950s, his illegal and illicit pursuits in Dallas, and his involvement in Cuban affairs, which involved gunrunning with Thomas Eli Davis and others. What he did during this period would ingratiate him with people who would later use him to silence Oswald. And he would have no choice but to comply.

There was also the rise of violence-prone radical right paramilitary and racist groups after the government forced racial desegregation in Little Rock, Arkansas schools in 1954. These groups became part of a southern movement, centered in Dallas and New Orleans, that thought violent insurrection against the Communists running Washington was the answer. The evidence will show they became known to powerful elements of the right-wing and were in a position to be taken advantage of when the time came.

Finally, we will discuss the increased discontent of the military and the CIA and how they increasingly hounded Eisenhower to drop nuclear weapons on the Chinese and the Soviets and created a different foreign policy from what Ike wanted to pursue. It culminated with Francis Gary Powers' U-2 plane's sabotage by U.S. intelligence to prevent Eisenhower from signing a nuclear test ban treaty with the Russians while Oswald was in the Soviet Union.

After examining all the evidence presented in Volume Two, there will no doubt in the reader's mind that by 1960, the groups were already in place and were becoming more aware of each other, who wanted to assassinate JFK. Three years later, elements from all these groups would join to do just that.

Notes

Introduction

1. Paget, Karen M., *Patriotic Betrayal*, New Haven, Connecticut, Yale University Press, 2015.

2. Williams, Paul L., *Operation Gladio, The Unholy Alliance between The Vatican, The CIA, And The Mafia*, Amherst, New York, Prometheus Books, 2015.

3. Prados, John, *Safe for Democracy, The Secret Wars of the CIA*, Chicago, Illinois, Ivan R. Dee, 2006.

4. Archer, Jules, *The Plot to Seize the White House, The Shocking True Story of the Conspiracy to Overthorw FDR*, New York, New York, Skyhorse Publishing, 2007.

5. Ibid.

6. Ibid.

7. Ibid.

8. Morton, Andrew, *17 Carnations, The Royals, The Nazis, and the Biggest Cover-Up in History*, New York New York, Grand Central Publishing, 2015.

9. Archer, *The Plot to Seize the White House*.

10. Scheim, David E., *Contract on America, The Mafia Murder of President John F. Kennedy*, New York, New York, Shapolsky Publishers, Inc., 1988, and Brands, H.W., *Traitor to his Class, The Privileged Life and Radical Presidency of Franklin Delano Roosevelt*, New York, New York, Doubleday, 2008.

11. Wallace, Max, *The American Axis, Henry Ford, Charles Lindbergh, and the Rise of the Third Reich*, New York, New York, St. Martin's Press, 2003.

12. Ayton, Mel, *Hunting the President, Threats, Plots, and Assassination Attempts from FDR to Obama*, New York, New York, Regnery History, 2014.

13. Archer, Jules, *The Plot to Seize the White House*.

14. Ibid.

15. White, Richard D. Jr., *Kingfish, The Reign of Huey P. Long*, New York, New York, Random House, 2006.

16. Archer, *The Plot to Seize the White House*.

17. Caufield, M.D., Jeffrey H., *General Walker and the Murder of President Kennedy, The Extensive New Evidence of a Radical-Right Conspiracy*, Moreland Press, 2015.

18. Parmet, Herbert S., *Eisenhower and the American Crusades*, New York, New York, The MacMillan Company, 1972.

19. Coffin, Tristram, *The Passion of the Hawks, Militarism in Modern America*, New York, New York, The MacMillan Company, 1964.

20. Ibid.

21. Amrose, Stephen E., *Eisenhower: The President*, New York, New York, Simon and Schuster, 1984.

22. Ibid.

23. Duignan, Brian, "Smith Act, United States [1940]," www.britannica.com/event/Smith-Act.

24. Douglass, James W., *JFK and the Unspeakable, Why He Died and Why it Matters*, Marknoll, New York, Orbis Books, 2014.

25. McMillan, Priscilla Johnson, *Marina & Lee*, New York, New York, Harper & Row, 1977.

26. Ibid.

27. Jones, J. Harry Jr., *The Minutemen*, Garden City, New York, Doubleday & Company, 1968.

28. LaFontaine, Ray and Mary, *Oswald Talked, The New Evidence in the JFK Assassination*, Gretna, Louisiana, Pelican Publishing Company, 1996.

29. McMillan, *Marina & Lee*.

30. Jones, *The Minutemen*.

31. *The New York Times* article, June 18, 1961.

32. Coffin, Tristram, *The Passion of the Hawks, Militarism in Modern America*.

33. Caufield, M.D., Jeffrey H., *General Walker and the Murder of President Kennedy, The Extensive New Evidence of a Radical-Right Conspiracy*.

34. Bamford, James, *Body of Secrets, Anatomy of the Ultra-Secret National Security Agency, From the Cold War Through the Dawn of a New Century*, New York, New York, Doubleday, 2001.

35. Ibid.

36. Raymond, Jack, *Power at the Pentagon*, New York, New York, Harper and Row Publishers, 1964.

37. Cottrell, Richard, *Gladio, Nato's Dagger at the Heart of Europe, The Pentagon-Nazi-Mafia Terror Axis*, San Diego, California, Progressive Press, 2015.

38. Schlesinger, Arthur M. Jr., *Robert Kennedy and His Times*, Boston, Massachusetts, Houghton Mifflin Company, 1978.

39. Russell, Dick, *The Man Who Knew Too Much*, New York, New York, Carroll & Graf Publishers, 1992.

40. Caufield, *General Walker and the Murder of President Kennedy*.

41. Ibid.

42. Russell, *The Man Who Knew Too Much*.

43. Caufield, *General Walker and the Murder of President Kennedy*.

44. Garrison, Jim, *On the Trail of the Assassins*, New York, New York, Warner Books, 1988.

45. *Hearings Before the President's Commission on the Assassination of President Kennedy*, Volume V, Washington D.C., Government Printing Office 1964.

46. Summers, Anthony, *Conspiracy*, New York, New York, McGraw-Hill Book Company, 1980.

47. Ibid.

48. Scott, Peter Dale, *Oswald, Mexico, and Deep Politics, Revelations from CIA Records on the Assassination of JFK*, New York, New York, Skyhorse Publishing, 2013.

49. Evans, Roland, and Novak, Robert, *Lyndon B. Johnson: The Exercise of Power*, New York, New York, Harper & Row, 1976.

50. Summers, Anthony, *Official and Confidential, The Secret Life of J. Edgar Hoover*, New York, New York, G.P. Putnam and Sons, 1993.

51. Hunter, Stephen, and Bainbridge, John Jr., *American Gunfight, The Plot to Kill Harry Truman and the Shoot-Out That Stopped It*, New York, New York, Simon & Schuster, 2005.

52. J. Edgar Hoover speech to Washington Hebrew Congregation, December 4, 1963, from North, Mark, *Act of Treason. The Role of J. Edgar Hoover in the Assassination of President Kennedy*, New York, New York, Carroll & Graf Publishers, Inc., 1991.

Chapter One: A New World Order

1. Gage, Beverly, *The Day Wall Street Exploded, A Story of America In Its First Age of Terror*, Oxford University Press, New York, New York, 2009, and Huchthausen, James P., *Imperialism, Corporatism, Militarism, An American Tragedy*, North Charleston, South Carolina, Createspace Publishing Platform, 2014.

2. Fried, Richard M., *Nightmare in Red, The McCarthy Era in Perspective*, New York, New York, Oxford University Press, 1990.

3. Bird, Kai, *The Chairman, John McCloy The Making of the American Establishment*, New York, New York, Simon & Schuster, 1992.

4. Ibid.

5. Ibid.

6. Brands, H.W., *Traitor To His Class, The Privileged Life and Radical Presidency of Franklin Delano Roosevelt*, New York, New York, Doubleday, 2008.

7. Mandel, Paul, "End to Nagging Rumors: The Six Critical Seconds," *Life Magazine* article, December 6, 1963.

8. Brands, *Traitor to his Class*.

9. Fried, *Nightmare in Red*.

10. Churchwell, Sarah, *Behold America, A History of America First and the American Dream*, London, England, Bloomsbury Publishing, 2018.

11. Ibid.

12. Ibid.

13. Ibid.

14. Wallace, Max, *The American Axis, Henry Ford, Charles Lindbergh, and the Rise of the Third Reich*, New York, New York, St. Martin's Press, 2003.

15. Thomas, Gordon, and Morgan-Witts, Max, *The Day the Bubble Burst, A Social History of the Wall Street Crash of 1929*, Garden City, New York, Doubleday & Company, Inc., 1979.

16. Talbot, David, *The Devil's Chessboard, Allen Dulles, the CIA, and the Rise of America's Secret Government*, New York, New York, Harper Collins Publishers, 2015.

17. Ibid.

18. Corsi, Jerome R., P.H.D., *Who Really Killed Kennedy?, 50 Years Later, Stunning New Revelations about the JFK Assassination*, Washington, D.C., WND Books, 2013.

19. Talbot, *The Devil's Chessboard*.

20. Collier, Peter, and Horowitz, David, *The Kennedys – An American Drama*, New York, New York, Summit Books, 1984.

21. Goodwin, Doris Kearns, *The Fitzgeralds and the Kennedys – An American Saga*, New York, New York, Simon & Schuster, 1987.

22. Collier and Horowitz, *The Kennedys – An American Drama*.

23. Goodwin, *The Fitzgeralds and the Kennedys – An American Saga*.

24. Ibid.

25. Ibid.

26. Thompson, Laura, *The Six, The Lives of the Mitford Sisters*, New York, New York, St. Martin's Press, 2015.

27. Ibid.

28. Ibid.

29. Preston, Paul, *The Spanish Holocaust, Inquisition and Extermination in Twentieth Century Spain*, New York, New York, W.W. Norton & Company, 2012.

30. Ibid.

31. Ibid.

32. Manchester, William, *The Last Lion, Winston Churchill, Alone, 1932-1940*, Boston, Massachusetts, Little, Brown and Company, 1988.

33. Cooney, John, *The American Pope, The Life and Times of Francis Cardinal Spellman*, New York, New York, Times Books, 1984.

34. Kertzer, David I., *The Pope and Mussolini, The Secret History of Pius XI and the Rise of Fascism in Europe*, New York, New York, Random House, 2014.

35. Ibid.

36. Ibid.

37. Ibid.

38. Black, Edwin, *War Against the Weak: Eugenics and America's Campaign to Create a Master Race*, New York, New York, Four Walls Eight Windows, 2003.

39. Churchwell, *Behold America, A History of America First and the American Dream*.

40. Ibid.

41. Black, *War Against the Weak: Eugenics and America's Campaign to Create a Master Race*.

42. Ibid.

43. Ibid.

44. Preston, *The Spanish Holocaust, Inquisition and Extermination in Twentieth Century Spain*.

45. Olson, Lynne, *Those Angry Days, Roosevelt, Lindbergh, and America's Fight Over World War II*, 1939-1941, New York, New York, Random House, 2013.

46. Brands, *Traitor to His Class, The Privileged Life and Radical Presidency of Franklin Delano Roosevelt*.

47. Olson, *Those Angry Days, Roosevelt, Lindbergh, and America's Fight Over World War II, 1939-1941*.

48. Thomas and Morgan-Witts, *The Day the Bubble Burst, A Social History of the Wall Street Crash of 1929*.

49. Brands, *Traitor to His Class, The Privileged Life and Radical Presidency of Franklin Delano Roosevelt*.

50. Kruse, Kevin M., *One Nation Under God, How Corporate America Invented Christian America*, New York, New York, Basic Books, 2015.

51. Archer, Jules, *The Plot to Seize the White House, The Shocking TRUE Story of the Conspiracy to Overthrow FDR*, New York, New York, Skyhorse Publishing, 2007.

52. Evica, George Michael, *A Certain Arrogance; The Sacrificing of Lee Harvey Oswald and the Cold War Manipulation of Religious Groups by US Intelligence*, Walterville, Oregon, TrineDay, 2011.

53. Williams, Paul L., *Operation Gladio, The Unholy Alliance between The Vatican, The CIA, And The Mafia*, Amherst, New York, Prometheus Books, 2015.

54. Wallace, *The American Axis, Henry Ford, Charles Lindbergh, and the Rise of the Third Reich.*

55. Olson, *Those Angry Days, Roosevelt, Lindbergh, and America's Fight Over World War II, 1939-1941.*

56. Bird, *The Chairman, John McCloy The Making of the American Establishment.*

57. McCoy, Alfred W., *The Politics of Heroin in Southeast Asia*, New York, New York, Harper and Row, 1972.

58. Bird, *The Chairman, John McCloy The Making of the American Establishment.*

59. Ibid., and www.wilkileaks.org

60. Bird, *The Chairman, John McCloy The Making of the American Establishment.*

61. McCoy, *The Politics of Heroin in Southeast Asia.*

62. Williams, *Operation Gladio, The Unholy Alliance between The Vatican, The CIA, And The Mafia.*

63. Ambrose, Stephen E., *Eisenhower: The President*, New York, New York, Simon & Schuster, 1984.

Chapter Two: Strange Bedfellows

1. Waller, Douglas, *Wild Bill Donovan, The Spymaster who Created the OSS and Modern American Espionage*, New York, New York, Free Press, 2011.

2. Ibid., and Riebling, Mark, *Wedge, The Secret War Between the FBI and CIA*, New York, New York, Alfred A. Knopf, 1994.

3. Riebling, Mark, *Church of Spies, The Pope's Secret War Against Hitler*, New York, New York, Basic Books, 2015, and Cooney, John, *The American Pope, The Life and Times of Francis Cardinal Spellman*, New York, New York, Times Books, 1984.

4. Riebling, *Church of Spies.*

5. Ibid.

6. Ibid.

7. Ibid.

8. Wallace, Max, *The American Axis, Henry Ford, Charles Lindbergh, and the Rise of the Third Reich*, New York, New York, St. Martin's Press, 2003.

9. Williams, Paul L., *Operation Gladio, The Unholy Alliance Between The Vatican, The CIA, And The Mafia*, Amherst, New York, Prometheus Books, 2015, and Cooney, *The American Pope, The Life and Times of Francis Cardinal Spellman.*

10. Caufield, M.D., Jeffrey H., *General Walker and the Murder of President Kennedy, The Extensive New Evidence of a Radical-Right Conspiracy*, Moreland Press, 2015.

11. Preston, Paul, *The Spanish Holocaust, Inquisition and Extermination in Twentieth Century Spain*, New York, New York, W.W. Norton & Company, 2012.

12. Gentry, Curt, *Hoover: The Man and the Secrets*, New York, New York, W.W. Norton & Company, 1991.

13. Cooney, *The American Pope, The Life and Times of Francis Cardinal Spellman.*

14. Ibid.

15. Ibid.

16. Russell, Dick, *The Man Who Knew Too Much*, New York, New York, Carroll & Graf Publishers/ Richard Gallen, 1992.

17. Stone, I.F., *The Hidden History of the Korean War, 1950-1951, A Nonconformist History of Our Times*, Boston, Massachusetts, Little, Brown and Company, 1952, and Mellen, Joan, *The Great Game in Cuba, How the CIA Sabotaged Its Own Plot to Unseat Fidel Castro*, New York, New York, Skyhorse Publishing, 2013.

18. Binder, L. James, *Lemnitzer, A Soldier for His Time*, Washington, D.C., Brassey's, 1997.

19. Ibid.

20. Fleming, Thomas, *The New Dealers' War, F.D.R. and the War Within World War II*, New York, New York, Basic Books, 2001.

21. Talbot, David, *The Devil's Chessboard, Allen Dulles, the CIA, and the Rise of America's Secret Government*, New York, New York, Harper Collins Publishers, 2015., and Williams, *Operation Gladio, The Unholy Alliance Between The Vatican, The CIA, And The Mafia.*

22. Ibid.

23. Talbot, *The Devil's Chessboard, Allen Dulles, the CIA, and the Rise of America's Secret Government.*

24. Woods, Randall B., *Shadow Warrior, William Egan Colby and the CIA*, New York, New York, Basic Books, 2013.

25. Beavan, Colin, *Operation Jedburgh, D-Day and America's First Shadow War*, New York, New York, The Penguin Group, 2006, and Woods, *Shadow Warrior, William Egan Colby and the CIA*.

26. Williams, *Operation Gladio, The Unholy Alliance Between The Vatican, The CIA, And The Mafia*.

27. Woods, *Shadow Warrior, William Egan Colby and the CIA*.

28. Riebling, *Church of Spies, The Pope's Secret War Against Hitler*.

29. Ibid.

30. Talbot, *The Devil's Chessboard, Allen Dulles, the CIA, and the Rise of America's Secret Government*.

31. Cooney, *The American Pope, The Life and Times of Francis Cardinal Spellman*.

32. Riebling, *Church of Spies, The Pope's Secret War Against Hitler*.

33. McCoy, Alfred W., *The Politics of Heroin in Southeast Asia*, New York, New York, Harper and Row, 1972.

34. Valentine, Douglas, *The Strength of the Wolf, The Secret History of America's War on Drugs*, London, England, Verso, 2004.

35. McCoy, *The Politics of Heroin in Southeast Asia*.

36. Williams, *Operation Gladio, The Unholy Alliance Between The Vatican, The CIA, And The Mafia*.

37. Ibid., McCoy, *The Politics of Heroin in Southeast Asia*.

38. McCoy, *The Politics of Heroin in Southeast Asia*.

39. Willliam B. Herlands, Commissioner of Investigations, Executive Department, State of New York, "Report," *Thomas E Dewey Papers*, September 17, 1954, University of Rochester, from McCoy, *The Politics of Heroin in Southeast Asia*.

40. Valentine, *The Strength of the Wolf, The Secret History of America's War on Drugs*.

41. Ibid., and *McCoy, The Politics of Heroin in Southeast Asia*.

42. Ibid., and *Williams, Operation Gladio, The Unholy Alliance Between The Vatican, The CIA, And The Mafia*.

43. Valentine, *The Strength of the Wolf, The Secret History of America's War on Drugs*.

44. Albarelli, H.P. Jr., *A Terrible Mistake, The Murder of Frank Olson and the CIA's Secret Cold War Experiments*, Walterville, Oregon, Trine Day, 2009.

45. Ibid.

46. Valentine, *The Strength of the Wolf, The Secret History of America's War on Drugs*.

Chapter Three: The Evil Empire Emerges

1. Dobbs, Michael, *Six Months in 1945, From World War to Cold War*, New York, New York, Alfred A. Knopf, 2012.

2. Swanson, Michael, *The War State, The Cold War Origins of the Military-Industrial Complex and The Power Elite, 1945-1963*, North Charleston, South Carolina, CreateSpace Independent Publishing Platform, 2013.

3. Dobbs, *Six Months in 1945, From World War to Cold War*.

4. Ibid.

5. Ibid.

6. Talbot, David, *The Devil's Chessboard, Allen Dulles, the CIA, and the Rise of America's Secret Government*, New York, New York, Harper Collins Publishers, 2015.

7. Black, Edwin, *War Against the Weak: Eugenics and America's Campaign to Create a Master Race*, New York, New York, Four Walls Eight Windows, 2003.

8. Ibid.

9. Leffler, Melvyn P., *For the Soul of Mankind, The United States, the Soviet Union, and The Cold War*, New York, New York, Hill and Wang, 2007.

10. Dobbs, *Six Months in 1945, From World War to Cold War*.

11. Ibid.

12. Prados, John, *Safe for Democracy, The Secret Wars of the CIA*, Chicago, Illinois, Ivan R. Dee, 2006.

13. Dobbs, *Six Months in 1945, From World War to Cold War*.

14. Leffler, *For the Soul of Mankind, The United States, the Soviet Union, and The Cold War*.

15. Dobbs, *Six Months in 1945, From World War to Cold War*.

16. Manchester, William, and Reid, Paul, *The Last Lion, Winston Spencer Churchill, Defender of the Realm, 1940-1965*, New York, New York, Little, Brown and Company, 2012.

17. Beisner, Robert L., Dean Acheson, A Life in the Cold War, New York, New York, Oxford University Press, 2006.

18. Gaddis, John Lewis, *George F. Kennan, An American Life*, New York, New York, The Penguin Press, 2011.

19. Beisner, *Dean Acheson, A Life in the Cold War.*

20. Gaddis, *George F. Kennan, An American Life.*

21. Ibid.

22. Ibid.

23. Ibid.

24. Ibid.

25. Cohen, Andrew, *Two Days in June, John F. Kennedy and the 48 Hours That Made History*, Toronto, Canada, McClelland & Stewart, 2014.

26. Douglas, James, W., *JFK and the Unspeakable, Why He Died & Why It Matters*, Maryknoll, New York, Orbis Books, 2008.

27. Clarke, Thurston, *JFK's Last Hundred Days, The Transformation of a Man and the Emergence of a Great President*, New York, New York, The Penguin Press, 2013.

28. Riebling, Mark, *Wedge, The Secret War Between the FBI and CIA*, New York, New York, Alfred A. Knopf, 1994.

29. Trento, Joseph J., *The Secret History of the CIA*, New York, New York, MJF Books, 2001, and Trento, Joseph J., *Prelude to Terror, The Rogue CIA and the Legacy of America's Private Intelligence Network*, New York, New York, Carroll & Graf Publishers, 2005.

30. Riebling, *Wedge, The Secret War Between the FBI and CIA.*

31. Ibid.

32. Jacobsen, Annie, *Operation Paperclip, The Secret Intelligence Program That Brought Nazi Scientists to America*, New York, New York, Littler, Brown and Company, 2014.

33. CIA.gov, *The CIA Official Website.*

34. Leffler, *For the Soul of Mankind, The United States, the Soviet Union, and The Cold War.*

35. Truman, Harry S., *Harry S. Truman, Memoirs: Years of Trial and Hope, 1946-1952*, New York, New York, Signet, 1956, from Leffler, For the Soul of Mankind, The United States, the Soviet Union, and The Cold War.

36. Ibid.

37. Marton, Kati, *The Polk Conspiracy, Murder and Cover-Up in the Case of CBS News Correspondent George Polk*, New York, New York, Farrar, Straus & Giroux, 1990.

38. Ibid.

39. Manchester and Reid, *The Last Lion, Winston Spencer Churchill, Defender of the Realm, 1940-1965*, and Avalon.law.yale.edu, "The Avalon Project," Yale Law School, Lillian Goldman Law Library.

40. Beisner, *Dean Acheson, A Life in the Cold War.*

41. Gaddis, John Lewis, *Strategies of Containment, A Critical Appraisal of Postwar American National Security Policy*, New York, New York, Oxford University Press, 1982.

42. Gaddis, *George F. Kennan, An American Life.*

43. Binder, L. *James, Lemnitzer, A Soldier for His Time*, Washington, D.C., Brassey's, 1997.

44. Gaddis, *Strategies of Containment, A Critical Appraisal of Postwar American National Security Policy.*

45. Ibid.

46. Manchester and Reid, *The Last Lion, Winston Spencer Churchill, Defender of the Realm, 1940-1965.*

47. Bird, Kai, *The Chairman, John McCloy The Making of the American Establishment*, New York, New York, Simon & Schuster, 1992.

48. Riebling, *Wedge, The Secret War Between the FBI and CIA.*

49. Gaddis, *George F. Kennan, An American Life.*

50. Ibid.

51. Osgood, Kenneth, *Total Cold War, Eisenhower's Secret Propaganda Battle at Home and Abroad*, Lawrence, Kansas, University Press of Kansas, 2006, and Gaddis, *George F. Kennan, An American Life.*

52. Miller, Scott, *Agent 110, An American Spymaster and the German Resistance in WWII*, New York, New York, Simon & Schuster, 2017, & Trento, *The Secret History of the CIA.*

53. Ganis, Major Ralph P., USAF, Ret., *The Skorzeny Papers, Evidence for the Plot to Kill JFK*, New York, New York, Skyhorse Publishing, 2018.

54. Riebling, *Wedge, The Secret War Between the FBI and CIA.*

55. Williams, *Operation Gladio, The Unholy Alliance between The Vatican, The CIA, And The Mafia.*

56. Ganis, *The Skorzeny Papers, Evidence for the Plot to Kill JFK.*

57. Ibid.

58. Riebling, *Wedge, The Secret War Between the FBI and CIA.*

59. Ibid.

60. Marton, *The Polk Conspiracy, Murder and Cover-Up in the Case of CBS News Correspondent George Polk.*

61. Ibid.

62. Ibid.

Chapter Four: The Enemy of My Enemy is My Friend

1. Bird, Kai, *The Chairman, John McCloy, The Making of the American Establishment*, New York, New York, Simon & Schuster, 1992.

2. Ibid.

3. Jacobsen, Annie, *Operation Paperclip, The Secret Intelligence Program That Brought Nazi Scientists to America*, New York, New York, Littler, Brown and Company, 2014.

4. Simpson, Christopher, *Blowback, The First Full Account of America's Recruitment of Nazis, and its Disastrous Effect on Our Domestic and Foreign Policy*, New York, New York, Weidenfeld & Nicolson, 1988.

5. Jacobsen, *Operation Paperclip, The Secret Intelligence Program That Brought Nazi Scientists to America.*

6. Ibid.

7. Ibid.

8. Bird, *The Chairman, John McCloy, The Making of the American Establishment.*

9. Simpson, *Blowback, The First Full Account of America's Recruitment of Nazis, and its Disastrous Effect on Our Domestic and Foreign Policy.*

10. Ibid.; Applebaum, Anne, *Iron Curtain, The Crushing of Eastern Europe, 1944-1956*, New York, New York, Doubleday, 2012; and Paget, Karen M., *Patriotic Betrayal*, New Haven Connecticut, Yale University Press, 2015; and Beisner, Robert L., *Dean Acheson, A Life in the Cold War*, New York, New York, Oxford University Press, 2006; and Jacobsen, *Operation Paperclip, The Secret Intelligence Program That Brought Nazi Scientists to* America.

11. Beisner, *Dean Acheson, A Life in the Cold War.*

12. LeMay, General Curtis, *America is in Danger*, New York, New York, Funk and Wagnalls, 1968.

13. Simpson, *Blowback, The First Full Account of America's Recruitment of Nazis, and its Disastrous Effect on Our Domestic and Foreign Policy.*

14. Osgood, Kenneth, *Total Cold War, Eisenhower's Secret Propaganda Battle at Home and Abroad*, Lawrence, Kansas, University Press of Kansas, 2006.

15. Ibid.

16. *The Washington Post*, article, March 4, 1947.

17. Gaddis, John Lewis, *George F. Kennan, An American Life*, New York, New York, The Penguin Press, 2011.

18. Ibid.

19. Osgood, *Total Cold War, Eisenhower's Secret Propaganda Battle at Home and Abroad.*

20. Talbot, David, *The Devil's Chessboard, Allen Dulles, the CIA, and the Rise of America's Secret Government*, New York, New York, Harper Collins Publishers, 2015.

21. Cooney, John, *The American Pope, The Life and Times of Francis Cardinal Spellman*, New York, New York, Times Books, 1984.

22. Williams, Paul L., *Operation Gladio, The Unholy Alliance Between The Vatican, The CIA, And The Mafia*, Amherst, New York, Prometheus Books, 2015.

23. Ibid.

24. Ibid.

25. Ibid.

26. Ganis, Major Ralph P., USAF, Ret., *The Skorzeny Papers, Evidence for the Plot to Kill JFK*, New York, New York, Skyhorse Publishing, 2018.

27. McCoy, Alfred W., *The Politics of Heroin in Southeast Asia*, New York, New York, Harper and Row, 1972.

28. Thomas, Evan, *The Very Best Men, Four Who Dared: The Early Years of the CIA*, New York, New York, Simon & Schuster, 1995, and Simpson, Blowback, *The First Full Account of America's Recruitment of Nazis, and its Disastrous Effect on Our Domestic and Foreign Policy.*

29. Thomas, *The Very Best Men, Four Who Dared: The Early Years of the CIA*.

30. Simpson, *Blowback, The First Full Account of America's Recruitment of Nazis, and its Disastrous Effect on Our Domestic and Foreign Policy*.

31. Ibid.

32. Raigorodsky, Paul, testimony of, *Hearings Before the President's Commission on the Assassination of President Kennedy*, Washington D.C., Government Printing Office, 1964

33. Kluckhohn, Clyde, "Russian Research at Harvard," *World Politics, A Quarterly Journal of International Relations*, Cambridge University Press, January 1949, Volume 1, Number 2.

34. Diamond, Sigmund, *Compromised Campus, The Collaboration of Universities With the Intelligence Community, 1945-1955*, New York, New York, Oxford University Press, 1992.

35. Ibid.

36. "FBI Report, Special Agent in Charge, Richmond, Virginia, May 1, 1951", *The Black Vault*, www.theblackvault.com/documentarchive/.

37. Diamond, *Compromised Campus, The Collaboration of Universities With the Intelligence Community, 1945-1955*.

38. Bird, Kai, *The Color of Truth, McGeorge Bundy and William Bundy: Brothers in Arms*, New York New York, Simon & Schuster, 1998; and Bauer, Raymond A., *Nine Soviet Portraits*, The MIT Press, Cambridge, Massachusetts, 2018; and *Diamond, Compromised Campus, The* Collaboration of Universities With the Intelligence Community, 1945-1955.

39. Ibid.

40. Ibid., and Thomas, *The Very Best Men, Four Who Dared: The Early Years of the CIA*.

41. Thomas, *The Very Best Men, Four Who Dared: The Early Years of the CIA*.

42. Simpson, *Blowback, The First Full Account of America's Recruitment of Nazis, and its Disastrous Effect on Our Domestic and Foreign Policy*.

43. Ibid.

44. Albarelli, H.P. Jr., *A Terrible Mistake, The Murder of Frank Olson and the CIA's Secret Cold War Experiments*, Walterville, Oregon, Trine Day, 2009.

45. Thomas, *The Very Best Men, Four Who Dared: The Early Years of the CIA*.

46. Simpson, *Blowback, The First Full Account of America's Recruitment of Nazis, and its Disastrous Effect on Our Domestic and Foreign Policy*.

47. Ibid.

48. Bird, *The Chairman, John McCloy, The Making of the American Establishment*.

49. Simpson, *Blowback, The First Full Account of America's Recruitment of Nazis, and its Disastrous Effect on Our Domestic and Foreign Policy*.

50. Diamond, *Compromised Campus, The Collaboration of Universities With the Intelligence Community, 1945-1955*.

51. Russell, Dick, *The Man Who Knew Too Much*, New York, New York, Carroll & Graf Publishers/ Richard Gallen, 1992.

52. Ibid.

53. Evica, George Michael, *A Certain Arrogance; The Sacrificing of Lee Harvey Oswald and the Cold War Manipulation of Religious Groups by US Intelligence*, Walterville, Oregon, TrineDay, 2011, and Ganis, Major Ralph P., USAF, Ret., *The Skorzeny Papers, Evidence for the Plot to Kill JFK*, New York, New York, Skyhorse Publishing, 2018.

54. Russell, *The Man Who Knew Too Much*.

55. Ibid.

56. Caufield, M.D., Jeffrey H., *General Walker and the Murder of President Kennedy, The Extensive New Evidence of a Radical-Right Conspiracy*, Moreland Press, 2015.

57. Newman, John, *Oswald and the CIA*, New York, New York, Carroll & Graf Publishers, Inc., 1995.

58. Ibid.

Chapter Five: A Difference of Opinion in Defending the Pacific

1. Beisner, Robert L., Dean Acheson, *A Life in the Cold War*, New York, New York, Oxford University Press, 2006.

2. Ibid.

3. Stone, I.F., *The Hidden History of the Korean War, 1950-1951, A Nonconformist History of Our Times*, Boston, Massachusetts, Little, Brown and Company, 1952.

4. Osgood, Kenneth, *Total Cold War, Eisenhower's Secret Propaganda Battle at Home and Abroad*, Lawrence, Kansas, University Press of Kansas, 2006.

5. Beisner, *Dean Acheson, A Life in the Cold War.*

6. Gaddis, *John Lewis, Strategies of Containment, A Critical Appraisal of Postwar American National Security Policy*, New York, New York, Oxford University Press, 1982.

7. Ibid.

8. Syngman, Rhee, *Encyclopedia of Korean Culture, Academy of Korean Studies*, Retrieved March 13, 2014; and Cummings, Bruce, "38 degrees of separation: a forgotten occupation," *The Korean War: A history, Modern Library*, ISBN 978-0-8129-7896-4, 2010; and Hastings, Max, *The Korean War*, Simon and Schuster, New York, New York, 1988.

9. "A Divided Korea Heads for War: 1948-1950," *Korean War Reference Library*, encyclopedia.com, December 7, 2018.

10. Stone, *The Hidden History of the Korean War, 1950-1951, A Nonconformist History of Our Times.*

11. Ibid.

12. Ibid.

13. Manchester, William, and Reid, Paul, *The Last Lion, Winston Spencer Churchill, Defender of the Realm, 1940-1965*, New York, New York, Little, Brown and Company, 2012.

14. Stone, *The Hidden History of the Korean War, 1950-1951, A Nonconformist History of Our Times.*

15. Brands, H.W., *The General vs. the President, MacArthur and Truman at the Brink of Nuclear War*, New York, New York, Doubleday, 2016.

16. Carrozza, Anthony R., *William D. Pawley, The Extraordinary Life of the Adventurer, Entrepreneur, and Diplomat Who Cofounded the Flying Tigers*, Washington D.C., Potomac Books, 2012.

17. Ibid.

18. Thomas, Evan, *Ike's Bluff, President Eisenhower's Secret Battle to Save the World*, New York, New York, Little, Brown and Company, 2012.

19. Gaddis, John Lewis, *George F. Kennan, An American Life*, New York, New York, The Penguin Press, 2011.

20. Valentine, Douglas, *The Strength of the Wolf, The Secret History of America's War on Drugs*, London, England, Verso, 2004.

21. Carrozza, Pawley, *The Extraordinary Life of the Adventurer, Entrepreneur, and Diplomat Who Cofounded the Flying Tigers*, and Stone, *The Hidden History of the Korean War, 1950-1951, A Nonconformist History of Our Times.*

22. Stone, *The Hidden History of the Korean War, 1950-1951, A Nonconformist History of Our Times.*

23. Bird, Kai, *The Chairman, John McCloy, The Making of the American Establishment*, New York, New York, Simon & Schuster, 1992.

24. Ibid.

25. Ibid.

26. Gaddis, John Lewis, *Strategies of Containment, A Critical Appraisal of Postwar American National Security Policy.*

27. Ibid.

28. Stone, *The Hidden History of the Korean War, 1950-1951, A Nonconformist History of Our Times.*

29. Ibid.

30. Ibid..and Morris, Seymour Jr., *Supreme Commander, MacArthur's Triumph in Japan*, New York, New York, Harper Collins Books, 2014.

Chapter Six: How Do You Solve a Problem Like Korea?

1. Beisner, Robert L., *Dean Acheson, A Life in the Cold War*, New York, New York, Oxford University Press, 2006.

2. *National Security Agency, Central Security Service*, "The Korean War: The SIGINT Background," NSA.gov website.

3. Merrill, John, *Korea: The Peninsular Origins of the War*, Newark, Delaware, University of Delaware Press, 1989.

4. Beisner, *Dean Acheson, A Life in the Cold War.*

5. Merrill, *Korea: The Peninsular Origins of the War.*

6. Stone, I.F., *The Hidden History of the Korean War, 1950-1951, A Nonconformist History of Our Times*, Boston, Massachusetts, Little, Brown and Company, 1952.

7. Ibid.

8. Ibid.

9. Brands, H.W., *The General vs. the President, MacArthur and Truman at the Brink of Nuclear War*, New York, New York, Doubleday, 2016.

10. Stone, *The Hidden History of the Korean War, 1950-1951, A Nonconformist History of Our Times.*

11. Brands, H.W., *The General vs. the President, MacArthur and Truman at the Brink of Nuclear War.*

12. Ibid.

13. Binder, L. James, *Lemnitzer, A Soldier for His Time*, Washington, D.C., Brassey's, 1997.

14. Gaddis, John Lewis, *Strategies of Containment, A Critical Appraisal of Postwar American National Security Policy*, New York, New York, Oxford University Press, 1982.

15. Ibid.

16. Stone, *The Hidden History of the Korean War, 1950-1951, A Nonconformist History of Our Times.*

17. Ibid.

18. Ibid.

19. Brands, H.W., *The General vs. the President, MacArthur and Truman at the Brink of Nuclear War.*

20. Weintraub, Stanley, *MacArthur's War and the Undoing of an American Hero*, Simon & Schuster, New York, New York, 2000

21. Wallace, Max, *The American Axis, Henry Ford, Charles Lindbergh, and the Rise of the Third Reich*, New York, New York, St. Martin's Press, 2003.

22. Bamford, James, *Body of Secrets, Anatomy of the Ultra-Secret National Security Agency, From the Cold War Through the Dawn of a New Century*, New York, New York, Doubleday, 2001.

23. Stone, *The Hidden History of the Korean War, 1950-1951, A Nonconformist History of Our Times.*

24. Ibid.

25. Ibid.

26. Ibid.

27. Ibid.

28. Ibid.

29. Gaddis, *Strategies of Containment, A Critical Appraisal of Postwar American National Security Policy.*

30. Stone, *The Hidden History of the Korean War, 1950-1951, A Nonconformist History of Our Times.*

31. Gaddis, *Strategies of Containment, A Critical Appraisal of Postwar American National Security Policy.*

32. *Stone, The Hidden History of the Korean War, 1950-1951, A Nonconformist History of* Our Times.

33. Ibid.

34. Ibid.

35. Ibid.

36. Ibid.

37. Ibid.

38. Carrozza, *Pawley, The Extraordinary Life of the Adventurer, Entrepreneur, and Diplomat Who Co-founded the Flying Tigers*, and Stone, *The Hidden History of* the Korean War, 1950-1951, A Nonconformist History of Our Times.

39. Stone, *The Hidden History of the Korean War, 1950-1951, A Nonconformist History of Our Times.*

Chapter Seven: The War Machine

1. Romerstein, Herbert, and Breindel, Eric, *The Venona Secrets, Exposing Soviet Espionage and America's Traitors*, Washington, D.C., Regency Publishing, Inc., 2000, and Farrell, Joseph P., *The Third Way, The Nazi International, European Union, and Corporate Fascism*, Kempton, Illinois, Adventure Unlimited Press, 2015.

2. Fried, Richard M., *Nightmare in Red, The McCarthy Era in Perspective*, New York, New York, Oxford University Press, 1990.

3. Leffler, Melvyn P., *For the Soul of Mankind, The United States, the Soviet Union, and The Cold War*, New York, New York, Hill and Wang, 2007.

4. Romerstein and Breindel, *The Venona Secrets, Exposing Soviet Espionage and America's Traitors.*

5. Leffler, *For the Soul of Mankind, The United States, the Soviet Union, and The Cold War.*

6. Ibid.

7. Parmet, Herbert S., *Eisenhower and the American Crusades*, New York, New York, The MacMillan Company, 1972.

8. Beisner, Robert L., *Dean Acheson, A Life in the Cold War*, New York, New York, Oxford University Press, 2006.

9. Parmet, *Eisenhower and the American Crusades.*

10. Farrell, *The Third Way, The Nazi International, European Union, and Corporate Fascism.*

11. Parmet, *Eisenhower and the American Crusades.*

12. Nichols, David, A., *Ike and McCarthy, Dwight Eisenhower's Secret Campaign Against Joseph McCarthy*, New York, New York, Simon & Schuster, 2017.

13. Parmet, *Eisenhower and the American Crusades.*

14. Mills, C. Wright, *The Power Elite*, New York, New York, Oxford University Press, 1956.

15. Beisner, *Dean Acheson, A Life in the Cold War.*

16. Ibid.

17. Beschloss, Michael R., *May-Day, Eisenhower, Khrushchev and the U-2 Affair*, New York, New York, Harper & Row Publishers, 1986.

18. Osgood, Kenneth, *Total Cold War, Eisenhower's Secret Propaganda Battle at Home and Abroad*, Lawrence, Kansas, University Press of Kansas, 2006

19. Gaddis, John Lewis, *Strategies of Containment, A Critical Appraisal of Postwar American National Security Policy*, New York, New York, Oxford University Press, 1982.

20. Talbot, David, *The Devil's Chessboard, Allen Dulles, the CIA, and the Rise of America's Secret Government*, New York, New York, Harper Collins Publishers, 2015.

21. Nichols*, Ike and McCarthy, Dwight Eisenhower's Secret Campaign Against Joseph McCarthy.*

22. Ambrose, Stephen E., *Eisenhower: The President*, New York, New York, Simon and Schuster, 1984.

23. Swanson, Michael, *The War State, The Cold War Origins of the Military-Industrial Complex and the Power Elite, 1945-1963*, North Charleston, South Carolina, CreateSpace Independent Publishing Platform, 2013.

24. Applebaum, Anne, *Iron Curtain, The Crushing of Eastern Europe,1944-1956*, New York, New York, Doubleday, 2012.

25. Leffler, *For the Soul of Mankind, The United States, the Soviet Union, and The Cold War.*

26. Nichols, David A., *Eisenhower 1956, The President's Year of Crisis, Suez and the Brink of War*, New York, New York, Simon & Schuster, 2011.

27. Leffler, *For the Soul of Mankind, The United States, the Soviet Union, and The Cold War.*

28. Gaddis, *Strategies of Containment, A Critical Appraisal of Postwar American National Security Policy.*

29. Leffler, *For the Soul of Mankind, The United States, the Soviet Union, and The Cold War.*

30. Bird, Kai, *The Chairman, John McCloy The Making of the American Establishment*, New York, New York, Simon & Schuster, 1992.

31. Osgood, *Total Cold War, Eisenhower's Secret Propaganda Battle at Home and Abroad.*

32. Leffler, *For the Soul of Mankind, The United States, the Soviet Union, and The Cold War.*

33. Ibid.

34. Binder, L. James, *Lemnitzer, A Soldier for His Time*, Washington, D.C., Brassey's, 1997.

35. Thomas, Evan, *Ike's Bluff, President Eisenhower's Secret Battle to Save the World*, New York, New York, Little, Brown and Company, 2012.

36. Ibid., and Gaddis, *Strategies of Containment, A Critical Appraisal of Postwar American National Security Policy.*

37. Ibid.

38. Fleming, Thomas, *The New Dealers' War, FDR and the War Within World War II*, New York, New York, Basic Books, 2001.

39. Swanson, *The War State, The Cold War Origins of the Military-Industrial Complex and the Power Elite, 1945-1963.*

40. Mills, *The Power Elite.*

41. Ambrose, *Eisenhower, The President.*

42. Arthur Krock, "Eisenhower Crticized On Leadership; Complaints Are Directed Against His Handling of Security Policy and His Part in Latest McCarthy Incident," *The New York Times*, April 5, 1953.

43. Mills, *The Power Elite.*

44. Thomas, *Ike's Bluff, President Eisenhower's Secret Battle to Save the World.*

45. Mills, *The Power Elite.*

46. Ibid.

47. Leffler, *For the Soul of Mankind, The United States, the Soviet Union, and The Cold War.*

48. Parmet, *Eisenhower and the American Crusades.*

49. Coffin, Tristram, *The Passion of the Hawks, Militarism in Modern America*, New York, New York, The MacMillan Company, 1964.

50. LeMay, General Curtis, *America is in Danger*, New York, New York, Funk and Wagnalls, 1968.

51. Parmet, *Eisenhower and the American Crusades.*

52. Ambrose, *Eisenhower, The President.*

53. LeMay, *America is in Danger.*

54. Ambrose, *Eisenhower, The President.*

55. Nichols, *Eisenhower 1956, The President's Year of Crisis, Suez and the Brink of War.*

56. Ibid.

57. Ibid.

58. Beschloss, *May-Day, Eisenhower, Khrushchev and the U-2 Affair.*

59. Ibid.

60. Thomas, *Ike's Bluff, President Eisenhower's Secret Battle to Save the World.*

61. Douglas, James, W., *JFK and the Unspeakable, Why He Died & Why It Matters*, Maryknoll, New York, Orbis Books, 2008.

62. Ambrose, *Eisenhower, The President.*

63. Encyclopedia Britannica, www.britannica.com/topic/fascism.

64. Coffin, Tristram, *The Passion of the Hawks, Militarism in Modern America.*

65. *Hearings Before the President's Commission on the Assassination pf President Kennedy*, Volume V, 1964.

66. Summers, Anthony, *Conspiracy,* New York, New York, McGraw-Hill Book Company, 1980.

Chapter Eight: Organized Crime—Don't Dance with the Devil

1. Valentine, Douglas, *The Strength of the Wolf, The Secret History of America's War on Drugs*, London, England, Verso, 2004.

2. Ibid.

3. McCoy, Alfred W., *The Politics of Heroin in Southeast Asia*, New York, New York, Harper and Row, 1972.

4. Huchthausen, James P., *Imperialism, Corporatism, Militarism, An American Tragedy*, North Charleston, South Carolina, Createspace Publishing Platform, 2014.

5. Rovner, Eduardo Saenz, *The Cuban Connection, Drug Trafficking, Smuggling, and Gambling in Cuba from the 1920s to the Revolution*, Chapel Hill, North Carolina, The University of North Carolina Press, 2008.

6. Ibid.

7. McCoy, *The Politics of Heroin in Southeast Asia.*

8. Waldron, Lamar, *The Hidden History of the JFK Assassination, The Definitive Account of the Most Controversial Crime of the Twentieth Century*, Berkeley, California, Counterpoint, 2013.

9. Williams, Paul L., *Operation Gladio, The Unholy Alliance Between The Vatican, The CIA, And The Mafia*, Amherst, New York, Prometheus Books, 2015.

10. Rovner, *The Cuban Connection, Drug Trafficking, Smuggling, and Gambling in Cuba from the 1920s to the Revolution.*

11. Russell, Dick, *The Man Who Knew Too Much*, New York, New York, Carroll & Graf Publishers/ Richard Gallen, 1992.

12. Albarelli, H.P. Jr., *A Terrible Mistake, The Murder of Frank Olson and the CIA's Secret Cold War Experiments*, Walterville, Oregon, Trine Day, 2009.

13. Ibid.

14. Albarelli, H.P. Jr., *A Secret Order, Investigating the High Strangeness and Synchronicity in the JFK Assassination*, Walterville, Oregon, Trine Day, 2013.

15. Russell, Dick, *On the Trail of the JFK Assassins, A Groundbreaking Look at America's Most Infamous Conspiracy*, New York, New York, Skyhorse Publishing, 2008.

16. Albarelli, *A Terrible Mistake, The Murder of Frank Olson and the CIA's Secret Cold War Experiments*

17. Valentine, *The Strength of the Wolf, The Secret History of America's War on Drugs.*

18. Ibid.

19. "FBI Memorandum, March 15, 1951," *The Black Vault*, www.theblackvault.com/document-archive/.

20. McCoy, *The Politics of Heroin in Southeast Asia.*

21. "FBI Letter to J. Edgar Hoover, July 2, 1953," *The Black Vault*, www.theblackvault.com/document-archive/

22. "FBI Memorandum, August 5, 1953," *The Black Vault*, www.theblackvault.com/documentarchive/

23. "FBI Memorandum, August 14, 1953," *The Black Vault*, www.theblackvault.com/document-archive/.

24. "FBI Memorandum, February 28, 1952," *The Black Vault*, www.theblackvault.com/document-archive/.

25. Valentine, *The Strength of the Wolf, The Secret History of America's War on Drugs.*

26. Russell, *On the Trail of the JFK Assassins, A Groundbreaking look at America's Most Infamous Conspiracy.*

27. Ibid.

28. Ibid.

29. Albarelli, *A Terrible Mistake, The Murder of Frank Olson and the CIA's Secret Cold War Experiments.*

30. Ibid.

31. Ibid.

32. Ibid.

33. Ibid.

34. Russell, Dick, *The Man Who Knew Too Much*, New York, New York, Carroll & Graf Publishers/Richard Gallen, 1992.

35. Ibid.

36. Ibid.

37. Albarelli, A Terrible Mistake, The Murder of Frank Olson and the CIA's Secret Cold War Experiments.

38. Mellen, Joan, A Farewell to Justice, Jim Garrison, JFK's Assassination, and the Case That Should Have Changed History, New York, New York, Skyhorse Publishing, 2013.

39. Ibid.

40. Mellen, A Farewell to Justice, Jim Garrison, JFK's Assassination, and the Case That Should Have Changed History.

41. Ibid.

42. Waldron, Lamar, and Hartmann, Thom, *Ultimate Sacrifice, John and Robert Kennedy, the Plan for a Coup in Cuba, and the Murder of JFK*, New York, New York, Carroll & Graf Publishers, 2005.

43. Russell, *The Man Who Knew Too Much.*

44. Waldron, *The Hidden History of the JFK Assassination, The Definitive Account of the Most Controversial Crime of the Twentieth Century.*

45. Valentine, *The Strength of the Wolf, The Secret History of America's War on Drugs.*

46. Ibid.

47. Ibid.

48. Ibid.

49. Waldron, *The Hidden History of the JFK Assassination, The Definitive Account of the Most Controversial Crime of the Twentieth Century.*

50. Ibid.; North, Mark, *Act of Treason, The Role of J. Edgar Hoover in the Assassination of President Kennedy*, New York, New York, Carroll & Graf Publishers, 1991, and Shaw, Mark, *The Reporter Who Knew Too Much, The Mysterious Death of What's My Line TV Star and Media Icon Dorothy Kilgallen*, New York, New York, Post Hill Press, 2016.

51. Waldron, *The Hidden History of the JFK Assassination, The Definitive Account of the Most Controversial Crime of the Twentieth Century.*

52. Valentine, *The Strength of the Wolf, The Secret History of America's War on Drugs.*

53. Ibid.

54. Waldron and Hartmann, *Ultimate Sacrifice, John and Robert Kennedy, the Plan for a Coup in Cuba, and the Murder of JFK.*

55. Scheim, David E., *Contract on America, The Mafia Murder of President John F. Kennedy*, New York, New York, Shapolsky Publishers, Inc., 1988, and Albarelli, *A Terrible Mistake, The Murder of Frank Olson and the CIA's Secret Cold War Experiments.*

56. Benson, Michael, *Who's Who in the JFK Assassination, An A-to-Z Encyclopedia*, New York, New York, Carol Publishing Group, 1993.

57. Summers, Anthony, *Conspiracy*, New York, New York, McGraw-Hill Book Company, 1980.

58. *Report of the Select Committee on Assassinations, U.S. House of Representatives*, Volume IX, Section V, 1979.

59. *Report of the Select Committee on Assassinations, U.S. House of Representatives*, 1979.

60. New York Times (editor), *The Witnesses: The Highlights of Hearings Before the Warren Commission on the Assassination of President Kennedy*, New York, New York, Mc-Graw Hill Book Company, 1965.

61. Scheim, *Contract on America, The Mafia Murder of President John F. Kennedy.*

62. Scheim, *Contract on America, The Mafia Murder of President John F. Kennedy.*

63. *Report of the Select Committee on Assassinations, U.S. House of Representatives*, 1979.

64. Ibid.

65. Summers, *Conspiracy.*

66. Blakey, G. Robert, and Billings, Richard N., *The Plot to Kill the President, Organized Crime Assassinated J.F.K.*, The Definitive Story, New York, New York, Times Books, 1981.

67. Ibid.

68. Scheim, *Contract on America*, The Mafia Murder of President John F. Kennedy.

69. Summers, *Conspiracy.*

70. Ibid.

71. Waldron, *The Hidden History of the JFK Assassination, The Definitive Account of the Most Controversial Crime of the Twentieth Century.*

72. Ibid.

73. North, *Act of Treason, The Role of J. Edgar Hoover in the Assassination of President Kennedy.*

Chapter Nine: Deep in the Heart of Texas

1. Mellen, Joan, *The Great Game in Cuba, How the CIA Sabotaged Its Own Plot to Unseat Fidel Castro*, New York, New York, Skyhorse Publishing, 2013.

2. Ibid.

3. Caro, Robert, *The Years of Lyndon Johnson: The Path to Power*, Alfred A. Knopf, New York, New York, 1982.

4. Carleton, Don E., *Red Scare, Right-Wing Hysteria, Fifties Fanaticism, and Their Legacy in Texas*, Austin, Texas, Texas Monthly Press, 1985.

5. Ibid.

6. Ibid.

7. Simkin, John, *Spartacus Educational*, www.spartacus-educational.com, 2017; and Hughes-Wilson, Colonel John, *JFK, An American Coup D' Etat, The Truth Behind the Kennedy Assassination*, London, England, John Blake Publishing Ltd., 2015, and North, Mark, *Betrayal in Dallas, LBJ, The Pearl Street Mafia, and the Murder of President Kennedy*, New York, New York, Skyhorse Publishing, 2011.

8. Mellen, Joan, *A Farewell to Justice, Jim Garrison, JFK's Assassination, and the Case That Should Have Changed History*, New York, New York, Skyhorse Publishing, 2013.

9. Mellen, *The Great Game in Cuba, How the CIA Sabotaged Its Own Plot to Unseat Fidel Castro.*

10. Manchester, William, *American Caesar, Douglas MacArthur 1880-1964*, New York, New York, Dell Publishing Group, 1978.

11. Caufield, M.D., Jeffrey H., *General Walker and the Murder of President Kennedy, The Extensive New Evidence of a Radical-Right Conspiracy*, Moreland Press, 2015.

12. Ibid.

13. Marrs, Jim, *Crossfire, The Plot That Killed Kennedy*, New York, New York, Carroll & Graf Publishers, Inc., 1989; Scheim, David E., *Contract on America, The Mafia Murder of President John F. Kennedy*, New York, New York, Shapolsky Publishers, Inc., 1988; and Summers, Anthony, *Conspiracy*, New York, New York, McGraw-Hill Book Company, 1980.

14. Russell, Dick, *The Man Who Knew Too Much*, New York, New York, Carroll & Graf Publishers/Richard Gallen, 1992.

15. North, *Betrayal in Dallas, LBJ, The Pearl Street Mafia, and the Murder of President Kennedy.*

16. Ibid.

17. Ibid.

18. Russell, *The Man Who Knew Too Much.*

19. North, *Betrayal in Dallas, LBJ, The Pearl Street Mafia, and the Murder of President Kennedy.*

20. Scheim, *Contract on America, The Mafia Murder of President John F. Kennedy.*

21. Caufield, *General Walker and the Murder of President Kennedy, The Extensive New Evidence of a Radical-Right Conspiracy.*

22. Russell, *The Man Who Knew Too Much.*

23. Ibid., and Benson, *Who's Who in the JFK Assassination, An A-to-Z Encyclopedia*.

24. Benson, *Who's Who in the JFK Assassination, An A-to-Z Encyclopedia*.

25. Albarelli, H.P. Jr., *A Terrible Mistake, The Murder of Frank Olson and the CIA's Secret Cold War Experiments*, Walterville, Oregon, Trine Day, 2009.

26. Mellen, Joan, *Our Man in Haiti, George de Mohrenschildt and the CIA in the Nightmare Republic*, Walterville, Oregon, Trine Day, 2012.

27. Ibid.

28. Baker, Russ, *Family Secrets, The Bush Dynasty, America's Invisible Government, and the Hidden History of the Last Fifty Years*, New York, New York, Bloomsbury Press, 2009.

29. Mellen, *Our Man in Haiti, George de Mohrenschildt and the CIA in the Nightmare Republic*, and Newman, *Oswald and the CIA*.

30. Albarelli, H.P. Jr., *A Secret Order, Investigating the High Strangeness and Synchronicity in the JFK Assassination*, Walterville, Oregon, Trine Day, 2013.

31. Ibid.

32. Ganis, Major Ralph P., USAF, Ret., *The Skorzeny Papers, Evidence for the Plot to Kill JFK*, New York, New York, Skyhorse Publishing, 2018.

33. Albarelli, *A Secret Order, Investigating the High Strangeness and Synchronicity in the JFK Assassination*.

34. Waldron, Lamar, and Hartmann, Thom, *Ultimate Sacrifice, John and Robert Kennedy, the Plan for a Coup in Cuba, and the Murder of JFK*, New York, New York, Carroll & Graf Publishers, 2005, and North, *Betrayal in Dallas, LBJ, The Pearl Street Mafia, and the Murder of President Kennedy*.

35. Mellon, Joan, *Faustian Bargains, Lyndon Johnson and Mac Wallace in the Robber Baron Culture of Texas*, New York, New York, Bloomsbury USA, 2016.

36. Trouillot, Michel-Rolph, "Haiti, State Against Nation, The Origin and Legacy of Duvalierism," New York, *New York, Monthly Review Press*, 1990.

37. Mellon, *Faustian Bargains, Lyndon Johnson and Mac Wallace in the Robber Baron Culture of Texas*.

38. "That High-Living Baker Boy Scandalizes The Capital," *Life Magazine* article, November 8, 1963.

39. Mellon, *Faustian Bargains, Lyndon Johnson and Mac Wallace in the Robber Baron Culture of Texas*.

40. Ibid.

41. Ibid.

42. Zirbel, Craig I., *The Texas Connection: The Assassination of John F. Kennedy*, Scottsdale, Arizona, The Texas Connection Company Publishers, 1991.

43. Evans, Rowland, and Novak, Robert, *Lyndon B. Johnson: The Exercise of Power*, New York, New York, The New American Library, 1966.

44. Marrs, *Crossfire, The Plot That Killed Kennedy*.

45. North, *Betrayal in Dallas, LBJ, The Pearl Street Mafia, and the Murder of President Kennedy*.

46. Zirbel, *The Texas Connection: The Assassination of John F. Kennedy*.

47. Evans and Novak, *Lyndon B. Johnson: The Exercise of Power*.

48. Davis, John H., *Mafia Kingfish, Carlos Marcello and the Assassination of John F. Kennedy*, New York, New York, Penguin Books USA Inc., 1989.

49. Ibid.

50. Kaiser, David, *The Road to Dallas, The Assassination of John F. Kennedy*, Cambridge, Massachusetts, The Belknap Press of Harvard University Press, 2008.

51. Davis, *Mafia Kingfish, Carlos Marcello and the Assassination of John F. Kennedy*.

52. "Baker Hearing Delayed," *The New York Times* article, November 9, 1963.

53. Kenworthy, E.W., "Baker Is Linked To Import Deal; Justice Department Studies Report of Influence For Haitian Meat Company Baker Is Linked To," *The New York Times* article, November 13, 1963.

54. Summers, Anthony, *Official and Confidential, The Secret Life of J. Edgar Hoover*, New York, New York, G.P. Putnam and Sons, 1993.

55. Ibid.

56. Ibid.

57. Ibid.

58. Ibid.

59. Valentine, Douglas, *The Strength of the Wolf, The Secret History of America's War on Drugs*, London, England, Verso, 2004.

60. Marrs, *Crossfire, The Plot That Killed Kennedy*.

61. Talbot, David, *The Devil's Chessboard, Allen Dulles, the CIA, and the Rise of America's Secret Government*, New York, New York, Harper Collins Publishers, 2015.

62. Ibid.

63. Hughes-Wilson, *JFK An American Coup D'Etat, The Truth Behind the Kennedy Assassination.*

64. McClellan, Barr, *Blood, Money & Power, How L.B.J. Killed J.F.K.*, New York, New York, Hanover House, 2003, and Zirbel, The Texas Connection: The Assassination of John F. Kennedy.

65. Ibid.

66. Stone, Roger, with Mike Colapietro, *The Man Who Killed Kennedy, The Case Against LBJ*, New York, New York, Skyhorse Publishing, 2013.

67. Evica, George Michael, *A Certain Arrogance; The Sacrificing of Lee Harvey Oswald and the Cold War Manipulation of Religious Groups by US Intelligence*, Walterville, Oregon, TrineDay, 2011.

68. Escalante, Fabian, *The Secret War: CIA Covert Operations Against Cuba, 1959-62*, Ocean Press, 1995.

69. Baker, *Family Secrets, The Bush Dynasty, America's Invisible Government, and the Hidden History of the Last Fifty Years.*

70. Ibid.

71. Carrozza, Anthony R., *William D. Pawley, The Extraordinary Life of the Adventurer, Entrepreneur, and Diplomat Who Cofounded the Flying Tigers*, Washington D.C., Potomac Books, 2012.

72. Ibid.

73. Russell, *The Man Who Knew Too Much.*

74. Ganis, *The Skorzeny Papers, Evidence for the Plot to Kill JFK.*

75. Russell, *The Man Who Knew Too Much.*

76. Ibid.

77. Ibid.

78. Ibid.

79. Ganis, *The Skorzeny Papers, Evidence for the Plot to Kill JFK.*

Chapter Ten: The Best Laid Plans of Mice and Men

1. Truman, Harry S, "Limit CIA Role to Intelligence," *The Washington Post* article, December 22, 1963.

2. Powers, Thomas, *The Man Who Kept the Secrets, Richard Helms and the CIA*, New York New York, Alfred A. Knopf, 1979.

3. Carrozza, Anthony R., *William D. Pawley, The Extraordinary Life of the Adventurer, Entrepreneur, and Diplomat Who Cofounded the Flying Tigers*, Washington D.C., Potomac Books, 2012.

4. Swanson, Michael, *The War State, The Cold War Origins of the Military-Industrial Complex and the Power Elite, 1945-1963*, North Charleston, South Carolina, CreateSpace Independent Publishing Platform, 2013.

5. Ranelagh, John, *The Agency, The Rise and Decline of the CIA*, New York, New York, Simon and Schuster, 1986.

6. Swanson, *The War State, The Cold War Origins of the Military-Industrial Complex and the Power Elite.*

7. Mellen, Joan, *The Great Game in Cuba, How the CIA Sabotaged Its Own Plot to Unseat Fidel Castro*, New York, New York, Skyhorse Publishing 2013.

8. Osgood, Kenneth, *Total Cold War, Eisenhower's Secret Propaganda Battle at Home and Abroad*, Lawrence, Kansas, University Press of Kansas, 2006.

9. Ibid.

10. Valentine, Douglas, *The Strength of the Wolf, The Secret History of America's War on Drugs*, London, England, Verso, 2004.

11. Talbot, David, *The Devil's Chessboard, Allen Dulles, the CIA, and the Rise of America's Secret Government*, New York, New York, Harper Collins Publishers, 2015.

12. Huchthausen, James P., *Imperialism, Corporatism, Militarism, An American Tragedy*, North Charleston, South Carolina, Createspace Publishing Platform, 2014.

13. Thomas, Evan, *Ike's Bluff, President Eisenhower's Secret Battle to Save the World*, New York, New York, Little, Brown and Company, 2012.

14. Farrell, Joseph P., *The Third Way, The Nazi International, European Union, and Corporate Fascism*, Kempton, Illinois, Adventure Unlimited Press, 2015.

15. Ganis, Major Ralph P., USAF, Ret., *The Skorzeny Papers, Evidence for the Plot to Kill JFK*, New York, New York, Skyhorse Publishing, 2018.

16. Ibid.

17. Ibid.

18. Thomas, Evan, *The Very Best Men, Four Who Dared: The Early Years of the CIA*, New York, New York, Simon & Schuster, 1995; Talbot, *The Devil's Chessboard, Allen Dulles, the CIA, and the Rise of America's Secret Government*; and Huchthausen, *Imperialism, Corporatism, Militarism, An* American Tragedy.

19. Valentine, *The Strength of the Wolf, The Secret History of America's War on Drugs*.

20. Corsi, Jerome R., P.H.D., *Who Really Killed Kennedy?, 50 Years Later, Stunning New Revelations about the JFK Assassination*, Washington, D.C., WND Books, 2013.

21. Thomas, *The Very Best Men, Four Who Dared: The Early Years of the CIA*.

22. Beisner, Robert L., *Dean Acheson, A Life in the Cold War*, New York, New York, Oxford University Press, 2006.

23. Thomas, *Ike's Bluff, President Eisenhower's Secret Battle to Save the World*.

24. Fursenko, Aleksandr, and Naftali, Timothy, *Khrushchev's Cold War, The Inside Story of an American Adversary*, New York, New York, W.W. Norton & Company, 2006.

25. Corsi, *Who Really Killed Kennedy?, 50 Years Later, Stunning New Revelations about the JFK Assassination*.

26. Waldron, Lamar, *The Hidden History of the JFK Assassination, The Definitive Account of the Most Controversial Crime of the Twentieth Century*, Berkeley, California, Counterpoint, 2013.

27. Ibid.

28. Huchthausen, *Imperialism, Corporatism, Militarism, An American Tragedy*, and Farrell, *The Third Way, The Nazi International, European Union, and* Corporate Fascism.

29. Paget, Karen M., *Patriotic Betrayal*, New Haven Connecticut, Yale University Press, 2015.

30. Prados, John, *Safe for Democracy, The Secret Wars of the CIA*, Chicago, Illinois, Ivan R. Dee, 2006.

31. Thomas, *Ike's Bluff, President Eisenhower's Secret Battle to Save the World*, and Prados, *Safe for Democracy, The Secret Wars of the CIA*.

32. Huchthausen, *Imperialism, Corporatism, Militarism, An American Tragedy*.

33. Prados, *Safe for Democracy, The Secret Wars of the CIA*.

34. Ibid.

35. Woods, Randall B., *Shadow Warrior, William Egan Colby and the CIA*, New York, New York, Basic Books, 2013.

36. Ibid.

37. Powers, *The Man Who Kept the Secrets, Richard Helms and the CIA*.

38. Ranelagh, *The Agency, The Rise and Decline of the CIA*.

39. Jeffrey-Jones, Rhodri, *The CIA & American Democracy*, New Haven, Connecticut, Yale University Press, 1989, and Powers, *The Man Who Kept* the Secrets, Richard Helms and the CIA.

40. Bird, Kai, *The Color of Truth, McGeorge Bundy and William Bundy: Brothers in Arms*, New York New York, Simon & Schuster, 1998.

41. Albarelli, H.P. Jr., *A Terrible Mistake, The Murder of Frank Olson and the CIA's Secret Cold War Experiments*, Walterville, Oregon, Trine Day, 2009.

42. Ibid.

43. Rust, William, J., "Operation Iceberg, Transition into CIA: The Strategic Services Unit in Indonesia," *Studies in Intelligence, Journal of the American Intelligence Professional, Vol 60, No 1*, March 2016.

44. Ranelagh, *The Agency, The Rise and Decline of the CIA*

45. Albarelli, *A Terrible Mistake, The Murder of Frank Olson and the CIA's Secret Cold* War Experiments.

46. "James Forrestal," *The New York Times* article, May 23, 1949

47. Martin, David, *The Assassination of James Forrestal*, Hyattsville, Maryland, McCabe Publishing, 2019.

48. *Chicago Tribune* article, April 1, 1951

49. Woods, *Shadow Warrior, William Egan Colby and the CIA*.

50. Ibid.

51. Janney, Peter, *Mary's Mosaic, The CIA Conspiracy to Murder John F. Kennedy, Mary Pinchot Meyer, and Their Vision for World Peace*, New York, New York, Skyhorse Publishing, 2012.

52. Ibid.

53. Ibid.

54. Ibid.

Chapter Eleven: CIA and the Rule of Lawlessness

1. Morris, Seymour Jr., *Supreme Commander, MacArthur's Triumph in Japan*, New York, New York, Harper Collins Books, 2014.

2. Jacobsen, Annie, *Operation Paperclip, The Secret Intelligence Program That Brought Nazi Scientists to America*, New York, New York, Littler, Brown and Company, 2014, and Albarelli, H.P. Jr., A *Terrible Mistake, The Murder of Frank Olson and the CIA's Secret Cold War Experiments*, Walterville, Oregon, Trine Day, 2009.

3. Albarelli, H.P. Jr., *A Secret Order, Investigating the High Strangeness and Synchronicity in the JFK Assassination*, Walterville, Oregon, Trine Day, 2013.

4. Blum, William, *Rogue State: A Guide to the World's Only Superpower*, London, England, Zed Books, 2006.

5. Mangold, Tom, and Goldberg, Jeff, *Plague Wars: A True Story of Biological Warfare*, New York, New York, MacMillan Books, 2000.

6. Blum, *Rogue State: A Guide to the World's Only Superpower*.

7. Jacobsen, *Operation Paperclip, The Secret Intelligence Program That Brought Nazi Scientists to America.*

8. Albarelli, *A Terrible Mistake, The Murder of Frank Olson and the CIA's Secret Cold War Experiments.*

9. Hess, Stephen, *America's Political Dynasties*, New York, New York, Doubleday, 1966.

10. Roosevelt, Archibald, and Dobbs, Zygmund, *The Great Deceit, Social Psedo-Sciences*, Sayville, New York, The Veritas Foundation 1964.

11. Trento, Joseph J., *The Secret History of the CIA*, New York, New York, MJF Books, 2001.

12. Jacobsen, *Operation Paperclip, The Secret Intelligence Program That Brought Nazi Scientists to America.*

13. Ibid..

14. Ibid., Albarelli, *A Terrible Mistake, The Murder of Frank Olson and the CIA's Secret Cold War Experiments.*

15. Jacobsen, *Operation Paperclip, The Secret Intelligence Program That Brought Nazi Scientists to America.*

16. Albarelli, *A Terrible Mistake, The Murder of Frank Olson and the CIA's Secret Cold War Experiments.*

17. Russell, Dick, *On the Trail of the JFK Assassins, A Groundbreaking look at America's Most Infamous Conspiracy*, New York, New York, Skyhorse Publishing, 2008.

18. Huchthausen, James P., *Imperialism, Corporatism, Militarism, An American Tragedy*, North Charleston, South Carolina, Createspace Publishing Platform, 2014.

19. Albarelli, H.P. Jr., *A Secret Order, Investigating the High Strangeness and Synchronicity in the JFK Assassination.*

20. Albarelli, *A Terrible Mistake, The Murder of Frank Olson and the CIA's Secret Cold War Experiments.*

21. Baumeister, Alan A., "The Tulane Electric Brain Stimulation Program. A Historical Case Study in Medical Ethics," *Journal of the History of the Neurosciences*, 2000.

22. Valentine, Douglas, *The Strength of the Wolf, The Secret History of America's War on Drugs*, London, England, Verso, 2004.

23. Albarelli, H.P. Jr., *A Secret Order, Investigating the High Strangeness and Synchronicity in the JFK Assassination.*

24. Weidling, Paul, "The Origins of Informed Consent – Nuremberg Code," *Bulletin of the History of Medicine*, 2001.

25. Albarelli, H.P. Jr., and Kaye, Jeffrey S., "The Hidden Tragedy of the CIA Experiments on Children," *Truthout.org*, 2010.

26. Epstein, Edward Jay, *Legend, The Secret World of Lee Harvey Oswald*, New York, New York, Mc-Graw-Hill Book Company, 1978.

27. Ibid.

28. Testimony of Hartogs, Dr. Renatus, *Hearings Before the President's Commission on the Assassination of President Kennedy*, Volume VIII, Washington D.C., Government Printing Office, 1964.

29. Ibid.

30. Albarelli, *A Terrible Mistake, The Murder of Frank Olson and the CIA's Secret Cold War Experiments.*

31. Friedman, John S., *The Secret Histories: Hidden Truths that Challenged the Past and Changed the World*, New York, New York, Macmillan Books, 2005.

32. Albarelli, H.P. Jr., *A Secret Order, Investigating the High Strangeness and Synchronicity in the JFK Assassination.*

33. Ibid.

34. Shenon, Philip, *A Cruel and Shocking Act, The Secret History of the Kennedy Assassination*, New York,

New York, Henry Holt and Company, 2013.

35. Albarelli, H.P. Jr., *A Secret Order, Investigating the High Strangeness and Synchronicity in the JFK Assassination.*

36. Ibid.

37. Russell, Dick, *The Man Who Knew Too Much*, New York, New York, Carroll & Graf Publishers/ Richard Gallen, 1992.

38. Ibid.

39. Mellen, Joan, *Our Man in Haiti, George de Mohrenschildt and the CIA in the Nightmare Republic*, Walterville, Oregon, Trine Day, 2012.

40. Ibid.

Chapter Twelve: Third World Unres Threatens the New World Order

1. Porch, Douglas, *The French Secret Service, A History of French Intelligence from the Dreyfus Affair to the Gulf War*, New York, New York, Farrar, Straus and Giroux, 1995.

2. McCoy, Alfred W., *The Politics of Heroin in Southeast Asia*, Chicago, Illinois, Lawrence Hill Books, 2003.

3. Kinzer, Stephen, *The Brothers, John Foster Dulles, Allen Dulles, and Their Secret World War*, New York, New York, Henry Holt and Company, 2013.

4. Prouty, L. Fletcher, *JFK, The CIA, Vietnam and the Plot to Assassinate John F. Kennedy*, New York, New York, Carol Publishing Group, 1992.

5. Kinzer, *The Brothers, John Foster Dulles, Allen Dulles, and Their Secret World War.*

6. Prouty, *JFK, The CIA, Vietnam and the Plot to Assassinate John F. Kennedy.*

7. Beisner, Robert L., *Dean Acheson, A Life in the Cold War*, New York, New York, Oxford University Press, 2006.

8. Porch, *The French Secret Service, A History of French Intelligence from the Dreyfus Affair to the Gulf War.*

9. Kinzer, *The Brothers, John Foster Dulles, Allen Dulles, and Their Secret World War.*

10. Leffler, Melvyn P., *For the Soul of Mankind, The United States, the Soviet Union, and The Cold War*, New York, New York, Hill and Wang, 2007.

11. Ibid.

12. Porch, *The French Secret Service, A History of French Intelligence from the Dreyfus Affair to the Gulf War.*

13. Horne, Alistair, *A Savage War of Peace, Algeria, 1954-1962*, New York, New York, The Viking Press, 1977.

14. Ibid.

15. Ibid.

16. Ibid.

17. McMillan, Priscilla Johnson, *Marina & Lee*, New York, New York, Harper & Row, 1977.

18. Ibid.

19. Weberman, Alan Jules, *The Oswald Code*, Createspace Independent Publishers, 2014, and Caufield, M.D., Jeffrey H., *General Walker and the Murder of President Kennedy, The Extensive New Evidence of a Radical-Right Conspiracy*, Moreland Press, 2015.

20. Caufield, *General Walker and the Murder of President Kennedy, The Extensive New Evidence of a Radical-Right Conspiracy.*

21. Osgood, Kenneth, *Total Cold War, Eisenhower's Secret Propaganda Battle at Home and Abroad*, Lawrence, Kansas, University Press of Kansas, 2006.

22. Nichols, David A., *Eisenhower 1956, The President's Year of Crisis, Suez and the Brink of War*, New York, New York, Simon & Schuster, 2011.

23. Ibid.

24. Ibid.

25. Fursenko, Aleksandr, and Naftali, Timothy, *Khrushchev's Cold War, The Inside Story of an American Adversary*, New York, New York, W.W. Norton & Company, 2006, and Smith, Kathleen E., Moscow 1956, *The Silenced Spring*, Cambridge, Massachusetts, Harvard University Press, 2017.

26. Ibid.

27. Prados, John, *Safe for Democracy, The Secret Wars of the CIA*, Chicago, Illinois, Ivan R. Dee, 2006.

28. Fursenko and Naftali, *Khrushchev's Cold War, The Inside Story of an American Adversary.*

29. Ibid..

30. Prados, *Safe for Democracy, The Secret Wars of the CIA.*

31. Ibid.

32. Thomas, Evan, *The Very Best Men, Four Who Dared: The Early Years of the CIA*, New York, New York, Simon & Schuster, 1995.

33. Ibid.

34. Quinn, Ruth, "This Week in History, Dorothy K. Matlack, A Pioneer and Champion of Army HUMINT," *The United States Army*, , https://www.army.mil/article/97889, March 6, 1963.

35. Woods, Randall B., *Shadow Warrior, William Egan Colby and the CIA*, New York, New York, Basic Books, 2013.

36. Prados, *Safe for Democracy, The Secret Wars of the CIA.*

37. Applebaum, Anne, *Iron Curtain, The Crushing of Eastern Europe,1944-1956*, New York, New York, Doubleday, 2012.

38. Ranelagh, John, *The Agency, The Rise and Decline of the CIA*, New York, New York, Simon and Schuster, 1986.

39. Bocca, Geoffrey, *La Legion! The French Foreign Legion and the Men Who made It Glorious*, New York New York, Thomas Y. Crowell Company, 1964.

40. Horne, *A Savage War of Peace, Algeria, 1954-1962.*

41. Ibid.

42. Paget, Karen M., *Patriotic Betrayal*, New Haven Connecticut, Yale University Press, 2015.

43. Horne, *A Savage War of Peace, Algeria, 1954-1962.*

44. Ibid.

45. Ibid.

46. Ibid.

47. Sully, Francois, *Age of the Guerilla, The New Warfare*, New York, New York, Parents' Magazine Press, 1968.

48. Ibid.

49. Mellen, Joan, *Our Man in Haiti, George de Mohrenschildt and the CIA in the Nightmare Republic*, Walterville, Oregon, Trine Day, 2012.

50. Ibid.

51. Porch, *The French Secret Service, A History of French Intelligence from the Dreyfus Affair to the Gulf War.*

52. Mellen, *Our Man in Haiti, George de Mohrenschildt and the CIA in the Nightmare Republic.*

Index

About the Author

Walter Herbst has been researching the assassination of President John F. Kennedy for thirty-eight years and is passionate about uncovering the truth behind the greatest crime in American history. Through the years, his investigation expanded to include related topics, such as America's role in assassinations and government overthrows around the world, the hidden history of the U.S. military and CIA, anti-communism, the civil rights movement, and the rise of the radical right throughout the twentieth century.

He enjoys writing books that reveal the truth about America's secret past, for, like most Americans, he cares deeply about fairness. As a result, his works will appeal to readers who are unwilling to accept the sanitized version of American history and want to know the truth about the nation's sometimes checkered past. Walter lives with his wife Margaret in Mahwah, NJ.

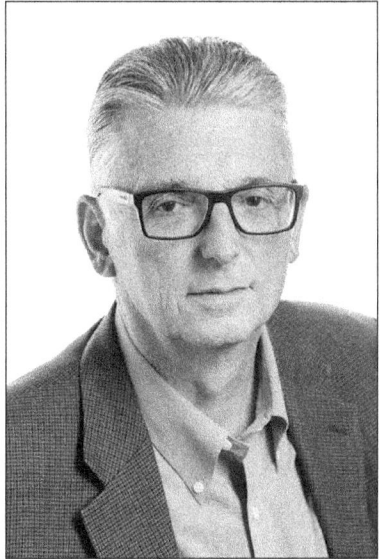

Learn more at herbstbooks.com.

www.ingramcontent.com/pod-product-compliance
Lightning Source LLC
Chambersburg PA
CBHW031233090426
42742CB00007B/185